Science 8

Directions

Science Directions 7
Science Directions 8
Science Directions 9

Science Directions 7 Teacher Resource Package
Science Directions 8 Teacher Resource Package
Science Directions 9 Teacher Resource Package

John Wiley & Sons Canada Limited/Arnold Publishing Ltd.

SI Metric

Our Cover Photograph

Does the photograph on our cover show something that is living or non-living, natural or human-made? In fact, the photograph is a highly magnified view of a fastening device you've probably used. Invented only in recent years, "Velcro" is its trade name. This type of fastener quickly gained popularity and has replaced zippers, snaps, buttons, and laces for many uses. One such use is shown on the back cover of this book.

How does this handy fastener work? The picture shows a small section of two strips of Velcro when they are apart. The top strip consists of loops of thick nylon that have been snipped open during manufacture, forming tiny hooks. The loops at the bottom are made from multiple strands of thinner cotton that can pass through the gaps in the hooks and so become attached to them.

Velcro is a new technology for an old problem—how to keep two materials together yet also be able to separate them easily. What will the next invention be? Will it result from scientific research, technological problem solving, or both?

Science Directions 8

PROGRAM CONSULTANT
Douglas A. Roberts
Faculty of Education, University of Calgary

AUTHOR TEAM
Mary Kay Winter • Gordon R. Gore
Eric S. Grace • H. Murray Lang
William MacLean

PUBLISHING CONSULTANT
Trudy L. Rising

John Wiley & Sons
Toronto   New York   Chichester
Brisbane   Singapore

Arnold Publishing
Edmonton

All Activities in this text have been designed to be as safe as possible, and have been reviewed by professionals specifically for that purpose. The introductory section, *Safety in the Science Classroom*, provides appropriate safety procedures and specifies how they are highlighted in the text. Even though the publisher has taken these measures, safety of students remains the responsibility of the classroom teacher, principal, and school board.

Canadian Cataloguing in Publication Data

Main entry under title:

Science directions 8

ISBN 0-471-79579-8

1. Science—Juvenile literature. 2. Science—Problems, exercises, etc.—Juvenile literature.

I. Roberts, Douglas A., 1936-   . II. Winter, Mary Kay, 1942-   .

Q161.2.S34   1990   J500   C90-093598-7

Science Directions 8 Project Team

Project Director: Trudy Rising
Project Manager: Grace Deutsch
Project Editor: Jane McNulty
Designer: Julian Cleva
Production Co-ordinator/Art Director: Francine Geraci
Developmental Editors: Jane McNulty, Lesley Grant
Bias Review: Jane McNulty, Lesley Grant
Copy Editor: Lily Fong
Word Processing: Diane Klim
Production Assistants: Cheryl Teelucksingh, Gail Copeland
Proofreader: Susan Marshall
Picture Research: Delores Gubasta, Natalie Pawlenko
Typesetting: Lithocomp
Assembly: Full Spectrum Art
Film: Graphitech
Manufacturing: Arcata Graphics
Field Test Preparation Co-ordinator: Shona Wehm
Workshop Co-ordinator: Janet Mayfield
Field Test Design and Preparation: Arnold Publishing Ltd.,
   Presentation Plus Desktop Publishing Inc.

Written, designed, and illustrated in Canada

Printed and bound in the United States of America

10 9 8 7 6 5 4 3 2 1

Contents

Acknowledgements

Science Directions 8 is the result of the efforts of a great many people. First, we would like to thank Alberta Education for reviewing this project at its various stages of development. We thank particularly the Alberta Junior High Science Advisory Committee and Bernie Galbraith, Program Manager, for their thorough analysis of the first draft, the field test (pilot) material, and the final pages.

The efforts of many other educators were invaluable in developing the book. The Teacher Resource Package authors reviewed each Unit and made helpful suggestions throughout manuscript development. They are: David Gue, Medicine Hat; Van McPhail, Calgary; Paul Stevenson, Lethbridge; Alex Penner, Calgary; Monika Amies, Calgary; and Stephen Beare, Slave Lake.

Each Unit of **Science Directions 8** has been field-tested. We would very much like to thank the following teachers and their students for using our materials in draft form and giving us their reactions to assist us in the development of the final text: Darrin De Grand, Blessed Sacrament School, Wainwright (Units One and Two); Pat Ternan, J. R. Harris Junior High School, Barrhead (Units One and Two); Marion Jacobsen, John Ware Junior High School, Calgary (Units One and Four); Jim Ryan, Blessed Sacrament School, Wainwright (Units One and Four); Shayne Page, Lorne Aikens Junior High School, St. Albert (Unit Two); Craig Herbert, Winterburn School, Winterburn (Units Two and Six); John Osborne, J. R. Harris Junior High School, Barrhead (Units Three and Four); Karen Loerke, Dickinsfield School, Fort McMurray (Units Three and Five); Alex McIntosh, Sherwood Heights Junior High School, Sherwood Park (Units Three and Five); Mary Goede-Kohn, Prairie River Junior High School, High Prairie (Units Four and Six); Stan Walchuk, Prairie River Junior High School, High Prairie (Units Five and Six); and Alberta Education field test teachers and their students (all six Units).

We are grateful to the following reviewers for assisting us in ensuring that the content was pedagogically sound and scientifically accurate: John Eix (Unit One); Dr. Margaret Ann Armour, University of Alberta (safety review, Unit One); Jean Bullard (Unit Two); Rick Buchannan (Unit Two); Hank Stratton (Unit Two); Phil Dupuis, Director of Research, Consumers' Association of Canada (Unit Three); Bernice Browne, Manager, Consumer Services, Canadian Standards Association (Unit Three); Fred McGuire, Consumer and Corporate Affairs Canada (Unit Three); Dr. Bruce Gurney (Unit Four); and Dr. Nancy Flood (Units Five and Six).

Science and Technology in Society features were written by Valerie Wyatt (Unit One), Lesley Grant (Units Two, Three, Four, and Six), and Mark Fawcett (Unit Five). Mike Quinn of Prairie for Tomorrow kindly provided information on Operation Burrowing Owl in Unit Six. The Career Profiles for all Units were written by Lesley Grant. We extend thanks as well to each of the individuals whose careers are featured.

We would also like to thank the following for use of their material in adapted form: Gerry Sieben (for the illustration from *Science Probe 8* used in Activity 6–11); Dr. James D. Rising (for use of text, illustrations, and activities from *Science Probe 8*); John Wiley & Sons Canada Limited (for the use of text, illustrations, and activities from *Science Probe 9*, Unit IV for use throughout Unit Four); Marion Gadsby of *Science Explorations 9* and E. Usha R. Finucane of *Science Ideas and Applications 9* (for portions of the Skillbuilders).

Lastly, we thank the committed editors, production co-ordinator, designer, and artists who helped us produce this textbook.

The Authors

This is a very exciting time to be teaching science. It is also a very demanding time. Science educators all over the world are being challenged to rethink the goals, purposes, and processes of science teaching, and thus their teaching approaches. The importance of scientific literacy for all citizens has become increasingly clear. As well, the challenge to demonstrate the relationships between science and technology, and their role in the societal decision-making process is generally accepted as essential in the teaching of science.

Science Directions responds to these new challenges. This program gets students involved in the processes of science, in technological problem solving, and in discussions relating science and technology to social issues. I have found it very impressive to watch teachers working with these materials. I have seen students develop and defend different viewpoints on issues. And I have seen both girls and boys equally involved in the activities.

Science Directions provides a balanced approach to science by emphasizing three important goals of science education in each book. Some Units concentrate on the nature of science and science processes. Others place their main emphasis on the relationship between science and technology. And still others expose students to issues related to science, technology, and society (STS). Together these approaches are designed to develop students' critical thinking abilities. That is, students learn to identify scientific questions, technological problems, and STS issues, and to recognize the underlying assumptions of each. They develop the ability to identify and to gather appropriate data, and to draw inferences from these data. Likewise, they are encouraged to analyse issues by identifying different viewpoints, and evaluating evidence on specific issues.

It has been a pleasure for me to work with these creative, solid, and very teachable materials. With texts of this kind, science teachers can provide the kind of balanced program that meets the challenges and demands of science education for the 1990s and well into the 21st century.

Douglas A. Roberts
Program Consultant

- **Science Directions 8** has six Units. Each uses an appropriate major emphasis: nature of science; science and technology; or science, technology, and society (STS). Each is designed to develop students' critical thinking abilities.
- Many and varied *Activities* are included in each Unit: formal investigations, informal discoveries, technological challenges, among others. Some Activities invite the students to solve practical problems; others provide opportunities for them to design their own experiments.
- The Activities are followed by three levels of questioning: *Finding Out* leads students to consolidate their results and observations; *Finding Out More* challenges them to reach logical conclusions and to reason beyond the immediate and obvious results they have obtained; *Extension* encourages investigations or explorations in new directions. They should be considered optional.
- Within the text, *Probing* questions help enhance the students' understanding of textual and/or visual material by leading them to think through related problems. These questions, designed to be optional, can serve as reinforcement, a basis for independent investigations, or research.
- The *Did You Know?* heading introduces brief statements of scientific, technological, or societal interest related to the concepts under discussion.
- After every two Topics within a Unit, a *Checkpoint* set of questions provides review and reinforcement of the ideas discussed.
- Each Unit ends with a *Unit Review* consisting of three parts. The *Focus* presents the subject matter in point form. The *Backtrack* enables students to review the general content and process skills taught in the Unit. The *Synthesizer* challenges the students to think through and often apply the knowledge, skills, and processes that have been developed in the Unit.

- Within each Unit is a two-page special feature entitled *Science and Technology in Society*. While the text at all times attempts to use concrete examples to explain abstract concepts, the special features emphasize actual situations and highlight real-life applications of the scientific ideas under consideration in the Unit. This helps the students understand that the concepts they are investigating may have an immediate impact on their society and themselves.
- Each Unit also contains a career feature, entitled *Working with . . ., Working at . . .,* or *Working in . . .,* which encourages students to consider how they might develop their own interests and capabilities into rewarding careers related to science.
- Throughout the text, new terms are presented in **boldfaced** type and defined in context; they also appear in the *Glossary* and in the *Index*.
- Appendices called *Skillbuilders* include text and Activities on the SI units, models in science, measurement, graphing, and use of the microscope. The Skillbuilders provide useful support and reference for the students. This material may be used to introduce the course, or it may be used as needed to enhance skills throughout the course.
- The text opens with extensive discussions of the safety rules to be observed at all times in science classes. The students should become thoroughly acquainted with these safety rules, and the reasons for them, at the beginning of the school year. In addition, a **CAUTION** is included within the text's Activities when special care must be taken in using equipment or materials. Any Activity that could potentially be dangerous is designated as a **Demonstration** to be carried out by the teacher.
- The *Teacher Resource Package* provides the teacher with information on the emphases of the program and offers various teaching strategies. The package is designed to provide a wealth of information for both experienced science teachers and those new to the program.

Safety in the Science Classroom

Before You Begin an Activity

- Read through the entire Activity so that you know what to do.
- Make sure the work area is clean before you start. Clear away everything from the work area (books, papers, and personal belongings) except your textbook, your notebook, and a pen or pencil.
- Do not begin an Activity until you are instructed to do so.

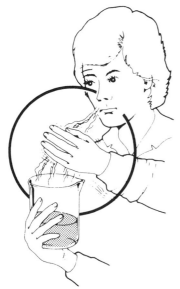

If you test an odour, do so cautiously.

The Activities in this textbook are safe, so long as they are done with proper care. When special attention is needed, you will see the word **CAUTION** with a note about the particular care this Activity requires.

Your teacher will give you specific information about the safety routines used in your school and will make sure that you know where all the safety equipment is. Follow these guidelines and general safety rules, along with your own school's rules.

General Safety Precautions

- Work quietly and carefully; accidents, as well as poor results, can be caused by carelessness. Never work alone; if you have an accident, there will be no one there to help you.
- Tie back loose hair, roll back and secure loose sleeves, and make sure you are wearing shoes that cover your feet as much as possible. Don't wear scarves or ties, baggy clothing, earphones, or jewellery in the laboratory — these can catch on equipment and cause spills or damage.
- Wear safety glasses during experiments involving chemicals or breakable glass.
- Inform your teacher of any allergies, medical conditions, or other physical problems you may have.
- Never eat or drink in the laboratory.
- Do not do laboratory experiments at home unless instructed to do so by your teacher.
- Touch substances only when told to do so. What looks harmless may, in fact, be dangerous.
- When you are instructed to smell a substance in the laboratory, ensure that you hold the container a good distance from your nose, *not* up close. Wave your hand in order to waft the fumes towards your nose.
- Never pour liquids while holding the containers close to your face. Place a test tube in a rack before pouring liquids into it.

- If any part of your body comes in contact with any harmful chemical or specimen, rinse the area immediately and thoroughly with water. If your eyes are affected, do not touch them, but rinse them with water immediately and continuously for at least 10 min.
- Wash your hands after you handle substances and before you leave the laboratory.
- Clean up any spilled substances immediately, as instructed by your teacher.
- Never pour harmful substances into the sink. Follow your teacher's instructions about how to dispose of them.

Handling a Heat Source
- Whenever possible, use electric hot plates with thermostatic controls.
- To heat a test tube using a hot plate, place the test tube in a beaker of water on the hot plate.
- Use only heat-resistant glass containers when you are heating material. Make certain the glass you use for heating is Pyrex or Kimax, and is not cracked.
- Always keep the open end of a test tube pointed away from other people and from yourself.
- Never allow a container to boil dry.
- Pick up hot objects carefully by using tongs or gloves.
- Make sure that the hot plate is turned off when not in use.
- Always unplug electric cords by pulling on the plug, not the cord. Report any frayed cords to your teacher.
- Be careful how the cord from the hot plate to the electrical outlet is placed. Make sure no one will trip over it.
- If you burn yourself, immediately apply cold water or ice.

Rules for Using an Open Flame
- Before using any open flame, be sure that you know the location of the nearest fire extinguisher and/or fire blanket.
- If Bunsen burners are used in your science classroom, use them only when instructed to do so. Obtain instructions from your teacher on the proper method of lighting and using the Bunsen burner, and make sure you understand the instructions.
- Be sure there are no flammable substances in the room before you light the flame.

Compressed Gas

Flammable and
Combustible Material

Oxidizing Material

Corrosive Material

Poisonous and Infectious
Material Causing
Immediate and Serious
Toxic Effects

Poisonous and
Infectious Material
Causing Other
Toxic Effects

Biohazardous Infectious
Material

Dangerously Reactive
Material

WHMIS symbols.

- Use a test tube holder to hold a test tube that is being heated in the flame. Point the open end of the test tube away from yourself and from other people, and move the test tube back and forth over the flame so that heat is distributed evenly. Be ready to extinguish the flame immediately if necessary.
- Never leave a flame unattended.
- Never heat a flammable substance over an open flame.
- Follow your school's rules in case of fire.

Other Recommendations

- Never use cracked or broken glassware. If glass does break while you are using it, follow your teacher's instructions in disposing of it.
- Watch for sharp or jagged edges on equipment. Report such problems to your teacher.
- After each experiment, clean all equipment and put it away. Do not leave unused equipment lying around the work area.
- Report to your teacher all accidents (no matter how minor), broken equipment, damaged or defective facilities, and suspicious-looking chemicals. In this way, you will be taking responsibility not only for your own safety, but also for the safety of those who use the laboratory after you.

Handling Materials

- Examine the WHMIS (Workplace Hazardous Materials Information System) safety symbols shown here. Be sure that you understand these symbols. If you see any of them on containers in your science classroom, use appropriate safety precautions as you handle the materials. These safety symbols appear on many potentially hazardous substances. You may also find these symbols posted on walls to alert people that such materials are on the site. You should be familiar as well with the consumer product safety symbols, found on many consumer products. These symbols are shown on page 134.

The four liquids in this container do not mix, thus forming distinct layers.

In order to drill for oil, many technological problems had to be solved.

When you walk into a lunchroom where someone is eating a pizza, you probably detect the aroma before you actually see the pizza. How does the aroma leave the slice of pizza? And how does it reach the sense receptors in your nose that allow you to smell it? In Unit One, you will learn about the process that makes it possible for you to smell a pizza—or any other substance. As well, you'll investigate mixtures and determine how mixtures can be separated. Why do some materials mix completely with others—giving us mixtures like the gases in the air we breathe—whereas other materials do not mix? You'll study this question and others that will help you to see how mixtures and the separation of mixtures can benefit us in practical ways.

The **Science Directions Program** gives you an opportunity to see how both science and technology have helped shape the world in which we live. In Unit One, your investigations will use a scientific approach. **Science** is a search for explanations about how and why structures and patterns occur in the natural world. Scientific inquiry results from people's curiosity and their willingness to explore all possible explanations. For example, why certain substances mix together, whereas other substances do not, is a question of science.

In Unit Two, you'll be investigating several questions, using a **technological** approach rather than a scientific one. How are these approaches different? Quite simply, if you are using a technological approach to answer a question, you are looking for a practical solution to a practical problem. A scientific question, on the other hand, is not asked in order to solve a practical problem. A scientific question is asked simply to discover how things in nature function. You will use a technological approach to solve practical problems when you learn about machines in Unit Two.

In Unit Three, you'll be using the third approach to inquiries upon which your junior high science studies are based. This approach is known as **STS** (science, technology, and society). You'll be using both science and technology to help analyse some issues that affect the society we live in. **Issues** are topics on which there is more than one opinion or viewpoint. How does science try to ensure that the products we buy are as safe, reliable, and effective as their advertisements claim they are? For example, what kind of scientific testing is done to ensure that a toy is safe for a young child to play with? What can we do to minimize the waste generated by disposable consumer items? Unit Three investigates these kinds of issues and gives you a chance to make some choices for yourself.

The spectacular results of a volcanic eruption or the aftermath of an earthquake show us clearly the tremendous forces within the Earth's interior. Why and how do such dramatic events occur? The materials forming the Earth and the structure of its surface give us clues. You will investigate the Earth's materials, as well as changes in the Earth's crust, in Unit Four.

Aftermath of the San Francisco/ Oakland earthquake, October 1989.

In Unit Five, you will again use your technological problem-solving skills to determine how to grow healthy plants. For successful growth, how much water does a certain kind of plant need? How much light? What kind of soil? In this Unit, you will decide on the conditions you think are important by being responsible for the growth of some plants.

Unit Five looks mainly at how to produce and grow the healthiest plants for human use, but your studies in Unit Six take you back to "the wild." Using a scientific approach, you'll study the interactions among living and non-living things in nature. You'll also investigate some cases of human influence on these relationships in the natural environment.

The Skillbuilders at the end of this book are for your reference whenever you need them. For example, when you need to review the SI units, refer to Skillbuilder One. To better understand the use of models in science, read Skillbuilder Two. Do you know how to measure mass and volume? If you need to learn how, go to Skillbuilder Three. When you obtain data from experiments, do you know how to present the data most clearly? To review graphing, a way of presenting data, go to Skillbuilder Four. To improve your microscope skills and to learn about cell structure, go to Skillbuilder Five.

We hope you enjoy **Science Directions 8**.

The Authors

Matter and Mixtures

Matter is all around you. You eat it, breathe it, wear it, and sleep on it. Everything is made of matter—including your own body, the Earth, and the entire universe. Many different kinds of substances make up matter.

In this Unit, you'll learn about substances that are mixtures—how to make them, as well as how to separate them. You'll be able to explain the techniques shown in these photographs. For example, why is swishing a pan of sand and water from a stream an effective means of separating gold from other materials? Why doesn't ice cream taste salty, even though so much salt is used in an ice-cream maker? What does the designer of a surgical mask need to know about mixtures in order to design the mask? Why might you dissolve sugar in *hot* water when you're making *cold* lemonade?

Questions like these can be answered if you know something about matter and mixtures. You'll use some of the processes shown here in the experiments that you do. And you'll tie it all together with a theory about the nature of matter.

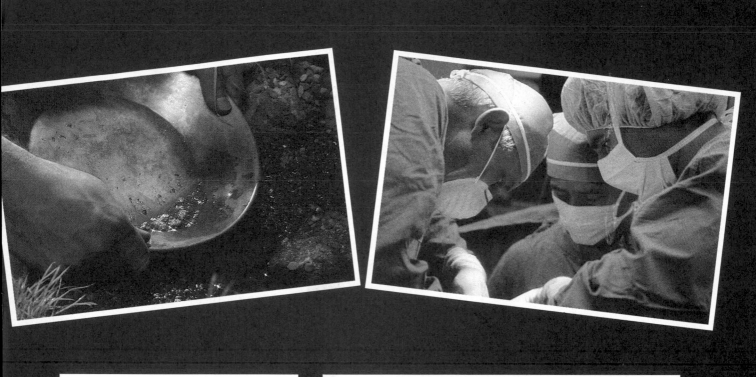

Observing Matter

Matter is anything that has mass and occupies space. You can *see* the difference between solid matter and liquid matter, but how can you explain the difference?

The photographs summarize some characteristics of solids, liquids, and gases. Scientists have tried to explain the differences among them. For example, why does a gas always expand to fill whatever container it is in? Exactly what is happening when a substance changes its state (for example, when ice melts or when water boils)?

Scientists use their senses to make careful observations of matter and of how it behaves. They then try to develop **inferences**, reasonable conclusions or explanations about what they have observed. See what inferences you can make to explain your observations of matter in the following Activity.

A gas has no definite volume (always fills its container) and no definite shape (takes the shape of its container).

A solid has a definite volume and a definite shape.

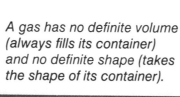

A liquid has a definite volume but no definite shape (takes the shape of its container).

Colouring Water

Problem
What causes two substances to gradually mix together?

Materials
crystal of potassium
   permanganate, or another
   coloured crystal
petri dish
forceps or scoopula
water

Procedure
1. Half-fill a petri dish with water. Let it sit on a level surface for about 1 min to let the water become perfectly still.
2. Using forceps or a scoopula, carefully place one crystal of potassium permanganate in the centre of the dish.
3. Leave the petri dish undisturbed for 5 min.

> **CAUTION:** Potassium permanganate stains skin and clothing. Do not handle it with your fingers. The mixture of water and potassium permanganate will stain skin and clothing. Handle it according to your teacher's directions.

Finding Out
1. (a) Sketch the contents of the petri dish just as you add the potassium permanganate to the water, and sketch the contents again after 5 min.
(b) In a sentence or two, describe how the colour spread in the dish.

Finding Out More
2. Sketch the mixture in the dish as you predict it would look in (a) 30 min and (b) 24 h.
3. What could have caused the water and the potassium permanganate to gradually mix together?
4. (a) How do you predict your results might have differed if you had used hot water?
(b) Explain your prediction.

gas
liquid

after about 1s

later

If you allowed enough time, particles of perfume would spread completely through the room, mixing with the other gases in the air.

A chain of paper clips can be used to illustrate the hypothesis of Democritus. Each paper clip represents one particle. You can divide the chain into two chains, which can be divided into smaller and smaller chains. Eventually the chain will be broken into individual paper clips. If you break a paper clip, it will no longer have the characteristics of a paper clip. Similarly, there is a limit to how far matter can be subdivided and still retain the characteristics of that type of matter.

Diffusion

The gradual mixing that you observed in Activity 1-1 is commonplace. Many substances mix together in the same way as potassium permanganate and water, without any stirring or shaking. For example, if someone opens a bottle of perfume in one corner of your classroom, you are soon aware of it. The fragrance spreads in all directions. This gradual mixing of substances is called **diffusion**.

How do scientists explain diffusion? They think that tiny particles of perfume are continually moving about and bumping into each other. When the perfume bottle is closed, the particles remain squeezed together inside. They collide with other particles and are bounced about in all directions. When the bottle is opened, the particles gradually spread out, moving away from the crowded bottle, to spaces where there are fewer particles. If the bottle were left open, this process would continue until the particles of perfume were equally distributed throughout the air in the room.

Thinking About Matter

More than 2000 years ago in ancient Greece, a thinker named Democritus hypothesized that all matter is made up of tiny particles too small to be seen. (A **hypothesis** is a set of ideas that provide a possible explanation of why something occurs in the natural world.) Democritus thought that if you kept cutting and cutting a substance into smaller and smaller pieces, you would eventually come to the smallest possible particles. He called these tiniest particles "*atomos*" (meaning "indivisible"), from which we get our English word "atom."

Over the centuries, scientists have carried out many investigations of matter. So far, no results have suggested that the hypothesis suggested by Democritus is false. A hypothesis that is supported again and again by experimental results is called a **theory**. This hypothesis—that matter is made up of tiny particles—has become widely accepted as the *particle theory of matter*. The theory has proved useful in explaining many observations of matter.

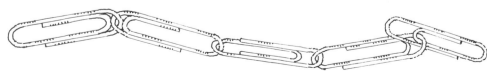

The Particle Theory of Matter

Today we call the particles mentioned in the particle theory *atoms* and *molecules*. Experiments have indicated that the water in one ordinary drinking glass has about 10 000 000 000 000 000 000 000 molecules (that's 10 million million million million). Could you count that high? Suppose you start when you are born, counting one every second. In one year, you would count to 31 557 600. If you lived to 316, you would reach 10 thousand million (10 billion). By the time you finished counting up the number of molecules in the glass of water, you would be 3 160 000 000 000 years old!

1. All matter is made up of tiny particles.
2. All the particles in a substance are the same; different substances are made of different particles.
3. There are attractive forces among particles—these attractions may be strong or weak.
4. The particles are always moving; the more energy the particles gain, the faster they move.
5. There are spaces among the particles.

Solids, Liquids, and Gases

The particle theory is useful in explaining the differences among solids, liquids, and gases. Solids have a definite shape and volume because the particles of a solid can move only a little. They vibrate back and forth, but strong forces hold them in fixed positions.

ONE MILLION FIVE HUNDRED FORTY-SEVEN, ONE MILLION FIVE HUNDRED FORTY-EIGHT...

Illustrations such as these help to clarify the particle theory.

A liquid takes the shape of its container because the particles can move around more freely than they can in solids. A liquid's particles are held together by strong attractions to each other, so a liquid, like a solid, occupies a definite volume.

A gas always fills whatever container it is in. The attractions among the particles of a gas are so weak that individual particles are quite far apart, with spaces among them. Since gas particles are moving constantly and randomly in all directions, they spread throughout their container, no matter what its shape and volume.

Changes of State and the Particle Theory

According to the particle theory, particles with more energy move faster. One way of adding energy to a substance is to heat it. As a solid is heated, the particles vibrate faster and faster until they have enough energy to break away from their fixed positions. When this happens the particles can move about more freely; we say the substance has **melted**. The reverse of this process is the change of state called **freezing**; as the particles in a liquid lose energy, they move more and more slowly. When the attraction between particles pulls them into fixed positions, the liquid has frozen or solidified.

Some solids can change directly to a gas, a change of state called **sublimation**. In sublimation, individual particles of a solid gain enough energy to break completely away from the other particles. The reverse process—a direct change of state from a gas to a solid—is also called sublimation.

As a liquid is heated, the particles move about more and more quickly. Some particles gain enough energy to break free of the attractions of the other particles. When this happens, the liquid changes to a gas, a change called **evaporation**. The reverse process is called **condensation**.

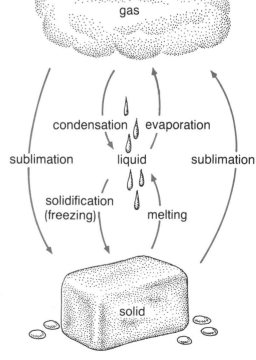

Changes of state.

During a cool night, this stream lost heat to the air. At the stream's surface, the water froze; that is, the water particles lost some of their freedom of movement, and became held in fixed positions.

This frost pattern is a result of sublimation. Water particles in the air in gaseous form changed to solid ice, without becoming a liquid first.

Each substance has its own characteristics, depending on the nature of its particles. If the attractions among the particles of a substance are relatively weak, the substance is a gas at ordinary temperatures. The oxygen we breathe is one such substance. Solid substances, such as metals, wood, and plastic, have much stronger attractions among their particles.

Looking at Mixtures

Very few substances in our environment are completely pure. For example, cosmetics are made of many substances including colouring materials and perfumes. Foods contain preservatives and other additives. And even fruit juice labelled "100% pure" is actually a mixture of water, citric acid, and other substances. A **mixture** is made up of two or more substances. Because there are so many common mixtures, it's useful to group similar ones together—that is, to **classify** them—when we study them.

You're probably familiar with many ways of classifying things. Libraries, for example, classify books as fiction or non-fiction. These categories are then further subdivided: young adult books, mystery stories, science fiction, biography, large-print books, and so on. Without this classification system, imagine how difficult it would be to locate books on the shelves.

Classification helps to make sense of the multitude of mixtures that you could investigate in a science laboratory. In the following Activity, make some mixtures and classify them into categories according to your observations.

In a music store, tapes within each category of music are classified alphabetically. When you look for a certain tape, the classification system simplifies your search. Similarly, classifying matter simplifies our understanding of it.

Most of the substances that you use every day are mixtures.

Making and Classifying Mixtures

Problem

How can you classify mixtures?

Materials

6 test tubes
test tube rack
rubber stoppers for test tubes
tape for labels (or wax pencil)
scoopula
graduated cylinder
a variety of solids and liquids:
   table salt, sand, pepper, salad
   oil, vinegar, copper(II) sulphate,
   sugar, ethanol, water

Table 1-1

SUBSTANCES MIXED	HOW MANY PARTS ARE VISIBLE?	DOES THE MIXTURE CONTAIN SOLIDS OR LIQUIDS OR BOTH?	DESCRIBE ANY CHANGES DURING MIXING.
1. Salt and sand	2	2 solids	No change
2. Copper(II) sulphate and water			
3. Salad oil and vinegar			
4. Vinegar and sugar			
5. Water and ethanol			
6. Pepper and water			

Procedure

1. Set up six test tubes and label them from 1 to 6.
2. Copy Table 1-1 into your notebook.
3. Make each mixture by combining the two substances in the appropriate test tube. Use 10 mL of each substance that is a liquid and one scoop of each substance that is a solid. For example, in test tube 1, mix one scoop of salt and one scoop of sand; in test tube 2, mix one scoop of copper(II) sulphate and 10 mL of water.

CAUTION: Copper(II) sulphate and ethanol are poisonous. Do not touch them. Ethanol is flammable! Be sure there are no open flames in the room.

4. To mix the two substances in each test tube, put the stopper in the test tube and turn the test tube upside down several times. As you do this, hold the stopper with your thumb (see the illustration). Then turn the test tube right side up and remove the stopper.

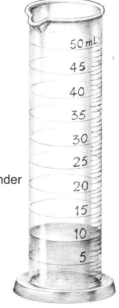

graduated cylinder

scoopula

Hold the test tube like this when you turn it upside down.

5. Record detailed observations of each mixture as you make it. (See the sample entry for mixture 1.)
6. Dispose of or save the mixtures according to your teacher's directions.

Finding Out

1. Classify the mixtures that you made. List the ones:
   (a) that were made from two solids;
   (b) that were made from two liquids;
   (c) that were made from a solid and a liquid;
   (d) in which one of the substances could no longer be seen; and
   (e) in which one of the substances appeared to change colour.
2. Think of at least one other way of classifying the mixtures, besides those in Question 1. Compare your idea with those of your classmates.
3. Classify the mixtures shown in the photographs on this page.

Stainless steel.

Vinegar.

Cement.

Seashells.

Classifying Mixtures

One way in which scientists classify mixtures is to group them according to their appearance. A **mechanical mixture** is a mixture in which two or more parts can be seen with the unaided eye. Granola cereal is an example of a mechanical mixture. A **solution** is a mixture that appears to be all one substance. The parts of a solution are so completely mixed that they cannot be seen even under a microscope. Clear fruit juice (a liquid), clean air (a gas), and stainless steel (a solid), are all examples of solutions. More examples are listed in Table 1-2.

Table 1-2

MECHANICAL MIXTURES	SOLUTIONS
orange juice containing pulp	clear, tinned apple juice
dirty, sooty air	clear air
salad	vinegar (a solution of water and acetic acid)
cornflakes and milk	
concrete (cement, sand and gravel)	tea
	bronze (a solid solution)
sand and pebbles	clear shampoo

Reread the observations you recorded in Activity 1-2. Which of the six mixtures would you classify as solutions? Which would you classify as mechanical mixtures? (Liquids are often the most difficult to classify. A rule of thumb may help you: Liquid solutions are always clear—that is, you can see through them. They may be coloured, like one of the solutions in Activity 1-2, but they are never cloudy.)

Classifying mixtures is not always as straightforward as you might expect. For one thing, mixtures often have more than two parts. For another, a mechanical mixture may contain a solution within it! As one example, when oil and vinegar are combined they make a mechanical mixture, but the vinegar itself is a solution of acetic acid in water. As another example, if clear tea contains dissolved sugar, the tea is a solution; if milk is added, the tea becomes cloudy, so it is no longer a solution.

Classification of Matter

Did You Know?

Your body contains many solutions. You've probably noticed the taste of tears, caused by dissolved salt. Saliva, sweat, and urine are all solutions. Blood is a mechanical mixture. It consists of many kinds of cells— including red cells that give the blood its colour—suspended in a clear yellow solution of proteins, sugars, and other substances.

One classification system for matter is based on its observable properties and is summarized in the chart shown here. Throughout this Unit, you'll deal with mechanical mixtures and solutions; in further studies of chemistry you will learn more about pure substances.

Classification of Matter

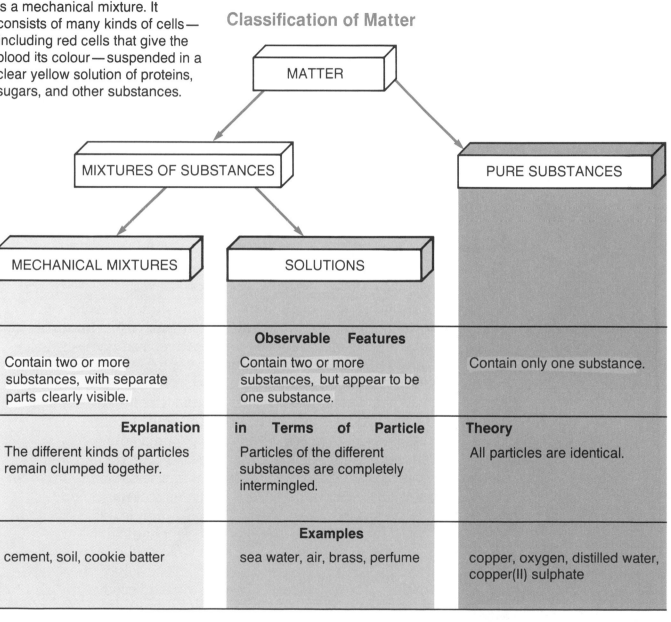

MECHANICAL MIXTURES	SOLUTIONS	PURE SUBSTANCES
Observable Features		
Contain two or more substances, with separate parts clearly visible.	Contain two or more substances, but appear to be one substance.	Contain only one substance.
Explanation in Terms of Particle Theory		
The different kinds of particles remain clumped together.	Particles of the different substances are completely intermingled.	All particles are identical.
Examples		
cement, soil, cookie batter	sea water, air, brass, perfume	copper, oxygen, distilled water, copper(II) sulphate

Solutions

Sugar dissolving in water. You can see solid sugar, but when it dissolves it seems to disappear. This is because the individual sugar particles are so tiny and so far apart from each other that they cannot be seen.

● sugar particle

○ water particle

Why does a sugar cube become invisible when it is placed in water? When it disappears, where has it gone? How could a magician make the cube reappear? It is not magic that causes the disappearance of the sugar, but the fact that both sugar and water are made up of tiny particles.

According to the particle theory, sugar particles are held together by attractive forces. But when sugar mixes with water, the sugar particles are more strongly attracted to the water particles than they are to themselves. The sugar granules are "ripped apart" as the particles move off into the water. Individual sugar particles are much too small to be seen, so the sugar seems to disappear.

Many other substances form solutions with water; that is, they dissolve in water. **Dissolving** is the complete intermingling of the tiny particles of two or more substances. For example, in Activity 1–2, copper(II) sulphate particles and ethanol particles were attracted to water particles; these two substances formed solutions with water.

Another way of saying that a substance dissolves in water is to say that it is **soluble** in water. An **insoluble** substance is one that does not dissolve. You have seen that copper(II) sulphate and ethanol are soluble in water, while pepper, sand, and oil are insoluble in water.

When a solid dissolves in a liquid, the liquid that does the dissolving is called the **solvent**, and the solid that dissolves is the **solute**. For example, in a solution of copper(II) sulphate and water, water is the solvent and copper(II) sulphate is the solute. Water is a common solvent, but many other substances can act as solvents, too.

water

sugar

Using Different Solvents

Problem

Which is the more effective solvent: water or salad oil?

Materials

4 small disposable cups
markers for labelling
salad oil
petroleum jelly
copper(II) sulphate
4 popsicle sticks

Procedure

1. Copy Table 1–3 into your notebook.
2. Label the four cups 1, 2, 3, and 4. Pour salad oil into cups 1 and 2 to a depth of about 2 cm. Pour the same amount of water into cups 3 and 4.
3. Using the popsicle sticks, add the same amount of copper(II) sulphate to cups 1 and 3 and a little petroleum jelly to cups 2 and 4, as shown. Stir each mixture thoroughly.
4. Examine the contents of each cup and record whether the solute has been dissolved completely, partially, or not at all. Describe each mixture carefully in your table.

Table 1–3

CUP	SOLUTE	SOLVENT	OBSERVATIONS
1			
2			
3			
4			

Finding Out

1. In which liquid was the petroleum jelly more soluble? What observation suggests this?
2. Which solvent dissolved more copper(II) sulphate? What observation suggests this?
3. Are particles of petroleum jelly attracted more strongly to the water particles or to the oil particles? Which observation leads you to this inference?

Finding Out More

4. Look at the photograph of the pieces of cloth. All three samples of cloth had identical tar stains, which were then treated in different ways. Compare the effect of washing the cloth in Varsol with the effect of washing it in water. Use the words "solvent" and "dissolve" in your answer.

unwashed   tar stain   tar stain
tar stain   washed in Varsol   washed in water

All Kinds of Solutions

Solids, liquids, and gases can all form solutions. In Activity 1–2, you made a solution of liquid in liquid (ethanol in water) and a solution of solid in liquid (copper(II) sulphate in water). Did you know that soft drinks are solutions of gas (as well as solids) in liquid? The solvent is water. Besides various flavourings, colourings, and sugars, a gas—carbon dioxide—is also dissolved in the water. When you open a soft-drink bottle or can, you can see bubbles of carbon dioxide separating from the solution. This gives the soft drink its fizz.

In any solution, the substance that does the dissolving—the solvent—is always present in a larger quantity than the solute. Clean air is a solution of about 80% nitrogen and 19% oxygen, along with carbon dioxide and other gases. Nitrogen is considered to be the solvent because it makes up the largest part of the mixture. Oxygen and the other gases are the solutes.

Many of the metals we use most commonly are actually mixtures called **alloys**. To produce an alloy, the metals are heated together until they melt and form a liquid solution. When the solution is cooled, it changes to a solid.

There are many different kinds of steel, but all are alloys containing mostly iron.

Brass is an alloy made of copper with zinc dissolved in it. Adding zinc makes the alloy stronger than copper alone, and also makes it resistant to corrosion. Brass is used to make ornamental objects such as door knockers, house numbers, and inexpensive gold-coloured jewellery.

Solute and Solvent

Copy Table 1-4 into your notebook. Using the information on page 14, as well as your general knowledge, complete the table by naming the solute and the solvent for each solution. If you can think of any other solutions, add them to the list.

Table 1-4

SOLUTION	SOLVENT	SOLUTE
Tea		
Air		
Ocean water		
Soft drink		
"Gold" jewellery		
Brass		

Did You Know?

Some skin-care products such as sunscreens and body lotions contain substances dissolved in alcohol. In these products, several kinds of alcohol (for example, *ethanol* and *propanol*) are used as solvents. Most alcohols are poisonous if swallowed, so skin-care products containing these solvents are labelled "for external use only."

This "gold" jewellery is made from an alloy of copper in gold. The copper makes the jewellery less expensive. Also, because copper is a much harder metal than gold, it makes the jewellery stronger.

Alloys of aluminum contain other metals such as silicon, copper, magnesium, or manganese. Because these alloys are strong and light, they are used in making aircraft bodies.

Solutions **15**

Mixtures, Solutions, and the Particle Theory

Some mixtures have characteristics of both solutions and mechanical mixtures. These mixtures may be *suspensions, emulsions, colloids,* or even several kinds of mixtures all at the same time. Use the Glossary at the end of this book to find the meaning of these three new terms. In your notebook, list the example given in the Glossary for each term, along with one more example of your own. You may need to consult a reference book to find other samples.

Why do some substances form solutions in which the parts are not visible, while other substances form mechanical mixtures in which the parts can be seen? How can the particle theory help to explain this?

If substances are made up of particles that are attracted to water particles—for example, table salt, sugar, and copper(II) sulphate—they are soluble in water. Sand is an example of a solid substance that is *not* soluble in water. Sand doesn't dissolve in water because the particles of sand are more strongly attracted to each other than they are to the particles of water. Similarly, oil does not form a solution with water because the oil particles are not attracted to water particles. Oil can dissolve petroleum jelly, however, because particles of oil and particles of petroleum jelly attract each other.

Generally, a solution forms if the particles of the solute are more strongly attracted to the solvent particles than they are to each other. In solutions, the tiny particles of both the solvent and the solute are completely intermingled. In mechanical mixtures, the particles remain clumped together, so the parts of the mixture can be seen with the unaided eye.

Why can't you see the solute after it has dissolved? Because the individual particles of the solute are too small and too far apart to be visible. However, you can make some observations that indicate that the solute is still present. Sometimes you can taste the solute; for example, sugar dissolved in your tea, or salt in your soup. (Remember that taste is not a characteristic that should be tested in your science classroom.) Sometimes the solute particles colour the solution. Recall the solution of water and copper(II) sulphate that you made in Activity 1–2; although you could not see any copper(II) sulphate, the blue colour of the liquid indicated that this solute was present.

1. (a) You have learned about mixtures whose parts cannot be seen. Four words related to such mixtures begin with *s-o-l*. Find the four words in this book, and write a definition for each one in your notebook.

   sol ■ ■ ■ ■ ■
   sol ■ ■ ■ ■
   sol ■ ■ ■ ■
   sol ■ ■ ■

   (b) You have learned two other words that also contain *s-o-l*. Find the two words in this book, write them in your notebook, and explain what they mean.

   ■ ■ sol ■ ■ ■ ■
   ■ ■ ■ sol ■ ■

2. (a) Describe how a solution differs from a mechanical mixture.
   (b) How does the particle theory explain this difference?

3. Reread the key points of the particle theory on page 5.
   (a) Which part(s) of the theory account(s) for what happens when liquid candle wax solidifies? Give a reason for your answer.
   (b) Use the particle theory to explain what happens when oil and vinegar are mixed together.

4. Most of the sentences shown on the right contain errors or are incomplete. In your notebook, write the complete, correct version of each sentence.

5. Give examples of:
   (a) three solid solutions;
   (b) two liquid solutions that do not contain water; and
   (c) a solution that is a gas.

6. Identify the solute and the solvent in the following situations.
   (a) Baking soda forms a solution in water.
   (b) Varsol dissolves the grease from a mechanic's clothes.
   (c) Air is made up of about 80% nitrogen and 19% oxygen.
   (d) Ocean water tastes salty.
   (e) Bubbles of gas are produced when a soft-drink bottle is opened.
   (f) Some "gold" jewellery is really made of copper and gold.
   (g) Tea is a clear, brownish liquid.

7. Examine the graduated cylinders in the illustration. Twenty minutes before this photograph was taken, two different solids were dropped into each cylinder.

(a) What is happening in the cylinder on the left? Use the particle theory to explain this.
(b) Explain how the particles of the two solids must be different.

8. Sugar dissolves more quickly in tea if the solution is stirred. Explain this in terms of the particle theory, using a sketch as part of your explanation.

potassium permanganate   stone

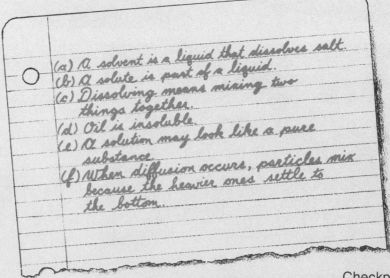

(a) A solvent is a liquid that dissolves salt.
(b) A solute is part of a liquid.
(c) Dissolving means mixing two things together.
(d) Oil is insoluble.
(e) A solution may look like a pure substance.
(f) When diffusion occurs, particles mix because the heavier ones settle to the bottom.

Separating Mechanical Mixtures

The photographs show how some mixtures are separated into their parts. How many other ways of separating mixtures can you think of? Suppose some sand was accidentally mixed into your sugar, or some small foreign coins were mixed with Canadian coins in your wallet. What could you do to remove the unwanted materials? In the next Activity, try to devise some ways to separate the parts of mixtures.

Filtration

Would you drink the water from this river? It probably contains a mixture of soil, algae, micro-organisms, and dissolved chemicals. Many communities get their water supply from a source such as this. One of the techniques used to make the water drinkable is **filtration**. Larger particles in the mixture are held back or screened out. The material that does not pass through the filter is called the **residue**, and the material that passes through the filter is called the **filtrate**.

A filter can be made from a screen or mesh with holes, but it can also be made of a material such as sand or charcoal. Sand is used for filters in water treatment plants. In Activity 1–6, see how sand can function as a filter.

Did You Know?

Water-treatment plants use simple separation methods to produce clean, drinkable water from muddy lakes or rivers. Intake pipes covered with screens filter out coarse materials such as plants, fish, or pieces of debris. In a process called sedimentation, a chemical called a flocculator is added to the water to make small pieces of mud stick together in clumps so they can be removed. The water then passes through sand filters that remove tiny bits of dirt from the water. Finally, small amounts of chlorine are added to kill micro-organisms, and fluorine may be added to help prevent tooth decay.

E.L. Smith Water-Treatment Plant in Edmonton.

Inside a water-treatment plant.

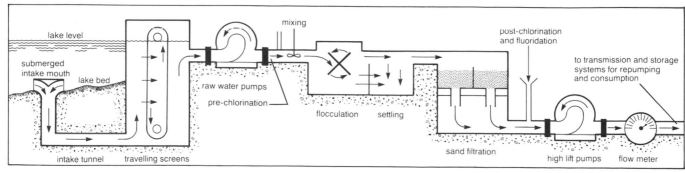

Making a Filter

Problem

How can you make an effective sand filter?

Materials

plastic bottle (transparent if possible) with bottom cut off
clay
fine sand
coarse sand
small stones
large stones
muddy water (or water and sawdust)
support stand
ring clamp
250 mL beaker
timing device with a second hand

Procedure

1. Design a sand filter to separate the residue from the muddy water, using the set-up shown below the Materials list.
2. Make a filter, try it out, and modify it if necessary.
3. Fill a 250 mL beaker with the mixture to be filtered. Pour it through your filter and record the number of seconds it takes for all the water to pass through.

Finding Out

1. Examine your filtrate. Compare it with the original mixture and rate the effectiveness of your filter in separating solid material from the water. Use a scale from 0 to 10, as shown in the diagram on the right.

2. On the chalkboard, one student will record the filtering time and the effectiveness rating for each of the filters made by the class.
3. What materials or combination of materials made the most effective filters? Explain why you think these were the most effective.
4. (a) How long did it take your group to filter 250 mL of water?
   (b) How long did it take to filter 250 mL of water using the least effective filters?
   (c) More effective filters are often slower than less effective ones. Was this true in your class? If so, explain why.

plastic bottle (bottom removed)

ring clamp

support stand

beaker

WON'T THE SAND WASH OUT OF THE BOTTLE?

WHICH WOULD BE FASTER – SAND OR CLAY?

WHAT IF THE DIRT COMES THROUGH AS WELL?

Effectiveness of Filter

10 The filtrate is perfectly clear.

5

0 All the dirt came through. (The filter is totally ineffective.)

Filters

Filters are commonly used whenever solid pieces of a substance must be removed from other solids, liquids, or gases. Air is filtered in car engines, industrial smokestacks, and hospital operating rooms. Window screens act as filters, preventing the entry of annoying insects. Workers who use spray paint wear face masks so they don't breathe in droplets of paint. Tea bags keep tea leaves out of tea, and coffee filters keep coffee grounds out of coffee.

To remove extremely tiny particles, a filter with extremely small holes is needed. Paper can do the job. You've probably seen filter papers used in coffee makers. Try using laboratory filter paper in the following Activity.

Car engines contain filters like these for air, fuel, and oil.

Industrial smokestacks have filters to remove some of the soot and ashes from the air that's released.

Using Filter Paper

Problem

How can filter paper be used to separate mixtures?

Materials

filter paper
funnel
support stand
ring clamp
250 mL beaker
stirring rod
liquid mixture (e.g., tomato juice; soil and water; flour and water; charcoal powder and water)

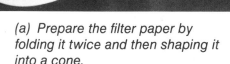

(a) Prepare the filter paper by folding it twice and then shaping it into a cone.

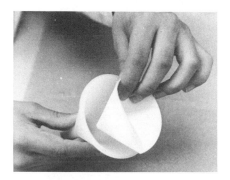

(b) Wet the funnel and fit the cone of filter paper into it.

Procedure

1. Set up a support stand, ring clamp, and funnel. Place an empty beaker under the funnel.
2. Prepare the filter paper by folding it twice and then shaping it into a cone, as shown.
3. Wet the funnel and fit the cone of filter paper into it. Set the funnel in the ring.
4. Stir the mixture assigned to your group, then pour it into the funnel and collect the filtrate in the beaker. Pour slowly so that the level of the liquid in the funnel stays below the edge of the filter paper.

5. While the mixture is being filtered, prepare a table in your notebook with these headings: "Mixture," "Appearance of Filtrate," and "Appearance of Residue."

Finding Out

1. In your table, list all the mixtures that were filtered by the class. Describe the appearance of each filtrate and each residue.
2. What similarities, if any, do you observe in the appearance of the filtrates?
3. For any filtrate that appears cloudy, suggest what causes its cloudiness.
4. Draw a labelled diagram of the equipment you used in this Activity. (Hint: Scientific drawings may be simple. They need not be elaborate. They should, however, be accurate.)

Finding Out More

5. (a) List one advantage of filter paper compared with a sand filter.
   (b) List one advantage of a sand filter compared with filter paper.
6. List as many kinds of filters as you can. Ask your family and friends for suggestions, and get examples from mechanics, cooks, factory workers, engineers, and people in other occupations as well. Make a sketch of each type of filter, and explain why it is effective.

When Is Filtration Effective?

Even very small bits and pieces of substances can be removed from mixtures by filtration if the filtering material has small enough holes. According to the particle theory, liquids and gases pass through a filter because they are made of tiny individual particles that move about separately. In other words, liquids and gases have no bits and pieces that can be held back by a filter. Filtration is effective, however, in separating solids from mechanical mixtures. Filters cannot separate the parts of solutions, in which the tiny particles of different substances are completely intermingled.

Probing

In the food industry, certain substances are used to prevent the separation of mixtures. In some salad dressings, for example, oil and vinegar remain mixed together because another substance called an emulsifier is present in the mixture. You can observe the action of an emulsifier on your own:

- In one test tube, mix oil and vinegar as you did in Activity 1–1; in another test tube, mix oil, vinegar, and two drops of egg yolk.
- Describe in your own words the effect of the emulsifier.
- Egg yolk, gelatin, corn syrup, and corn starch are all common emulsifiers. In your kitchen at home, find five products that contain one or more of these emulsifiers, and list the products in your notebook.

Egg yolks are often used as emulsifiers in salad dressings.

Separating Solutions

It's not always a simple matter to tell whether a material is a solution or a pure substance. For example, water with nothing dissolved in it is a pure substance, but most water, even rainwater, contains dissolved substances. As rain or snow falls, it dissolves some carbon dioxide from the air. Upon reaching the ground, the rainwater trickles over soil and rocks, dissolving minerals as it goes. (Minerals are pure, solid substances that occur naturally in the Earth.) The familiar taste of your drinking water is caused by the combined presence of these solutes.

The characteristics of the particles in a mixture determine whether or not different substances will form solutions. In the same way, characteristics of the particles determine how parts of solutions can be separated. Generally, the separation methods involve changes of state. For example, particles of one of the substances in a liquid solution might be more likely than particles of the other substance to escape from the liquid. That is, one substance might *evaporate* more readily. Or particles of one of the substances might be strongly attracted to each other. Under certain conditions, these particles might group together, crystallize, and form a solid. In this Topic, you'll investigate evaporation, crystallization, and other methods of separating the parts of solutions.

In oil refineries like this one at Edmonton, Alberta, many substances are separated out of the complex mixture called crude oil.

Read Pat's description, then try to answer the following questions.

1. Was the blue liquid in the dish a mechanical mixture, a solution, or a pure substance? Give a reason for your answer.

2. What has happened to the liquid? (Explain, using the particle theory.)

3. What difference between the particles of solute and the particles of solvent caused them to separate?

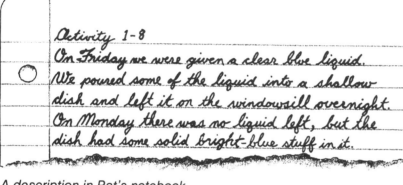

Activity 1-8
On Friday we were given a clear blue liquid. We poured some of the liquid into a shallow dish and left it on the windowsill overnight. On Monday there was no liquid left, but the dish had some solid bright-blue stuff in it.

A description in Pat's notebook.

Did You Know?

Potash is a valuable mineral found in large underground deposits and used widely as a fertilizer. About 25% of all the world's potash is produced in Canada, mainly from mines in Saskatchewan. Scientific evidence suggests that more than 350 million years ago this potash was once dissolved in the water of the Devonian Seas that covered a large part of what is now the Canadian Prairies. When the sea water evaporated, the potash was left behind. Later, it was buried under soil washed down from the Rocky Mountains.

Removing potash from the ground.

Have you ever been on a trip and noticed that the water in another town or city tastes strange? In a different part of the country, with different rocks and soils, the water has dissolved a different combination of minerals. The water may taste strange to you, but it seems quite normal to someone who is accustomed to it. Pure water, with almost nothing dissolved in it, has quite a different taste.

When part of a solution evaporates, the solute may begin to **crystallize** (form crystals). **Crystals** are naturally occurring, regular-shaped pieces of a solid, with straight edges, flat sides, and regular angles. Crystals of a particular substance always have the same shape, determined by the characteristics of the particles in the crystal. Crystals of table salt are cubic, for example, while copper(II) sulphate crystals have a distinctive, non-cubic shape. There are many kinds of crystals in nature, displaying a variety of shapes and colours. Some crystals are soluble in water, and some are insoluble. From some solutions, you can "grow" crystals (that is, separate them from the solvent). Try this in the next Activity, using alum or some other suitable substance.

Crystals of table salt viewed under specialized light conditions.

Alum crystals.

Crystals of copper(II) sulphate.

Calcite crystal.

Your body produces a solution, called urine, as a way of disposing of soluble waste products. Under normal conditions, the waste products remain dissolved in the liquid. Sometimes, however, substances that were once dissolved in urine may solidify. This material can form a lump, called a kidney stone, within the kidney. If this lump blocks the flow of urine, intense pain can result. Occasionally a stone passes down through the urinary system and out of the body along with the urine. Most often, a doctor must use ultrasound to break up the stone, or must operate to remove it.

Activity 1-9

Growing Crystals

Problem

How can you "grow" some large crystals?

Materials

alum solution (or other solution)
tall narrow jar
pencil
10 cm string
paper clip, or seed crystal

Procedure

1. Tie one end of the string to the paper clip and the other end around the middle of the pencil. Hang the paper clip in the jar as shown. Adjust the length of the string so that it does not touch the bottom or sides of the jar. Remove the pencil, string, and paper clip, and set them aside.
2. Carefully pour alum solution into the jar to a depth of about 5 cm.
3. Set the pencil across the top of the jar with the paper clip hanging into the solution, and leave the jar in a place where it will be undisturbed for several days.

Finding Out

1. Each day, observe the string and make a sketch of what you see.

Finding Out More

2. How does the meaning of "grow" in "growing crystals" differ from its meaning in "growing up"?
3. Use the particle theory to explain the difference between the growth of a crystal and the growth of an animal or plant.

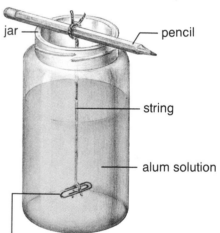

jar — pencil
string
alum solution
paper clip (hanging near the bottom of the jar, but not touching the glass)

Distillation

You have seen how evaporation and crystallization can separate the parts of a solution so that the *solute* is recovered. Using the process of **distillation**, you can separate the parts of a solution and recover the *solvent*. The material collected during distillation is called the **distillate**. The mixture that remains in the original container is called the **residue**.

Distillation: Demonstration

Problem

How is the solvent in a solution recovered by means of distillation?

Procedure

1. Your teacher will set up the apparatus as shown, heat the solution until it boils, and then turn down the heat and allow the solution to boil gently.

> **CAUTION:** The heat must be turned off while there is still liquid in the flask. The flask must not be allowed to boil dry.

2. The heat will be turned off while there is still solution to a depth of about 1 cm in the flask.

Finding Out

1. Describe the solution in the flask at the beginning of the demonstration.
2. Describe any way in which the residue appears different from the original solution.
3. Describe the distillate. How is it different from the original solution in the flask?
4. (a) What observation indicates that the solute and the solvent have separated?
   (b) Which was recovered— solute, solvent, or both?
5. (a) In what state (solid, liquid, or gas) was the distillate while it was moving into the test tube?
   (b) How many changes of state occurred during the distillation?
   (c) What are these changes called and where did they occur?

Finding Out More

6. Why must the heat be turned off while there is still solution in the flask?
7. Four safety precautions are included in the diagram on this page. For each precaution, suggest what danger or problem is prevented.
8. Use the particle theory to explain what happens during distillation.
9. If the solution had had some soil mixed with it, would: (a) the residue, and (b) the distillate, appear different? Explain your answers.

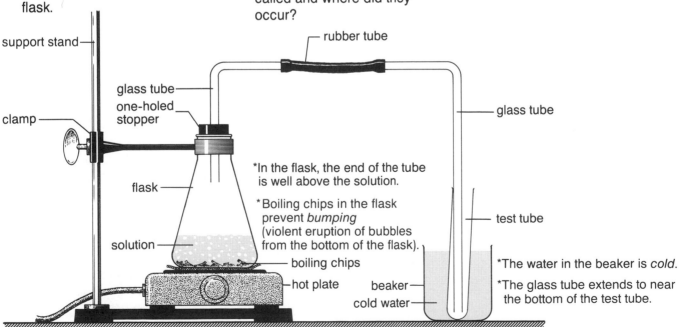

support stand

clamp

glass tube
one-holed stopper

flask

solution

rubber tube

glass tube

*In the flask, the end of the tube is well above the solution.

*Boiling chips in the flask prevent *bumping* (violent eruption of bubbles from the bottom of the flask).

boiling chips

hot plate

beaker

cold water

test tube

*The water in the beaker is *cold*.

*The glass tube extends to near the bottom of the test tube.

Separation Techniques: A Summary

You have now learned about several ways to separate the parts of mixtures and solutions, and you have tried several techniques yourself. Here is a summary of some separation methods that can be used:

- dissolving one substance but not the other
- filtration (using a variety of filters)
- attracting one of the substances to a magnet
- picking apart the bits and pieces (with or without a hand lens)
- floating and/or sinking the parts in water
- evaporating one part
- crystallizing one part
- distilling a solution

Now try to design an efficient and practical way to solve a separation problem.

Activity 1-11

Using Separation Methods

Problem

How can you separate a mixture of three or more substances?

Materials

mixture of three or more substances

your choice of the equipment available

Procedure

1. Examine your mixture carefully. In your group, list the characteristics of the various substances in it. Then brainstorm methods to separate your mixture.

> **CAUTION:** Check with your teacher about safety precautions.

2. List the steps in the separation procedure you have devised. Beside each step, predict what you think it will accomplish.
3. Obtain your teacher's go-ahead; then carry out your procedure.

Finding Out

1. (a) Several groups will list their separation procedures on posters or on the chalkboard.
   (b) Discuss each procedure. What problems occurred? Was anything omitted? Could the separations be accomplished more efficiently by modifying the apparatus or procedure? How?

Checkpoint

1. In your notebook, write the descriptions in List A and match each description with a separation technique in List B.

LIST A	LIST B
(a) One substance changes to a gas, and then changes back to a liquid.	crystallization
(b) The solute separates from the solvent, forming a solid.	filtration
(c) One substance is made of iron and the other is a non-metal.	evaporation
(d) One substance changes to a gas more readily than the other.	magnetism
(e) The pieces of one of the substances in a mixture are larger than those of the other substance(s).	distillation

2. Describe how you would separate the parts of the following mixtures. For each mixture, explain what makes the separation method effective.
   (a) sand and salt
   (b) brass bolts and iron bolts, all painted the same colour
   (c) dust in a fluffy blanket
   (d) sawdust and sand
   (e) pebbles and sand

3. Explain the meaning of: filtrate, distillate, crystal. If you like, use diagrams in your explanations.

4. A vacuum cleaner contains a filter. Where is this filter located and what does it filter? What problems would occur if the filter were too fine or too coarse?

5. For any two of the separation methods listed in Question 1, describe what occurs in terms of the particle theory of matter.

6. Examine the diagram of a "solar still," a device used to produce pure water from sea water. This device is sometimes included in survival kits for sailors.
   (a) What mixture is being separated?
   (b) What is the effect of the heat from the Sun?
   (c) What separation process does the solar still use?
   (d) Identify the distillate from the separation process.
   (e) How is the residue different from the original mixture?

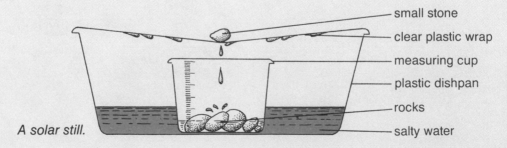

A solar still.

- small stone
- clear plastic wrap
- measuring cup
- plastic dishpan
- rocks
- salty water

Chew a Petroproduct

Did you chew some gum today? Or listen to music on a tape player? If so, you used some "petroproducts." In fact, you use hundreds of products made from petroleum every single day.

The products of petroleum (crude oil) range from fuels for cars, planes, and other vehicles to plastics and synthetic fibres such as nylon, to sunscreen lotions, paints, cosmetics, dental floss, plastic pens and tapes, medicines, glues, mattresses, food preservatives, and even one of the ingredients in chewing gum. These diverse products have one thing in common: they all start out deep underground as crude oil.

Changing a blob of crude oil into useful products doesn't require any magic. All it takes is some science and technology. Crude oil is a mixture of valuable substances that need to be separated before being refined and processed.

Separating crude oil into its liquid parts, or fractions, occurs in an oil refinery in a process called fractional distillation. This technique takes advantage of the fact that different liquids have different boiling points.

Recall that the boiling point is the temperature at which heat causes a liquid to change rapidly to a gas. This is the same temperature at which the gas condenses back to a liquid during cooling.

At the beginning of the process, the petroleum is heated to a temperature so high—about 400°C—that most of it vaporizes. The vapours are channelled into the bottom of a tall tower called a fractionating column. As the vapours rise in the column, they cool and condense back into liquids. Each substance in the crude oil condenses at a different temperature and therefore at a different level in the fractionating column. Trays located at various heights in the column collect the different liquids. Then pipes

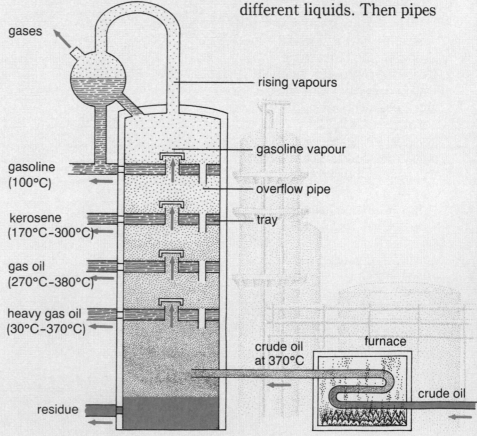

gases

rising vapours

gasoline vapour

overflow pipe

gasoline (100°C)

kerosene (170°C–300°C)

tray

gas oil (270°C–380°C)

heavy gas oil (30°C–370°C)

crude oil at 370°C

furnace

crude oil

residue

A cross section of a fractionating column.

Crude oil is separated and processed in an oil refinery. Notice the tall fractionating columns.

transport the liquids away for further processing.

Some of the liquids are blended and purified to make fuels such as gasoline, kerosene, propane, motor oil, and home heating oil. Others are used as petrochemicals, the building blocks of plastics, vinyls, synthetic fibres, and many other petroproducts.

This climber's life depends on a petroproduct. Her nylon rope is stronger and longer-lasting than natural hemp.

Think About It

1. Do some research and list as many petrochemical products as you can. Check off the products you have used.
2. Imagine what a day in your life would be like without petroproducts. Write a short story or poem about your day.
3. Check out the petroleum in your wardrobe: Which clothes are made of synthetic fibres? List the names of the synthetic materials that are printed on the labels.

Dissolving

What can you do to speed up the dissolving process? Would you heat the solution or cool it, stir it or shake it, put it in the dark or in the light, transfer it to a larger or a smaller container, grind up the solute or leave it in large pieces? How can you compare different solutes? Is there a fixed limit to how much will dissolve, and is this limit the same under all conditions? By using measuring devices such as those shown here, and changing various conditions, you will find answers to these questions.

In this Topic, you'll see how the particle theory can be used to predict answers to these questions. As you test your predictions, you'll be making measurements, so you may wish to refer to Skillbuilder Three, *Measuring Matter*, on page 333.

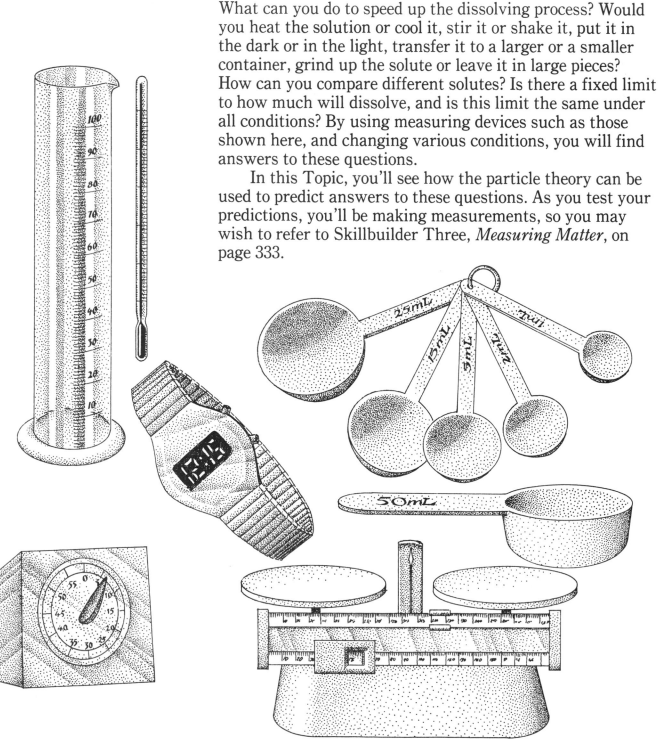

There is a limit to how concentrated a solution can become. When a solution contains as much solute as it can possibly hold at that temperature, it is said to be **saturated**. If more solute is added, it simply doesn't dissolve. The amount of solute needed to saturate a certain volume of solution varies enormously. A solution of one substance in water, for example, may be saturated when only a little of it has been dissolved. On the other hand, a saturated solution of another substance may contain a lot of solute. Why is this so?

In terms of the particle theory, each substance has its own unique type of particle. Particles of one substance may be strongly attracted to each other and only slightly attracted to water particles. Particles of another substance may be more strongly attracted to the water particles than to each other; this substance could form a more concentrated solution in water before becoming saturated.

Did You Know?

The concentration of a solution can be estimated using a device called a hydrometer. You may have seen someone using a hydrometer to test the concentration of the antifreeze solution in a car, or the concentration of acid in the car's battery.

A hydrometer is a long hollow tube with a weight at one end. The more concentrated the solution, the higher the hydrometer floats.

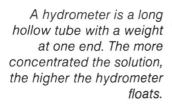

Comparing Solutes

Problem

How are saturated solutions of various solutes different from one another?

Materials

test tube
stopper for test tube
graduated cylinder
solid solute (e.g., table salt, sugar, potassium chloride, aluminum sulphate, or other substance)
scoopula or 2 mL measuring spoon

Procedure

1. Each group of students will use a different solute. To compare the results of different groups, all groups must use standardized methods of measuring and mixing. Decide exactly how large "one scoop" of solute is, how to mix the solution, and how much time to allow for the last bits of solute to dissolve.
2. Pour 10 mL of water into the test tube. Add 1 scoop of the solute assigned to your group, insert the stopper, mix the contents, and then remove the stopper.
3. If all the solute dissolves, add another scoop, insert the stopper, and mix.
4. Repeat Step 3 until some undissolved solute remains in the test tube. (The solution is now saturated.)
5. Record the total number of scoops of solute that dissolved.

Save or dispose of your solution as your teacher directs.
6. The class results will be summarized in a table on the chalkboard.

Finding Out

1. Record the number of scoops of the various solutes that were needed to make a saturated solution in 10 mL of water. List the solutes used by your class, in order, from the most soluble to the least soluble.

Finding Out More

2. Draw a bar graph to illustrate how many scoops of the various solutes were required to make a saturated solution in 10 mL of water. Label the bars and complete them for each solute you select.

3. Read the following statements. For each situation, indicate which solution is more dilute and which is more concentrated.
   (a) Rainwater contains a small amount of dissolved carbon dioxide, but a soft drink contains much more of this gas.
   (b) Amin mixed so much sugar with his tea that he could hardly stir it, but Rachel added only one lump of sugar to hers.
   (c) Angela thought the fruit punch was much too sweet; the apple juice was more to her liking.
   (d) Industrial sewage flows into a river. Tests show that the water downstream from the sewage outlet contains tiny amounts of harmful chemicals.

4. Which solution(s) in Question 3 is (are) probably saturated? Give a reason for your answer.
5. (a) Of the solutes investigated in your class, which has particles that seem to be most attracted to water particles?
   (b) Which solute has particles that seem to be least attracted to water particles? Explain your answers.

Extension

6. "Dilute" and "concentrated" are used to describe solutions *qualitatively*, that is, without measurements. A *quantitative* description involves numbers. Think of a way to describe the concentration of a solution quantitatively. You could say, for example, that a certain saturated solution contained "six scoops of dissolved solute per litre of solution." Include information about both the amount of solute and the amount of solvent or solution. (Hint: There are several possibilities, involving measurements of mass and/or volume.)

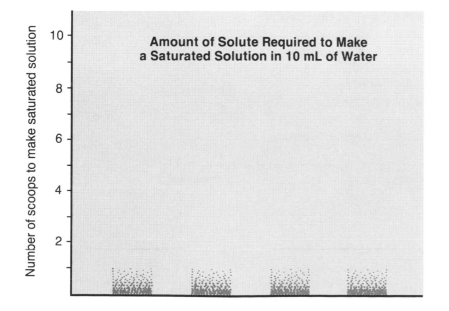

Amount of Solute Required to Make a Saturated Solution in 10 mL of Water

Number of scoops to make saturated solution

Solute

Solubility

Table 1-5 shows data from an investigation carried out by a class of Grade 8 students. They added six different solutes to 10 mL samples of water until no more of the solutes would dissolve. All the solutions were then saturated. All six substances are soluble in water. However, for each substance, only a certain amount dissolved. In other words, each substance has a different solubility in water. **Solubility** is the maximum amount of solute that will dissolve in a specific quantity of solvent at a specific temperature.

1. Table 1-5 shows that the saturated solution of table salt contained less solute than the saturated solution of sugar. In other words, salt is *less soluble* in water than sugar is.
   (a) Compare the solubilities of sugar and baking soda in water at 20°C. Which is more soluble?
   (b) Which is more soluble in water at 20°C: copper(II) sulphate or potassium nitrate?

   (c) Which is less soluble in water at 20°C: table salt or baking soda?
2. (a) In this investigation, what was the manipulated variable? (For a review of variables, refer to Skillbuilder Four, *Graphing*, on page 338.)
   (b) What was the responding variable?
   (c) List as many variables as you can think of that were kept constant in this investigation.
3. The solubilities in this investigation are given as grams of solute that dissolved in 10 mL of water. Solubility is often expressed as grams of solute that dissolve in 1 L of solvent. For example, the solubility of sugar is 20 g/10 mL, or 2000 g/L.
   (a) In your notebook, list all the substances from Table 1-5. In a column beside the list, write the solubility of each substance expressed as g/10 mL.
   (b) In a second column, write the solubility of each substance expressed as g/L.

Table 1-5 *Amount of Solute that will Dissolve in 10 mL of Water at 20°C to Form a Saturated Solution*

SOLUTE	MASS OF SOLUTE (g)
Sugar	20
Baking soda	7
Potassium nitrate	6
Table salt	4
Copper(II) sulphate	3
Alum	1

Temperature and Solubility

Problem

How does temperature affect the solubility of a solute?

Materials

graduated cylinder
3 test tubes
rubber stopper for test tubes
thermometer
ice
3 beakers (each 250 mL)
appropriate solute (e.g., hydrated sodium carbonate or sodium sulphate)
scoopula or 2 mL measuring spoon
hot plate

Procedure

1. Half fill the three beakers with water. Add ice to one beaker, leave one beaker at room temperature, and heat the third beaker on a hot plate.

cold water bath   room-temperature water bath

hot water bath

Table 1-6

TEMPERATURE (°C)	NUMBER OF SCOOPS OF SOLUTE ADDED TO 10 mL OF WATER	NUMBER OF SCOOPS OF SOLUTE DISSOLVED IN 10 mL OF WATER

2. Pour 10 mL of water into each test tube. Place one test tube in each of the three water baths. Leave the test tubes there while you copy Table 1-6 into your notebook.
3. When the temperature of the water in the cold test tube has fallen below 5°C, record the temperature in your notebook.
4. Remove the test tube from the water bath, and add one scoop of solute. *Quickly* insert the stopper, turn the test tube upside down several times, and put the test tube back in the same water bath. Remove it *briefly* to check whether or not all the solute has dissolved. If it has, add another scoop of solute, and mix and check the solution as before. Repeat this process until some solute remains undissolved in the test tube. Record the number of scoops of solute that you added.
5. Note the temperature of the water in the test tube at room temperature, and repeat Step 4.
6. Note the temperature of the water in the heated test tube (it should be between 40°C and 60°C), and repeat Step 4.

7. For each temperature, record in your table the number of scoops of solute that dissolved (that is, one less than the number of scoops added).
8. Put all three test tubes into the ice water bath. In your notebook, record what you observe.

Finding Out

1. (a) How does higher temperature affect the solubility of the solute in water? Use data from this Activity as evidence for your answer.
   (b) How does lower temperature affect the solubility of the solute in water? Again, give evidence for your answer.
2. (a) Why did you return the test tube to the water bath each time, after you added a scoop of solute?
   (b) If you had forgotten this step with the cold solution (Step 4), how might your results have been affected?
   (c) If you had forgotten this step with the hot solution (Step 6), how might your results have been affected?
   (d) Explain why the instructions "quickly" and "briefly" are included in Step 4. For which temperature (cold, room temperature, or hot) are these instructions least important?

Finding Out More

3. (a) Suppose you have a friend who carries out a similar investigation in another school. In your friend's class, the number of scoops of solute that would dissolve at each temperature is quite different. What could cause this difference?
4. Table 1-7 on page 40 shows data obtained by students doing an experiment similar to this one, but using potassium nitrate as the solute. Draw a graph of the solubility of potassium nitrate, setting up the axes, as shown on page 40. After plotting the four points on the graph, draw a smooth curve to join them.

Solubility Graphs

Table 1-7

TEMPERATURE (°C)	NUMBER OF SCOOPS OF POTASSIUM NITRATE THAT DISSOLVED IN 10 mL OF WATER
4	2
18	4
37	7
52	11

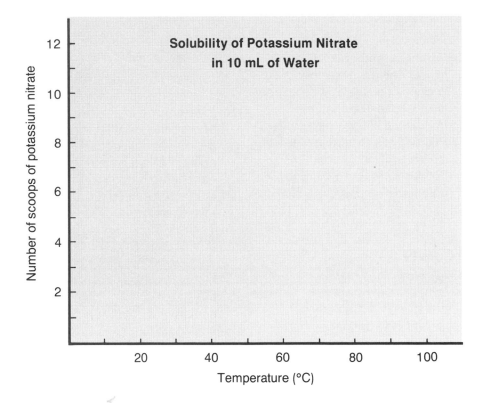

Solubility of Potassium Nitrate in 10 mL of Water

1. In Activity 1-15 you measured solubility as "number of *scoops* that dissolved in 10 mL of water." It is more common to measure the *mass* of solute that will dissolve in a given amount of solvent. In the graph shown on page 41, solubility is expressed as "number of *grams* that will dissolve in *100 mL* of water." Use this graph to estimate answers to the following questions:

   (a) How many grams of potassium nitrate will dissolve in 100 mL of water at the following temperatures?
   - 15°C
   - 30°C
   - 50°C

   (b) What is the lowest temperature at which the following amounts of potassium nitrate will dissolve in 100 mL of water?
   - 40 g
   - 65 g
   - 80 g

   (c) Which of the following are saturated solutions in 100 mL of water?
   - 30 g of potassium nitrate at 18°C
   - 43 g of potassium nitrate at 50°C
   - 80 g of potassium nitrate at 48°C
   - 90 g of potassium nitrate at 55°C

5. Use your graph from Question 4 to estimate answers to the following questions:

   (a) How many scoops of potassium nitrate would dissolve in 10 mL of water at 10°C?

   (b) How many scoops of potassium nitrate would dissolve in 10 mL of water at 95°C?

(d) At what temperature would 52 g of potassium nitrate make a saturated solution in 100 mL of water?

(e) How many grams of potassium nitrate must be used to produce a saturated solution in 100 mL of water at 20°C? If this solution were cooled to 10°C, what would you probably observe? Explain your answer.

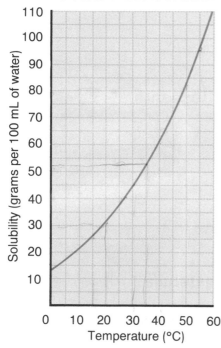

Solubility of Potassium Nitrate in Water

2. In a high-school chemistry laboratory, students investigated the solubility of alum and obtained the data shown in Table 1-8. Use this data to plot a solubility graph for alum. Then use your graph to answer the following questions:

(a) If you want to dissolve 25 g of alum in 100 mL of water, how hot must the water be?

(b) How much alum will dissolve in 100 mL of water at 15°C?

(c) Extend the curve of your graph to higher temperatures. Then predict how much alum would dissolve in 100 mL of water at 70°C.

3. Examine the data for the solubility of table salt in Table 1-9. Plot this data on the graph you made in Question 2, using a different colour from the line you drew for alum. Refer to your graph to answer these questions:

(a) At the following temperatures, which contains more dissolved solute: a saturated solution of alum or a saturated solution of table salt?
- 20°C
- 60°C

(b) For which substance, alum or table salt, is solubility more affected by changes in temperature?

Table 1-8 *Solubility of Alum in 100 mL of Water*

TEMPERATURE (°C)	ALUM (g)
0	5
10	7
20	10
30	14
40	22
50	30
60	47

Table 1-9 *Solubility of Table Salt in 100 mL of Water*

TEMPERATURE (°C)	TABLE SALT (g)
0	35.7
10	35.8
20	36.0
30	36.2
40	36.5
50	36.7
60	37.3

Summary: Factors Affecting Solubility

In several Activities you have seen three main factors that affect solubility: the solvent, the solute, and the temperature. Activity 1–3 showed that the *solvent* affects solubility. You found that copper(II) sulphate dissolves in water, but not in salad oil. Activity 1–13 showed that different *solutes* have widely differing solubilities, even in the same solvent at the same temperature. For example, you can dissolve more baking soda than alum in water at 20°C. Activity 1–15 showed that *temperature* affects solubility. Most solids are more soluble in water at higher temperatures.

Any quantitative statement about solubility must mention all three of these factors. For example, instead of saying "a lot of salt dissolved," you can be more precise and say "36.0 g of salt dissolved in 100 mL of water at 20°C."

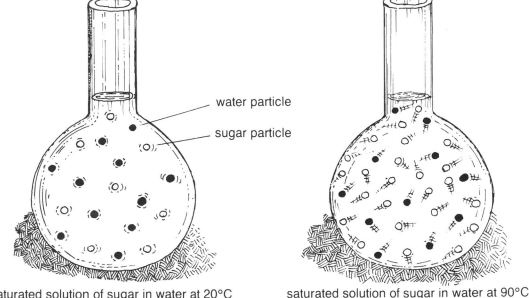

water particle

sugar particle

saturated solution of sugar in water at 20°C   saturated solution of sugar in water at 90°C

At a higher temperature, more sugar can dissolve in the same volume of water.

Designing Solutions

Your challenge in this Topic is to design a solution and demonstrate that it freezes at exactly –2°C. You have already prepared for this challenge by studying Topics One to Five. You'll be even better prepared after doing the two preliminary investigations that follow.

Maybe this solution will solidify!

Freezing Point and Melting Point

If you have lived for more than a year in Canada, you've observed melting and freezing. During the regular cycle of the seasons, snow and ice disappear, only to reappear a few months later. Changes in the weather cause water to change state again and again. Some substances (antifreeze, for example) can remain liquid even in the coldest winter. Other substances remain solid in both winter and summer. The characteristics of different types of matter differ because the tiny particles that make them up differ from substance to substance.

The particle theory provides a reasonable explanation for changes of state (page 6). Many observations have shown that pure substances have a specific temperature at which they change from one state to another. The **freezing point** is the temperature at which a liquid changes to a solid. Pure liquid water at sea level, for example, freezes into a solid (ice) at 0°C. The **melting point** is the temperature at which a solid changes to a liquid. Pure ice melts into liquid water at 0°C. The **boiling point** is the temperature at which a liquid changes rapidly to a gas. Pure water at sea level boils at 100°C. Now try some experiments to find out about the freezing point of solutions.

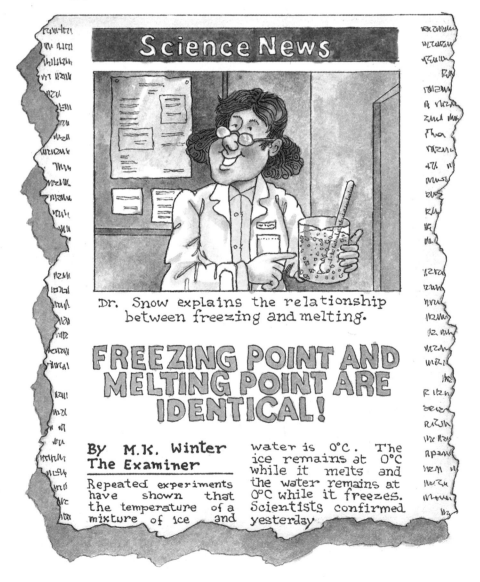

Science News

Dr. Snow explains the relationship between freezing and melting.

FREEZING POINT AND MELTING POINT ARE IDENTICAL!

By M.K. Winter
The Examiner

Repeated experiments have shown that the temperature of a mixture of ice and

water is 0°C. The ice remains at 0°C while it melts and the water remains at 0°C while it freezes. Scientists confirmed yesterday

You could verify the scientist's results at home, using ice cubes in a cold drink.

Activity 1-17

Preliminary Investigation #1

Problem

How does dissolved salt affect the freezing point of water?

Materials

4 large beakers (each 400 mL)
crushed ice
salt (sodium chloride)
large scoop
thermometer
stirring rod (made of unbreakable material)

Procedure

1. Copy Table 1–10 into your notebook.
2. Put identical amounts of crushed ice into four beakers.
3. To the first beaker, add two scoops of salt; to the second beaker, add one scoop of salt; and to the third beaker add ½ scoop of salt. Add nothing to the fourth breaker.

CAUTION: Do not use the thermometer to stir the solutions in the beakers.

4. Use a stirring rod to stir each beaker thoroughly.
5. After about 2 min, observe and record the temperature of each solution. Look carefully to compare the amount of ice left in each beaker, and record your observations.

Table 1-10

AMOUNT OF SALT ADDED	TEMPERATURE (°C)	OTHER OBSERVATIONS
2 scoops		
1 scoop		
$\frac{1}{2}$ scoop		
none		

Finding Out

1. For the beaker containing no salt, did your results agree with the news flash in the cartoon on page 44? List reasons for any difference between your results and those in the newspaper headline.

2. (a) In the beaker with the lowest temperature, was there any liquid?
   (b) Would pure water stay liquid at this temperature?
   (c) Is the freezing point of salt water lower or higher than that of pure water?

Finding Out More

3. Draw a bar graph to illustrate your results.

4. How is the freezing point of a salt solution related to the concentration of salt?

5. Your observations in this lab were quantitative. You measured equivalent volumes of water and equal-sized scoops of salt, and you obtained numerical values for the temperatures. However, the experiment was not completely controlled. Describe how you could improve this investigation so that the results could be checked by other groups using different equipment.

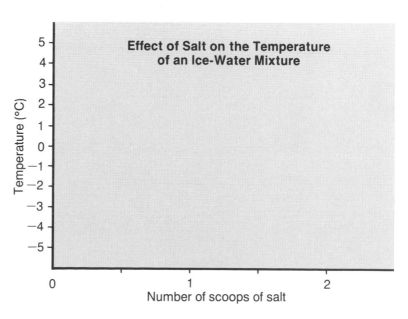

Did You Know?

The substance that has been called "table salt" or "salt" in this Unit has the chemical name *sodium chloride*. Table salt is purified sodium chloride, usually with a little sodium iodide added. Road salt is also mainly sodium chloride.

Salting Roads

In winter, snow and ice can make driving hazardous. To combat these hazards, salt is often spread on roads. As the solid salt comes in contact with the snow, some of the snow melts because salt lowers the snow's melting point. The resulting salt solution spreads out and prevents falling snow from sticking to the surface of the road. Snowploughs can then easily remove the mixture of unmelted snow and salt-water solution.

Salting roads makes driving safer, but it also causes some serious problems. Where salt is used, cars rust much more quickly. Also, salt damages metal bridges, concrete parking garages, and the pavement itself. Salt spray from passing cars damages plant life up to 500 m from the road. If the concentration of salt in soil and streams increases, it can make the water in springs and wells unfit to drink.

When winter deicing salt penetrates through tiny openings in reinforced concrete, it can speed up the rusting of the steel reinforcements. The rust takes up more space than the steel, and the force of this expansion can cause the concrete to crumble.

Probing

When the temperature is below −15°C, salt is no longer effective in melting ice. In which of the five cities listed in Table 1–11 do you think salt is used regularly to melt the ice on roads? Explain your answer.

Table 1–11

	MEAN JANUARY TEMPERATURE	MEAN JANUARY SNOWFALL
Calgary	−12°C	21 cm
Edmonton	−15°C	27 cm
Toronto	−7°C	33 cm
Montreal	−10°C	53 cm
Halifax	−4°C	46 cm

Preliminary Investigation #2

To design a solution that will freeze at -2°C, you could use salt, but maybe you could use some other solute more easily. Try the following investigation before you decide.

Problem

Do other dissolved substances affect the freezing point of water in the same way that salt does?

Materials

4 large beakers (each 600 mL)
stirring rod
thermometer
crushed ice
substance that is soluble in water (e.g., sugar, baking soda, alum, or any substance suggested by your teacher)
device for measuring amount of solute (e.g., scoop, graduated cylinder, balance, etc.)

Procedure

> **CAUTION:** Do not use the thermometer to stir the solutions.

1. Repeat the procedure used in Activity 1-17, but use a solute other than salt. Be sure to measure the amount of solute added to each beaker.

2. Make a table for your observations. Compare the temperatures and the amounts of ice remaining in the beakers after 2 min.
3. If necessary, repeat one or both of these preliminary investigations in order to decide exactly how much of which solute is needed to make a solution that freezes at -2°C.

Finding Out

1. List the solutes and quantities used in both these preliminary investigations, along with the freezing temperature of each solution. Suggest possible "recipes" for your solution with a freezing point of -2°C.

Extension

2. Would a mixture of solutes, rather than only one solute, make the temperature of a solution colder? Design an investigation to find out.

In western Canada, where temperatures often fall below -15°C, calcium chloride is sometimes spread on roads. While calcium chloride is more effective than salt at colder temperatures, it does cost more, and it causes similar environmental damage. Research is under way to find another solute that would work as well as salt and calcium chloride, but would be relatively inexpensive and cause less damage to cars, bridges, pavement, and living organisms.

Antifreeze

The cooling system of a car contains liquid that circulates through the engine. The moving liquid removes heat from the engine and transfers it to air passing through the radiator. If pure water were used as the coolant, the water would freeze when the engine was shut off in the winter. Solid water (ice) would be useless in the cooling system—it could not circulate through the radiator. To prevent the liquid in the engine from freezing, **antifreeze** (ethylene glycol) is added to the water to lower its freezing point. Depending on the lowest temperature expected, different concentrations of antifreeze are used (see Table 1–12).

(see Table 1–12)

On a hot summer day, especially in stalled traffic, the engine temperature of your car can rise above 100°C, the boiling point of water. If the liquid in your car's cooling system boils, it soon evaporates, causing the engine to overheat and be damaged. Antifreeze is left in the engine's cooling system in the summer as well as in the winter, because the antifreeze in the solution raises the boiling point above 100°C.

Table 1-12

PROPORTION OF SOLVENT AND SOLUTE		PROTECTION AGAINST FREEZING AT TEMPERATURES ABOVE:
WATER	ETHYLENE GLYCOL	
65 parts	35 parts	-18°C
60 parts	40 parts	-24°C
50 parts	50 parts	-36°C
40 parts	60 parts	-64°C

Even in winter, the engine of a car gets very hot. A properly working cooling system that contains antifreeze prevents the engine from overheating.

Antifreeze is useful in summer as well as in winter. It raises the boiling point of the liquid in the cooling system of a car's engine.

The Challenge

Problem

How can you make and freeze a solution with a freezing point of exactly -2°C?

Materials

large beaker
crushed ice
stirring rod
solute
timing device with a second hand
measuring device (e.g., scoop, graduated cylinder, or balance)

Procedure

1. Decide exactly how to define "frozen" in this investigation. (This step is important—without it, the challenge could be like a marathon without a finishing line.)
2. Plan your procedure. (Hint: Make an ice bath, combining what you learned in Activity 1-15, with equipment from Activity 1-17 or 1-18.)
3. Obtain your teacher's go-ahead, and try out your procedure.

Finding Out

1. Which solutes, at what concentration, were used by groups that designed a solution successfully?
2. Write your results on the chalkboard in a table that summarizes the results of the entire class.
3. List any factors that the successful procedures had in common.
4. If any solutions froze at temperatures other than -2°C, suggest how the solutions could be changed so that they would freeze at -2°C.

Finding Out More

5. How would the solubility of a particular solvent affect its suitability for lowering the freezing point of water?
6. What might be one advantage of a liquid solute over a solid solute in the design of this experiment?

At ski resorts, artificial snow is made by spraying water into the air from high-pressure equipment. The water freezes in the cold air, forming crystals and falling as snow. Ski-resort operators want ice to form as quickly as possible, even when the temperature is relatively warm. Researchers in a private company, working with the Alberta Research Council, have developed a product that speeds up the formation of ice crystals. When this product, which is made from a type of dead bacteria, is mixed with the spray, snow-making becomes more efficient.

Working with Glass

Sometimes, when lightning strikes a beach, sand, lime, and soda ash fuse together, producing thin tubes of glass. About 3500 years ago, the Egyptians studied these natural occurrences and learned to make glass.

Today, glass blowers like Daniel Crichton heat these same substances together in a special fire-brick furnace to make a glass that has the consistency of thick molasses. Because of the intense heat (temperatures up to 2400°C are reached), glass blowers wear safety glasses and lightweight cotton clothing.

When the glass melt is ready, it is gathered on the end of a stainless-steel blowpipe. The pipe is rolled back and forth to shape the gather of glass. The glass can then be hollowed out and expanded by blowing into the pipe. Most of the tools used to work the glass are stainless steel because it can be heated and cooled repeatedly without deteriorating.

Daniel first became interested in glass during daily walks around the city he lives in. "I really enjoyed looking at the colourful stained-glass windows in the old houses." He now teaches a three-year community college program in glass arts and design. Besides learning

A fragment of a fish-shaped Egyptian glass vase (from about 300 A.D.).

the skills needed to work with glass, his students explore the nature and history of glass, artistic expression, drawing, photography, and how to deal with galleries and shops. Community colleges in Alberta, Quebec, and Ontario offer courses in glass arts. Most graduates of these programs become self-employed artisans, although a variety of careers can be pursued in arts and design.

Daniel Crichton at work in his studio.

Some students go on to take apprenticeship programs in scientific glass blowing, learning how to make highly specialized laboratory equipment.

The unique and mysterious properties of glass continue to fascinate Daniel. "Glass is a mixture of 70% silica sand, 20% soda ash, and about 10% limestone. By adding different elements such as cobalt or copper to this mixture, you can get many different colours and alter the transparency of the glass. Glass has interesting properties. For example, the hotter glass gets, the softer and more fluid it becomes. There is a broad temperature range within which you can manipulate it. It gets soft at about 550°C to 600°C, and from there up, it gets softer and softer.

"What I enjoy about glass blowing is that it is a blend of the artistic and the scientific. If you are interested in arts, crafts, and design, try to make sure that your high-school program is balanced, by taking courses in both arts and sciences. There are literally thousands of different types of glass, each with its own special physical and chemical characteristics, and you need to understand these in order to be a successful glass artisan."

Checkpoint

1. Write an accurate statement containing all the words in each list below.
   (a) dilute, solvent, solute
   (b) concentrated, dilute, solution
   (c) saturated, solvent
   (d) solubility, solvent, solute, temperature
   (e) diffusion, soluble
   (f) saturated, solubility
2. The illustration shows identical uncooked eggs—one in a beaker of pure water and one in a beaker of salt water. Which beaker contains which liquid? Explain your answer.

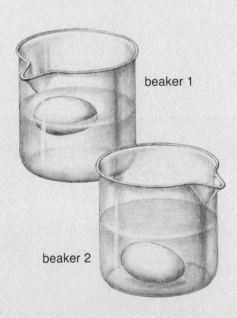

beaker 1

beaker 2

3. (a) What three factors affect the solubility of a solid in a liquid?
   (b) Examine the photograph of the two flasks. Both water and ethanol are clear, colourless liquids. What can you infer about the solubility of iodine in these two substances?

4. Read these statements written in a student's notebook. Decide which are correct, which are incorrect, and which are incomplete. If the statement is wrong or incomplete, write the correct or complete version in your notebook.
5. (a) Suppose you had a test tube of water with some undissolved alum at the bottom. How could you make the alum dissolve?
   (b) Would the same method work as well for undissolved salt? Explain your answer.
6. Use the particle theory to explain what happens when a solid dissolves in a liquid. Include a sketch in your answer.

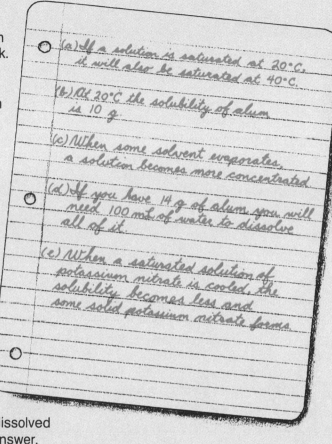

(a) If a solution is saturated at 20°C, it will also be saturated at 40°C.

(b) At 20°C the solubility of alum is 10 g.

(c) When some solvent evaporates, a solution becomes more concentrated

(d) If you have 14 g of alum, you will need 100 mL of water to dissolve all of it.

(e) When a saturated solution of potassium nitrate is cooled, the solubility becomes less and some solid potassium nitrate forms.

IODINE + ETHANOL

IODINE + WATER

Brainstorming Separation Methods

Problem

How can you separate the parts of mixtures?

Procedure

1. Examine the illustrations. Brainstorm ways in which the parts of each mixture could be separated. (Hint: Think of the properties of each substance. Does the substance float or sink in water? Does one of the substances dissolve? Could you separate the parts with forceps? Would a magnet attract one of the substances?)

2. Discuss the separation methods suggested. Predict whether or not these methods would be practical and effective. Try to think of equally effective alternative methods.

Finding Out

1. (a) Make a list of the separation methods suggested by the class.
   (b) For each method, identify the properties of the substances that make the separation possible.

Extension

2. Using only a cardboard box, cardboard, scissors, and tape, construct a mechanical sorter for pennies, nickels, dimes, quarters, and loonies.

(a) marbles and styrofoam balls

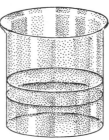
(d) oil and water

(b) soil and water

(f) wood chips and pieces of brick

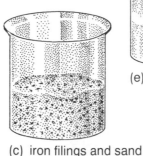
(c) iron filings and sand

(e) salt and pepper

Activity 1-12

Testing Hypotheses

Problem

What factors affect the speed of dissolving?

Materials

solid solute
beakers, test tubes, stirrers, etc., as needed
timing device with a second hand

Procedure

1. Refer to the key points of the particle theory on page 5. Use them to make a hypothesis about at least two procedures that might make a solid dissolve faster in water.
2. For *one* of the procedures, design an experiment that will allow you to test your hypothesis. Be sure that you control all variables except one.
3. Check your procedure with your teacher; then try it out. Carefully time how long the dissolving process takes, from the time the solute is added to the water, until it has completely dissolved.

Finding Out

1. On the chalkboard, list all the procedures tested by everyone in the class. Beside each procedure, indicate whether or not it affected the speed of dissolving and, if so, whether it speeded up or slowed down the dissolving process.

Finding Out More

2. Suggest at least two procedures that you hypothesize would have no effect on the speed of dissolving. Explain why you think they would have no effect.

Concentration of Solutions

The terms **dilute** and **concentrated** are used to compare the amount of solute in different solutions. Whatever the volume of two solutions being compared, the solution with less solute is said to be more dilute, and the one with more solute is said to be more concentrated. For example, lemonade with a small amount of sugar dissolved in it is a more dilute solution than lemonade with a lot of sugar dissolved in it. The lemonade with lots of dissolved sugar in it is more concentrated and tastes sweeter, compared with the more dilute solution. You can compare the concentrations of solutions in this way, using any volume—ranging from large quantities as in the cartoon, to small samples in test tubes, as in Activity 1-13.

When you add sugar to your lemonade, do you prefer a more dilute or a more concentrated solution?

Focus

- According to the particle theory, all matter is made up of tiny particles.
- The particle theory helps to explain the characteristics of matter.
- Matter can be classified as pure substance, mechanical mixture, or solution.
- The solutes and solvents in solutions may be solid, liquid, or gas.
- The parts of mixtures and solutions can be separated in several ways; the properties of the substances in a particular mixture determine which separation methods will be effective.
- Concentration of solutions and solubility of solutes can be expressed both qualitatively and quantitatively.
- Knowledge of mixtures and solutions is applied in many everyday applications.
- Some solutions, such as antifreeze, are designed with specific properties for specific purposes.

Backtrack

1. Write the letters (a) to (e) in your notebook and read the following statements. Beside each letter, write T if the statement is true and F if the statement is false. Rewrite each false statement to make it accurate.
   (a) "Mixing" and "dissolving" have the same meaning.
   (b) In both the process of filtration and the process of distillation, there is a residue.
   (c) Water dissolves most solids.
   (d) Solubility is the amount of solute that will dissolve in a particular solvent at a specific temperature.
   (e) Antifreeze is a pure liquid that never changes to a solid.
2. (a) How can you tell whether a mixture is a solution or a mechanical mixture?
   (b) How can you distinguish a solution from a pure substance?
3. (a) State the particle theory of matter. (Include all key points.)
   (b) Use the particle theory to explain the differences among mechanical mixtures, solutions, and pure substances.
4. What separation methods could you use most easily to separate the parts of the following mixtures and solutions?
   (a) sand and salt
   (b) copper(II) sulphate and water
   (c) water and sugar
   (d) oil and water
   (e) feathers and sand
   (f) wood chips and brick chips
   (g) iron nails and iron bolts
5. Name a solution that:
   (a) you eat;
   (b) you wear;
   (c) you breathe; and
   (d) is produced in your body.
6. Name a mechanical mixture that:
   (a) you eat;

   (b) is used as a construction material; and
   (c) can be made fit to drink.
7. (a) Write a definition of solubility.
   (b) What factors affect the solubility of a substance?
   (c) Name one substance that is insoluble in water but soluble in oil.
   (d) Name one substance that is more soluble in hot water than in cold water.
8. Use the solubility graph below to answer the following questions.

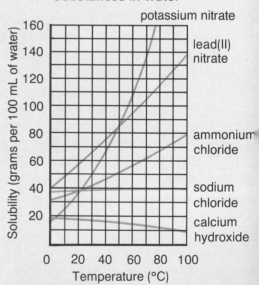

Solubility of Five Substances in Water

(a) For which of the substances is the solubility most constant as the temperature of the water changes?
(b) For which substance does the solubility decrease as the temperature increases?
(c) What is the solubility of ammonium chloride at 50°C?

(d) At what temperature do potassium nitrate and lead(II) nitrate have the same solubility?

(e) If you dissolved 50 g of lead(II) nitrate in 100 mL of water at 60°C, how much more solute would you have to add to the water in order to have a saturated solution?

(f) A chemical engineer, involved in a company's financial planning, is calculating how much solute can be recovered and reused in an industrial process. From a saturated solution of lead(II) nitrate in 100 mL of water at 60°C, how much solute would be recovered if the temperature were lowered to 2°C?

9. (a) How is the freezing point of water affected by dissolved solutes?

(b) Describe two ways in which we make use of this effect of solutes on freezing point.

Synthesizer

10. Reread the four questions on the opening page of this Unit about panning for gold, ice-cream makers, surgical masks, and lemonade. Using your knowledge of mixtures and solutions, write answers to the questions.

11. Often, the soil around a potted house plant appears white after the surface of the soil has dried out. Explain what causes this.

12. Sewage is an interesting mixture of substances! Besides food scraps, human waste, and chemicals, it also contains things that are dropped into street sewers — for example, wallets, coins, watches, and even dentures. Design a method of separating and treating sewage so that it can be returned to the river or lake as clean water. Your method may be similar, but not identical, to the treatment of drinking water.

13. Have you ever noticed that honey, once it starts to crystallize, rapidly becomes solid? It may remain liquid for months, then solidify in a week. Why does this happen so quickly? Try putting two samples of liquid honey in clean jars. To one jar, add a spoonful of solid honey. Store both jars in the same place. After you have completed your observations, develop a hypothesis to explain what happened.

How does adding solid honey affect the crystallization of liquid honey?

14. Soft drinks contain a lot of dissolved carbon dioxide. What keeps this gas dissolved in the liquid? Examine some pop bottles and cans and discuss the following questions with your class.

(a) In large pop bottles, why is the glass so thick?

(b) Why do bottled soft drinks go "flat" if the top is not replaced tightly?

(c) Why are soft drinks not sold in cardboard containers like milk cartons?

(d) Which remains fizzy for a longer time: cold pop or pop at room temperature?

(e) For solutions of gas in liquid, what is the fourth factor that affects solubility?

(f) Sketch and describe your own design for a new soft-drink container. It should be:

- reusable (so the materials are not wasted);
- cheap (so you will make a profit on sales); and
- in one piece (so that discarded lids will not litter the landscape).

Evaluate the designs suggested by your classmates. Think of other features besides those mentioned here that you want to include in your own design.

Energy and Machines

It's 7:30 in the morning. Sarah's alarm clock rings. She flicks the switch on her bedroom wall to turn on the light. She walks to the bedroom door and turns the doorknob. Then she goes into the bathroom, closes the door, turns the handle on the tap, and washes her face.

The day has barely started, and Sarah has already used five machines. Think of all the other machines she will use before she leaves home and heads off to school.

In a single day, you use dozens of machines. You may use a pencil sharpener, stapler, bicycle, car, train, skateboard, door hinge, wrench, screwdriver, and front door key. All are machines. So are pulleys, crowbars, scissors, wheelbarrows, nutcrackers, and automobile jacks. Your list of machines would be very lengthy if you tried to name all the machines you know.

In this Unit, you'll learn about many kinds of machines, how they help us accomplish tasks, and how combinations of simple machines can produce more complex machines. You will design, build, and test some mechanical devices made up of simple machines, to gain experience first-hand. How do you fix that broken gadget? How do you invent your own machine? Read on to find out!

What Is a Machine?

A **machine** is any device, simple or complicated, that uses energy to perform a useful task or function. The energy the machine uses may be chemical energy (from a fuel), light, electricity, or some other form of energy. Later in this Unit, you'll learn more about **energy**, which scientists sometimes define as the ability to do work.

In science, work has a special meaning. **Work** is done on an object (1) if a force is exerted on the object, and (2) if the object moves for a distance in the general direction of the force. Recall from your previous studies that to change the motion of an object a force (pushing or pulling on the object) is required. Forces are measured in newtons (N).

In the cartoon, Hasan and Andrea have lifted a rock from the ground up onto the truck. They have done work on the rock, because they have exerted a force on it (equal to the force of gravity on the rock), and they have also lifted the rock a certain distance (equal to the height of the tailgate of the truck).

On the other hand, Maria and David have been pushing on their car for 15 min, but it hasn't moved at all. Therefore, they have not done any work on the car.

Hasan and Andrea together exert a force, and are able to lift a rock a distance equal to the height of the tailgate of the truck. By using their energy they have caused this movement of the rock. They therefore have done work on the rock.

Maria and David have also exerted a force by pushing hard to get the car moving, but the car has not moved. They therefore have not done any work on the car.

Systems and Subsystems

Even the most complicated machine is just a combination of simple machines. Each of the nonsense machines built by Roland Emett, like the one shown in the photograph, is really made up of many simple machines. The six most common simple machines are the ramp, the pulley, the lever, the wheel-and-axle, the wedge, and the screw. You'll learn more about each of these simple machines later in this Unit.

Think of a complicated machine as a **system**. Its working parts make up the **subsystems** of the machine. How do the subsystems—the basic simple machines or components that make up complex machines—ensure that the whole system performs a certain task or function?

Simple machines use energy to do work in a variety of ways. For example, in the following Activity, try to solve this problem: Imagine that a block of wood is a heavy crate that you must lift a certain height onto a truck. You cannot lift this heavy load without using some sort of machine. As you do the Activity, you will experiment with two common simple machines: the **inclined plane** (more commonly called a ramp) and the **pulley** (a rotating wheel with a grooved rim). You will measure the force you have to exert to move a load, with and without the help of a machine. The force you exert is called your **effort force**.

This contraption was designed by British inventor Roland Emett.

Ramps and Pulleys

Problem

How can you lift a load with the help of a ramp and a pulley?

Materials

smooth board for ramp (an unused bookshelf will do)
single pulley
string (about 1.5 m)
block of wood with a hook on it
5 N spring scale
several books
support stand
C-clamp
protractor (to measure the angle of the ramp)

Procedure

1. Copy Table 2-1 into your notebook.
2. Use the spring scale to lift the block straight up, as in diagram (a). In your table, record the force of gravity exerted on the block.

3. To get the load onto the truck, you could use a ramp. Set the board at an angle of about 30° to the surface of your work area, as in diagram (b). Pull the block up the ramp at a steady speed, using the spring scale. Determine how much force you need to pull the load up to the (imaginary) truck. Record this force in Table 2-1.

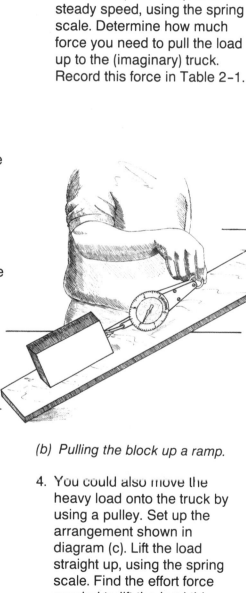

(c) Using a movable pulley to help lift the block.

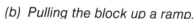

(b) Pulling the block up a ramp.

4. You could also move the heavy load onto the truck by using a pulley. Set up the arrangement shown in diagram (c). Lift the load straight up, using the spring scale. Find the effort force needed to lift the load this time. Record this force in Table 2-1.

5. Find out what happens if you combine both the ramp and the pulley into one lifting system. Set up the arrangement in the illustration. Use the spring scale to pull the load up the ramp at a steady speed, as shown in diagram (d). Record the effort force in Table 2-1.
6. Perhaps you can think of a way to make raising the load onto the (imaginary) truck easier still. If so, ask your teacher for appropriate materials, then try out your improved system.

(a) Lifting the block straight up.

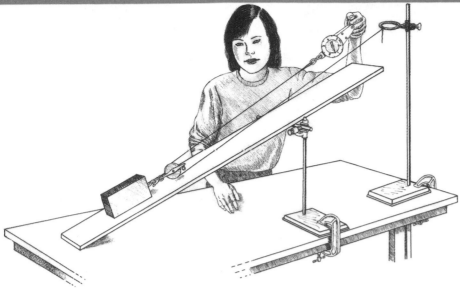

(d) Using both a ramp and a pulley to lift the block.

Table 2–1

	EFFORT FORCE NEEDED (N)
to lift the block straight up	
to pull the block up a ramp	
to lift the block using a pulley	
to pull the block up a ramp using a pulley	

Finding Out

1. (a) What was the force of gravity on the load you lifted?
   (b) When you lifted the load without the help of a machine, what was your effort force?
   (c) What was your effort force when you used the ramp to help you lift the load?
   (d) By about how much did the ramp reduce the effort force you had to exert: by about one-quarter, one-third, or one-half?
2. (a) When you lifted the load using only the pulley, what effort force did you exert?
   (b) By how much did the pulley reduce the effort force you had to exert: by about one-quarter, one-third, or one-half?
3. (a) When you used both the ramp and the pulley, what effort force did you have to exert?
   (b) By how much did the system of the ramp plus the pulley reduce the effort force you had to apply: by about one-quarter, one-third, or one-half?
4. Was there any practical advantage in using a combination of two different machines? If so, what was this advantage?

Finding Out More

5. (a) If you tried to improve the system (Step 6), describe what you did.
   (b) How did your improved method affect the force you had to exert to lift the load?

Extension

6. See if you can devise a system to lift a given load to a certain height, using the least effort force possible. (You may wish to try this project after you learn about other simple machines that might be used, in the Topics that follow.)

This pulley system, called a block and tackle, is used to lift heavy loads.

Easing the Task with Levers

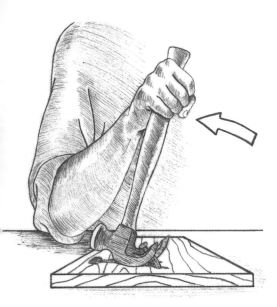

You have seen how using a ramp or a pulley can reduce the force you need to exert (often called your effort force). Another effort-reducing simple machine is the lever. In its simplest form, a **lever** might be a wooden rod used to pry a rock loose in a garden or field. A crowbar is a typical lever, but many mechanical devices can be used as levers. A hammer, for example, can be used as a lever to pull out a crooked nail.

Levers appear in a variety of "disguises": a seesaw, a balance scale, a bottle opener, a can opener, a nutcracker, a wrench, bolt cutters, scissors, a golf club, a hockey stick, a tennis racket, a baseball bat . . . and, believe it or not, your arms, legs, and jaws are all levers!

In the next Activity, you will see how levers can do work for you.

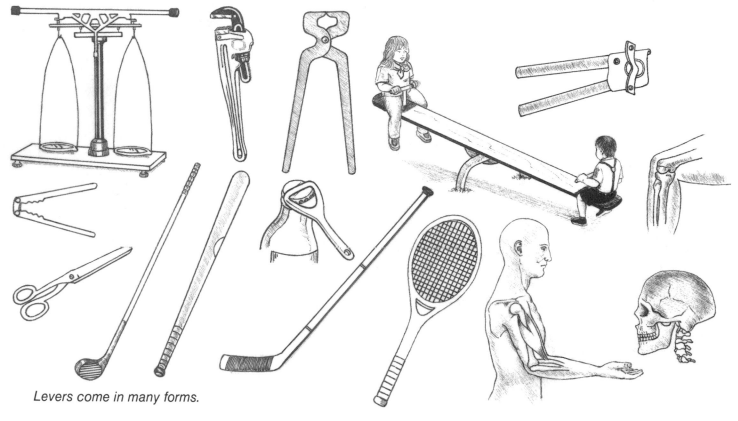

Levers come in many forms.

Experimenting with Levers

Problem

How can a lever be used to make it easier to lift a load?

Materials

metre stick
fulcrum (pivot)
200 g mass
1 kg mass
20 N spring scale
set of small masses
supporting wire or thread loops

Procedure

PART A

1. Set up the lever arrangement shown in illustration (a). Note the position of the **fulcrum**. This is the point that supports the lever and upon which it turns, or pivots. The fulcrum, in this set-up, is close to the 50 cm mark, where the metre stick remains balanced; that is, it tends not to rotate one way or the other.

2. Hang a 200 g mass (the load) from one end of the metre stick. Predict what mass you will need at the other end of the stick to make it balance again. Test your prediction.

3. Use the spring scale to measure the force of gravity on this balancing mass, and on the mass at the other end of the stick.

4. Make a simple sketch of the lever, and label it to show the two forces on it, in newtons (N). (Show the force on the 200 g load, and your effort force.)

5. Move the fulcrum from the 50 cm mark to the 25 cm mark. Hang the 200 g mass at 0 cm, as in illustration (b). Predict what will happen when you try to lift the 200 g mass by adding a mass near the 100 cm mark. Will the balancing mass be more than before, the same as before, or less than before?

6. Test your prediction. Now use the spring scale to measure the force of gravity on the balancing mass. Sketch the lever and label it to show the force on the 200 g load, and the effort force.

7. Experiment to see what you must do to make it easy to lift a heavy load with a lever (the metre stick).

(a)

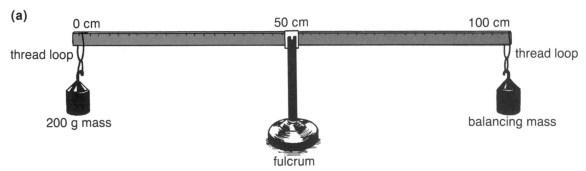

A simple lever system, with the fulcrum in the middle of a metre stick.

(b)

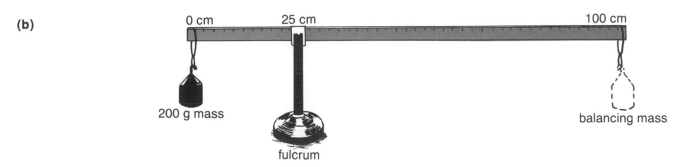

8. See if you can balance the 200 g mass using only the metre stick itself, with no added masses.
NOTE: When a lever's fulcrum is between the load and the effort force, it is called a **Class 1 lever** (see the diagram).

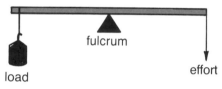

Class 1 lever.

Finding Out

1. How would you use the lever if you want to lift a heavy load with the smallest possible effort force? (Make a simple labelled diagram to illustrate your answer.)
2. How might you change the lever itself to make lifting the load even easier?

PART B

1. Measure the force of gravity on a 1 kg mass, using a 20 N spring scale.
2. Set up the lever arrangement shown below, with the 1 kg load at the 50 cm mark, and the fulcrum at the 0 cm mark. Predict what will happen when you try lifting the load by applying an upward force at the 100 cm mark.
3. Test your prediction. Use the spring scale to measure the effort force needed to lift the load.
4. Sketch the lever you used, and label it to show the force on the 1 kg load and your effort force.

5. Experiment to see how you could use this lever arrangement to make your effort force as small as possible. Note the position of the best place to put the load. Record where you should apply the effort force.
NOTE: When a lever is arranged with the fulcrum at one end, the load in the middle, and the effort force at the opposite end from the fulcrum, it is called a **Class 2 lever** (see the diagram).

effort

load

fulcrum

Class 2 lever.

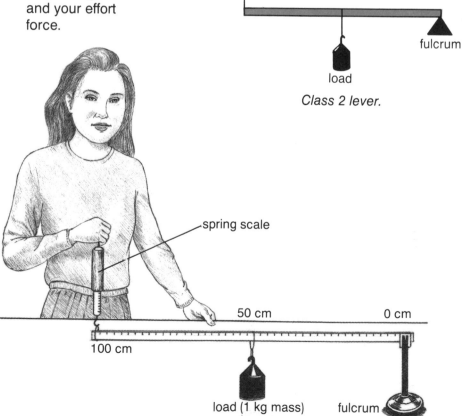

spring scale

50 cm

0 cm

100 cm

load (1 kg mass)

fulcrum

Finding Out

1. A wheelbarrow is actually a lever much like the one you just set up.
   (a) If you have to move a heavy load, where in the wheelbarrow will you put the load? Explain your answer.
   (b) Make a simple labelled diagram to show where the effort, load, and fulcrum are located in a wheelbarrow.

A wheelbarrow is a Class 2 lever.

2. When a can opener like this one is used, where is the fulcrum, where is the load, and where is the effort force applied? Draw a simple labelled sketch to illustrate your answers.

PART C

1. Set up the lever arrangement shown in the illustration. The fulcrum is at 0 cm again, but the 1 kg load is at 100 cm.
2. Exert an effort force at 50 cm by pulling the spring scale upward. Predict whether the effort force will be more than the force on the load, the same as the force on the load, or less than the force on the load. Test your prediction.
3. Experiment to see what happens when you leave the load where it is, but apply the effort force at different places between the fulcrum and the load.

NOTE: When a lever's effort force is between the fulcrum and the load, it is called a **Class 3 lever** (see the diagram).

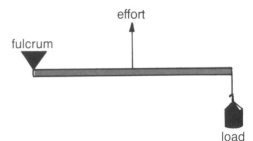

Class 3 lever.

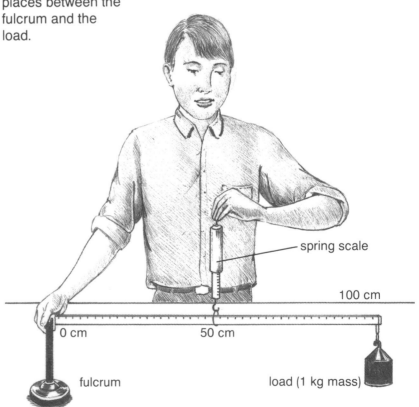

Finding Out

1. In a Class 3 lever, is the effort force ever less than the force exerted on the load?
2. A Class 3 lever may seem rather pointless at first glance, because it does not make lifting a load easier. However, it is the most frequently used class of lever. If a Class 3 lever does not reduce your effort force, what kind of benefit does it give you? (Hint: When you used this type of lever to lift a load, how far did the load move when you exerted your effort force just a small distance?)
3. A golf club and a baseball bat are Class 3 levers. List at least four other examples of Class 3 levers.
4. (a) Sketch a human arm lifting a book. Label the sketch to show where the fulcrum is, where the load is, and where the effort force is applied.
   (b) Repeat (a), but this time sketch a leg kicking a soccer ball.

Finding Out More

5. Levers were probably one of the first simple machines used. What tools do you think early people might have used that were really levers?

The importance of levers was recognized thousands of years ago. No doubt, various simple tools were used as levers in ancient times. Levers are seen in Egyptian sculptures dating back 5000 years. Aristotle of Greece mentions the lever in his writings, and Archimedes, another famous Greek thinker (287–212 B.C.), studied the mathematics of levers. Archimedes is said to have made this statement about levers: "With a lever long enough and a point to stand upon, I could move the world."

What You've Learned About Levers

You now know the following facts about levers:
- There are three types of levers.
- They are formed by varying the arrangement of three things: the load, the fulcrum, and the effort force.
- The arrangement of these three things depends on the lever's function.

   The next two Topics discuss three more simple machines and the work they do for us.

Checkpoint

1. In your notebook, copy the words in the left-hand column below. Beside each word or words, write the best matching description from the right-hand column.

2. Suppose that lifting a load straight up requires a force of 600 N. If the same load is pushed up a ramp, will the effort force be 600 N, more than 600 N, or less than 600 N?

3. Describe three situations in which you have seen ramps used to help people move heavy objects to higher levels.

4. Describe three situations in which pulleys are used to make lifting objects easier.

5. The photographs show some devices that are levers, or that include levers in their design. Try to identify the class of lever in each device (Class 1, Class 2, or Class 3).

(a) effort force	a device that uses energy to perform a useful function
(b) fulcrum	done when a force is exerted over a distance in the general direction of the force
(c) inclined plane	unit of measurement of a force
(d) jaw	a simpler part of a complex machine
(e) machine	the scientific term for a ramp
(f) newton	the force you exert to operate a simple machine
(g) seesaw	the point on which a lever pivots, or turns
(h) subsystem	an example of a Class 1 lever
(i) wheelbarrow	an example of a Class 2 lever
(j) work	an example of a Class 3 lever

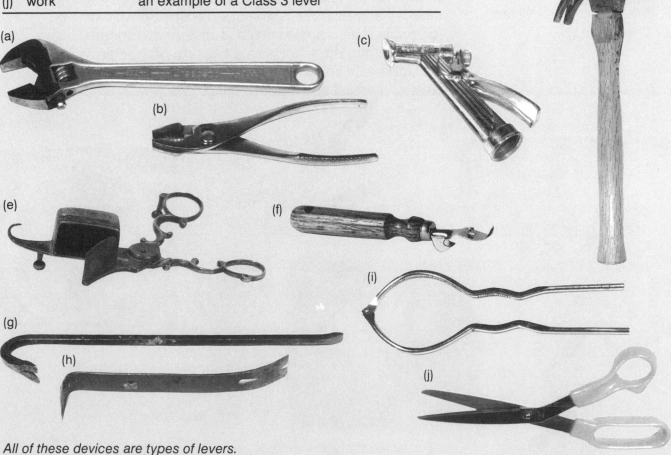

All of these devices are types of levers.

The Wheel-and-Axle

A basic wheel-and-axle diagram showing:
- wheel
- axle
- load
- effort force applied here
- front view
- effort force / load
- side view

A basic wheel-and-axle.

Imagine trying to open a door without a doorknob! Doorknobs are an example of another simple machine you use every day—the wheel-and-axle.

The diagram shows a basic **wheel-and-axle**. A rope passes over a large wheel. The effort force is exerted on this rope. The load is attached to the axle, which is a smaller wheel. The photographs show a variety of devices that include wheels-and-axles.

Quite often, a wheel-and-axle is used to overcome a large force by applying a smaller effort force, for example, when you use a doorknob. This is called a **force advantage**. Sometimes, though, a wheel-and-axle is used to increase speed—in other words, to obtain a **speed advantage**. (Speed is the distance travelled in a given amount of time.) For example, the wheels on a car or a bicycle provide a speed advantage. In Activity 2–3 you will investigate these two uses of a wheel-and-axle.

wind-up toy car

can opener

key and doorknob

hand brace (drill)

water faucet

steering wheel

Try to locate the wheel-and-axle in each of these devices.

How the Wheel-and-Axle Works

PART A

Problem

How is a wheel-and-axle used to gain a force advantage?

Materials

model wheel-and-axle
500 g load
5 N spring scale
box of masses
metre stick or ruler
string
felt marker
selection of devices that include wheels-and-axles, e.g.:
    key with padlock, can opener with rotating handle, pencil sharpener, doorknob, old-fashioned hand drill, screwdriver, hand-operated food mixer, simple wing nut

Procedure

1. Copy Table 2-2 into your notebook.
2. The diagram shows a typical model wheel-and-axle. The axle has a small radius, while the wheel has a larger radius. The load to be lifted is attached to the axle, while the effort force is exerted at the edge of the wheel.
3. Hang a load of 500 g from the axle. This load exerts a downward force of 5 N on the axle.
4. Measure what mass is needed at the wheel to balance the 500 g load. Record this mass in your notebook.

Table 2-2

FORCE EXERTED AT AXLE (N)	RADIUS OF AXLE (cm)	FORCE EXERTED AT WHEEL (N)	RADIUS OF WHEEL (cm)
5			
5			
5			

5. Measure the force of gravity on the balancing mass, using the spring scale. Record this force in Table 2-2.
6. Measure the radius of (a) the axle and (b) the wheel, in centimetres. Record these measurements in Table 2-2.

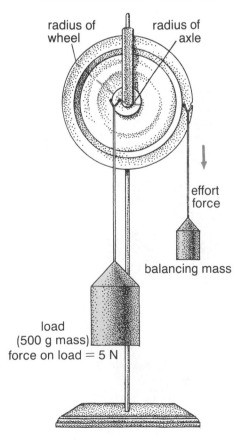

radius of wheel   radius of axle

effort force

balancing mass

load (500 g mass)
force on load = 5 N

7. If the model wheel-and-axle has several different sizes of wheels, measure the balancing effort force at the edge of each wheel. Do this by hanging masses from the wheel until you find the one that balances the 500 g load.
8. Measure the force of gravity on the balancing mass, using the spring scale. Record this force each time in Table 2-2. Measure and record the wheel radius for each trial as well.

Finding Out

1. (a) In Step 4, if the force on the balancing mass is the effort force, was the effort force less than, the same as, or greater than the force on the load?
   (b) Why is the wheel-and-axle said to give a force advantage when used this way?
2. In Step 7, you used wheels of different radii. What happens to the size of the effort force when the radius of the wheel is increased, while the same axle is used?

PART B

Problem

How is a wheel-and-axle used to gain a speed advantage?

Procedure

1. Copy Table 2–3 into your notebook.
2. Set up the wheel-and-axle with the 500 g mass at the axle, and a suitable balancing mass at the edge of the largest wheel.
3. Mark the starting positions of the bottom edge of both the 500 g mass and the balancing mass.
4. Now pull the 500 g mass down 1 cm. Measure how far up the balancing mass moves.
5. Repeat this, pulling the 500 g mass down through distances of 2 cm and 3 cm. Record the distance the balancing mass moves up in each case.

Finding Out

1. In Steps 4 and 5, you applied an effort force at the axle instead of at the wheel. This makes it harder to move the load (which is now at the wheel). Why is this arrangement said to give a speed advantage instead of a force advantage? (Recall that speed is equal to distance travelled in a given amount of time.)

Table 2–3

FORCE EXERTED AT AXLE (N)	DISTANCE MASS AT AXLE MOVES (cm)	FORCE EXERTED AT WHEEL (N)	DISTANCE MASS AT WHEEL MOVES (cm)
5	1		
5	2		
5	3		

2. (a) From the photographs on page 66, select any three examples of wheels-and-axles. Sketch each one. Show where the load is and where the effort force is applied.
(b) State whether each example gives a force advantage or a speed advantage.

Finding Out More

3. (a) Name several wheels-and-axles you can identify on this bicycle.
(b) Where on a bicycle is a wheel-and-axle used for a force advantage?
(c) Where on a bicycle is a wheel-and-axle used for a speed advantage?

Completing Your Survey of Simple Machines

So far, you have looked closely at four types of simple machines: (1) the ramp (or inclined plane); (2) the pulley; (3) the lever (three classes); and (4) the wheel-and-axle.

Before you look at more complex mechanical devices, and begin to design a device of your own, you need to know about two more simple machines you can use in your designs. These machines are so simple that it's hard to think of them as machines. Yet they are—each reduces the effort force required to perform certain tasks.

One of these is the **wedge** (see the diagram). A wedge is similar to an inclined plane, except that a wedge normally moves into an object (for example, an axehead cuts into a block of wood), while an inclined plane stays still and objects move along it. The photographs show some devices that involve wedges in their design.

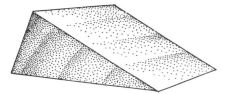

The simple machine known as a wedge is similar to an inclined plane.

golfer's sand wedge

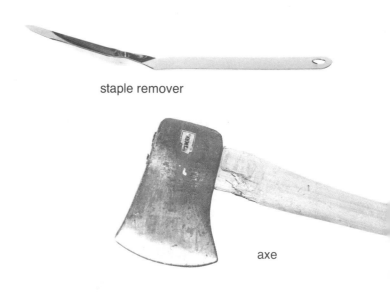

staple remover

axe

wood-chopping wedge

These common devices feature wedges as part of their structures.

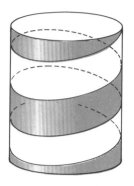

A screw can be thought of as an inclined plane that has been wrapped around a cylinder.

Finally, a sixth type of simple machine is the **screw**. This machine is an inclined plane that is wrapped around a cylinder (see the illustration). A wood screw can penetrate even hardwoods (such as the wood of oak or maple trees) quite easily. This is because the screw is made of such a long inclined plane that the effort force needed to turn it is greatly reduced.

An inclined plane may be as simple as a plank used to roll a motorbike onto a trailer, or it could appear as a path winding up a steep hill. A wedge can be thought of as a two-sided inclined plane. A screw is really a spiralling inclined plane.

Many devices can be classified as screws.

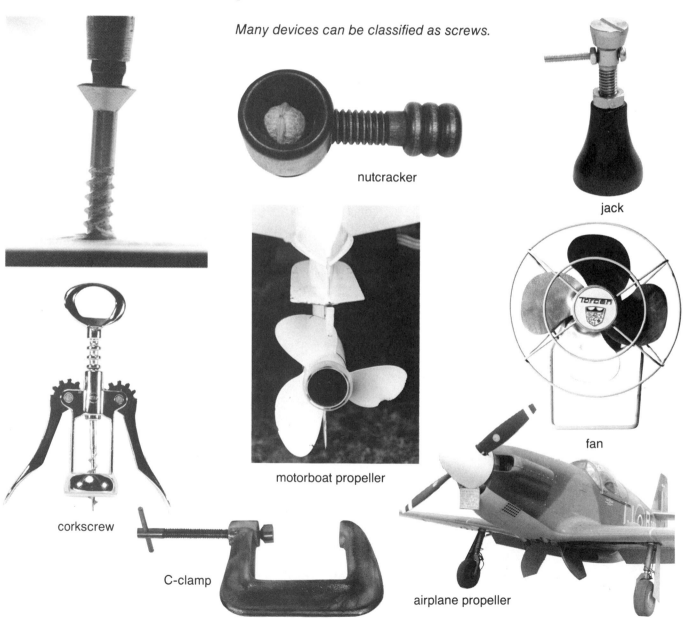

nutcracker

jack

motorboat propeller

fan

corkscrew

C-clamp

airplane propeller

The water faucet is an application of the simple screw. When you turn off a tap, a screw or threaded bolt with a washer at its lower end is screwed down by the handle, which presses the washer into a hole. This shuts off the flow of water. When the tap is turned on, the bolt is unscrewed, the washer comes out of the hole, and the water runs out the tap. If the washer wears out and does not close the hole properly, the result is a tap that leaks.

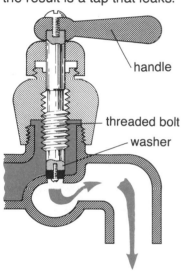

handle

threaded bolt

washer

Making Machines

Commercial construction kits are excellent for inventing your own complex machines made up of the simple machines to which you have now been introduced. The photographs show two student inventions, each using a different construction kit: Lego Technic and fischertechnik.

This machine was built with a Lego Technic construction kit.

This machine was built with a fischertechnik construction kit.

Today there are contests for young inventors, just as there are Science Fairs and Science Olympics. One recent winner of such a contest, Amy Seiden, invented a way to save herself time and energy. Her father liked to practise golf putting. Her task—a boring one—was to retrieve the golf balls for reuse. What did she do? She attached a fishing reel to the shaft of the putter, just below the grip on the handle, and she then attached the fishing line to a golfball. This enabled her father to retrieve the ball by reeling in the line. Simple, but effective. In fact, the invention has been patented and is now being manufactured and sold! Amy was only nine years old when she came up with this idea. Keep an eye out for such contests if you like to invent things.

Amy Seiden and her invention.

An Egyptian pyramid was built before 2000 B.C. It is made of millions of carefully shaped stones, each as massive as 1000 kg. Details of how these huge stones were transported to the site and moved into place are not known for sure. Suggest possible ways that simple machines or combinations of simple machines might have been used to construct a pyramid.

Building with Simple Machines

Problem

How can you design and build a machine that uses at least three of the simple machines you've learned about?

Materials

construction kit such as Lego Technic or fischertechnik; or laboratory equipment and materials from other sources

Procedure

Decide on a simple task you would like a machine to do. Then design and build a machine to carry out the task. You may use either a small motor and batteries or your own energy (by turning a crank, for example) as the energy source to operate your machine.

After you have built and tested your machine, write a brief report on its operation. Include in your report any sketches that would help others understand how it functions. As well, include a trouble-shooting section in your report; for example: Did your design work? How well did it work? How do you think you could improve your design?

Who used the first machine? Put yourself in the position of an early human who had only his or her own arms, legs, and body to push or pull on objects to make a shelter for protection or to obtain food. We think the first machine was probably a tree branch or stone used as a lever. We know people began to use stone tools almost 2 million years ago. If you look closely at these stone tools, you will see that most of them, too, are simple machines.

Checkpoint

1. When you use a screwdriver to drive a screw into a wall, you use two kinds of simple machines. Draw a simple labelled diagram of a screwdriver to show where the simple machines are.
2. Name two simple machines involved when you use scissors to cut a piece of paper. Use a sketch to illustrate your answer.
3. (a) What kind of simple machine is your lower jaw?
   (b) Where in your mouth would you find a wedge?
4. When you use a simple hand-held pencil sharpener to sharpen a pencil, what kinds of simple machines are involved?
5. (a) Why does a ship often have a large steering wheel?

(b) In a modern car, the steering wheel is quite small compared to that of a ship. Why is a large steering wheel not needed in this case?
6. Where in these devices will you find a wheel-and-axle?
   (a) fishing rod
   (b) movie projector
   (c) meat grinder
   (d) radio or television set
   (e) tape recorder
7. What part of these devices consists of a screw? Illustrate your answer with a simple drawing.
   (a) water faucet
   (b) plumber's pipe wrench
   (c) boat motor
8. What kind of simple machine is a potato peeler?

9. Examine a selection of screwdrivers and screws (or refer to the photograph). One type of screw has a simple slotted head. Another type has an X-shaped depression in its head. This is called a Phillips head. A third type has a square, box-shaped depression. This is called a Robertson head.
   (a) What are the advantages and disadvantages of the various designs of screws?
   (b) Look at the screwdriver in the photograph. What design features make it especially versatile (that is, useful for a large number of functions)?

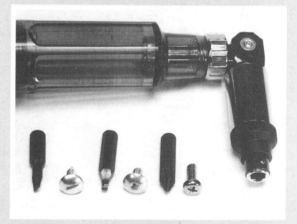

A versatile screwdriver, with a selection of screws.

The steering wheel of this ship is a large wheel-and-axle.

Examining Mechanical Devices

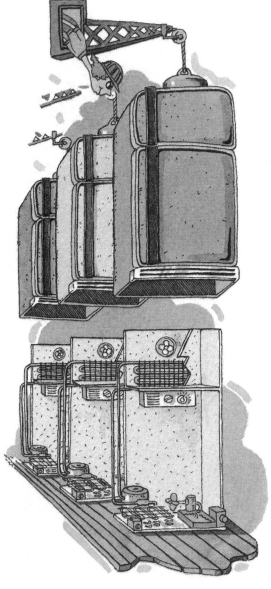

The mechanical devices (systems) you find in your home contain one or more subsystems made up of simple machines. Mechanical devices are usually made up of large numbers of such simple machines. If you look inside mechanical devices you can see examples of these machines, usually as a set of parts that are connected to each other. Sometimes there are also electrical parts to provide the energy for the machines or to help control their operation.

How can you understand how a mechanical device functions? One of the best ways is to examine what each of its subsystems do to help ensure the entire system operates as it should. Often you'll see that certain subsystems do one job and other subsystems do another. For example, a complex device such as a refrigerator is a system to cool food. It requires a subsystem to take away heat, a subsystem to circulate the cool air, a subsystem to permit the opening and closing of its door, and so on.

Many devices are designed to operate automatically—with controls that adjust them to perform properly what they are designed to do. For example, a refrigerator keeps food at a certain temperature. It is designed to shut off when the inside temperature is about 2°C, and to turn on again if the temperature becomes higher than that. Its internal light is designed to turn on when the door is opened and turn off when the door is shut. All this occurs automatically and continuously because of the refrigerator's efficient design and the constant supply of energy through the electricity that it receives.

Systems can operate automatically only if:
1. each subsystem performs the functions for which it is responsible;
2. the subsystems of the system work together as a whole;
3. the system has controls that are self-correcting (think of the refrigerator, for example); and
4. the system has a constant energy supply.

Systems such as the stapler need only (1), (2), and (3). Why? Because the energy is supplied only when the mechanical device is in use. Energy is supplied by a person when the stapler is needed.

The main subsystem of the stapler uses a lever. See illustration (a). When you push down on the end of the lever, a single staple is forced through a narrow opening, and the staple's pointed ends strike a plate called the **anvil**.

Illustration (b) shows two hollowed-out depressions in the anvil. These permit the staple to bend inward so that it attaches the pages together. Illustration (c) shows the staple just before it is bent at the anvil.

Illustrations (d) and (e) show the **channel** holding a strip of staples. A coiled spring pushes the staples toward the front of the stapler lever, so that the stapler is always "loaded."

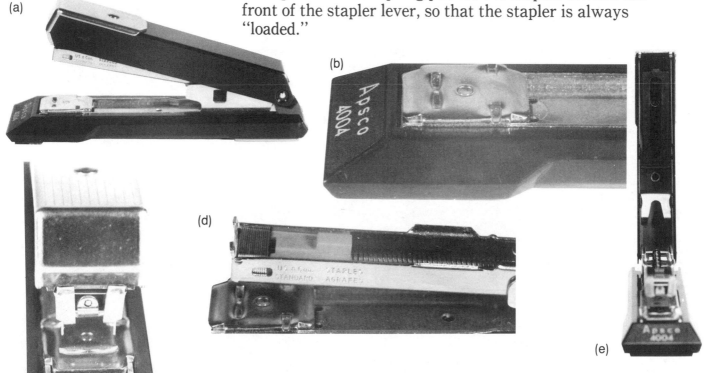

(a)

(b)

(d)

(e)

(c)

A stapler has several subsystems that allow it to perform its function.

The stapler has five subsystems:
1. a subsystem to hold the strip of staples and keep them in position in the channel;
2. a subsystem that uses a lever to deliver the force needed to free a single staple from the strip and drive it downward into the anvil;
3. a subsystem to deliver the staples one by one;
4. a subsystem to bend the staples so that they fasten sheets of paper together; and
5. a subsystem that uses a spring to return the lever to its starting position, ready to eject the next staple.

Systems and Subsystems in Everyday Devices

Now it's your turn to select a common mechanical device and analyse how its subsystems work together to perform a function. You may choose one of the devices shown here, or any other device you'd like to examine. Present your findings in the form of a report or a poster.

- Closely examine the device. Record all of its subsystems that work together to ensure the device functions as it should.
- Describe how each subsystem carries out its function as a part of the system.

- Describe or draw a flowchart that shows how all the subsystems work together.
- Be sure you include controls. In other words, what makes the system return to its starting position, ready to perform its function again?
- As part of your report, discuss how the size, structure, and materials of which the device is made are important in permitting all the subsystems to work together so that the system as a whole can function.

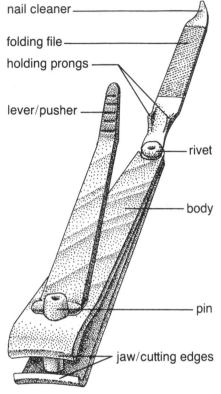

nail cleaner

folding file

holding prongs

lever/pusher

rivet

body

pin

jaw/cutting edges

Fingernail clippers.

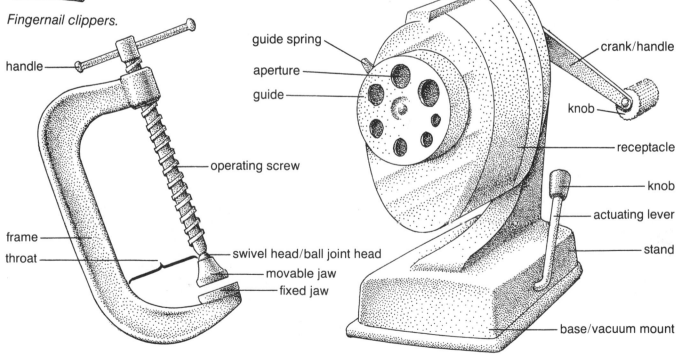

handle

guide spring

aperture

guide

operating screw

frame

throat

swivel head/ball joint head

movable jaw

fixed jaw

crank/handle

knob

receptacle

knob

actuating lever

stand

base/vacuum mount

C-clamp.

Pencil sharpener.

Extension

1. Look at the camper's can opener shown below.
   (a) What three functions does this device perform?
   (b) Identify and describe as many subsystems as you can.
2. Think of a musical instrument such as a guitar.
   (a) What subsystems can you identify?
   (b) What is the function of each subsystem? (If necessary, get help from a student who plays the instrument.)
3. What types of simple machines are used in (a) nail clippers? (b) a C-clamp? and (c) a screwdriver?
4. Examine a three-hole punch. How many parts or subsystems can you identify in it? What is the function of each subsystem?
5. Choose an example of a device in your home or classroom that operates automatically. List the subsystems that ensure it continues to operate.

Science and Technology in Society
"Magical" Machines

Did you have a special toy when you were younger, one that was magical or mysterious in some way? Now that you are older, perhaps you've been asked to fix a toy for a young child. If so, there's a good chance that the toy broke because its owner just needed to find out what was making it walk, swim, talk, spin, or growl!

In the 18th and 19th centuries, people were amazed by moving toys called automatons that seemed almost human. One such automaton was "The Writer," a child-like doll that could actually write a 50-word letter. Many people in these times didn't understand the new automated toys they were seeing. Magic, miracles, and witchcraft were thought to cause movement in the toys.

Another intriguing mechanical toy was "The Artist." This automaton could sketch the portraits of famous people of the 18th century, including King George III of England and Marie Antoinette of France!

All the complicated movements in these toys were accomplished by means of gears, levers, and pulleys. Stored energy for prolonged movement came from clockwork mechanisms. Some toys of this era relied on other sources of stored energy, such as wind, water, mercury, and sand. In the 19th century, toys with "sand motors" became popular. Sand trickling through small apertures (openings) caused tiny water wheels to spin and also enabled toy animals to perform many ingenious tricks.

The Writer *is found in the Museum of Neufchatel, Switzerland.*

The Artist *can also be seen at the Museum of Neufchatel, Switzerland.*

Trickling sand causes the monkey's arm to move up and down, so that the monkey appears to feed the kitten.

In 1887, the American inventor Thomas Edison developed the first speaking toy, by fitting a doll with a miniaturized phonograph and disc. The doll's chatter could be varied by simply changing the disc. These interesting dolls were often displayed at fairs and the following was said of them: "The pleasure of a child who has one of these dolls promises to be endless, if he or she can restrain the instinct to find out where the voice comes from!"

The mechanisms that make toys move are generally hidden from view, making them all the more mysterious. But just what does go on inside mechanical toys? In the case of the duck shown in the illustration, a spring is wound, which then releases its stored energy to drive the gear train. Another component, called a cam, converts the rotating motion of the gear train to back-and-forth motion in a lever. This lever drives the duck's feet . . . and off it scoots!

Although many modern toys have sophisticated electronic components, most mechanical toys still rely on the levers, gears, and pulleys that have been powering toys and delighting children—and adults—for many centuries.

Wind-up toys rely on levers, gears, and pulleys to function.

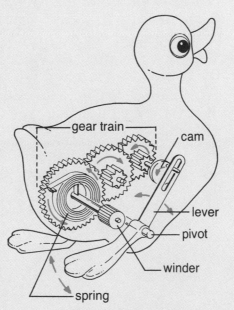

gear train — cam — lever — pivot — winder — spring

Edison's talking doll had a built-in gramophone turntable.

Today's toys might seem much more complex and perhaps more exciting than old-fashioned ones, but the mechanisms inside moving toys haven't changed very much in the past 400 years.

Think About It

Bring in some old wind-up toys from home—toys that could be taken apart to reveal their hidden mechanisms. See if you can discover what makes each toy "go." Try identifying the components by name, and explain with words and sketches how these components work together to make the toy move.

Science and Technology in Society 79

Using Gears

You probably know that cars and bicycles have subsystems of gears that control the transfer of energy from the engine or rider to the wheels of the vehicle. Many simpler devices also use gears of various types to perform particular functions.

A **gear wheel** is a wheel with precisely manufactured, identical teeth around its edge; see illustration (a). A gear wheel is used to transfer rotary motion and force from one part of a machine to another part. To do this, more than one gear wheel is needed. Two or more gear wheels form a **gear train**, as in illustration (b).

The gear wheels in a gear train must **mesh** (interlock neatly) as they rotate. If two meshing gear wheels are different sizes, the larger gear is called a **wheel**, and the smaller gear is called a **pinion**, as in illustration (c).

If you have ever used a push lawnmower, you know that the mower's wheels turn much more slowly than its blades. Why? This is due to the meshing of a gear ring that lines the inside of each wheel, with a pinion attached at either end of the cylinder of cutting blades. This meshing of gears allows the wheels to turn slowly while the blades spin much faster, cutting the grass. After you investigate driving gears and driven gears in this Topic, you'll have a better understanding of how devices like a push lawnmower make tasks easier.

(a) Gear wheel.

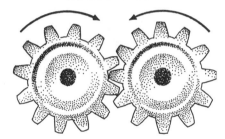

(b) Gear train.

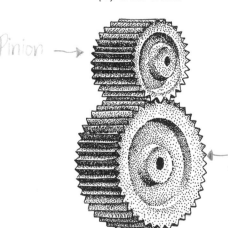

Pinion →

← Wheel

(c) Wheel and pinion.

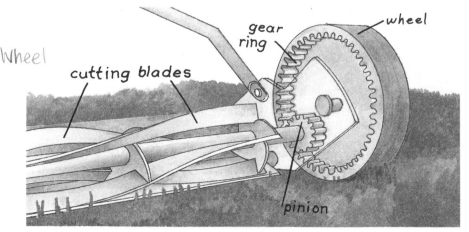

gear ring

wheel

cutting blades

pinion

In a push lawnmower, the gear ring inside each wheel meshes with a pinion attached to the cylinder holding the cutting blades.

driving gear   driven gear

The gear wheel that supplies the driving force is called the **driving gear**, while the gear wheel to which the force is applied is the **driven gear** (see the photograph on the left).

Look at the photograph of a hand-operated food mixer. Your hand turns the handle, which is really a kind of wheel-and-axle. The axle is connected to a large driving gear. The driving gear meshes with and turns the driven gears (which are also pinion gears, since they are smaller than the driving gear). The pinion gears are attached to the long shafts that have the beaters on their ends.

Notice that the driving gear has a large circumference. The driven gears, on the other hand, have small circumferences. This means that as you rotate the driving gear one turn, the driven gears will rotate more than one turn. In fact, the driven gears shown in the photograph rotate four turns for every turn of the driving gear. This gear arrangement produces an increased rotational speed in the beaters. In the next Activity, you will examine the gears in a food mixer more closely.

Driving gear and driven gears in a hand-operated food mixer.

Activity 2-6

Gears in a Food Mixer

Problem

How does a hand-operated food mixer work?

Materials

hand food mixer (a hand-operated drill can be substituted)
felt pen or marker

Procedure

1. Use a felt pen or marker to make small marks on both the driving gear and one of the

driven gears in a hand food mixer. Place the marks so that you can tell whether both gears have completed one full turn.
2. Slowly rotate the driving gear one full turn, by turning the handle of the mixer. Count how many times the driven gear turns while the driving gear turns only once. Record this number in your notebook.
3. Count and record the number of gear teeth on the driving gear.
4. Count and record the number of gear teeth on the driven gear.

Finding Out

1. In the food mixer, how many turns does the driven gear make for every one turn of the driving gear?
2. How many times more gear teeth does the driving gear have, compared with the driven gear?
3. How does your answer to Question 2 compare with your answer to Question 1?

Using Gears   **81**

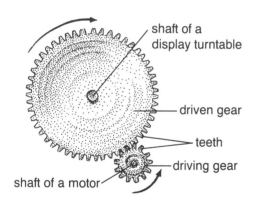

Multiplying gears in a hand-operated drill.

Reducing gears: The driving gear has a small circumference and few teeth; the driven gear has a large circumference and many teeth. The driving gear is the pinion, and the driven gear is the wheel.

shaft of a display turntable

driven gear

teeth

driving gear

shaft of a motor

Multiplying Gears and Reducing Gears

The pair of gears used in the food mixer works to increase rotational (turning) speed. These are examples of what engineers call **multiplying gears**. The illustration shows multiplying gears in a hand-operated drill.

Often the driving gear has fewer teeth than the driven gear (see the diagram). This causes the driven gear to rotate more slowly than the driving gear. Such gears are called **reducing gears**, because they reduce turning speed. A car or bicycle in low gear uses reducing gears.

Have you ever been in a store that displays items of merchandise on a slowly rotating tray? The tray is driven by an electric motor. The shaft of the motor rotates quite rapidly—too rapidly for the display to be effective. A gear system is used, therefore, to slow down the rotation. A driving gear on the motor shaft meshes with a driven gear on the turning axis of the tray. The driving gear has a much smaller circumference (and fewer teeth) than the driven gear. This device involves a reducing gear, therefore.

You have seen how a pair of gear wheels can increase rotational speed or decrease rotational speed. The illustration shows two identical gears—both the same size—meshing with each other. These gears are called **parallel gears**.

Suppose the gear on the left is the driving gear. Since the two gear wheels have the same size and number of teeth, the driven shaft will have the same rotational speed as the driving shaft. However, if the driving shaft were turning clockwise, then the driven shaft would turn counter-clockwise. Try to think of a use for such a gear system.

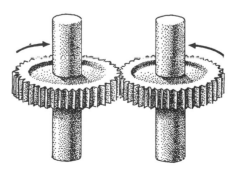

These parallel gears can be used to reverse the direction of rotation.

Gearing Up

Obtain a suitable commercial kit containing various gears, and construct gear arrangements that can be used to perform one of these tasks:
- speed up a rotary motion;
- slow down a rotary motion;
- reverse the direction of a rotary motion;
- change a rotary motion into a straight-line motion;
- transfer a rotary motion from one shaft to another shaft running parallel to it, without changing the direction of rotation;
- transfer a rotary motion from one shaft to another shaft that is at a right angle to the first shaft; or
- perform a task of your own choosing.

Extension

Would gears be useful in the machine that you invented in Activity 2-4? Either improve the machine, or use gears to produce a new machine for performing a certain task.

Gears in a Bicycle

A bicycle is an interesting example of yet another way to use gears. In a bicycle, the gears do not mesh directly with each other. Instead, a looped chain joins them (see the diagram). The gears are toothed discs, called **sprockets**. The front sprocket is attached to the pedal crank. The back sprocket is attached to the hub (axis) of the rear wheel.

When the rider pushes on the pedals, the front sprocket turns. This causes the chain to turn, which makes the rear sprocket turn. When the rear sprocket turns, the rear wheel also turns. This propels the bike forward.

A ten-speed bicycle has five sprockets on the rear wheel, and two sprockets on the pedal crank.

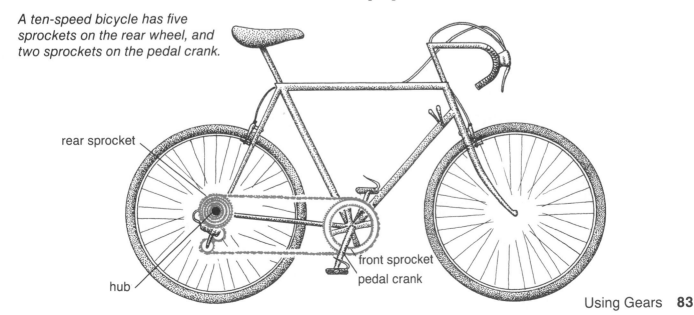

rear sprocket

hub

front sprocket

pedal crank

In a multi-speed bike, there are five sprockets on the rear wheel and two sprockets on the pedal crank. This means that there are ten possible combinations of gears.

Suppose a ten-speed bike is in the highest (tenth) gear. This means that the front sprocket with the larger circumference is used, and the rear sprocket with the smallest circumference is used. This combination gives the highest possible turn rate for the rear wheel. The bike can reach its highest possible speed when it is in tenth gear.

Highest gear.

The lowest gear (first gear) is used when it is more important to decrease effort than it is to increase speed. You use first gear when you ride a bike up a hill. In this gear, the front sprocket that has the smaller circumference is used, along with the rear sprocket that has the largest circumference. This means it is harder to achieve high speed, but the effort force needed to pedal the bike is less. The cyclist must make more turns of the pedal to travel a certain distance, but he or she will not have to push as hard on the pedals.

Lowest gear.

Examining a Bicycle

Problem

What simple machines are used to operate a bicycle?

Materials

one bicycle

Procedure

Examine the bicycle, and answer the following questions.

NOTE: Your answers to these questions may depend on the type of bicycle examined. Write down the type of bike used (ten-speed, five-speed, one-speed, mountain bike, BMX bike, etc.).

Finding Out

1. (a) How many examples of levers can you find on the bike?
   (b) Describe where the levers are and what they are used for.
2. (a) What part(s) of the bike can be classified as screws?
   (b) What is each part used for?
3. (a) How many individual gears or sprockets can you find?
   (b) What are their functions?

Finding Out More

4. Explain how a rider shifts gears when riding a multi-speed bike and describe the result of this action.
5. Describe the action of the brakes on the bike you examined.

1. What special design features does a trick riding BMX bike like the one in the photograph have that a regular bike does not have? (Discuss this with someone who does trick riding on a BMX bike.)
2. Design, on paper, a mechanical device that uses at least three kinds of simple machines. (Remember that the six main simple machines are the inclined plane, pulley, lever, wedge, screw, and wheel-and-axle. You can include gears as a type of simple machine, as well.) Your invention must perform a useful function. Here are some suggestions, but feel free to use your own ideas.
   - chalkboard cleaner
   - burglar alarm
   - peanut-shelling machine
   - fence-painting machine
   - lawnmower
   - window opener
   - wake-up alarm

   Your invention can be serious or funny. If possible, build a working model of your device.

This BMX trick rider has an unconventional way of riding his bike. Describe some design features that this type of bike must have.

Checkpoint

1. The photograph shows one type of food scoop. What is the function of the gear teeth in this device? How does the scoop perform its function?
2. Name any device that uses (a) multiplying gears; (b) reducing gears.
3. Besides increasing rotational speed or decreasing rotational speed, what is another use for gears?

5. The gears in the photograph below are found inside an electric food mixer. The centre gear is called a worm gear. The other two gears are called crown gears.
(a) The worm gear is the driving gear. If it rotates so as to make one of the crown gears turn clockwise, in what direction will the other crown gear turn?
(b) Is this gear combination a multiplying or a reducing gear arrangement? Explain your answer.

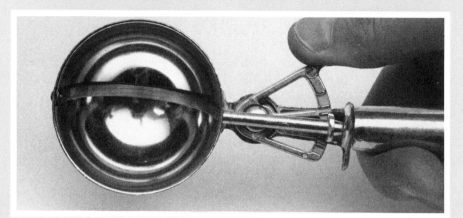

4. For what purpose might you use the device shown below? Are the gears reducing gears or multiplying gears? What other simple machine is used in this system?

6. In a bicycle, the gears do not mesh. How does one gear make the other gear turn?

This device is called a winch.

Sources of Energy to Run Machines

Chemical energy from a potato provides the energy to run this clock.

This toy motor is powered by the chemical energy from the dry cells in a battery.

This aircraft is solar-powered. Special batteries change light energy from the Sun into electricity, which runs the motor that turns the propeller. The aircraft in the photograph crossed the English Channel using only solar energy!

So far in this Unit, you have been the source of energy for most of the machines that have been discussed. You used your own energy to move a block up a ramp, or to operate devices such as a stapler, a pencil sharpener, or scissors. Where does this energy come from? The energy you have, as a living creature, is mainly chemical energy. Within the cells of your body, oxygen is used in a complex series of chemical reactions, producing carbon dioxide and water, and releasing energy. This energy is used to move your muscles, and they do the work necessary to operate a mechanical device.

However, many devices use sources of energy other than human chemical energy. An electric motor is one example. Think of the many devices in your home or car, for instance, that are operated by the electrical energy supplied by motors. The furnace in your home has a motor to drive the fan, which sends warm air throughout your building. Your refrigerator has a motor. An electric clock has a motor. A starter motor gets a car engine going. Clothes washers, hair dryers, record players, electric trains, and many toy cars have electric motors. You can probably think of many other devices operated by electric motors.

The photographs show some ways that electrical energy can be obtained from other forms of energy, in order to operate a motor.

The tides can be used as a source of energy. As the illustration shows, either a rising tide or a falling tide means that water will move a turbine in the generator. An advantage of using the mechanical energy of tides is that no resources are used up, and no harmful substances are produced. Tides are caused by the gravitational pull of the Moon on bodies of water during the various motions of the Earth and the Moon. The gravitational pull of the Sun is also a factor.

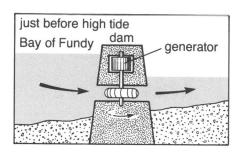

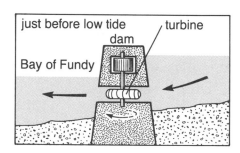

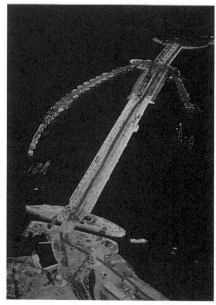

Canada's first tidal generating station is located in the Bay of Fundy, between New Brunswick and Nova Scotia. Tides here are the highest in the world.

Some Forms of Energy

Energy appears in many forms. Light and sound are forms with which you are familiar. Electricity and magnetism are two other forms. **Thermal energy** is the total energy of all the particles in a material or object. (You'll learn more about this in your Grade 9 studies.) Sometimes energy exists in a "stored" form. For example, chemical energy is stored in all kinds of foods and fuels. This chemical energy is "potentially available" to us if we release it by eating the food or burning the fuel. Stored energy is called **potential energy**.

One kind of potential energy is gravitational energy. A skier at the top of a hill has gravitational potential energy. As soon as she starts down the hill, her potential energy begins to be converted into energy of motion. Energy of motion is called **kinetic energy**. Anything that moves has kinetic energy.

When you wind up a spring, you store energy in the spring. This kind of potential energy is called **elastic potential energy**. When the spring is released, the potential energy is transformed into kinetic energy.

Mechanical energy is the type of energy we associate with mechanical devices. Mechanical energy can be kinetic energy (when the parts of the device are moving) or potential energy. (For example, when a grandfather clock's pendulum is at the top of its swing, its energy is potential energy.)

In Activity 2–9, you will examine a number of devices, called **energy converters**, that convert (change) energy from one form into another form.

For example, a solar-powered airplane converts the Sun's light energy into electrical energy to run a motor, which then turns the propeller. The turning propeller has mechanical energy, which is used to move the airplane forward. An electric train converts electrical energy into mechanical energy. A kerosene lamp converts chemical energy into light energy. The tidal generator shown on page 88 converts the mechanical energy of the tides into electrical energy. And when you ride your bicycle, it converts your body's chemical energy into mechanical energy.

Activity 2-9

Energy Converters

Problem

What forms of energy are involved in some energy converters?

Materials

the photographs shown here, or energy converters supplied by your teacher

Procedure

1. Copy Table 2-4 into your notebook, adding a row for each energy converter. In the first column, list the energy converters, adding any others available to you that are not in the photographs.

(a) angel chimes

Table 2-4

DEVICE	FORM(S) OF ENERGY USED (INPUT ENERGY)	FORM(S) OF ENERGY PRODUCED (OUTPUT ENERGY)
candle	chemical	thermal, light

2. Forms of energy used and produced by your devices might include the following: light, thermal, chemical, electrical, sound, gravitational, mechanical, elastic potential, and magnetic. Examine each device closely. Operate the device if possible. Then complete the table (see the sample response provided).

Finding Out

1. Name devices you use regularly that convert energy in each of these ways:
   (a) electricity into thermal energy
   (b) elastic potential energy into kinetic energy
   (c) electricity into light
   (d) chemical energy into kinetic energy
   (e) electricity into sound
   (f) elastic potential energy into gravitational energy

(b) spring-powered toy

(c) lightstick

(d) wind-powered water pump

(e) model helicopter powered by a rubber band

(f) hand-operated generator

(g) flashlight

The Law of Conservation of Energy

You have seen several ways in which energy can be changed from one form into another. Careful measurements by many scientists have convinced them that although energy may change its form, it is never "created" and never "destroyed." Scientists say that energy in a system is "conserved." This means that it is neither created nor destroyed, but transformed (changed from one form into another). This idea is called the *Law of Conservation of Energy*.

Activity 2-10

Designing Your Own Self-Propelled Machine

Problem

How can you construct, from simple materials, a vehicle that will transport a hard-boiled egg over a distance of at least 3 m, without damaging the egg?

NOTE: The vehicle must obtain its energy from one standard-sized elastic band that has been either stretched or wound to store potential energy in it.

Materials

one 15 cm elastic band
anything from which you can construct one homemade vehicle propelled only by the elastic band

Procedure

1. Design your vehicle (a) to go as far as possible, (b) to go as fast as possible, or (c) to go as slowly as possible. (Your class may decide on other design possibilities.) Keep in mind what you have learned about levers, wheels-and-axles, pulleys, and gears.
2. Think about various ways that you can propel the vehicle using the elastic potential energy in a stretched or wound elastic band. Your vehicle should be made from scrap materials, or from low-cost parts. Your teacher will place an upper limit on what you are allowed to spend on your vehicle. Use your ingenuity!

Finding Out

After you've designed, built, and tested your vehicle, describe any changes that you would now make to improve your design.

Selecting an Energy Source

1. Investigate the advantages and disadvantages of operating vehicles using any one of these sources of energy: (a) hydrogen gas as a fuel; (b) solar energy; (c) rechargeable batteries; (d) nuclear energy.
2. Read about pedal-powered airplanes. What is the world record for distance travelled by a pedal-powered plane? What are some of the design features a pedal-powered plane must have?

When any device requires energy to operate it, an appropriate form of energy must be chosen. For example, a province or other community needs electrical energy to operate all kinds of home appliances, to light streets and, in some cases, to provide energy for transportation vehicles. In some areas, the gravitational potential energy of water held in reservoirs is converted into electrical energy by generators (see the illustration).

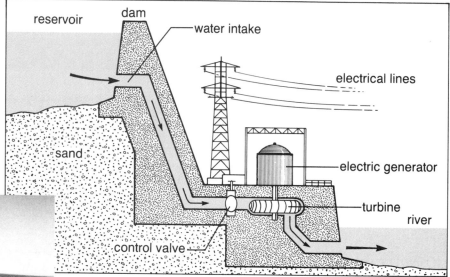

This generating station converts the gravitational energy of water in a reservoir into electrical energy.

This large field full of solar batteries provides enough electrical energy for 400 homes. At night, the community uses regular hydroelectric sources.

Some communities burn coal, and use the resulting thermal energy to change water to steam, which is then used to run electric generators.

In some provinces of Canada, atomic energy from radioactive uranium is converted into thermal energy, which is used to change water to steam, which drives generators.

Solar energy can be converted into electricity directly, by using large solar batteries. This system obviously works effectively in parts of the world that have a lot of sunny days.

In some places the Sun's light is reflected by large mirrors to a single boiler, where it changes water to steam. The energy of the steam is used to operate generators, which produce electricity.

This array of computer-controlled mirrors keeps reflected light from the Sun aimed at a single boiler. Superhot steam from the boiler is used to operate a generator.

In transportation systems, most vehicles are currently operated by energy obtained from burning gasoline or diesel fuels. For several reasons, this will have to change. For one thing, the world has a limited supply of petroleum, from which these fossil fuels are produced. Therefore, this non-renewable source of energy cannot last forever.

A second reason is the rise in temperature of the Earth. When fossil fuels are burned, they add excess carbon dioxide gas to the atmosphere. As more and more of our green forests are cut down to make way for dwellings or for growing food plants, there are fewer trees. Since leaves of trees absorb carbon dioxide and give off oxygen, fewer leaves mean more carbon dioxide in the air. (The process called photosynthesis, using energy from the Sun, changes carbon dioxide from the air and water from the soil into oxygen and simple sugar. You will learn more about photosynthesis in Unit Five.)

Excess carbon dioxide gas in the air causes the atmosphere to trap too much radiant heat. Some scientists think this is causing the temperature of the Earth's atmosphere to rise dangerously—the so-called "greenhouse effect."

A third reason to look for other sources of energy for transportation is the simple fact that gasoline engines are not very efficient. Most of the chemical energy in the fuel is converted into heat that is not used, rather than into useful mechanical energy to move the vehicles. You will learn more about efficiency in Topic Eight.

Did You Know?

Canada is a leader in the development of alternative energy sources. The photograph shows a vertical axis wind generator designed by Canada's National Research Council.

This vertical axis wind generator designed by Canada's National Research Council can rotate no matter which way the wind is blowing.

Making Your Own Transportation System

In Activity 2-11, you will have an opportunity to select your own energy source to solve a transportation problem.

Choosing an Energy Source

Problem

How can you move a wheeled cart a distance of 2 m using a source of energy other than your own chemical energy?

Materials

a wheeled cart (either homemade or a small lab cart)
a source of energy of your own choice

Procedure

Here are some suggestions for energy sources for your vehicle, but feel free to use any other safe means. Be sure to check your idea with your teacher.
1. Attach a sail to the cart and use the energy in wind from a fan to move your cart.
2. Use a solar-powered motor to drive a propeller, which will move the cart.
3. Use the potential energy of a wound or stretched elastic band to move the axle on the cart or to turn a propeller that will drive the cart.
4. Use the gravitational potential energy of a mass hanging from a string that is wrapped around the axle of the cart, thus propelling the cart forward.
5. Attach a string to the cart, and let the string go over a pulley at the edge of your work area. A mass hanging from the string will pull the cart along as it falls.
6. Use the energy stored in a strong spring (about the strength of one in a clothespin) to power your vehicle.

Finding Out

1. After all the students in your class have tested their propulsion systems, discuss the advantages and disadvantages of each system.

2. Which propulsion systems were the most effective? (Which ones seemed to make the most effective use of the energy supplied by the source?) Explain your answer.
3. (a) What worked best about your design?
   (b) How would you improve your design?

Extension

4. Use what you have learned from Activity 2-11 to improve your design. You could help organize a class, school, or even a district contest in several categories:
   (a) farthest distance travelled by a vehicle
   (b) fastest speed reached by a vehicle over a certain distance
   (c) slowest speed reached by a vehicle over a certain distance
   (d) most attractive design
   (e) most spectacular failure

Energy Use and Efficiency

How many devices will you use today that will do work for you, provide you with heat or light, or entertain you? Most of these devices use electrical energy to produce some other form of energy. Some devices use the chemical energy of fuels such as natural gas, wood, or gasoline. In Activity 2-12, think about all the ways you use energy from a variety of sources.

Activity 2-12

Using Energy Converters

Problem

In one day, how many devices do you use that change energy from one form into another?

Procedure

1. Copy Table 2-5 onto a full page in your notebook.
2. For 24 h, keep track of each and every device you use that converts energy from one form into another. List all the devices in your table.
3. Complete the table by including the form of energy the device used (input energy) and the form of energy it produced (output energy). In the table, list these under "Type of Input Energy" and "Type of Output Energy." Some examples are given in the table.

Table 2-5 *Energy Converters I Used On . . . (Date)*

TIME	DEVICE	TYPE OF INPUT ENERGY	TYPE OF OUTPUT ENERGY
07:00	alarm clock	electrical	sound
07:05	room light	electrical	light
07:10	toaster	electrical	heat
07:30	toothbrush	chemical	mechanical

Finding Out

1. In your table, what was the most common form of input energy?
2. What was the most common form of output energy?
3. List all the devices you would not be able to use if there was a power failure in your community.
4. If there was a lengthy power failure in your community, describe how you would adapt the way you get at least three tasks done, which normally require electricity.

What is Efficiency?

If a salesperson says an appliance is efficient, what does he or she mean? A certain amount of energy is required to operate any machine. If most of this input energy is useful—in other words, if it supplies the form of output energy for which the machine is designed—then we say the machine is efficient.

Efficiency can be measured by comparing the output energy with the input energy. You probably recall that the basic unit of measurement for energy is the joule (J). The energy of machines is most often measured in kilojoules (kJ) (1 kJ = 1000 J).

For example, a gasoline engine in a car may produce only 25 kJ of useful mechanical output energy for every 100 kJ of chemical input energy. The efficiency of the gasoline engine is, therefore:

$$\frac{25 \text{ kJ}}{100 \text{ kJ}} = 0.25$$

Expressed as a percentage, the efficiency of the gasoline engine is 25%.

If the efficiency of an engine is only 25%, this means that for every 100 kJ of input energy, 75 kJ are wasted! When we say "wasted," we mean that these 75 kJ of energy have been changed into a form that is not useful to us. In a gasoline engine, most of this wasted energy is in the form of heat that warms the environment. Heat is released when the gasoline burns. The exhaust gases in a gasoline engine are hot. Also, friction between moving parts of the engine generates more heat.

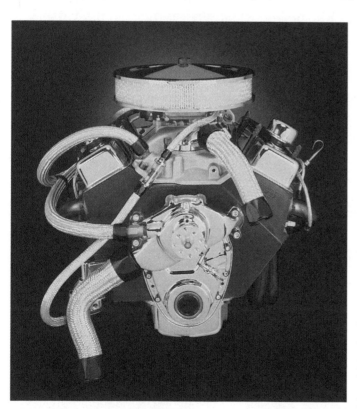

This gasoline engine for a sports car loses a great deal of heat as it functions. Thus, the engine is very inefficient.

A common device with a low efficiency rating is the standard light bulb. This type of bulb has a filament made of tungsten metal. Electrical current in the filament causes it to heat up until it glows white. Such a light is said to be **incandescent** (glowing hot). The incandescent light bulb is only about 5% efficient. This means that for every 100 J of input (electrical) energy, only 5 J of useful output (light) energy are produced. The other 95 J of energy are wasted as heat. (On the other hand, you could say that an incandescent light bulb is 95% efficient as a heat source!)

this is wrong!

Probing

1. What kind of lights are used in your home? in your classroom? Which type of light costs less? Why?
2. Why is leaving the lights on less "wasteful" in winter than in summer?

Measuring Efficiency

To measure the efficiency of a device, you must first measure how much energy is used to operate it (in a given amount of time), then measure how much useful energy it produces in the same amount of time. You can then calculate the efficiency of the device. The efficiency equals the energy produced by the device divided by the energy used to operate the device. To state the efficiency as a percentage, multiply the decimal fraction by 100.

$$\text{Efficiency} = \frac{(\text{Energy produced by the device})}{(\text{Energy used to operate the device})} \times 100\%$$

$$= \frac{(\text{Output Energy})}{(\text{Input Energy})} \times 100\%$$

It isn't practical to measure the efficiency of a complex machine, such as an engine, in a classroom. However, you can do simple classroom experiments to compare input energy with output energy, thus measuring efficiency.

Here's one example of how to measure efficiency: You can easily determine the "efficiency" of a bouncing ball. The input energy, which is gravitational potential energy, depends upon how high you lift the ball above the floor before letting it fall and bounce. The height to which the ball bounces after hitting the floor is a measure of the output energy. The output energy is what is left of the original gravitational potential energy after one bounce. To find out how efficient the ball is for bouncing, just divide the height to which the ball bounces by the height from which it was originally dropped. Then multiply by 100.

Did You Know?

A modern gasoline engine has a low efficiency, but an old-fashioned steam locomotive engine was even less efficient—only about 8%! For every 100 kJ of chemical energy in the coal that a steam engine burned, only 8 kJ were used to move the locomotive. The other 92 kJ were "wasted," mainly as heat given off to the surroundings.

Bouncing Balls

Problem

How energy-efficient are various types of balls when they are bounced off a hard floor?

Table 2-6 *Observations*

TYPE OF BALL	STARTING HEIGHT (cm)	AVERAGE REBOUND HEIGHT (cm)	EFFICIENCY
Ping-pong	100		
golf	100		
lacrosse	100		
Plasticine	100		
basketball	100		
large superball	100		
small superball	100		
sponge rubber	100		
tennis	100		

Materials

metre stick
a selection of balls: tennis ball, Plasticine ball, sponge rubber ball, lacrosse ball, golf ball, large superball, small superball, Ping-pong ball, basketball

Procedure

1. Copy Table 2-6 into your notebook.
2. Do this Activity with a partner. Hold a metre stick upright, against a hard concrete or wooden floor. Hold one of the balls above the floor so that the bottom of the ball is exactly 100 cm above the floor. Drop the ball. Have your partner observe the height to which the bottom of the ball bounces on the first bounce. This is called the ball's **rebound height**. Record this measurement in your notebook.
3. Repeat Step 2 four more times with the same ball. Find the *average rebound height*. To do this, add the five rebound height measurements and divide by five. Record the average rebound height in your table.
4. Repeat Steps 2 and 3 for all the balls. Record all the average rebound heights in your table.

The bottom of the ball is at the 100 cm mark before it is dropped. Measure the rebound height to the bottom of the ball, as well.

5. Calculate the efficiency of each ball: Divide the average rebound height by the starting height, then multiply by 100. For example: A certain ball, dropped from 100 cm, bounces to an average rebound height of 60 cm.

$$\text{efficiency} = \frac{(\text{rebound height})}{(\text{starting height})} \times 100\%$$

$$= \frac{(60 \text{ cm})}{(100 \text{ cm})} \times 100\%$$

The ball's efficiency is 60%.

Finding Out

1. Which ball was most efficient?
2. (a) Which ball was least efficient?
   (b) Where did its "wasted" energy go?
3. In what form was (a) the input energy? (b) the output energy?
4. Besides properties of the ball itself, what other factor helps determine how efficient each bouncing ball is?

Extension

5. Hold a small superball immediately above and touching a large superball. Drop the two superballs at the same time. Observe the height of the bounce of the small ball and the large ball. (You will have to practise this technique.) Try to explain the result of this experiment.

Efficiency of Some Common Devices

Some of the appliances and other energy converters you use in your home are very efficient. When purchasing a new appliance, it is always wise to compare different brands of that appliance to see which brand is the most efficient. New appliances sold in Canada have a special label on them with an "energy use" rating called the **Energuide Number**.

The Energuide Number tells you how much electrical energy the device will use, on average, in a month. This means you can compare the likely energy uses of competing brands of appliances, and see which one is the most efficient. The energy used is measured in units called kilowatt hours (kW·h). This unit is calculated using the joule. If a device uses energy at a rate of one joule per second, then its power rating is one watt (W). Energy for small appliances is sometimes stated in watt seconds. Since most appliances use a great deal of energy, the larger unit kilowatt hours is used on their Energuide labels.

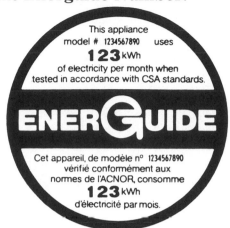

A typical Energuide label.

Table 2-7 lists approximate efficiencies of some common devices that convert energy from one form to another.

Table 2-7 *Efficiencies of Some Common Energy Converters*

CONVERTER	INPUT ENERGY	OUTPUT ENERGY	APPROXIMATE EFFICIENCY (%)
dry cell in a battery	chemical	electrical	90
gas furnace	chemical	thermal	90
oil furnace	chemical	thermal	70
diesel engine	chemical	mechanical	40
gasoline engine	chemical	mechanical	25
electric oven	electrical	thermal	99
incandescent lamp	electrical	light	5
fluorescent lamp	electrical	light	20

Working with Students

Do you like teaching other people new things? If so, you'll be interested in what Tracy Wong, a physics teacher at Provost Public School in Provost, Alberta has to say about her career in education.

One summer, when I was still a student in university, I was asked to tutor a Grade ten student in physics. It was then that I realized that teaching was for me. Now I teach physics, math, career and life management, and band.

Science is such a great area to get involved in. It's always changing—new discoveries are made every day that increase our understanding of the world. It's an exciting field.

Math and physics are subjects many people used to think were mainly for boys. I'm concerned that some people still seem to feel that way. If they looked at my physics classes, they'd see just how well girls do. I hope both boys and girls who enjoy these subjects will feel equally confident to take them and do well in them.

I like getting to know students best of all. Seeing students get excited about something they have just learned is so rewarding for me. Last year my students especially enjoyed the experiments on photoelectric effect, that is, seeing that light energy can be transformed into electrical energy. They were amazed to learn that this process is involved in the operation of televisions by remote control, as well as automatic garage-door openers.

These experiments were fun for me, too. I've always been fascinated by any type of electronic equipment. When I was younger I loved taking things apart. I fixed my neighbour's alarm clock and repaired some toy telephones that the manufacturer couldn't seem to fix.

We live in a society based on science. You can't cross the street without a stoplight (well, I guess you can in my small town!), but you can't do much without seeing evidence of applied science. That's why I think it's important for students to get involved in science. If you go into your studies with an open mind, you're bound to learn many things you can use throughout your life. You might even be able to answer many of the "how does this work?" questions that people are constantly asking!

Checkpoint

1. In your notebook, write the devices in List A and match them with the energy conversions in List B.

LIST A	LIST B
(a) whistle	Chemical energy is converted into mechanical energy.
(b) fan	Mechanical energy is converted into sound.
(c) tape recorder	Chemical energy is converted into gravitational energy.
(d) rocket	Electrical energy is converted into mechanical energy.
(e) motorcycle	Electrical energy is converted into sound.
(f) flashlight	Electrical energy is converted into light.

2. (a) If a reading lamp converts 100 J of electrical energy into 20 J of light, how efficient is the lamp?
(b) What kind of lamp is it likely to be?

3. What happens to most of the chemical energy used to operate a vehicle run by a gasoline engine?

4. Refer again to Table 2-7 to answer the following questions:
(a) What are the most efficient appliances in the list?
(b) If you could choose between the following, which would you use, and why:
- gas or oil furnace?
- diesel or gasoline engine?
- incandescent or fluorescent lamp?

5. A steel ball was dropped on a steel plate. If its starting height was 10 cm, and the rebound height was 9 cm, how efficient was the steel ball?

6. Describe the rubber-band-powered vehicle from Activity 2–10 that moved the fastest.
(a) What features made it possible for it to move so fast?
(b) What types of simple machines did it use?

7. Describe the rubber-band-powered vehicle from Activity 2–10 that travelled the greatest distance.
(a) What features made it possible for the vehicle to travel such a long distance?
(b) What types of simple machines did it use?

8. (a) Why are people concerned about the energy that is transformed to heat when a light bulb is lighted?
(b) What does the *Law of Conservation of Energy* state?

9. The popular toy shown in the photograph functions because of more than one energy conversion. List as many of these energy conversions as you can.

A toy energy converter.

Focus

- A machine is a device that uses energy to do useful work for us.
- You use many kinds of machines every day.
- There are six kinds of simple machines: inclined plane, pulley, lever, wheel-and-axle, screw, and wedge.
- Work is done when a force is exerted over a distance in the general direction of the force.
- Mechanical devices (systems) are made up of simpler parts (subsystems).
- Ramps (inclined planes) and pulleys can be used to reduce the effort force needed to lift a load.
- Levers can be used either to reduce effort force or to increase speed.
- The wheel-and-axle can be used either to reduce effort force or to increase speed.
- Wedges and screws are types of inclined planes.
- Gears can be used in a variety of ways, for example, to increase rotational speed, to reduce rotational speed, and to reverse the direction of a rotary motion.
- Many sources supply the energy needed to run machines.
- Energy converters are devices that change energy from one form into another form, usually in order to do work for us.
- The efficiency of a device is a measure of how much of the input energy is changed into the desired output energy.

Backtrack

1. What is the main reason for using a ramp to lift a load to a higher level?
2. Sketch a system that uses a ramp, a single pulley, and a lever to move a heavy load from a ditch to ground level.
3. The photograph shows a device used to pull a boat up onto its trailer. What kind of simple machine is this device?

A winch for pulling boats out of the water.

4. One corner of a mobile home is too low. Describe at least three ways that you could lift it, using simple machines or combinations of simple machines.
5. Which of these devices use multiplying gears, and which use reducing gears?
   (a) hand-operated food mixer
   (b) display turntable
   (c) hand-operated drill
6. What form of energy exists within a wound or stretched elastic band?
7. List five ways to make a small cart move along a table.

8. Describe the energy conversion that occurs when each of these devices is used:
   (a) battery-operated clock
   (b) firecracker
   (c) trombone
   (d) generator
   (e) television set
9. A salesperson says an appliance is extremely efficient. What does she mean?
10. Explain how the scientific meanings of the words "force," "work," and "energy" differ from one another.

Synthesizer

11. Suppose you must move a motorboat out of the water, up a bank, and onto the road. Design a system, made up of two or more simple machines, that will enable you to do this all by yourself. Sketch your system.
12. Sketch the nutcracker in the photograph. Label your sketch to show (a) where the fulcrum is, (b) where the effort force is applied, and (c) where the load is. What kind of simple machine is this?

13. The baseball bat in the photograph is a lever. Where is (a) the fulcrum? (b) the effort force? (c) the load?

14. The photographs show (a) pruning shears used to cut fairly thick tree branches, and (b) trimming shears used to cut long grass and weeds. Describe the main differences in the designs of the two cutting devices.

(a) Pruning shears.

(b) Trimming shears.

15. Sketch (a) a gear arrangement that will increase rotational speed and reverse rotational direction, and (b) one that will increase rotational speed without reversing rotational direction.

16. The photograph below shows a gear system. Describe one way in which this system might be used in a device.

17. A well-maintained bicycle is a very efficient machine. What does a cyclist do to ensure that his or her bicycle is kept in "energy-efficient" condition?

18. Identify the simple machines making up the camera tripod shown in the photograph below.

Camera tripod.

19. Discuss whether solar energy might be a practical way to obtain electrical energy for your community. How would you obtain electrical energy at night?

20. Look at the photograph below of the Canadarm on the U.S. space shuttle. Think of at least two simple machines that must form a part of this device, enabling it to move and to pick up objects.

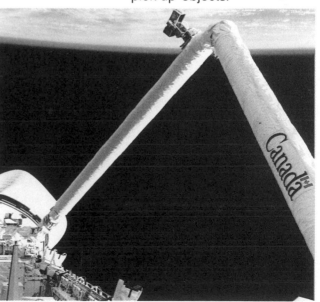

Consumer Product Testing

What does science have to do with shopping? For one thing, knowing how products are made and how they work can help you look critically at the things you buy. Are those boots really waterproof? Is that child's toy safe? Will that pen last for a long time? In this Unit, you will discover how scientific testing seeks to answer questions that you, as a **consumer**—a buyer of products and services—may have.

In some cases, manufacturers make certain claims for their products. Can those claims be defended using scientific evidence? You can evaluate products by comparing one with another, or by measuring the product against certain standards of quality and performance. You can also tell whether claims are scientific or not, and whether they can be proved or disproved.

Many of the products you see on store shelves have been tested, and meet government standards of safety and reliability. How can you tell? This Unit discusses what kind of information you can obtain from labels and packages. They may tell you what materials are in a product, whether the product has been tested, and how you can look after the product so that it lasts longer. You will also consider some of the ways in which consumer products affect the environment. The materials and energy used to make and operate products will be examined to determine what some of these effects are.

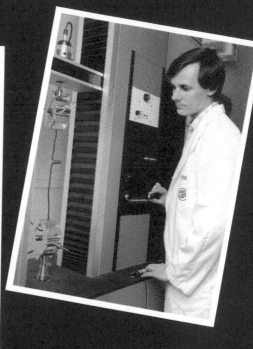

Going Shopping

Suppose you are shopping for a ballpoint pen. There are many types of pens in the store. Some have a medium point and others have a fine point. Some pens are disposable and others can be refilled. The pens have different colours of ink, and some have erasable ink. Some pens are more expensive than others. How do you decide which pen to buy?

The choice you make depends partly on which characteristics of a pen are most important to you. If you tend to lose pens, or if you don't have much money, a less expensive pen might be a better choice. If you like your writing to be extremely neat, you might want a pen with erasable ink. Decisions such as these are personal, and vary from individual to individual. Whichever pen you choose, however, you want to be sure it will work properly and that it is good value for your money. Here, science can help you make a decision.

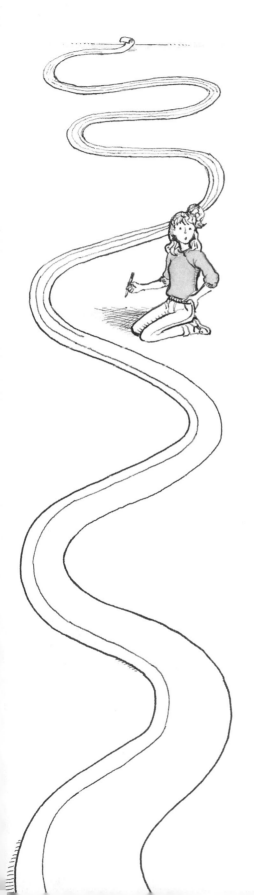

If you know something about the chemical composition of ink, you can determine which inks might fade and why. If you understand the properties of fluids, you can predict which ink will flow at the optimum rate. More practically, you can use scientific methods to measure and test these characteristics. You can carry out some simple tests for yourself before you buy an item. For example, you can scribble on a scratch pad with several different pens. This allows you to observe and compare the colour of the ink, the thickness of the line, and how well the ink flows.

Suppose you find two pens that look very similar. Both pens have the characteristics you want, but one pen costs twice as much as the other. Can you devise a test that will tell you which pen is the better value? To make your choice, you need to know how long each pen will last. One way of testing this would be to draw a straight, continuous line, using each type of pen until the ink ran out. Suppose someone tested the pens in this way. The results might show that the more expensive pen drew a 6 km line, and the cheaper pen drew a 2 km line. Which pen is the better buy?

As the example above shows, there may be many questions to answer before you choose the product you want. Only some of these questions can be answered by using scientific techniques. Consider the following questions about a selection of portable cassette players:

1. Will they work as they should?
2. Which one looks most attractive?
3. Is a loud one better than a quiet one?
4. Which one is loudest?

Questions 1 and 4 can be answered scientifically by observing, measuring, and testing the performance of each cassette player. The answers to Questions 2 and 3 are matters of personal choice.
In the next Activity, you will consider how science can help you choose among different products.

Considering Characteristics

NOTE: Later in this Unit, you will read about other factors to consider in choosing products, such as environmental effects. For now, just focus on product characteristics that appeal to you.

PART A

1. In your notebook, list two characteristics of a packaged loaf of bread that you can determine just by looking at the bread.
2. List two characteristics that cannot be determined from simply observing the bread.
3. Suppose you want to choose the freshest bread.
   (a) What would affect the freshness of the bread?
   (b) How might you discover the freshness of a loaf of bread without eating it?

PART B

You want to choose a car that will be economical to use.
1. List two characteristics of a car that affect the cost of operating it.

2. Write two questions that will help you choose the most economical car.
3. Describe a test that could answer one of your questions.

PART C

1. List three characteristics of a pair of jeans.
2. Name one factor that affects the strength of a pair of jeans.
3. Suppose you are comparing two pairs of jeans, both in your size.

(a) Choose one characteristic of the jeans that can be observed and measured scientifically. Briefly describe one way you could test that particular characteristic.

(b) Write a question about the jeans that cannot be answered by science.

PART D

1. For each of the products shown here, write down the most important characteristic you would consider when buying the product.
2. Briefly describe one way of measuring or testing each of these characteristics.

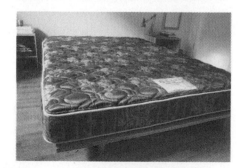

Designing a Fair Test

How dishwashing liquids clean your dishes—a close-up view of the tiny particles involved.

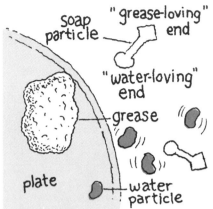

1. *Each soap particle in the dishwashing liquid has one end that is attracted to grease and one end that is attracted to water.*

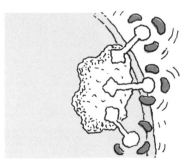

2. *The grease-loving ends attach themselves to greasy food particles on the dishes.*

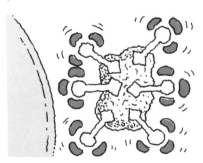

3. *Greasy food particles are pulled off the dishes by a cluster of soap particles. The food particles stay suspended in the water so they cannot be redeposited on the dishes.*

Once you have decided which characteristics of a product are related to its quality, how might you use science to help you test some of these characteristics? **Tests** help determine whether a product functions well.

How would you test the quality of dishwashing liquid? Because the function of this product is to clean dishes, your test should measure the characteristic of "cleaning power." The scientific explanation for the way dishwashing liquid works is illustrated in the diagram. The grease particles combine with soap particles to form a suspension in water. (A suspension is a mixture in which tiny solid pieces or droplets are scattered throughout another substance without dissolving.) Although all dishwashing liquids act in this way, there is a wide range of quality among different products. Some dishwashing liquids are more reliable and effective than others.

In order to conduct a fair test, you should be aware of all the variables that might affect your results. Your test might involve cleaning some dirty dishes with different brands of dishwashing liquid. Your materials are the dishes, the grease, the dishwashing liquid, and the water. What are the variables? They include:
- the number of dishes
- the size of the dishes
- the shape of the dishes
- the material from which the dishes are made
- the amount of grease
- the type of grease
- the way in which the grease covers the plates (for example, as a thin film or in thick globs)
- the amount and type of dishwashing liquid
- the amount of water
- the temperature of the water
- the type of cleaning implement

Other things that could affect your test results are the size, cleanliness, and material of the container in which you clean the dishes, how much you whisk up the suds, how long you wipe or scrub the dishes, and your judgement in determining how clean the dishes are when you've completed the test.

It is amazing how many variables can influence even the simplest test. But you do not really have to worry about all these things. To conduct a fair test, you must simply ensure that every time you carry out the test you conduct it in exactly the same way *except for the one variable you are measuring*. You **control** all other variables—that is, keep them the same. By doing this, you can conclude that any difference in results is due to the one factor (variable) you have changed and not to anything else.

For example, if you want to know which brand of dishwashing liquid works best, you should use the same type and amount of grease, and the same dishcloth, water, dishes, and basin in each test. Use exactly the same procedures as well. Change only the brand of dishwashing liquid. Compare how much of each brand you need to clean the dishes. Alternatively, you could use the same amount of each dishwashing liquid but change the amount of grease to be removed.

Is this a fair test?

Comparing Liquid Detergents

Problem

Which dishwashing liquid removes grease most effectively?

Materials

samples of 3 different dishwashing liquids, labelled A, B, and C

large mixing bowl or basin (at least 2 L capacity)

3 droppers

1 L beaker

beaker (any size)

80 mL grease paste (1 part flour to 2 parts oil)

graduated cylinder

stirring rod

Procedure

1. Measure 2 L of cold water into a clean mixing bowl.
2. Add 20 mL of grease paste to the water and stir.
3. Add two drops of one dishwashing liquid to the mixture. Stir up the mixture. If no suds appear on the surface of the water, add another two drops. Continue to add dishwashing liquid two drops at a time, until you produce just enough suds to completely cover the surface of the water. In your notebook, record the total number of drops of dishwashing liquid you used to achieve this result.
4. Empty and wash the bowl. Repeat Steps 1 to 3, using clean droppers and the other two samples of dishwashing liquid in turn. Record your results each time.

Finding Out

1. (a) Write a description for the effectiveness of a dishwashing liquid. (In your description, refer to the volume of dishwashing liquid needed to remove grease.)

   (b) Using your definition, rank the three dishwashing liquids in order of their effectiveness, from most effective to least effective.

   (c) Did everybody in the class rank the three samples of dishwashing liquid in the same order? Explain any differences that occurred.
2. Are there any differences in the characteristics of the three dishwashing liquids (such as their colour, odour, etc.) that might have allowed you to predict before the test which one would be most effective? Explain your answer.
3. Using your knowledge of the way soap particles combine with grease, explain the difference between a mixture with soap suds and a mixture that no longer has soap suds.

Finding Out More

4. Think of an alternative procedure for testing the effectiveness of dishwashing liquids. Write your ideas in your notebook.
5. Suppose two dishwashing liquids have the same effectiveness. What other characteristic might influence which product you choose? Explain your answer.

1 L beaker

beaker

dropper

grease paste

glass stirring rod

10 mL graduated cylinder

samples of dishwashing liquid

Finding Flaws

Have you ever used a new product for a short time and then had some part of it break, fall off, leak, stick, bend, tear, or stretch? Each of these problems indicates a **trouble spot** in the product—a single characteristic that is most likely to fail or wear out first. A trouble spot lowers the quality of a product and could make it unusable. A product is only as good as its weakest part, no matter how well the rest of it is made.

Can science help you predict trouble spots and test them? In some cases, knowledge of forces and structures can help you identify parts that may break under a load. Remember from your previous studies of structures and design that there may be several reasons why things fail. The more complex a product is, the more parts that can break down or wear out. More testing is needed to ensure safe, reliable performance.

In the next Activity, you will consider a range of products that differ in their design, materials, and complexity. Some of them perform similar functions in very different ways. You may want to bring samples of some of these products to class to examine them more closely. Try to determine the trouble spots in each product.

Looking for Trouble

Problem

What parts of various products are most likely to cause problems for consumers?

Procedure

1. Read the following list of consumer products and the functions they perform. For each product, identify and write in your notebook one potential problem that might occur when the product is used.

PRODUCT	FUNCTION
(a) paint brush	painting
(b) paint roller	painting
(c) paint spray can	painting
(d) electric fan	cooling
(e) air conditioner	cooling
(f) broom	sweeping
(g) vacuum cleaner	sweeping
(h) electric blanket	warming bed
(i) hot water bottle	warming bed
(j) clothes dryer	drying clothes
(k) clothesline	drying clothes

2. In your notebook, record whether each problem is most likely to result from (a) the material(s), (b) the design, or (c) the construction of the product.
3. Briefly describe a test that could be used to detect each potential problem you have identified.

There are several products used for painting. How might poor design, construction, or materials affect the performance of a brush, a roller, and a spray can?

Finding Out

1. How could each potential defect be avoided? [Your solution should specify an improvement or change in the material(s), the design, or the construction of the product.]
2. (a) Select one of the functions listed, then decide which product you would choose to perform that function.
(b) Write one or more scientific reasons for your choice.
(c) Write one personal reason for your choice.

Finding Out More

3. Prepare a short report on a product of your choice to identify its potential trouble spot(s). Your report should answer the following questions:
(a) Which part of the product will likely wear out first?
(b) Do some parts break off, tear, or get stuck easily?
(c) Are some parts too big, too small, or difficult to use?
(d) How might you test the durability of the product (that is, how long it will last)?
(e) Is the problem in the material(s), the design, or the construction of the product?
(f) Is it easy to tell where the problem is by looking at the product, or must the product be used before you can find out?
(g) How might you improve the product?
Here are some suggestions of products to examine: running shoes, tape recorder, bicycle, wallet, and paperback book.

Improving Products

Scientific tests that reveal trouble spots can help manufacturers improve their products. Common flaws may be eliminated by changes in design or materials. On the basis of scientific testing, many consumer products have changed and improved over the years. For example, early ballpoint pens often flowed unevenly and they leaked blobs of ink. This problem is now infrequent because manufacturers have improved the characteristics of the ink and the design of the rotating ballpoint tip.

New materials and technologies may revolutionize products that have been around for a long time. But new designs and materials may also lead to new problems. For example, consider the development of the phonograph record. Records produced in the early part of this century were made from a waxy material combined with clay. A major disadvantage of these records was that they broke easily if they were dropped.

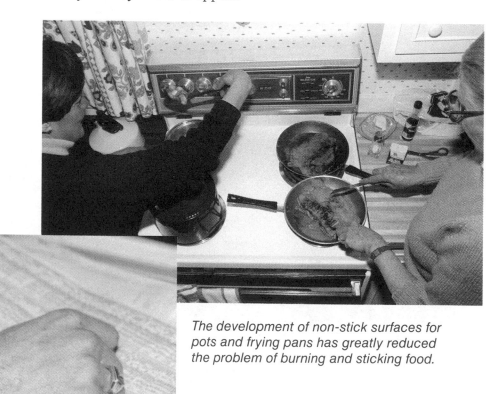

The development of non-stick surfaces for pots and frying pans has greatly reduced the problem of burning and sticking food.

Watches powered by miniature batteries have almost entirely replaced spring-wound wristwatches. What problem does this avoid? Do any new problems occur with battery-powered watches?

After the 1930s, plastics such as vinyl were used to make records. This change in materials made records difficult to break, but the grooves in the records could still become scratched or clogged with dirt, spoiling the quality of the sound. In addition, the vinyl records occasionally warped.

With the 1980s came the development of compact discs (CDs). These are also plastic discs, but their grooves are lined with a very thin layer of aluminum. Instead of using a stylus (needle) to track the groove, the compact disc player uses a beam of laser light that is reflected from the aluminum. The aluminum is protected by a coat of clear lacquer.

CD discs are designed to last longer and are more durable than the earlier style of record. Recent tests show, however, that CDs may also develop problems. Acidic ink on the disc label may slowly dissolve the plastic. Heating, cooling, or dropping the discs may eventually produce tiny cracks in the lacquer. If air reaches the aluminum through these cracks, oxygen in the air will combine with the aluminum to form aluminum oxide, a fine, white powder. Such deterioration in the disc distorts the sound. Often problems such as these become apparent only after the product has been in use for some time.

This old-fashioned phonograph reproduced sounds from a record by means of a needle.

A CD player uses a laser beam instead of a needle.

Testing and the Fabric Industry

Many of the materials in the clothes you wear were unknown to your great-grandparents. In their day, clothes were made only from natural materials such as cotton, wool, silk, leather, and fur. Although these materials are still used, most clothes now include at least some artificial materials.

Modern clothing fabrics such as nylon, polyester, and spandex were developed as a result of scientific studies of natural fibres. Scientists experimented with new combinations of chemicals, and produced new materials with different characteristics. For example, melting coloured pigments with artificial resins produces coloured fibres that do not need dyeing and have colours that do not run. (A resin is a sticky substance used to hold other materials in place.) Cloth manufacturers combine various natural and artificial fibres to produce materials with a wide range of characteristics. You can now choose clothes that are:

water-resistant	wrinkle-resistant	insulating
stretchable	windproof	crease-retaining
colourfast	drip-dry	dirt-resistant
flame-resistant	rot-resistant	pre-shrunk

Some characteristics of cloth come from the special ways the fibres are processed; one such process is shown below.

Fifteenth-century spinners and weavers of wool.

Permanent-press fabrics hold their creases even after washing. The fabric is soaked in a resin and dried before being made into a garment. The finished garment is then pressed and cured (baked).

These people are carding wool by hand. After it has been carded, the wool will be spun into yarn.

Other characteristics of cloth come from the fibres themselves, and some are a result of the way the fibres are woven together in the material. For example, very fine cloth is produced by using only long fibres of even thickness. Individual fibres are separated and made to lie parallel in a process called carding. Combing removes any short fibres, leaving a yarn that is both strong and flexible.

The quality of clothing fabrics can be assessed in three ways:
1. Durability: This includes tensile strength (resistance to lengthwise tearing), resistance to scraping, and colourfastness.
2. Utility: This includes the permeability (porousness) of the cloth to air and water, how well the cloth resists wrinkles and dirt, how well it insulates, and how much it shrinks.
3. Emotional appeal: This quality describes how a fabric looks and feels. For clothing fabrics, this can sometimes be more important than the other characteristics.

In the following Activity, you will test and compare some of these characteristics and decide which fabrics are most suitable for different uses.

Did You Know?

A sailmaker named Levi Strauss found a solution to the problem of trousers that ripped and came apart when worn by people doing rough outdoor work. He designed and made the famous blue jeans known as "Levi's." Strauss had moved to the West Coast during the California Gold Rush in the mid-1800s, taking with him a large supply of sailcloth. He found little demand for sails, but discovered that the gold miners and prospectors needed trousers that would stand up to a lot of wear and tear. He used his supply of sail canvas to make trousers, and employed a saddle-maker to reinforce the seams. In this way, Levi Strauss produced trousers with better-quality material, design, and workmanship. Levi's became a standard item of clothing for cowboys. Their popularity spread throughout the world, and today jeans are worn by many people in many countries.

An early Levi Strauss advertisement.

Fashion or Function?

Problem

Imagine that you are the buyer for a clothing factory that is planning to manufacture a jacket for spring/fall wear. You have samples of different fabrics to examine. Which characteristics in the jacket are important, and how can these characteristics be tested?

Materials

2 samples each of 3 different
   fabrics, such as polyester,
   cotton, and wool
3 beakers (each 250 mL)
small pieces of paper
laundry detergent
bowl or large beaker
stirring rod
forceps
waterproof marker
ruler
hair dryer
magnifying lens (optional)
white paper or cardboard
drawing paper

Procedure

1. Copy Table 3-1 into your notebook. Use it to record the results of your tests.
2. Your teacher will give you samples of three different materials. Using a waterproof marker, label your fabric samples A, B, and C. For each sample of material, carry out the four tests illustrated.

Table 3-1 *Comparison of Fabric Samples*

CHARACTERISTIC	SAMPLE A	SAMPLE B	SAMPLE C
crease resistance			
wind resistance			
colourfastness			
shrinkage			

TEST 1: Crease Resistance

1. Tie a knot in each sample of material and leave it for 5 min.
2. Untie the knot, smooth out the material, and note its appearance. Is there little sign of creasing or are many creases visible?
3. In your table, record each sample as good, moderate, or poor for this characteristic.

TEST 2: Wind Resistance

1. Hold a sample of fabric taut. With your lips touching the fabric, try to blow through it. Does the material resist air passing through it?
2. See if you can blow enough air through the fabric to move some small pieces of paper on the other side of the fabric. In your table, record each sample as having good, moderate, or poor wind resistance.

TEST 3: Colourfastness

1. Place a sample of each fabric in a separate beaker of hot water that contains 1 mL of laundry detergent. Let the samples soak for 5 min, stirring occasionally.
2. Observe whether any of the colour has been transferred to the water. Hold a white sheet of paper or cardboard behind the beaker to see the water colour more clearly. In your table, record the results as "colour bleeds" or "colour does not bleed."

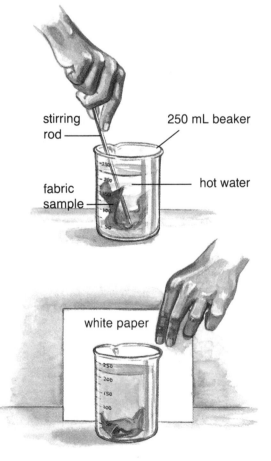

stirring rod

250 mL beaker

fabric sample

hot water

white paper

TEST 4: Shrinkage

1. Lay a flat, dry sample of each fabric on a separate sheet of paper and carefully trace around the edges of the samples. (Do not include the frayed ends in your outline.)
2. Soak one fabric sample in hot water for 5 min.
3. Use forceps to remove the fabric. Let it cool enough to touch safely and squeeze out the water. Dry the sample with hot air from a hair dryer.
4. Smooth out the dry fabric sample and place it back on the paper tracing. Measure and calculate any change in the size (area) of the sample; record the result.
5. Repeat the procedure for the other samples.

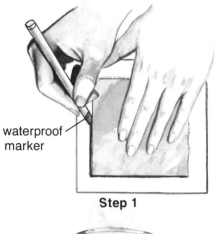

waterproof marker

Step 1

hot water

fabric sample

Step 2

Finding Out

1. Which of the fabric samples would you recommend using in a spring/fall jacket and why?
2. Which materials would you not recommend using? Give reasons for your answer.

Finding Out More

3. What other tests could you conduct on the fabrics?
4. Examine each type of material through a magnifying lens. Can you observe a relationship between any of the characteristics that you tested and:
   (a) the length and thickness of the fibres?
   (b) the way the fibres are woven or pressed together?
   (c) For (a) and (b), explain the relationship, if one exists.

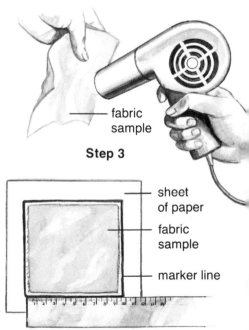

fabric sample

Step 3

sheet of paper

fabric sample

marker line

Step 4

Checkpoint

1. Listed below are three consumer products and some of their characteristics.
   (a) What is the function of each product?
   (b) Which of the characteristics listed are important to the function of the product?

PRODUCT	CHARACTERISTICS
pencil	hardness of lead length has eraser at end colour of lead colour of painted surface
sweater	colour size thickness of material designer's or manufacturer's name on label shape
desk	colour size material number of drawers size of drawers

2. Name two important characteristics you would want in a shirt worn:
   (a) at a school dance; and
   (b) on a camping trip in the mountains.
3. Name two important characteristics you would want in a radio to be used:
   (a) in your bedroom; and
   (b) on a camping trip in the mountains.
4. Which of the characteristics you listed in Questions 2 and 3 above can be scientifically tested?

5. Melanie was comparing different types of sugar to see how quickly they dissolve in hot water. She prepared three beakers, each containing the same amount of water at the same temperature. In one beaker, she placed a scoopula of icing sugar; in the second, she placed a scoopula of brown sugar; and in the third, she placed a cube of white sugar. She had determined that all three of her samples of sugar had the same mass. She started a timer and stirred each beaker in turn until all the sugar had dissolved. The icing sugar dissolved first, and Melanie concluded that icing sugar dissolves faster than either brown sugar or sugar cubes. Was this a fair test? Give a reason for your answer.
6. (a) Identify the possible trouble spots in each product shown below.

(b) Think about your previous studies of structures and design. Where in the products would you expect the greatest number of trouble spots?
(c) Think of two other products, and for each product, name:
   • the part that you would look at most closely for signs of defects or weakness; and
   • the characteristics you would test in that part.
7. Which of the three tubes of toothpaste in the illustration seems to be the best value for money? Explain how you arrived at your answer. What other factors might you consider in deciding which product gives you the best value for money?

Product Testing

Stores offer a wide choice of cameras, ranging from a pocket-sized, single-button, moulded plastic camera to a complex, highly technical camera with over a thousand different parts! How would you test a camera? Knowing the scientific principles by which a camera works can help you choose which characteristics to test and how to test them.

The function of a camera is, of course, to take photographs. In order to take a photograph, your camera needs only four basic parts, as shown in Table 3–2.

Table 3–2 *The Essential Parts of a Camera*

PART	FUNCTION
1. a dark box	holds a piece of light-sensitive film
2. light-sensitive film	records an image when light strikes it
3. a tiny hole (aperture) in the box	lets the light in and onto the film
4. a cover (shutter) over the hole	controls the length of time the film is exposed to light

Most cameras, however, have additional parts, such as:

- a diaphragm, which controls the size of the aperture;
- a viewfinder system, which allows you to see the image you are photographing; and
- a lens, which allows you to focus.

These basic technical features have been used in cameras from the time the camera was invented in 1826 until the present. No matter how complicated a modern camera is, or whatever technology it uses, a camera's essential parts must still carry out the functions listed in Table 3-2. Tests on a camera should answer questions about these functions. For example: Does the shutter open and close properly for the correct length of time? Does the camera casing allow any unwanted light to leak through onto the film? Scientific tests will answer questions such as these.

Testing Techniques

Tests may require elaborate laboratory equipment or almost no equipment at all. For example, measuring the speed and accuracy of a camera shutter requires video and computer equipment, as shown in the photograph. To test a camera casing for leakage of light into the camera, you can simply hang a camera, loaded with film, in the sun. If the film becomes fogged, you know that light entered the case.

Different tests on components are carried out at different stages of production, both while and after a product is manufactured. For example, a camera motor used for automatic film advance and rewind may be tested for speed and reliability before the camera is assembled. When the camera is complete, tests may be conducted to measure the sound level of the motor.

Camera shutter speed is tested in a high-speed instrumentation lab. A series of high-speed videos (1000 frames per second) are taken of the shutter, as it repeatedly opens and closes. The shutter blades travel at speeds close to 38 km/h. Computer analysis of the video checks that the shutter speeds are accurate and consistent (exactly the same each time) over thousands of repetitions.

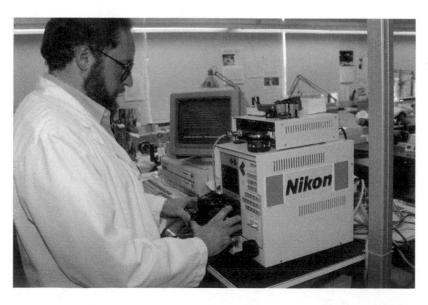

The more parts there are in a product, the more things there are to test. To maintain quality, manufacturers may test every part of every product several times. In order to be **reliable**, a scientific test must be **repeatable**; that is, the same results are obtained each time the test is carried out.

For mass-produced and inexpensive products, it may not be practical or necessary to test every item. The technique of **spot testing**, or **random sampling**, is an alternative way to monitor quality. A product is selected at random—that is, every so often—and tested. It is assumed that the randomly chosen product is typical of other identical items that are produced in the same way. The results of tests on the sample item are therefore assumed to hold true for identical, but untested, items.

One type of testing sometimes carried out on samples may actually damage the product. This technique, called **accelerated aging**, is used to determine how durable a product will prove over time. For example, a camera may undergo an endurance test by taking 2000 pictures one after the other. This ensures that the shutter and winding mechanisms of other cameras of the same type will continue to function properly after several years of normal use. A camera tested in this way is not distributed to a camera shop for sale, of course! One well-known furniture outlet tests chairs for durability by pummelling them up to 60 000 times with a 70 kg mass. They also test desk drawers by filling them with objects of a certain mass and sliding them in and out over and over again. With some products, samples are tested until they break in order to establish a maximum strength or capability.

How might you determine if a toaster's popping mechanism could withstand five years of use? You could begin by asking parents and neighbours how many times they use a toaster in a day. The average poppings per day and per year could then be calculated. A simple mechanical device could be devised to pop the toaster the required number of times over one or two days.

Another sampling technique used for new products is the **field test**. This is a test that is carried out under actual conditions of use, rather than in a laboratory. Field tests may reveal problems in the design of a product. For example, a camera may be well made and function properly, but it may not be comfortable to handle. It may be too heavy for some consumers, or the controls may be awkwardly

Bathtubs and other bathroom fixtures are tested by the Canadian Standards Association, using techniques such as the following:
- *A 133 kg mass is placed inside the bathtub to determine if the tub cracks or bends excessively under this load.*
- *The bathtub is scrubbed at least 10 000 times by mechanical brushes and cleansers to find out how well the tub's finish lasts when exposed to that amount of friction.*
- *Thirty-four different chemicals—from gasoline to mustard—are poured into the tub to find out how easily it stains as a result of the chemical reactions that occur.*

placed. Related to the field test is the **consumer survey**, in which a questionnaire is answered by people who have used a product. The survey results are analysed (using a type of mathematics called statistics) to find out if there are any recurring problems with a product. For example, every year the Canadian Automobile Association conducts a consumer survey of car owners. The durability of used cars is determined from this survey.

Manufacturers don't always test their products, however. They often depend on their suppliers to test the materials that go into making their products. So, for example, when a fabric arrives at the factory to be made into jackets, it is assumed to be of good quality. Similarly, a bicycle manufacturer knows that the frame, tires, and other components have all been rigorously tested before arriving at the factory for assembly. A test ride may be all that is required to ensure that the bike has been assembled properly.

As a consumer, you can perform informal tests yourself on some of the products you buy. In the next Activity, you will test the strength of facial tissues when they are dry and when they are wet.

Soft but Strong

Problem

How can you compare the strength of two brands of facial tissue?

Materials

samples of 2 different brands of facial tissue, A and B
coarse, dry sand or other mass (such as metal nuts)
metric measuring spoon
500 mL beaker
balance
water
dropper
masking tape

Procedure

PART A: DRY PAPER

1. Based on the appearance and feel of the tissues, predict which of the two brands will be the stronger. Record your prediction.
2. Find and record the mass of a clean, dry beaker.
3. Stretch a sheet of facial tissue A across the top of the beaker and tape it firmly in place.
4. Carefully place a spoonful of sand in the centre of the tissue, as shown. Continue adding sand, a little at a time, until the tissue tears.

NOTE: If the sand does not tear the tissue, use another material with greater mass that you can add a little at a time; or, if your samples are two-ply, use only one sheet of the tissue.

5. Determine the mass of the sand used and record it in your notebook.
6. Repeat the experiment with facial tissue B.

scoopula

sand

facial tissue

masking tape

PART B: WET PAPER

7. Stretch another sample of tissue A across the beaker as before.
8. Using the dropper, add ten drops of water to the tissue to make it evenly wet.
9. Repeat Steps 4 and 5.
10. Carry out the same test on facial tissue B.

Finding Out

1. Compare the strength of the two brands of facial tissue
   (a) when dry; and
   (b) when wet.
2. Was the stronger dry tissue also stronger when wet?
3. (a) Calculate the percentage loss in strength of each tissue when wet.
   (b) Which tissue—the stronger or the weaker—lost a larger percentage of its strength when wet?
4. Was there any relationship between the strength of the dry tissue and
   (a) the size of the sheets?
   (b) the thickness of the sheets?
5. Was there any other characteristic that you might have used in advance to predict strength?

Finding Out More

6. Find the cost of the two tissues. Which is the better buy? Explain your answer.
7. (a) Name a characteristic other than strength that might be important to consider when buying facial tissue. Explain.
   (b) Propose a test for this characteristic.

Testing and Consumer Groups

You might think that testing has been completed once a product is ready to be shipped to the stores. But at this stage, products may still be tested! Consumers do not depend entirely on the tests carried out by manufacturers. Government agencies also test products to ensure that they meet particular standards of safety or quality, and that the information on labels and in advertisements is accurate. You will read more about these standards in a later Topic. Besides government agencies, various consumer groups also test products to discover which ones perform best. The results of their tests are published in various magazines. You might like to look through some issues of consumer magazines in your library before you carry out the next Activity.

Consumer magazines such as these publish the results of tests that consumer groups and other organizations have conducted on different products. These results can help consumers decide which products are safest and most reliable.

Did You Know?

Not all testing involves complex scientific procedures. Some consumer items are tested by human senses. For example, certain people are employed as professional tasters or sniffers to evaluate the quality of products such as tea, wines, perfumes, deodorants, and water quality. In Edmonton, Alberta, professional sniffers test the quality of the city's drinking water. The testers sniff samples of water contained in 500 mL flasks, and then identify different smells as musty, oily, etc. The samples are rated and the values are compared with results from other sniffers in an effort to identify the origin of the odour. Water treatment procedures can then be modified to eliminate or reduce the odours. People with colds and allergies need not apply for this job!

You Be the Investigator

Imagine you are working for a consumer magazine. The editor of the magazine knows that you have learned how to conduct fair tests. She has asked you to choose a product, test it, and write up your findings for a special article in an upcoming issue of the magazine.

There are lots of products you can choose from, and lots of questions you can ask. Decide on something that interests you, and keep your questions simple. Consider carefully the product you choose.

- Which of its characteristics will you test?
- What is the function of that characteristic?
- What are the variables in your test?
- How will you control the variables?

Here are some suggestions of products to investigate. You may choose one of them, or something quite different.

- Which brand of detergent makes laundry the whitest?
- Which brand of paper towel absorbs the most liquid?
- Which brand of bread stays freshest the longest?
- Which building material is the best insulator?
- Which paper plate is the strongest?
- Which chewing gum keeps its flavour the longest?
- Which glue is the strongest?
- Which brand of battery lasts the longest? (You will need to consider a number of variables here, including shelf life, dates on the batteries, alkaline vs. dry cell, etc.)

Remember that to produce a recommendation that the readers of your magazine can rely on, you need to repeat your tests a few times. For this Activity, you may choose to work in a small group.

Procedure

1. Design a procedure for testing your product.
2. Write a list of the materials you will need to carry out your test.
3. Draw a table for recording your results.
4. Discuss your plans with your teacher.
5. Carry out your tests.
6. Present your findings in the form of a magazine article. Give it an appealing title, an illustration, and include recommendations based on your findings.

Product Safety and Standards

Every year, people are killed by electrocutions, suffocation, and by other means as a result of accidents involving consumer products. In this Topic, you will learn how product safety standards attempt to protect consumers from such terrible accidents.

Playing Safe

Extra care and attention to safety must go into the making and testing of products used by young children, because they are unable to read instructions or warning labels. Children may also use products in ways that were not intended. An adult probably warned you to be careful with toys that flew through the air, or had sharp edges. But there are less obvious dangers as well. For example, one toy company in the United States had to recall nearly half a million stuffed toys that were designed to hang on an elastic cord over a crib. The danger? A baby could be strangled by the cord.

Testing of products, and the careful selection of appropriate materials and design, can help prevent many potential accidents. At one time, for example, children ran the risk of suffering burns if they brushed too near a flame and their clothes caught fire. Today, clothing for children is made of materials that ignite less readily and burn more slowly than in the past. In Canada, the federal government does flammability testing on textile materials used for the outer covering of dolls, plush toys, and soft toys, as well as dolls' clothing and hair. If the material has a flame-retardant finish, a special laundering procedure is carried out prior to the test. This procedure helps ensure that toys covered with the finish do not lose their ability to resist fire after being washed.

Setting Standards

Suppose you are a safety inspector who must examine a new vacuum cleaner to ensure it is safe. What would you look for, and how would you test the product? Like any electrical appliance, a vacuum cleaner can give you a shock if part of the wire is exposed. It can also overheat and start a fire if it is poorly designed, or has a wire that is too small to carry the necessary voltage. In this particular vacuum cleaner, the wire and the plug look secure and well-insulated. But is that enough? When the vacuum cleaner is in use, it may be dragged from room to room, pulled up and down stairs, or pushed under furniture. Will it still be safe after months or years of use?

To answer these questions, and to set suitable standards, some tests are designed to duplicate or exceed the normal wear and tear that a product might undergo. For example, if a vacuum cleaner has a cord that automatically rewinds, a test could be conducted in which the cord is pulled out and rewound 6000 times to make sure it does not become detached, frayed, or broken. If the suction hose carries an electric current, it is dragged over rough emery paper 500 times, and twisted back and forth 20 000 times to make sure that live wires will not become exposed during normal use.

Tests like these are carried out by the Canadian Standards Association (CSA). They ensure that all electrical products are made to certain standards that have been legislated in Canada. The products must pass these tests before they can be offered for sale in this country. The tests specify requirements such as proper insulation around the wire; secure connections between the wire and the plug at one end and the appliance at the other; and a label on the equipment stating the maximum amount of voltage the wire can safely carry. As an added precaution, some electrical equipment includes a fuse that will cut off power if the wire becomes overloaded.

The technician is checking to see that the electrical cord is properly connected to the heating element of a kettle. A poorly made connection could electrocute a person using the kettle.

Look for CSA labels on several electrical appliances at home. A label means that the product has met the safety standards set by the Association. List or draw all the labels you can find. What information is on each label? What might happen if there were no safety standards or testing agencies? What might happen if you could not rely on the information on product labels?

If you see labels like these on a product, you know that it has passed a set of tests and has met the required standards of safety.

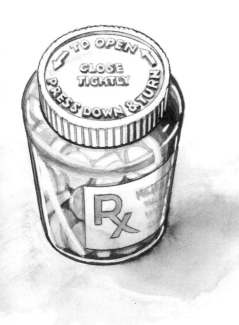

Designing for Safety

Designing products that reduce risk to consumers is a continual challenge for manufacturers. Government standards provide some good guidelines, based on experience and testing. But new products are always being developed, and old designs can always be improved. Improvements may come from new materials, such as flame-resistant cloth. They may also come from designs that have been developed to solve a particular problem or flaw. You have probably seen or used a bottle with a child-proof cap. The cap was designed for bottles that hold pills or other items that could be dangerous to children. In order to remove the cap, you must press down at the same time as you twist. This action is difficult or impossible for small children to carry out. In the next Activity you will face the challenges of a designer who is trying to invent a safe container.

What's in the Box?

Problem

How can you design a child-proof box?

Materials

cardboard
scissors
tape

Procedure

Your task in this Activity is to design a box that you can easily open and close, but that would be difficult for a small child to open. You cannot use a combination lock, or a lock and key.

Think about how this objective is achieved by the child-proof cap. To open the cap, you need a certain amount of strength and a grip that small children do not have. How can you achieve the same result in the design of your box?

You could devise a method of opening the box that:

- is too complicated for a small child to learn;
- requires more strength than a child has;
- hides the opening from the child in some way; or
- has parts that are physically difficult for a small child to handle (for example, by being too large or too small).

Three designs for boxes are illustrated below to help you start thinking about this problem. Some boxes open like drawers. Others have lids on the top. Where else could you have an opening? Could you combine two different designs? Sketch a design and then construct your child-proof box from cardboard.

Finding Out

1. In your notebook, write down the feature(s) of your box design that you think will make it difficult for a child to open the box.

Finding Out More

2. Have some young children try out your child-proof box.
3. How could you make a better child-proof box?

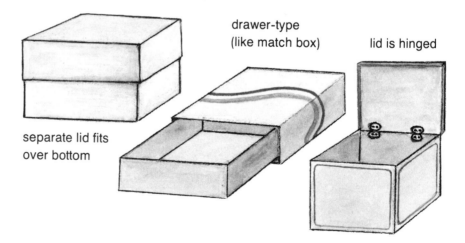

separate lid fits over bottom

drawer-type (like match box)

lid is hinged

Consumer Beware!

Safety standards help ensure that products are designed to be safe. But the consumer is responsible for using a product properly. What happens if a consumer uses a product in a way it was not designed for? For example, what if you use the blade of a penknife as a screwdriver? The blade and handle are not designed for this purpose. There is a risk that the blade may snap, or that it will slip and cut your hand.

Safety problems may also arise if products are poorly **maintained** (looked after and repaired). Something that is safe when new may wear out after years of use. Worn brakes, frayed electrical wire, blunt blades, rusted metal, and cracked parts are all potential hazards.

To avoid the dangers resulting from the improper use or poor maintenance of a product, many manufacturers include written instructions to guide consumers. What sort of information is needed by a consumer? In the next Activity you can find out.

Activity 3-8

Safety First

Problem

What kind of information do consumers need in order to use a bicycle safely?

A bicycle may be hazardous if it is not used and maintained properly. Write a sample set of instructions for a consumer who has just bought a bicycle, telling him or her how to use the bicycle safely. Think about the possible ways the consumer might misuse the bicycle, for example,

- using it in a way it was not designed for (such as riding over rocky ground);
- maintaining it poorly (so that the brakes become worn or the tires become soft); or
- using it without proper safety equipment (such as a safety helmet and night lights).

Write your instructions so that the consumer has enough information to use the bicycle safely. Compare your instructions with those written by your classmates. What were the most important safety concerns?

Bicycle Owner's Manual

Printed in Canada

RULES OF THE ROAD

1. Obey all traffic instructions, traffic signs, one-way streets, etc.

2. Keep right and ride single file. Do out, swerve or stunt in traffic. N on another vehicle.

3. For dusk, or night riding and w conditions warrant it, the bicy equipped with a white light i tor in the rear. (Lighting acc from your bicycle dealer.)

4. Take special precautions a all ways; be sure to use p indicate stopping and tu

5. Always give pedestrian

6. Watch out for cars pu doors opening on pa

7. Don't carry passen

8. Use carrier for ca packages that ob proper control o

Warning Signs

Many products, such as cosmetics and household cleaners, are not required to list all their ingredients on the package sold to consumers. Suppose you have an allergy to certain chemicals. How might you find out the contents of a product? Design a symbol that could be put on a package to indicate that some people may be allergic to the contents. The symbol should have an image that can be understood internationally.

Some products are particularly hazardous, and must be used with extreme care. Examples include power tools, fireworks, and products such as household cleaners and pesticides, which contain chemicals that may be flammable, toxic (poisonous), or harmful to health. Some materials, such as strong ammonia, are **corrosive**; that is, they can cause serious chemical burns to flesh. Some of these products are controlled by laws, and must have special warnings on their packages. The warning may include details of what to do in case of an accident.

Some harmful materials and designs are banned under a set of Canadian laws called the Hazardous Products Act, and these materials and designs cannot be used in consumer products at all. For example,

- children's products cannot be painted with coatings containing harmful amounts of lead or other poisonous metals;
- shower doors, storm doors, and bathtub enclosures must be made of safety glass that does not shatter into large, sharp pieces; and
- asbestos, which can cause lung disease, cannot be used in products such as children's toys and products for modelling and sculpture.

Symbols (below) used on potentially dangerous consumer products.

 Poison   Flammable   Explosive   Corrosive

 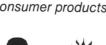

Danger   Warning   Caution

Compressed Gas  **Poisonous and Infectious Material Causing Other Toxic Effects**

Flammable and Combustible Material   **Biohazardous Infectious Material**

Oxidizing Material   **Corrosive Material**

Poisonous and Infectious Material Causing Immediate and Serious Toxic Effects  **Dangerously Reactive Material**

Symbols used on potentially dangerous products in the workplace.

Checkpoint

1. Describe a test that you could use to measure the quality of a sample of school chairs made of painted tubular steel, wood, and vinyl.
   (a) What part of the chair does your test measure?
   (b) Which characteristic of the chair are you testing?
   (c) Does your test result allow you to make an inference about the overall quality of the chair? Give a reason for your answer.

2. Chad and Jill each got a new backpack. Both packs were of the same design and made of the same material. After six months, Jill's backpack had a ripped seam and a broken zipper, while Chad's looked as good as new.
   (a) Suggest two reasons to account for this difference.
   (b) Describe a test that you could use to confirm one of your reasons.

3. "Modern products have better designs and materials, and they have fewer problems compared to products in the past." Explain why you agree or disagree with this statement.

4. Give an example of each of the following:
   (a) a product that must be individually tested;
   (b) a product that can be tested by random sampling; and
   (c) a product that could be field tested.

5. Analyse these manufacturers' claims. Do you think the claim would convince you that each manufacturer's testing was adequate? Explain why or why not.
   (a) "We know that our product is reliable. We have said that it is fireproof and we know it is because we have tested it repeatedly. In none of the over 1000 tests that we've done has the material caught fire."
   (b) "Our calculators can be depended on. We tested the first 100 that came off the assembly line and each of them worked perfectly for the period of time we guarantee."
   (c) "Our consumer survey of high school students throughout Canada showed that our brand of soft drink is their favourite—we are pleased to state categorically that Canadians prefer our brand."

6. Describe how an electric iron might be dangerous if
   (a) it is used in a way for which it was not designed; and
   (b) it is not maintained properly.

7. Write a set of instructions for consumers telling them how to use a hair dryer or a set of headphones safely.

8. Describe how you could change the materials or design of a pair of scissors in order to make them safer for young children to use.

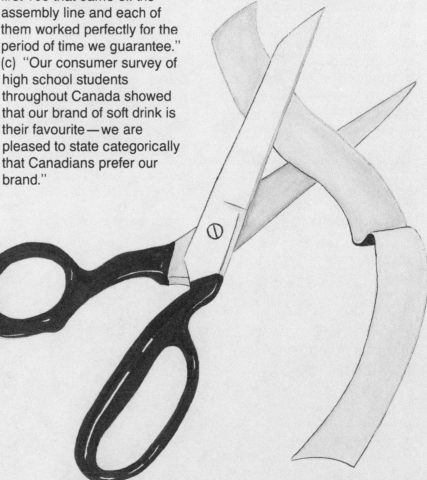

Science and Technology in Society

Looks Good . . . But Does It Work?

In 1917 the world was at war and Canadian soldiers were fighting in Europe. These soldiers had to use military equipment that was poorly designed and often didn't work properly. Standards for safety and performance were urgently needed to improve the equipment being manufactured. Concerned engineers and scientists met to consider the problem. They organized the forerunner to the Canadian Standards Association to promote the standardization of products.

Today, CSA tests a wide range of products, not only in Canada but also in 59 countries around the world. Household appliances, toys, elevators, safety boots, windows, amusement rides, and even sports equipment are just some of the products that undergo rigorous testing procedures to ensure their safety and quality. The CSA mark appears on more than 1 billion products a year! But CSA doesn't test everything. Most clothing, food, vehicles, and drugs are regulated, inspected, and/or tested by the government.

Let's look at just one product that CSA tests—eye

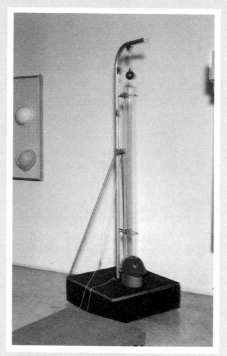

Testing the strength of a construction hard-hat.

protectors for racquet sports. Every year, many badminton, squash, and racquetball players suffer serious eye injuries. A racquetball travels much faster than a tennis ball—reaching speeds of 190 km/h!—so reliable eye protectors are a must. At one time players bought "lensless" goggles, believing that these would protect their eyes. Many people learned too late that these goggles were not safe. This prompted CSA to develop a national standard on racquet-sports eye protection. This standard specifies exactly the kinds of tests that eye protectors must pass.

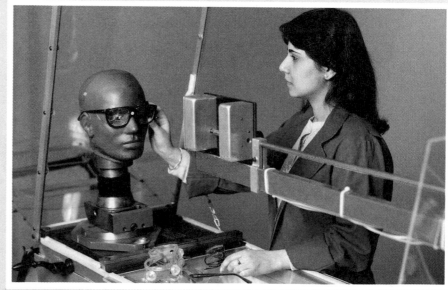

Testing eye protectors used in racquet sports.

How would you test a pair of eye protectors? Some students have suggested jumping on them, hitting them, or throwing balls at them. The CSA uses an air cannon that fires a ball at speeds of 40 m/s or 145 km/h at eye protectors placed on a special head form. Tissue paper is taped over the eyes of the head form and carbon paper is placed on top of this. If the tissue paper is marked by the carbon, this tells the technicians that the eye protector touched the head form's eyes and, therefore, failed the test.

Another product that must be strong and durable is, surprisingly, a TV set. The TV screen must be strong enough to withstand a sudden change in air pressure if the TV tube inside should happen to implode (burst inward). The technicians at CSA want to make sure that if a TV screen shatters for any reason, glass will not be scattered. To test this, a mechanical arm hurls a steel ball at the TV screen and technicians observe what happens on impact. If the glass breaks but does not fly outward too far, the TV screen has passed the test.

In the late 1960s, a number of fatalities and injuries occurred on amusement rides. It became clear that these rides had to be inspected regularly for safety. The CSA's Safety Code for Amusement Rides covers the design and manufacture of the rides, as well as the setting up, inspection, maintenance, and dismantling of this equipment.

Across Canada, organizations such as CSA, as well as numerous government departments, are hard at work putting products through rigorous tests to help ensure that the majority of products we buy are safe, effective, and reliable.

Think About It

It would be an overwhelming task for any one organization to test all the products available to consumers. Many organizations and government departments are involved in product testing. Choose one department, such as the Department of Consumer and Corporate Affairs, Health and Welfare Canada, Transport Canada, or Agriculture Canada. Find out about the important product regulation and testing that this department carries out.

Testing the durability of a TV screen.

Amusement rides must be tested for safety.

Advertisements and Labels

"Buy product A! It has more vitamins than product B!"
"Buy product B! It's good for you!"
Think about something you bought recently. Why did you buy that particular product? What effect did advertising have on your choice? Are advertisements an accurate source of information about products?

Consider the two advertising claims above. Could you test these claims? The claim for product A—"It has more vitamins than product B!"—can be tested. You can read the list of ingredients, or analyse the product, to confirm whether product A has more vitamins than product B. What about product B? It claims to be good for you. If may well be, but how could you test that claim? You may consume product B and feel good. But how do you know that feeling good was a result of consuming product B? You could have had the same feeling after consuming something else—or even after consuming nothing at all! This claim would be hard to test.

Some television advertisements claim to show products being tested. A car is dropped from a helicopter; a wristwatch is strapped to a deep-sea diver; a spot of glue is used to suspend a construction worker from a girder. Many TV commercials show "tests" in which one product is compared with another: one detergent washes whiter than another; a soft drink tastes better than that of its competitors; one brand of battery lasts longer than others. In another advertisement, a battery manufacturer claims that its brand of battery was not included in the famous comparison test shown in the advertisements of its rival. Are these tests fair? Do you have enough information to evaluate such tests? Knowing how scientific tests are designed will help you to assess the information presented in advertisements.

Analysing Advertisements

Problem

Are advertisements an accurate source of information about products?

Procedure

1. Select three or four advertisements from television, radio, newspapers, or magazines to analyse.
2. Record what facts, if any, each advertisement tells you about the product.
3. Record in detail the people, activities, and background in each advertisement (for example, a young woman with a baby is shown using the product in a kitchen; a group of three young women and three young men are shown splashing in the surf on a beach while the product is shown in a separate scene; a famous sports figure is shown talking about the product he is holding up in a locker-room).
4. Record whether any scientific terms or claims are featured in the advertisements.

Finding Out

1. (a) Do the advertisements show or tell you how the product is used?
   (b) If not, how would you obtain this information?
2. (a) Is the product compared to other, similar products?
   (b) If so, how is this done?
   (c) Is the comparison fair?
3. (a) What sex and age group use the product?
   (b) Is this the same sex and age group as the people (if any) shown in the ad?
4. Is the background or setting of the advertisement relevant to the way the product is used?
5. (a) Are any claims made about the performance of the product?
   (b) Can these claims be scientifically tested?
   (c) Outline an experimental design for testing one claim used in an advertisement.

Extension

6. Form small groups in class. Based on your analysis of the advertisements, debate the proposal: "Only factual statements should be allowed in advertisements." Have some students argue in favour of the proposal and some against it.

Looking at Labels

What do labels and packaging tell you about a product? Can you use this information to help you decide which products to buy? For example, the list of ingredients on a container of orange drink tells you if the drink contains pure juice or artificial flavouring and colouring. Other labels warn people who have allergies to certain chemicals, or those who want to reduce the sugar or salt in their diet. The labels inside clothing tell you the size of the clothes, what materials they are made from, and usually how to clean and look after them.

Have you seen products with labels that say "vitamin enriched" and "pH balanced"? These terms sound scientific, but what do they mean? Are they relevant to what you want from the product? If a product has "with vitamin C" on its label, does that mean that similar products without this claim do not have vitamin C? You will compare products with different labels in the next Activity.

Testing Scientific Claims

Problem

Do drinks that claim to be enriched with vitamin C have more of this ingredient than drinks that do not make this claim?

Materials

starch suspension
iodine solution
8 test tubes
test tube rack
vitamin C solution (made by dissolving a 100 mg vitamin C tablet in 100 mL of water)
250 mL beaker
stirring rod
10 mL measuring cylinder
medicine dropper
two brands of apple or orange drinks from containers that say "with vitamin C" on the label
two brands of apple or orange drinks from containers that do not say "with vitamin C" on the label

Procedure

1. Half fill a beaker with starch suspension. Add one or two drops of iodine solution and stir the mixture gently until it is a deep purple-blue colour. When vitamin C is added to this mixture, it will react to produce a colourless mixture.

2. Pour 5 mL of the starch-iodine mixture into a test tube. Add one drop of vitamin C solution to the mixture and shake the tube gently. Repeat, counting the number of drops added, until the colour has been bleached out. Record the total number of drops used. This tells you how much vitamin C of a known concentration is needed to produce a colourless mixture. You can now compare this result against the unknown concentrations of vitamin C in the different drinks.

3. Obtain two test tubes for each sample of juice you are testing. Set aside a control sample of each juice. Pour 5 mL of the starch-iodine mixture into the other test tubes.

4. Add one drop of the juice to be tested to the starch-iodine mixture in the test tube and shake gently to mix it well. Repeat this procedure, counting the number of drops added, until the purple-blue colour disappears. Remember that the drink has a colour of its own, so the bleached solution will not be colourless. Match the colour of the sample being tested to that of the control sample of juice you set aside. Record the number of drops used.

5. Follow the same procedure for each drink to be tested.

Finding Out

1. (a) Which drink appeared to have the most vitamin C?
   (b) On what evidence did you base your inference?
2. Which drink appeared to have the least amount of vitamin C?
3. Was there a large or a small difference between the amounts of vitamin C in the different drinks you tested?
4. Did the drinks that mentioned vitamin C on their labels have more vitamin C than those that did not mention it?
5. (a) What are the variables in this experiment?
   (b) Is this a controlled experiment? If not, how would you change it to make it controlled?

Step 1

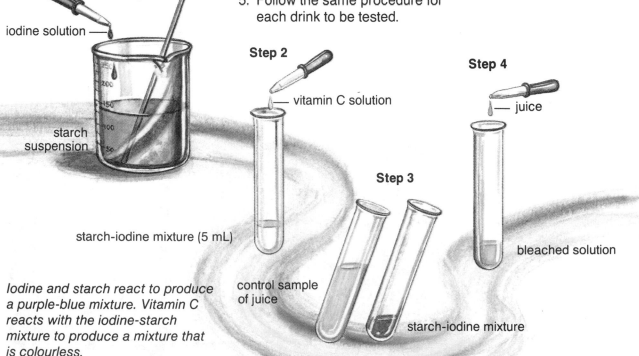

stirring rod

iodine solution

starch suspension

starch-iodine mixture (5 mL)

Iodine and starch react to produce a purple-blue mixture. Vitamin C reacts with the iodine-starch mixture to produce a mixture that is colourless.

Step 2

vitamin C solution

control sample of juice

Step 3

starch-iodine mixture

Step 4

juice

bleached solution

Labels and Laws

Before you can make a well-informed product choice, you must be sure the information conveyed to you is accurate. If a manufacturer labels a package "mixed nuts," and the package contains 95% peanuts and 5% almonds, hazelnuts, and cashews, you would be misled. To avoid this problem, the government has passed laws that help consumers obtain accurate information from labels. The Consumer Packaging and Labelling Act requires manufacturers to print the following information on packages:

- the quantity of the product (so you cannot be misled by finding a small amount of a product inside a large container);
- the name and address of the manufacturer (so you know where to complain if you have problems with the product); and
- the identity of the product (so you know what is inside the package or container).

Government inspectors examine and test products to make sure the descriptions on the packages match the product. For example, eggs labelled "large" must be a certain minimum size. If a drawing or photograph on a package containing a construction toy shows 12 different parts, there must be at least 12 different parts inside. If inspectors discover that a manufacturer's labels contain false or misleading information, the government can prosecute the manufacturer.

Probing

What visual information is on these book covers? Is there any relationship between the images and written information on the covers and the actual products inside? Can you judge the quality of the product from the information given? If so, how? Bring one or two of your favourite paperback books or record or CD album covers to class. Discuss whether the appearance of the cover and the information on it influenced your decision to buy.

Products and the Environment

You might be surprised to find out how many different countries around the world were involved in making some of the products you buy and use. Your bicycle may contain steel from Canada or the United States, chromium from Zimbabwe, and rubber from Malaya. Some of your clothing may have been produced in India or Korea. Parts of your radio may have come from Germany or Japan. The sugar in a chocolate bar may have come from the Caribbean, the cocoa from Africa, the milk from Switzerland, and the aluminum in the wrapping from a mine in Jamaica. Every time you buy or use a product, you have an impact on the world far beyond your own town or city. The materials that go into a product may be part of a dwindling world supply. Both materials and the energy used to make or operate a product may cause **pollution**. (Pollution is the addition of anything to the environment that is harmful to living things.) What difference do these factors make when you decide to choose one product over another?

The business of making and selling products uses energy at several stages. It takes energy to extract, transport, and process the raw materials. It takes energy to make, package, and transport the final product. Many consumers and manufacturers are concerned about the environmental effects of using large amounts of energy. Some of this energy comes from burning coal, oil, or gas. What will happen when these supplies are used up?

When energy is used, waste products are produced. If these wastes are not properly treated or disposed of, they may end up as pollutants in the air, soil, or water. These concerns have led many people to look for ways of conserving our energy resources. One way is to buy products that use the least amount of materials and use the least amount of energy in their manufacturing and operation. In the next Activity you will calculate the amount of energy used to manufacture a typical ballpoint pen.

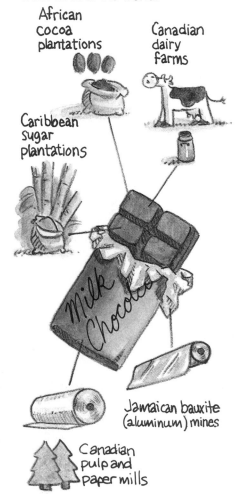

The production of a single consumer item such as a chocolate bar involves materials from all over the world.

African cocoa plantations

Canadian dairy farms

Caribbean sugar plantations

Jamaican bauxite (aluminum) mines

Canadian pulp and paper mills

Milk Chocolate

Making a Pen

Problem

How much energy is needed to make a ballpoint pen?

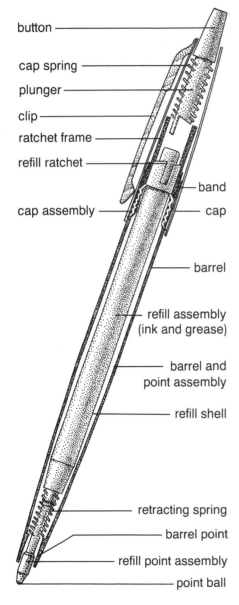

The parts of a ballpoint pen manufactured by the Parker Pen Company.

Procedure

1. The chart below shows the amount of energy needed to make or assemble each part of a pen. The energy is expressed in kilowatt hours, and the material used is shown in brackets. Study the chart carefully before proceeding. If necessary, refer to the diagram of the pen to identify the different parts of the pen listed in the chart.

2. Calculate the total energy (in kilowatt hours) used to make and assemble:
   (a) the cap;
   (b) the barrel; and
   (c) the refill.

3. Determine the total energy used to make and assemble the pen. Include the final assembly.

4. Seven parts of the pen are made of metal and four are made of plastic.
   Calculate:
   (a) how much energy is used to make the metal parts; and
   (b) how much energy is used to make the plastic parts.

5. There are six assembly steps in the chart. Calculate the total energy used in assembling the pen.

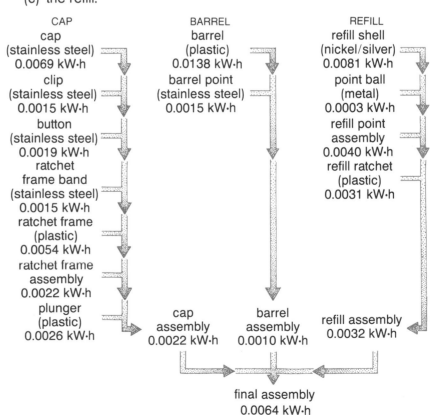

Energy for Packaging and Operating Products

Which takes more energy to make, a plastic bottle or a glass bottle? A comparison of these two materials shows that it takes twice as much energy to produce a 2 L glass bottle as a plastic bottle of the same size. It takes three times as much energy to produce an aluminum can compared with a plastic container. On the other hand, a paper cup takes half the energy to make compared with a plastic cup. These comparisons may help a consumer decide whether a particular product is "environmentally friendly" or not.

Finding Out

1. (a) Is more energy used to make the different parts of the pen or to assemble the pen?
   (b) Try to give a reason for the answer to (a).
2. (a) Does it take more energy to make plastic or metal parts?
   (b) Try to give a reason for the answer to (a). (Hint: Think about the size of the parts and the heat needed to melt the material.)

Finding Out More

3. The Parker Pen Company can manufacture 3000 of these pens in an hour.
   (a) Calculate the total energy consumed per hour to manufacture these pens.
   (b) Calculate the total energy used to manufacture these pens during one eight-hour work shift.

Extension

4. Examine the materials and purchase price of a number of different ballpoint pens. Do you think there is any relationship between the cost of each pen and:
   (a) the materials used to make it?
   (b) the amount of energy used to manufacture it?
   (c) the length of time the pen is likely to last?
   Explain your answers.

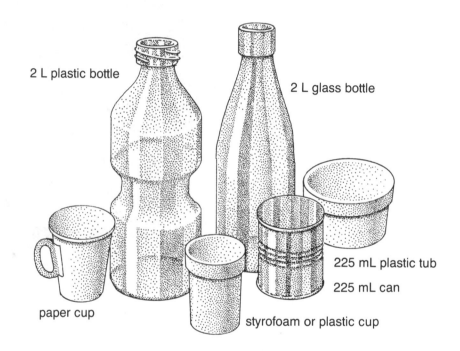

2 L plastic bottle

2 L glass bottle

225 mL plastic tub

225 mL can

paper cup

styrofoam or plastic cup

Some products require energy to operate. For example, an automobile uses gas, and a refrigerator uses electricity. Improved designs and materials allow products such as these to operate more efficiently on less energy. People can also save energy by not leaving electrical appliances, such as televisions and lights, turned on when they are not in use. As you learned in your study of energy and machines, new appliances sold in Canada have Energuide labels that tell you how much energy each appliance uses. You may find such a label inside your refrigerator or on your furnace.

Products and Waste

Children's bicycles, TV sets, radios, chairs, toasters, toys, toboggans, and clothing are among the items that people throw out as garbage. These used products, some of them easily fixed, may end up buried in the ground or burned in an incinerator. What effect does the disposal of waste products have on the environment? Is there an alternative to throwing out the products and packages that we no longer want?

The other side of consuming—most products that we buy are eventually disposed of.

Every time a product is manufactured, it uses up some of the Earth's material resources. Some materials, such as minerals, metals, and oil (from which plastics are made), exist in a limited amount in the Earth's crust. When these materials are mined and used, there is less left for the future. Recall that such materials are called **non-renewable resources**. Other materials come from living organisms. These include silk, cotton, wool, leather, paper, wood, some natural oils and resins, bone, and ivory. If properly managed, these materials can be "harvested" from generation to generation for an unlimited time. These are called **renewable resources**.

This label will help you find "planet-friendly" products.

An old tire can be reused to make a swing.

Why is it important to distinguish between these two types of resources? As some non-renewable materials become increasingly scarce and expensive, manufacturers may have to look for alternative materials for some products. Consumers may decide to choose products made from renewable resources, or to select longer-lasting items, rather than throw out products made from non-renewable materials after using them only once or twice.

For help in choosing products that are less harmful to the environment, consumers can now look for the new EcoLogo. This label will appear on products that are energy efficient, use recycled materials, and minimize the use of environmentally hazardous substances.

The average Canadian household of four produces about two tonnes of domestic refuse every year. Much of this waste could be reduced by reusing some items and recycling others. **Reusing** means using a product more than once. For example, many people save boxes, cookie tins, and jars and use them as storage containers. An old tire can be reused to make a planter or a child's swing. Old tires may also be shredded and used as material for highway construction. Paper and cardboard can be reused for insulation. Returnable bottles can be cleaned and refilled with beer or soft drinks. Clean, used oil can be sprayed in mines and fertilizer plants to control dust. All these activities reduce waste and pollution, and reduce the demand for new raw materials.

Recycling means using a material to make more of the same material. Materials that can be successfully recycled include paper, glass, metals, and oil. Recycling saves energy as well as materials, because recycled materials do not need as much processing as the original raw materials. For example, if broken glass is added to the materials used to make new glass, the mixture melts at a lower temperature. The old glass also helps to produce a more uniform new glass. Producing aluminum from scrap aluminum cuts energy use by about 95 per cent.

Through reusing and recycling, a discarded product may become raw material for another product. In the next Activity, you will use your imagination to find a way of reusing or recycling a common product.

Waste Not, Want Not

Problem

How can different consumer products be reused or recycled?

Procedure

1. Choose a product that many households have and may eventually throw out, for example, shoes, jackets, toboggans, skateboards, radios, baby strollers.
2. Imagine you are starting a company to make a new product. Your raw material is the discarded product that others throw out. Do not think of it as a waste product. Consider the parts and materials it is made of. They

are cheap and usable. How could you use manufactured parts such as wheels or buttons? How might you use materials such as metal, plastic, or leather? In a report or a poster, show how you would convert some or all of the discarded product into a new product that you have designed.

Finding Out

1. (a) Name two advantages of using discarded products as a starting point for making new products.
   (b) Name two disadvantages.

Making Choices

Before consumers can make wise choices, they need to be well informed. When people have been given enough information, many of them choose products that are less harmful to the environment, compared to the alternatives. In recent years, for example:

- Some people stopped buying products in aerosol spray cans. They had learned that the gases used in the cans damage the layer of ozone that is found high in the Earth's atmosphere. The ozone layer filters out the Sun's ultraviolet light, which in excessive amounts is harmful to living things. An alternative to aerosol sprays is an air pump mechanism.
- Some people have chosen products that break down rapidly when discarded, rather than those made of materials that may remain in the environment for many years. Disposable diapers, for example, may take

300 years to decompose. Cloth diapers can be reused after washing, and decompose relatively rapidly.

- Some people have chosen not to buy products that contain harmful chemicals. For example, many toxic household cleansers can be replaced by ammonia, vinegar, or baking soda, which are less harmful to living things. Toxic chrome cleaner can be replaced by rubbing alcohol.
- Some people have chosen to buy detergents that do not contain phosphates. When phosphates in the waste water from households and factories get into rivers and streams, they cause algae to grow rapidly. This chokes waterways and kills many small organisms and fish. You will learn more about this process in later studies.

In some cases, people have chosen not to buy products for **ethical** reasons (having to do with standards of right and wrong). For example, some people are concerned about the way animals are used in research to test cosmetic products. They feel that the research causes suffering. They argue that the animal tests are not necessary, and are not justified because cosmetic products are not essential to human existence. There are other brands of cosmetics that do not involve tests on animals. Manufacturers and researchers in cosmetic companies sometimes argue that the tests do not cause suffering, and that they are designed to protect people from using harmful products. Concerned consumers can analyse the information from both sides, and decide for themselves which products to buy.

These examples show that what you buy can directly affect the environment and other people. When people stop buying a product for environmental or political reasons, they are said to **boycott** the product. If many people boycott a product, they may force the manufacturer to change the product or go out of business.

What you buy and why you buy it are influenced by many factors, including your attitudes and those of your friends and family, the community you live in, and advertisements. Since the amount of money you have to spend on products is limited, you must always make choices about what to buy and use. Science can help you make some of these choices by giving you information about the safety, reliability, and effectiveness of products, as well as their effect on the environment.

Working with New Products

Irma Vescan is a certification engineer in the consumer product testing division of the Canadian Standards Association. In a recent interview she had this to say about her job.

When my teenage daughter and son come to my office, the first place they want to visit is the lab. Here TV screens are being smashed, appliances erupt into flames, and there is a good chance they'll get some popcorn if corn poppers are being tested. The lab is definitely where the action is!

My job involves checking the construction of electrical appliances and then determining what tests need to be done—tests that will reveal any problems in the operation of the appliance. Once the product passes the tests, it can be certified (approved) and sold to the public.

In my department, we test appliances mainly for fire or shock hazard. We have lots of controlled fires! First we test the product under normal operating conditions. Not everyone will follow the manufacturer's recommendations for safe use of the product, so next we try to

Irma Vescan and technician Ed Lee check a stove top to ensure that it is properly grounded.

think of the worst operating conditions possible, something that would produce a shock or a fire hazard.

What might happen, for instance, if you left a curling iron on all day with a bath towel on top of it? Would the towel smoulder? Would it ignite? To answer these questions, we try to recreate this scenario in the laboratory, where we can safely control any problems that might arise. We put a curling iron on tissue paper and place a piece of cheesecloth on top of it. Then we leave it for seven hours,

roughly the time you might expect someone to be away from home. If the paper smoulders at all, the curling iron cannot be approved.

With a toaster oven, for example, we cook fatty hamburgers and let all the grease accumulate. Then we leave the oven on for seven hours to see if the grease catches fire. With corn poppers, we look at what might happen if the popped corn is left in the appliance. Will it burn? Many products fail the test. When a product fails, we let the manufacturer know. The manufacturer redesigns the product and brings it back to us for further testing.

The lab technicians must wear safety shoes, safety glasses, and, in some cases, insulating gloves to protect them during the tests.

In school, I always liked math and science. I knew I wanted to pursue a career that involved these subjects. As I got older it became clear to me what that career might be—electrical engineering.

My job is so interesting for many reasons, but especially because I get to see the new products before they are available in the stores!

Checkpoint

1. • "More people choose brand X than any other leading brand."
    • "Brand Y gets your bathroom cleaner, faster."
    • "Dogs live longer if they eat brand A dog food."
    Which of the advertising claims above are testable and which are not? Explain your answer.

2. (a) List, in order of their importance to you, three things that might be printed on a package of breakfast cereal.
    (b) Explain why each item is important.
    (c) Name one thing printed on the package that is not important to you. Explain.

3. A brand of sunscreen advertises that its chemical ingredient provides more protection from sunburn than any other brand. How might you test this claim?

4. You want to buy 1 L of juice. You can get it in either of the two ways shown here.
    (a) Under what circumstances would you buy the glass bottle of juice?
    (b) Under what circumstances would you buy the cardboard containers?
    (c) Which form of packaging do you think has the least harmful effect on the environment? Why?

5. Draw a series of flowcharts to show the different industries involved in the manufacture of a skateboard, from the raw materials to the finished product. (Hint: Begin by listing the different parts of a skateboard and the materials they are made of.)

6. You want to buy a razor as a gift. You have a choice between a package of disposable razors and one that uses replaceable blades. You are concerned about which of these alternatives is less harmful to the environment. Give one reason:
    (a) to choose the disposable razors;
    (b) not to choose the disposable razors;
    (c) to choose the razor with replaceable blades; and
    (d) not to choose the razor with replaceable blades.

Focus

- Some characteristics of consumer products are important to their function, and some are not.
- Products may be compared and evaluated by means of fair tests.
- Products may have flaws as a result of poor design, materials, or construction.
- The development and testing of new materials and designs can help improve the quality, safety, and reliability of products.
- Products may be tested at different stages both while and after they are manufactured.
- Some products may be individually tested, while other products are tested by random sampling.
- Consumer groups and publications give consumers information about products and tests.
- Government standards for labelling help ensure that there is complete and accurate information about the product that is inside a package.
- Standards are used to ensure that products offered for sale are safe.

- Products can be dangerous if they are used in the wrong way, or if they are not maintained properly.
- The manufacturing and operation of certain products can damage the environment.
- Consumers may choose not to buy products for ethical reasons.

Backtrack

1. If you are a rock climber, dangling from a cliff, you need a rope that is [mystery word]. When you have completed the puzzle in your notebook, the highlighted letters will spell this word. Use the definitions to find the correct words for the puzzle.

   (a) ■■■■■■■■□ ■■■■■■
   (b) ■■■■ ■□■■■■■
   (c) ■■■■■■ ■■■■□■■
   (d) ■■■■■■■□■
   (e) ■■■■■□■■■
   (f) ■■■■■■■■□■
   (g) ■■■□■ ■■■■
   (h) ■□■■■■■■■

   (a) to test a product, people who have used the product answer a questionnaire
   (b) another term for random sampling
   (c) a product is taken at random and is tested
   (d) substances that can cause serious chemical burns to the flesh

   (e) resources that can be harvested from generation to generation, if they are properly managed
   (f) a test that must have the same results again and again
   (g) a test on a product carried out under actual conditions of use
   (h) using a material to make more of the same material

2. What is essential in a fair test?

3. What do the following symbols on a product indicate?

(a)

(b)

(c)

(d)

4. List three characteristics of a bicycle
   (a) that can be scientifically tested; and
   (b) that are matters of personal choice.
5. You are using a stapler that keeps jamming. List two reasons why this product may be faulty.
6. Explain why you agree or disagree with each of the following statements.
   (a) Proper product testing requires elaborate laboratory equipment.
   (b) All products need to be tested only once before they are ready to be sold.
   (c) Many individual products do not need to be tested if spot testing is used.
   (d) Field tests are unnecessary.
7. Name two different ways in which a consumer can obtain reliable information about the quality and safety of a product.
8. (a) Write an example of an advertising claim that can be scientifically tested.
   (b) Describe how you would test the claim.
9. (a) Give two examples of ways in which the production, use, or disposal of consumer products can affect the environment.
   (b) Suggest how the effects on the environment you have described may be reduced or eliminated.

Synthesizer

10. Look around the room you are in and choose one of the manufactured products you see. Analyse the product and write a complete report on it, describing:
    (a) the materials it is made of;
    (b) how those materials may be obtained;
    (c) the characteristics of the product related to its function;
    (d) how you would test one of the characteristics; and
    (e) how you might improve the product by changing its design or materials.

11. Design your own symbol to communicate to consumers that a product has been specially designed to have a minimum impact on the environment.
12. Write or draw an advertisement for a pair of running shoes, using a statement:
    (a) that will make the product sound appealing to consumers; and
    (b) that can be scientifically tested.
13. Design a fair test that will allow you to compare the quality of three different makes of bicycle safety helmets.

The Earth's Crust

If you were to dig a deep hole near where you live, would you be likely to find gold? Or diamonds? Or would you find only clay, sand, or granite? Why are precious materials found only in some places in the Earth, and not in others? Where do the different materials that make up the Earth's crust come from? Have they always been where they are found today—or was there a time when they were not there?

On the time scale of a human life, the solid surface of the Earth does not seem to change very much. Rocks and boulders, gold and diamonds, all appear to last forever. The mountains, valleys, continents, and oceans seem fixed in place. Only a few dramatic events, such as an exploding volcano or a violent earthquake, hint that the seemingly solid ground may be moved by powerful forces from deep inside the planet.

In this Unit, you will journey from the top of the world's highest mountains to the floor of the deepest oceans—and below. You will look at evidence that shows how rocks are produced, how mountains are formed, and how continents move over the surface of the planet. The processes that caused these dramatic changes in the Earth's crust in the past are not unusual in our dynamic world. The same processes continue today. With a little probing, you can discover them for yourself.

Rocks and Minerals

Anywhere you stand on the surface of the planet Earth, a layer of rock extends down 5 km to 60 km beneath your feet. This "shell" of rock around the Earth is called the **crust**. Buried within the crust are all the metals, gems, oil, coal, gas, and many other materials that our industries and economy depend on. Also buried in the crust are clues to the long history of our planet. In these rocks, you can read stories of earthquakes and volcanoes, of the building of mountains and continents, and of different forms of life that once lived on the Earth. Your exploration begins when you pick up and examine a piece of rock.

Rocks contain clues about the Earth's past—and its future.

Some rocks are white or colourless, some are black, and others are brightly coloured. Some appear dull and soft, while others are hard and shiny. The appearance and properties of a rock depend on the particular materials of which it is made. The building blocks of rock are pure, naturally occurring solid materials called **minerals**. A **rock** is a combination of two or more minerals in various proportions. Although more than 3000 different minerals have been identified, most of them are quite rare. Only a few minerals, such as quartz and mica, are common and widespread throughout the Earth's crust.

You have probably seen the type of rock called granite. Polished granite is often used in buildings and at the base of statues. If you look at granite closely, you will see tiny sparkling grains, mixed with glassy-looking crystals, and some silvery-white or black flakes. The sparkling grains are a mineral called feldspar. The glassy crystals are quartz and

This granite rock contains the minerals mica, quartz, and feldspar.

the flakes are pieces of mica. Each of these minerals may also be found in other rocks, either on its own or with other minerals.

Some minerals, such as sulphur, copper, and gold, consist of a single chemical element. An **element** is a pure substance that cannot be further broken down into other substances by chemical means. The majority of minerals are combinations of two or more elements. The mineral quartz, for example, is made up of the elements silicon and oxygen. The chemical composition and structure of each mineral give it distinctive properties.

Properties of Minerals

To identify most minerals, not just one but several properties must be examined:

- **Lustre** is a word used to describe the surface of a mineral when light strikes it. A mineral may have a shiny, metallic lustre, like gold or silver, or a non-metallic lustre, like soapstone.
- **Streak** describes the powdery mark that some minerals leave when they are scratched against a hard surface, such as a piece of unglazed tile. The colour of the streak may be the same as the colour of the mineral, or it may be different.
- Some minerals are harder than others. The **hardness** of a mineral can be determined by scratching one mineral against another. The harder mineral leaves a scratch on the softer one. The relative hardness of a mineral is measured with a scale developed by a German scientist named Friedrich Mohs. **Mohs' hardness scale** consists of ten minerals ranked in order of hardness. These ten are used as standards against which all other minerals are compared. For example, the hardness of calcite is greater than that of gypsum, so it will scratch gypsum but not fluorite, which has greater hardness. The complete scale is shown in Table 4-1, which includes an alternative hardness chart made of materials you can easily find for yourself. Now you can begin to identify some minerals.

Table 4-1

MOHS' HARDNESS SCALE		HARDNESS CHART MADE OF THINGS YOU CAN EASILY FIND
1. talc	SOFTEST	soft pencil point
2. gypsum		fingernail
3. calcite		copper coin
4. fluorite		
5. apatite		pocket-knife blade
6. feldspar		steel file
7. quartz		sandpaper
8. topaz		
9. corundum		emery paper
10. diamond	HARDEST	

Mineral Mystery

Problem

How can you tell different minerals apart?

Materials

set of numbered mineral samples
streak plate (unglazed tile)
Mohs' scale set of minerals (or substitutes)

You can identify many different minerals using simple equipment and your senses of sight and touch.

Procedure

1. Make a table in your notebook with column headings as shown in Table 4-2. Include a row in the table for each of your mineral samples.
2. Take a mineral sample and record its number in the first column of your table.
3. Record the mineral's colour.

Table 4-2

MINERAL NUMBER	COLOUR	LUSTRE	STREAK	HARDNESS	OTHER	MINERAL NAME

4. Record one of the following descriptions that best describes the lustre of your sample.
   * metallic (like polished metal)
   * brilliant (like diamond)
   * glassy (like the broken edge of a piece of thick glass)
   * waxy (like polished wax)
   * pearly (like mother of pearl)
   * silky (like the shine on a piece of silk fabric or fibreglass cloth)
   * greasy or oily (like a piece of fat or soapstone)
   * dull (with no lustre at all, like a piece of hard clay)
5. Scrape the mineral once across the streak plate and brush off the excess powder. Record the colour of its streak, if any.
6. Scratch your sample with Mohs' mineral #5 (or the pocket-knife blade). If that doesn't leave a scratch or groove on your sample, continue along the scale toward #10; if mineral #5 does leave a scratch on your sample, move along the scale toward #1. Rank the hardness of your sample. (It will be between two numbers unless your sample is identical to one of the samples in Mohs' scale.)

Table 4-3 *Characteristics of Some Common Minerals*

MINERAL	COLOUR	LUSTRE	STREAK	HARDNESS
graphite	black	almost metallic	grey/black	1-2
halite	white	glassy	white	2-3
biotite	black	glassy/brilliant	white	2-3
galena	grey	metallic	dark grey	2.5-3
calcite	white	glassy	colourless	3
serpentine	green/white/ brown/red/black	silky/waxy	colourless	3-4
hematite	red	metallic	red/black	5-6
feldspar	white to greenish-white	pearly	white	6-6.5
pyrite	yellow	metallic	brown/ black	6-6.5
quartz	colourless/ violet/brown/ green/rose	glassy	colourless/ white	7

7. Repeat Steps 2 to 6 for the remaining mineral samples in your set.
8. Identify your samples by comparing their properties with those listed in Table 4-3.

Finding Out

1. Name (a) one advantage and (b) one disadvantage of using colour to identify a mineral.
2. Did lustre help you to identify any minerals? If so, which one(s)?
3. Is streak a more reliable characteristic for identifying minerals than colour or lustre? Give a reason for your answer, using an example.
4. In your own words, define the properties of "hardness," including how to test for it and what to observe.

Did You Know? ————

In some rocks, metal-bearing minerals are found in high concentrations. When the concentration is high enough to make it profitable to extract the mineral by mining, the rock is called an ore. The mined ore may need further treatment to separate and purify the metal.

Crystals

All minerals occur in the form of crystals, although some crystals are too small to be seen without magnification. Each type of mineral has crystals of a distinctive geometrical shape, such as a cube or pyramid. A well-formed crystal has smooth, flat sides, or **faces**. If you drop and break a mineral, you may observe that each fragment still has these smooth surfaces. This tendency of a mineral to split most easily along a plane (flat surface) parallel to its crystal faces is called **cleavage**.

Not all minerals break in this way. Minerals that break into fragments with rough, uneven surfaces are said to **fracture**. Cleavage and crystal shape are two more properties that can be used to identify minerals. Both properties can be explained by the mineral's crystal structure.

Iron ore being mined.

Mineral crystals have regular geometric shapes and smooth flat faces. These photographs show crystals of (a) fluorite, (b) selenite, (c) pyrite, and (d) wulfenite.

(a)

(b)

(c)

(d)

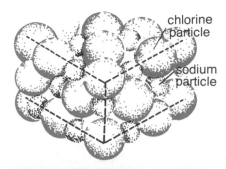
chlorine particle
sodium particle

As this simple model shows, the arrangement of particles in a mineral such as halite (rock salt) gives the crystals their characteristic shape.

Crystals are made up of tiny particles of certain elements. Evidence indicates that electrically charged particles of elements stay together in fixed and orderly arrangements. The particular shape of the arrangement depends on the elements involved. For example, the mineral halite (rock salt) is made up of the elements sodium and chlorine. The illustration shows a simple model of the arrangement of sodium and chlorine particles making up each tiny salt crystal. Compare this with the external appearance of a large salt crystal shown in the photograph.

Cleavage takes place along planes where the forces of attraction among the particles are the weakest. For example, one of the easiest minerals to split is mica. Its crystals are made up of silicon and oxygen particles arranged in flat layers. The attraction among the particles *within* each layer is much stronger than the attraction of particles *between* layers. Therefore, mica can be easily broken apart into thin flakes.

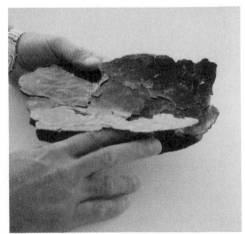

Mica is a mineral that cleaves easily into thin flat sheets.

Did You Know?

One of the hardest materials known is diamond. It is made entirely of the element carbon. But a very soft mineral called graphite (often used as pencil lead) is also made only of carbon. How can the same element produce such different materials? The explanation is that the carbon particles of the crystals of each material are in different arrangements.

You have looked at the structure and properties of minerals as a step toward understanding what rocks are made of. By describing and classifying various minerals, and mapping where they are found, scientists have built up a detailed picture of the Earth's crust. This knowledge allows Earth scientists, called **geologists**, to predict where to look for valuable minerals.

The composition of rocks also reveals a lot about conditions on the Earth in the past. For example, the size of the crystals in a rock can tell geologists how rapidly the Earth cooled in the area where the rock was formed. How does crystal size give them this information? You will be looking for an answer to this and other questions in the next Topic.

Rock Families

Although there are many different kinds of rock, they can all be grouped into three major **families** or types, depending on how the rocks were formed. The three families of rock are called **igneous**, **sedimentary**, and **metamorphic**. You can often determine to which family a rock belongs by its appearance. In this Topic, you will look at some scientific evidence used to unravel the mystery of how rocks originated.

Igneous Rock—"Born of Fire"

More than four-fifths of the Earth's crust is made up of **igneous rock**. The word igneous comes from the Latin word "*ignis*," meaning "fire." These rocks were formed by the cooling of melted rock material, either within the Earth's crust or after it had poured out onto the Earth's surface through volcanoes.

Hot magma erupting onto the Earth's surface cools and hardens to form igneous rock.

Obsidian is a dark, glassy rock. Although it is an igneous rock, it is smooth and shiny, with no visible crystals. It is produced by lava that cools so quickly that large crystals have no time to form.

The source of the melted rock lies many kilometres below the Earth's surface, where temperatures and pressures are high. The hot, molten (melted) rock found at these depths is called **magma**. This liquid material, which may contain suspended crystals and dissolved gases, is sometimes forced upward into the crust under high pressure. (Pressure is the force exerted on an area.) Wide fingers of magma make their way up through cracks in the rock, or displace or dissolve surrounding rock, making room for itself. From time to time, magma breaks through the Earth's surface. Then the magma loses some of its dissolved gases and water vapour, and is called **lava**. You may have seen films showing lava pouring from volcanoes in Hawaii or Iceland.

Igneous rock is classified into two groups, depending on whether it was formed below or on the Earth's surface. Rock formed from magma that cooled and hardened beneath the surface is called **intrusive rock**. This type of rock is found on the surface only where erosion has worn away the rock that once lay above it. Rock that was formed from lava cooling on the surface is called **extrusive rock**.

What evidence shows that igneous rock was formed in these ways? The most direct evidence comes from observation of lava flows and studies of newly cooled lava rock. Two hundred years ago, curiosity about these processes prompted scientists to collect different rock samples, melt their samples in the laboratory, and then cool and resolidify them. The scientists obtained glassy or crystalline minerals that differed in appearance depending on their rate of cooling.

Where would molten rock cool most quickly: below the Earth's surface or on the surface? What size of crystals would you expect to see in rocks formed in these two ways?

To test your predictions, you can try growing crystals under different conditions. In the next Activity, you will be working with a solution. Although a liquid solution is *not* the same as a melted pure substance, the relationship between crystal size and rate of cooling is the same in both types of liquid.

Two types of igneous rock.

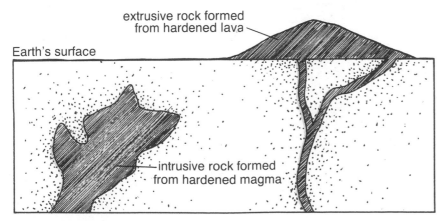

extrusive rock formed from hardened lava

Earth's surface

intrusive rock formed from hardened magma

Igneous Inquiry

Problem

How does the rate of cooling affect crystal size?

Materials

safety goggles
20 g copper(II) sulphate (in powder or granular form)
balance
2 test tubes
2 adhesive labels or masking tape
3 beakers (each 250 mL)
100 mL graduated cylinder
stirring rod
hot plate
scoopula
crushed ice
hand lens
tongs or gloves

Procedure

1. Label two test tubes A and B, and write your name on each label as well.
2. Measure 25 mL of water into a beaker.

> **CAUTION:** Do not touch copper(II) sulphate. If any gets on your hands, wash them thoroughly.

3. Measure 20 g of the copper(II) sulphate and add it to the beaker. Gently heat the solution while stirring. (If you need to review the use of a balance to measure mass, see Skillbuilder Three, *Measuring Matter*, on page 333.)

> **CAUTION:** Do not boil the solution.

4. When most of the copper(II) sulphate has dissolved, pick up the beaker with the tongs or gloves and carefully decant (pour off) equal amounts of the solution into each of the two test tubes. Be careful not to pour any undissolved solids into the test tubes.
5. Place test tube A in a beaker of crushed ice. Place test tube B in a beaker of warm water. Leave the test tubes for 24 h to allow crystals to form.
6. Tilt each test tube slightly, and using a hand lens, examine the crystals in each tube. In your notebook, make a drawing of what you see.

Finding Out

1. How did the rate of cooling affect the size of the crystals?
2. (a) Which sample of crystals could represent extrusive rock?
   (b) Which sample could represent intrusive rock?

Step 3

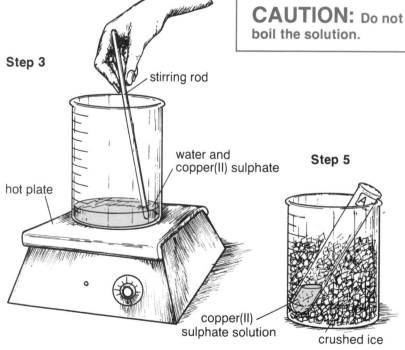

stirring rod

hot plate

water and copper(II) sulphate

Step 5

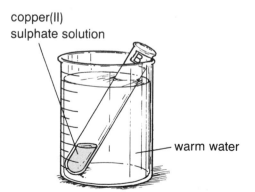

copper(II) sulphate solution

copper(II) sulphate solution

crushed ice

warm water

Sedimentary Rock—Layer Upon Layer

Have you ever looked at a cliff face or road cutting and seen rock stacked in layers like a pile of sandwiches? If you look closely at a sample of such rock, you may observe that it seems to be made from fragments of rock material closely packed and cemented together. In fact, that is probably how it was formed. Most layered rock is **sedimentary rock**, made from small fragments (sediments) of other rock. Although sedimentary rock is much less plentiful than igneous rock in the Earth's crust, sedimentary rock makes up about 75% of the rock that is exposed on the surface of the land.

Finding Out More

3. Look at the four photographs below. Which sample of rock appears to have cooled fastest? Describe its appearance and give a reason for your inference.

These are all igneous rocks. The appearance of these rocks depends on the conditions under which each rock was formed.

The layered appearance of this sedimentary rock is evidence of how it was formed.

To understand how sedimentary rock is formed, think of what you have learned about weathering and erosion in your previous studies. Small fragments of the Earth's surface are constantly being worn away and moved from one place to another by the action of wind and water. You can see these fragments in a dust storm or in the muddy silt carried along in a stream or river. Over time, huge quantities of eroded material are carried from the land into lakes and oceans, where they eventually settle to the bottom.

Rock Families **165**

(a)

(b)

(c)

Different types of sedimentary rock: (a) shale, (b) sandstone, and (c) conglomerate. Their appearance depends on the size of the fragments from which they were formed.

Blowing dust and sand granules that are carried into waterways may eventually become part of a sedimentary rock formation.

The layered appearance of sedimentary rock is produced by the slow accumulation of sediment settling on top of other sediment. The horizontal layers of rock are called **beds**.

How do all these piled-up fragments become rock? First, they are squeezed together or **compacted** by the mass of sediment and water on top of them. This process is similar to the way in which fresh snow turns from loose, fluffy flakes into a compacted solid when you stand on it. In some rocks, the fragments are further cemented together by chemical action.

The appearance of a sedimentary rock tells you the type of sediment from which it was formed. For example, sedimentary rock called **mudstone** or **shale** is formed from very fine grains of clay or mud. A harder, rougher rock called **sandstone** is formed from larger granules of sand, mostly made of quartz. Rounded pebbles and small stones cemented together form a type of rock called **conglomerate**.

Imagine that you could speed up time and watch the build-up and formation of a sample of sedimentary rock. You begin with a deposit of coarse sand near the mouth of a deep, wide river. Over time, the river mouth gets clogged and the river becomes slower and shallower. The slower water carries only fine sediments. These settle in a layer on top of the sand. Still later, the sea level rises and the mouth of the river is covered below several metres of water. Pebbles and stones are dragged and tossed by the waves along the shallow seabed. What will the rock formed in this area look like? It will consist of a layer of sandstone, covered by a layer of shale, and then a layer of conglomerate.

By observing the behaviour of sediments today, and studying rocks from different areas, geologists can infer the conditions under which different rocks were formed in the past. You may have observed the settling of sediments in your previous studies. If so, review how sediments settle by answering the questions at the end of the next Activity. If you have not observed the settling of sediments, you will do so in Activity 4-3.

Activity 4-3

Settling Sediments

Problem

How do sediments settle into layers?

Materials

mixture of clay, silt, sand, and fine gravel (about 1 L in volume)
large, clear glass jar (2 L or more) with screw cap
water
hand lens
sedimentary rock samples

Procedure

1. Fill the jar about three-quarters full with water.
2. Pour the mixture of sediments into the jar.
3. Cap the jar tightly, and shake it until all the sediment is moving about.
4. Set the jar down and observe the sediments settling. Record your observations.
5. Examine the sedimentary rock samples with a hand lens.

Finding Out

1. (a) Which size of sediment settled to the bottom of the jar first?
   (b) Which size of sediment settled last (or did not settle during your period of observation)?
2. How might the arrangement of sediments you obtained in your jar occur in nature?
3. What evidence from observation of your sedimentary rock samples allows you to infer that they were formed underwater?

Finding Out More

4. (a) Examine the photographs below and suggest how the features you observe in each rock sample were formed.
   (b) What evidence indicates that these rocks were formed in shallow water?
5. Name a natural force, other than running water, that might build up layers of sediment.

Metamorphic Rock—"Changing Form"

Near the beginning of this century, geologists walking along a sedimentary rock bed in Scotland noticed that the characteristics of the rock changed from one end of the bed to the other. The bed started out as fine-grained, sedimentary shale, but ended up some distance away as another type of rock called slate. **Slate** is a fine-grained, compact rock that is much harder than shale. How could shale and slate be in the same rock bed? The geologists' observations led them to conclude that the slate had been formed from shale. Slate is an example of the third family of rock, called metamorphic rock.

Metamorphic rock may be formed below the Earth's surface in several ways. When rock becomes buried at great depths, for example, it is subjected to increased heat and pressure. Earthquakes and intrusions of magma also squeeze and heat areas of nearby rock. Under these conditions, new minerals may be formed, and the rock may become harder. These changes take place while the rock remains solid.

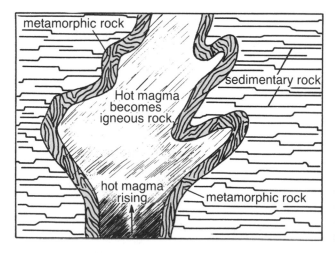

Metamorphic rock
may be formed
when intruding hot
magma heats and
squeezes the
surrounding layers
of sedimentary rock.

Some metamorphic rock has been altered so much that it no longer resembles the original or **"parent"** rock. Some minerals, such as asbestos and talc, are found only in metamorphic rock. Often, however, geologists can trace the relationships between metamorphic rock and the parent rock from which it was formed. For example, marble is a metamorphic rock that is formed from the sedimentary rock called limestone. Although they look different from one another, both rocks have some characteristics in common. Both rocks have a hardness of 3 and both are made of the mineral calcite (crystalline calcium carbonate). Both limestone and marble bubble and fizz if you place vinegar or hydrochloric acid on them. The fizz is caused by carbon dioxide given off by the chemical reaction between the mineral and the acid. In the next Activity, observe the differences between parent rocks and their metamorphic "children."

Activity 4-4

The Big Squeeze

Problem

What are the differences between a metamorphic rock and the parent rock from which it was formed?

Materials

labelled rock samples:
   slate, shale
   quartzite, sandstone
   gneiss, granite
   marble, limestone
   schist
hand lens (10x)

Procedure

1. Use your hand lens to examine each rock sample. Look for crystal structure, lustre, layering, and colour. Test the rocks for hardness. Observe and record any differences between the "parent" and the "child" in each pair.
2. Examine samples of gneiss and schist. Try to identify the minerals in each sample.

These photographs show one example of a change from an igneous rock, granite (shown in close-up on the left), to a metamorphic rock, gneiss.

Finding Out

1. What conditions do you think produced the differences you observed in Step 1? Give a reason for your answer.
2. (a) How are the gneiss and schist different from the other metamorphic rocks you examined?
(b) What does this tell you about the amount of change each rock has experienced?

Extension

3. Make a model of metamorphic rock using two colours of modelling clay. Use one colour to make a ball about the size of an apple. This represents a parent rock. From the second colour of clay, form about six pea-size balls. These represent mineral crystals. Carefully insert them into the "rock." Place the "rock" on a sheet of paper on the floor, and lay a board over it. Push or stand on the board. Note what happens to the "minerals." Compare your model with the samples of schist and gneiss.

The Rock Cycle

Your study of the three rock families has shown that rocks can change in structure and appearance. Not only metamorphic rocks do this. Any rock that is heated at great depths may melt into magma, and later form igneous rock. Any rock that is exposed on the Earth's surface may be broken into sediments, and may later become sedimentary rock. It is the physical environment that determines what type of rock is formed. If the environment of a rock changes, the rock also changes.

A rock may become so altered by a change in environment that it can no longer be classified in its original family. It has changed from one family to another. Over long periods of time, a single piece of the Earth's crust may be transformed into all three families of rock. Each family is linked to the others in a cycle. A diagram of this **rock cycle** summarizes all the processes of rock formation that you have learned thus far.

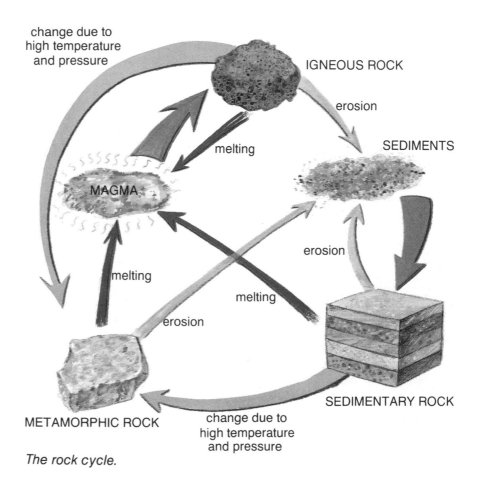

The rock cycle.

Checkpoint

1. Explain the statement: "You can have minerals without having a rock, but you cannot have a rock without having minerals."

2. A geologist found a rock that was shiny, black, and did not split easily.
   (a) What three mineral properties did the geologist notice?
   (b) Name two other properties that the geologist could examine.

3. Each of the following words is the correct answer to a question. Write a suitable question to match each answer.
   (a) lava
   (b) magma
   (c) intrusive rock
   (d) extrusive rock

4. What is the relationship between the size of mineral crystals in an igneous rock and the length of time it took the rock to form?

5. List ways in which metamorphic rock looks different from igneous rock.

The rock on the left is metamorphic and the one on the right is igneous.

6. Which family of rock is formed as a result of:
   (a) weathering and erosion;
   (b) pressure and heat; and
   (c) melting?

7. Do you think the terms "parent" and "child" are appropriate words to describe how metamorphic rock is formed? Explain why or why not.

8. Examine the illustration below. Describe what differences you might observe in sedimentary rock that was formed in shallow water near the shoreline and rock that was formed in deeper water. Explain what causes these differences.

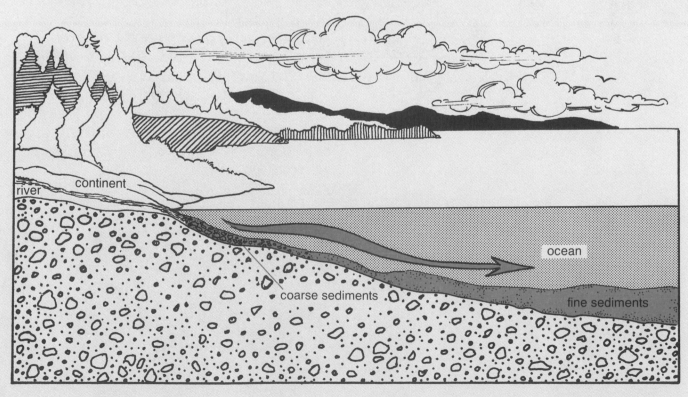

History Books in Stone

The processes that form rock have not stopped. You can see these processes at work today in the muddy waters washing into the sea or in the lava pouring from a volcano. Once you realize that the processes are continuous, you may come to an interesting conclusion: Rock is not all the same age! Different rocks were formed at different times in the past. We know that the youngest rocks on Earth are only a few years old. Geologists have observed the "birth" of these rocks as they cooled from red-hot lava. Scientists estimate that the oldest rocks on Earth may be about 4 billion years old. Since there were no geologists—or any other people— around at that time, the ages of these rocks must be inferred from different kinds of evidence.

You may find it hard to accept the idea of old rock and young rock because one rock appears very similar to another. You can see the difference between an old person and a young person. You can see the difference between an old tree and a young tree. But how can you tell the age of a rock?

Until recently, scientists had no way of knowing exactly how old different rocks are. To determine an exact or **absolute age**, you need some sort of calendar on which events are recorded.

You can then refer to the calendar and say, for example, that something happened exactly three years and two months ago. However, there is another way of talking about time. You have probably spoken of events that happened "before I was born." Or you may say that something took place "after I left Grade 7." These descriptions are not precise, but they describe the **relative age** of different events when compared with one another. It is possible to refer to relative age when speaking about rocks, too. Based on your knowledge of how rocks are formed, you can look for several clues indicating that certain rocks are older than others.

Activity 4-5

Which Came First?

Problem

How can you arrange events in a sequence of relative age?

Procedure

PART A: PERSONAL HISTORIES

1. Think of four important events that have occurred during your life and write them on a sheet of paper.
2. Write the most recent of these events at the top of a second sheet of paper.
3. At the bottom of the second sheet, write the event that happened longest ago.
4. With these two events as a "time frame," add the other two events in sequence on the sheet. Your list now tells you the relative ages of four events—in other words, the order in which they occurred.

5. Work in pairs and combine your lists. With your partner, determine the relative ages of all eight events. Record what questions you have to ask to determine the order of events from both lists.

PART B: WHICH ROCKS ARE OLDEST?

1. Look at the layered sedimentary rock in the diagram and answer the following questions about it.

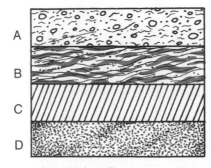

Layered sedimentary rock

Finding Out

1. (a) Which layer of sedimentary rock is probably oldest?
   (b) What is the evidence for your inference?
2. (a) Which layer of rock was probably formed most recently?
   (b) Give a reason for your answer.
3. What can you say about the relative ages of layers B and C?
4. Write down a general rule that you could use to determine the relative ages of rock in a sequence of layered sedimentary rock.

Finding Out More

5. Look back at the diagram on page 168, which shows three families of rock found together in one area. Using your knowledge of rock formation, list the relative ages of the three types of rock.

How Rocks Show Their Age

Imagine yourself stacking five books, one on top of the other, one at a time. Which book has been in the stack the longest? Which has been there for the shortest time? Now imagine you are studying a cross section of horizontal sedimentary rock layers. You know that the rock was formed by deposited sediment. Which layer of rock is probably the oldest? As you probably inferred in Activity 4–5, the oldest rock is at the bottom, and the youngest is at the top. A general rule for determining the relative ages of sedimentary rocks is called the **principle of superposition**. It states that any sedimentary rock in a horizontal section of layered rock is younger than the rock just beneath it.

Consider a section of sedimentary rock that has a band of intrusive igneous rock running through it, as shown in the diagram. Which rock is the youngest? The igneous rock intruded after the sedimentary rock was formed, so the igneous rock is younger than the rock that surrounds it.

Inferences such as those described above are useful for determining the relative ages of rocks that are found together. But how might you determine the relative ages of rocks from different locations? Is there a way of knowing whether a sample of rock from Alberta is older or younger than one from Ontario, a province a great many kilometres from Alberta? To answer this type of question, you must look at another piece of evidence found in sedimentary rock.

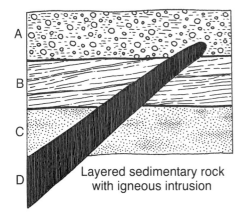

Layered sedimentary rock with igneous intrusion

Which is the youngest rock in this diagram?

Fossil Timekeepers

An important clue to the relative age of rocks was discovered in the early 1800s by an English surveyor named William Smith. Many canals were being dug in England at that time, and Smith had a chance to observe long sections of sedimentary rock that were exposed by the digging. Throughout the rock, he found many **fossils**, which are the remains or traces of prehistoric organisms. Smith carefully recorded the appearance of the fossils and where they were found. He gradually realized that certain fossils were always found in the same relationship to one another. Type A always occurred above Type B, which was always found above Type C. The same sequence was found in areas many

Discoveries about fossils have often been made in the course of digging tunnels, canals, and mines in the Earth.

kilometres apart. Eventually, when diggers unearthed Type A fossils in any location, Smith could predict that they would find Type B by digging a little deeper. By inferring that each type of fossil was found only in rock of a particular age, Smith could correlate the ages of rocks from different locations.

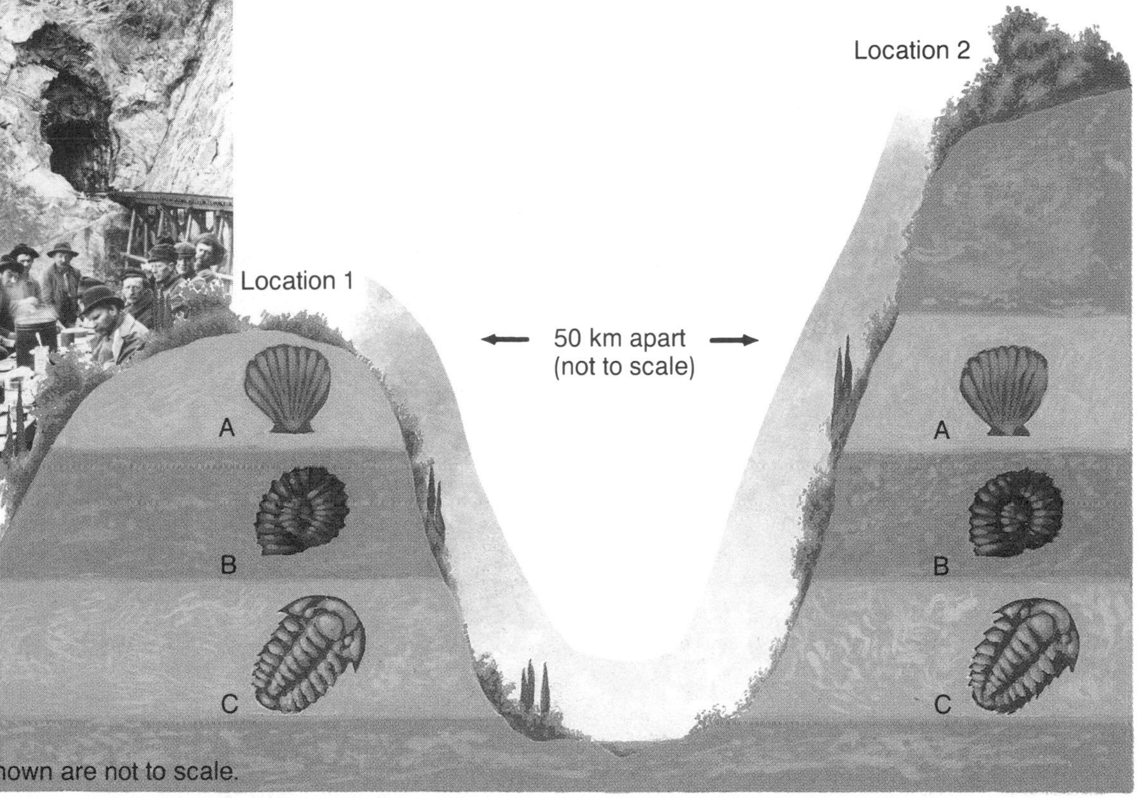

Location 2

Location 1

← 50 km apart →
(not to scale)

A

B

C

A

B

C

Fossils shown are not to scale.

By matching up similar fossils, geologists can compare the ages of rock in different locations. For example, Rock Layer A found on the surface in Location 1 is the same age as Rock Layer A found at a greater depth below the surface in Location 2.

Fossils are important clues to the history of the Earth. Each fossil can be thought of as a time capsule, buried at the time the organism died. Only a tiny fraction of organisms ever become fossilized. This is partly because the process usually works only on hard parts, such as teeth, bones, shells, and wood fibres, which many organisms do not have.

The fossilizing process also requires particular conditions. To become fossilized, an organism must be buried rapidly, before it begins to decay or gets eaten by scavengers. Burial may occur if the organism sinks into soft mud or sand, or is covered quickly by blowing sediment or volcanic ash. After it is buried, the organism may become fossilized in one of several ways.

Porous remains, such as bones, wood, and shells, may absorb water containing dissolved minerals. The minerals are deposited in the pores, forming a rocky framework throughout the remains. Bit by bit, the original material is replaced by more of the minerals. The final result is a **petrified fossil**, a rock that looks exactly like the original shell, bone, or piece of wood.

Petrified wood. Minerals have replaced the original piece of wood, preserving the details of its structure.

Another type of fossil is a **mould**, a cavity made by the imprint of an organism or its tracks. The fossil dinosaur footprint in the photograph was formed after a dinosaur walked through soft mud and left its imprint. The mud dried and hardened, then filled with sand or other rock fragments and was buried. After many hundreds of thousands of years, the mud and sand hardened into sedimentary rock, preserving the mould made by the original footprint. This fossil became exposed when the overlying rock was eroded away, millions of years after the dinosaur left its mark.

A third type of fossil is a **cast**, made when sediment slowly fills a mould, showing the original form of the organism. For example, sand might have filled a shell lying on an ancient beach. The shell became deeply buried, and the sand in it hardened under pressure. The shell eventually dissolved away, leaving a cast of sandstone that shows the shape of the inside of the shell. You can better understand how fossils were formed by imitating some of these processes in the next Activity.

A fossil dinosaur footprint.

Making Fossils

Problem

How might different fossils have been formed in nature?

Materials

250 mL fine sand
125 mL cement
mixing bowl
stirring rod or spoon
2 plastic or aluminum plates or
    dishes
petroleum jelly
125 mL water
sugar cube
various hard objects, such as
    shells, coins, keys, etc.

> **CAUTION:** Cement
> contains lime, which may
> be irritating to your eyes
> and skin. Do not allow the
> cement to contact your
> eyes or skin.

Procedure

1. Pour the sand and the cement into the mixing bowl.
2. Slowly add water, stirring constantly until you have a stiff mixture.

3. Pour the mixture into two paper plates. When the mixture begins to harden, push a sugar cube deep into the mixture in one plate, so that the cube is almost below the surface.

4. Lightly coat a small object, such as a shell or leaf, with petroleum jelly. Press the object into the surface of the mixture in the second plate.

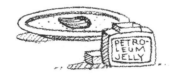

5. After the mixture in the first plate has hardened completely, dissolve the sugar cube by running hot water over it. Rinse out all the sugar. You are left with a concrete impression or mould of the sugar cube.

6. After the mixture in the second plate has hardened, remove the object you pressed into it. Lightly coat the inner surface of the mould with petroleum jelly.

7. Prepare another mixture of sand, cement, and water. Pour some of this mixture into the mould and leave it to harden overnight.

8. Carefully remove the hardened cast from the mould. You now have a concrete copy of the original object.

Finding Out

1. How are moulds formed in nature?
2. In your own words, define "cast" as it relates to fossil formation.

Finding Out More

3. The four illustrations show different stages in the formation of a fossil ichthyosaur. However, the illustrations are not in the correct order. Determine the proper sequence of events and indicate what order they should appear in. Describe what each illustration shows.

4. Name two parts of an animal or plant that are:
   (a) most likely to be preserved by fossilization; and
   (b) unlikely to be preserved by fossilization.
   Give a reason for each of your answers.

5. In which family of rock are fossils most likely to be found? Explain your answer.

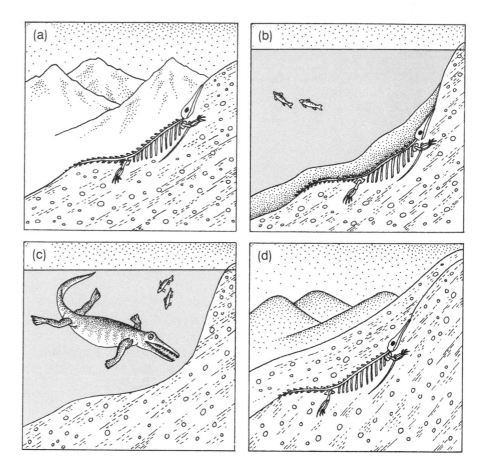

Geological Time Scale

The evidence of fossils shows that different **species** (kinds) of organisms have lived on the Earth at different times in the past. For example, the sea-living organisms called **trilobites** are very common as fossils, but no such organisms live in the world today. The same is true for many different kinds of giant reptiles such as dinosaurs.

As William Smith first realized, the fossils found in one layer of rock are different from those found in the rock above and below them. Furthermore, the sequence of fossils is the same in rocks from different parts of the world.

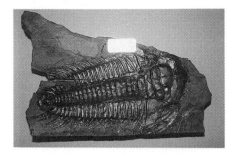

Fossils like these 500-million-year-old trilobites are valuable clues to the Earth's history. Trilobites are the ancient relatives of crabs, lobsters, and insects.

In areas where layers of sedimentary rock are deeply eroded, such as the Grand Canyon, scientists can study a continuous record of fossils going back several hundred million years. The oldest rock, at the bottom of the canyon, has no fossils. Just above the bottom, the oldest fossils start to appear. Many of these are trilobite fossils. In the more recent rock toward the top of the canyon, there are fossils of organisms similar to some living today. Reading from the bottom to the top, the fossils in the canyon walls are like a series of snapshots of changing life on Earth, from the distant past to the present.

Fossil bones of dinosaurs reconstructed in a museum at Drumheller in Alberta. Animals like these lived about 75 million years ago.

Layers of rock in the Grand Canyon hold fossils of different organisms dating back more than 500 million years.

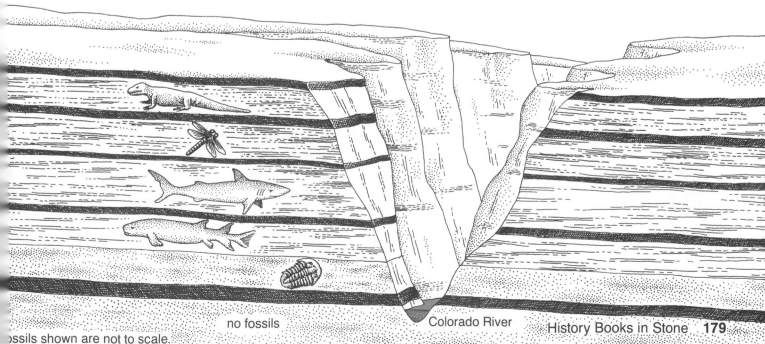

no fossils

Colorado River

fossils shown are not to scale.

Like historians who reconstruct human history from the remains of buildings and historical records, geologists began to reconstruct a history of the Earth from the evidence of rocks. This geological history of the Earth is called the **geological time scale**. As shown in Table 4-4, it is divided into large units called **eras**. Each era is identified by a particular name. Unlike days and years, eras are not all the same length. However, the time scale allows scientists in any country to name and date rock according to its type and the fossils it contains. The relative ages of the different eras were determined by the sequence of fossils in sedimentary rock layers. More recent evidence, which you will learn about in the next section, has allowed scientists to determine approximately how long ago each era began and ended.

Table 4-4 *Geological Time Scale*

ERA	MILLIONS OF YEARS AGO	FOSSIL RECORD OF MAJOR CHANGES IN LIFE ON EARTH
Cenozoic	65 to present	• appearance of most modern species • many more species of mammals • first grasses • first human-like species
Mesozoic	225 to 65	• many more species of plants, birds, and mammals • dinosaurs flourish and then become extinct • first flowering plants • first birds and mammals
Paleozoic	600 to 225	• first reptiles • first large land animals (amphibians) • first insects • first large land plants • first fish with jaws
Precambrian	4600 to 600	• first soft-bodied animals (those without backbones) • first simple organisms (bacteria) • formation of the Earth

Radioactivity—A Natural Clock

There are many ways to measure time—from the movement of hands on a clock face, to the dripping of sand through an hourglass, to the passage of the Sun across the sky. Whatever the method used, timekeeping depends on measuring something that happens at a fixed rate. Early in this century, it was discovered that certain forms of some elements give off matter and energy and, in doing so, are transformed into different elements. For example, some forms of the element uranium are **radioactive**. Because they give off energy and **decay** (are transformed) at a fixed and very slow rate, they can be used as "clocks" to measure the age of some rocks. This method of determining the age of a material is called **radioactive dating**.

samples of rock

Radioactive element "x" is formed. — time → It decays to element "y" at a constant rate.

Radioactive dating. A radioactive substance decays at a constant rate. By measuring the proportions of a radioactive substance and the substance it is transformed into, scientists can calculate when the rock was formed. The measurements show the length of time a mineral has contained its built-in radioactive "clock."

The radioactive "clock" starts when a mineral containing the radioactive form of the element is first crystallized. That happens when the rock is produced. At that time, the radioactive element is 100% pure and unchanged. It then begins the process of radioactive decay. Different radioactive elements decay at different rates. For example, it takes 4.5 billion years for one-half of the particles of radioactive uranium in a material to be transformed into the element lead. It takes about 1.3 billion years for one-half of the particles of radioactive potassium in a material to likewise decay. Other radioactive elements may take only days or hours to decay. The average length of time it takes for one-half of the particles of a radioactive element to decay is called its **half-life**. By knowing the rates of decay, and measuring the proportions of the original element (for example, uranium) and the transformed element (lead) in a sample of rock, geologists can calculate how long ago the rock was formed.

In the next Activity, you can analyse some of the Earth's major events by drawing a model of the history of life on the Earth. You will be using the geological time scale that has been produced using both fossil evidence and the radioactive dating of rocks.

A Model of Geological Time

Problem

What are the relative lengths of time between major events in the Earth's history?

Materials

5 m of adding machine tape
masking tape
metric tape measure or ruler
marking pen

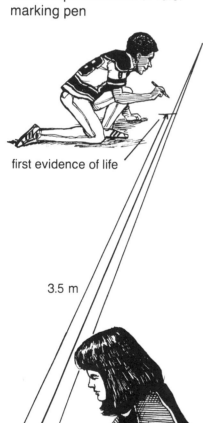

first evidence of life

3.5 m

present
day

Procedure

1. Roll out 5 m of adding machine tape in a convenient place on the floor, pull each end tight, and tape it down.
2. Draw a line at one end of the adding machine tape and label it "Present day."
3. Each metre on your tape is equal to 1 billion years of time. Using this scale, plot the information in Table 4-5 onto your tape. For example, draw a line 3.5 m from the line representing "Present day." Label this line "First evidence of life."

Finding Out

1. What can you conclude about the age of human history to date compared with
   (a) the length of time that dinosaurs lived on Earth; and
   (b) the age of the Earth?

Finding Out More

2. The first land plants appeared on the Earth before the first land animals. Do you think these events could have occurred in the reverse order? Explain your answer.

Table 4-5 *Milestones in Earth's History*

EVENT	NUMBER OF YEARS AGO
Last glaciers cover much of Canada	10 000
Earliest human-like species	10 000 000
Extinction of dinosaurs	65 000 000
Earliest evidence of birds	150 000 000
Earliest evidence of mammals	190 000 000
First dinosaurs	225 000 000
First land animals	350 000 000
First land plants	430 000 000
Earliest fish	500 000 000
First fossils of many-celled organisms	700 000 000
First evidence of life	3 500 000 000
Formation of Earth's crust	4 600 000 000

Mountains and Volcanoes

Buried in sedimentary rock high up Mount Everest in the Himalayas are fossil sea shells. How did the remains of organisms that lived undersea get to the top of the highest mountains in the world? It is almost impossible to imagine that the rock in these immense peaks was once on the bottom of a shallow sea. Yet the fossil shells and other evidence from around the world indicate that all the Earth's biggest mountain ranges have been lifted up out of the seas.

Much of the rock that forms Mount Everest originated below sea level.

The big mountain ranges of the Himalayas, Rockies, Andes, Alps, and Appalachians are made up mostly of sedimentary rock. Remember that this type of rock was formed from sediments that were deposited in layers and then compressed. At the mouths of rivers and along coasts, sedimentary rock is formed largely of gravel, sand, and mud. Elsewhere on the seabed, thick layers of sediment are built up mostly from countless millions of shells that were once part of various marine animals. Throughout the world's oceans, a constant "rain" of shells sinks down to produce vast underwater deposits as shell-bearing animals die. Along depressions in the sea floor, sediments have piled up to form rock layers 10 to 15 km thick.

In areas such as the Grand Canyon, you can clearly see horizontal layers showing how sediments were deposited on top of one another over hundreds of millions of years. But suppose you discover a sequence of sedimentary rock that is *not* in horizontal layers. The layers may be tilted at an angle, or even vertically, as shown in the photograph. Geologists call these rock formations **folds**. Could sediment settle in this pattern or was this rock formed in some other way?

Observations and experiments show that sediment does not build up in large quantities on slopes. It is pulled downward by gravity and settles in horizontal or near-horizontal layers. Furthermore, the fragments in folded rock appear the same as those in level sedimentary rock. You can therefore infer that this rock was moved and folded by some enormous force *after* it was formed. In the next Activity, you will see for yourself the effects of different forces on sedimentary rock.

How did this sedimentary rock become folded?

Activity 4-8

Folding Rocks

Problem

How do sedimentary rocks produce mountains?

Materials

2 foam blocks (each about 15 cm × 30 cm × 8 cm thick), each marked with lines as shown in the diagram

Procedure

1. Hold one end of a block still and push the other end towards it. What do you observe? Sketch your results. Notice what happens to the lines as folds occur.
2. Place two blocks end to end and push on the end of one block while holding the other block still. Sketch your results.
3. Together with some classmates, try to create formations that resemble those in the photograph on page 184 and in the illustrations below. Sketch your results and explain what you had to do to produce them.

Finding Out

1. What movements of the Earth's crust most likely produced folded rocks as shown in the photograph on page 184?
2. What might have happened to produce each of the mountains shown in the illustrations below?

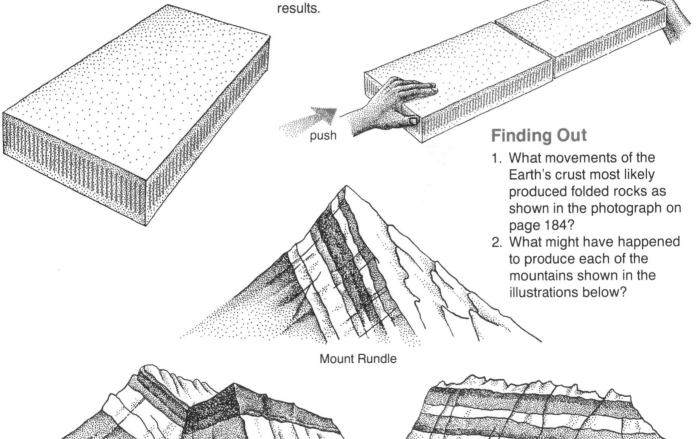

push

Mount Rundle

Mount Kerkeslin

Castle Mountain

Folds and Faults

When rock is put under great pressure and heat, it softens and bends like a piece of warm toffee. With increasing pressure, the soft rock may fold into curves that lift part of the rock up above the level of the rest to form a mountain. If you fly over some mountain ranges in an airplane, you can sometimes pick out rows of folds that look like waves. Geologists call the upfold on a curve an **anticline**. A trough-like downfold, or valley, is called a **syncline**.

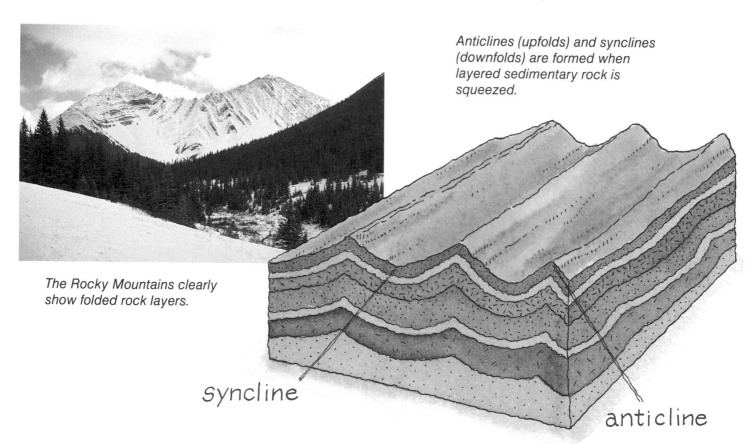

The Rocky Mountains clearly show folded rock layers.

Anticlines (upfolds) and synclines (downfolds) are formed when layered sedimentary rock is squeezed.

syncline

anticline

The tremendous forces that squeeze sedimentary rock into folds may change some of the rock into metamorphic rock. Mountains that show folding may therefore contain both these families of rock. But remember, the rock being folded does not melt. It remains in the solid state. In some cases, the rock under pressure may crack or break instead of folding. If pressure continues, a section of rock may move along the crack. A break in the Earth's crust along which rock moves is called a **fault**. Faults may be produced by either squeezing or stretching movements of the Earth's crust.

Rock movement along a fault can be vertical or horizontal. The amount of movement can range from a few centimetres to hundreds or thousands of metres. When a huge amount of rock is lifted along a fault a great distance relative to rock on the other side of the fault, it produces a **fault-block mountain**. In larger movements, older rock may be pushed up and tilted on top of younger rock.

These processes can be used to explain the appearance of the peaks in the Rocky Mountain range shown in the illustrations on page 185. The flat sedimentary layers seen in Mount Rundle have been lifted and then sharply tilted. Castle Mountain is an example of a mountain that has been uplifted with its sedimentary layers remaining almost horizontal. Mount Kerkeslin clearly shows folding. Its sedimentary layers have been squeezed sideways to form a syncline.

Geologists can sometimes trace the amount of movement along a fault by matching up the layers of rock on opposite sides. Horizontal movement of more than 100 km has been traced along some faults. Rapid movements along a fault may produce earthquakes, which you will learn more about in Topic Five.

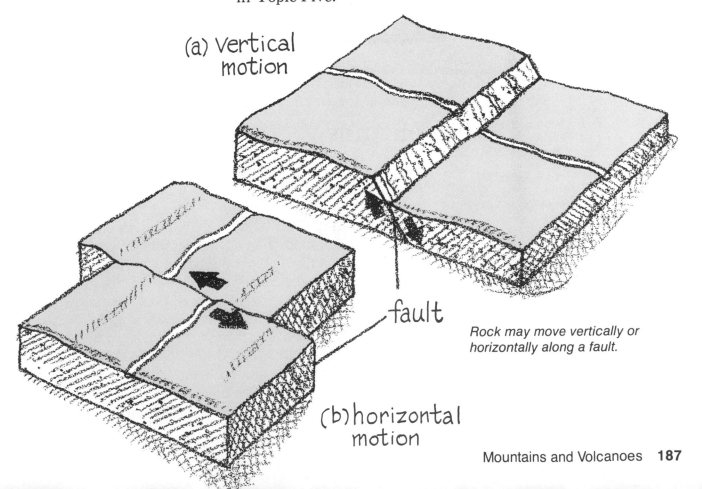

(a) vertical motion

fault

(b) horizontal motion

Rock may move vertically or horizontally along a fault.

Geologists have determined that the Appalachian Mountains in eastern North America were formed between 250 and 300 million years ago. The Rockies, by comparison, are much younger. This western mountain range was formed between 55 and 155 million years ago. In fact, measurements show that peaks in the Coast Range of British Columbia are still growing higher by about a metre per century!

The Ages of Mountains

You have learned that rocks are not all the same age. If you think about it, the same must be true of mountains. Younger mountains are being pushed upward even today, while older mountains have been worn down by centuries of erosion. What differences would you expect to see in the appearance of older and younger mountains? Compare the rugged peak of Mount Everest on page 183, with the smooth, rounded appearance of the Appalachian Mountains shown here. Which mountains do you think are older—the Himalayas or the Appalachians? How can you tell?

The Appalachian Mountains, a range that extends along much of eastern North America.

Volcanoes

If the idea of mountains that grow seems startling, it may help you to think of another type of mountain that people have actually observed growing. A volcano in Mexico named Paricutin began in 1943 when red-hot cinders shot out of a hole in a farmer's field. The surprised farmer tried to fill the hole, but within a day it had opened into a crater more than 2 m across. The crater continued to toss out hot ashes and stones, which piled up to form a small dome around the hole. Within days, explosions filled the air and the crater started spewing out lava. In a year, the volcano had built up a cone-shaped mountain 430 m high and nearly 1 km across at the base! The lava, rocks, and ashes destroyed and buried two small villages nearby. Nine years after it began, the eruption suddenly ended and the volcanic mountain stopped growing at a height of more than 500 m.

Many cone-shaped mountain peaks were formed by volcanic eruptions. All have a funnel-shaped depression at the top of the cone, marking the crater from which the volcanic material erupted. Three different types of volcanoes can be distinguished from their appearance and structure.

The smallest and most common types of volcanoes are called **cinder cones**. They are built up from small, hot bits of material that are hurled into the air and pile up around the crater. These fragments cool rapidly to produce a cone-shaped mass of cinder-like rock. Paricutin is an example of a cinder cone.

The largest volcanoes in the world are called **shield cones**. They are made almost entirely from lava flows, which build up gradually in layers on the sides of the volcanoes to produce mountains with gently sloping sides. The broad and low shape of these volcanoes resembles that of shields lying on the ground. The Hawaiian Islands in the Pacific Ocean were produced by shield volcanoes. The biggest of these, Mauna Loa, rises more than 9200 m from the sea floor—a height greater than Mount Everest! More than half its height, however, is below sea level.

Paricutin volcano in Mexico is one of the youngest volcanoes on Earth. It began to erupt in an open field in 1943 and continued to grow for nine years. This photograph shows a church buried by lava that spewed from the volcano.

The Hawaiian Islands are the tops of huge volcanoes (such as the one shown here) that rise from the ocean floor.

The third type of volcanoes, called **composite cones**, are made from alternating layers of cinder rock and hardened lava. Most of the famous and violent types of volcano are of this type, including Mount St. Helens in the state of Washington, Mount Fujiyama in Japan, and Mount Vesuvius in Italy.

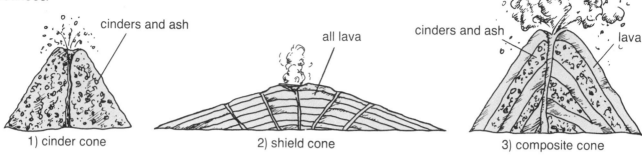

There are three main types of volcanoes.

1) cinder cone   2) shield cone   3) composite cone

Lava Floods and Explosions

Volcanoes may produce two different types of lava—one that flows freely and easily, and one that is thick and sticky. Free-flowing lava may flood out in a sheet over the land instead of piling up into a cone. One of the biggest such outpourings of lava in the history of the Earth took place in the area of the northwestern United States between 10 to 25 million years ago. The lava flood covered large parts of what are now the states of Washington and Oregon, building up a plateau of rock that is up to 4 km deep in places. Some of the volcanoes of the Cascade Range, such as Mount St. Helens, sit on this volcanic plateau.

Thick lava, with the consistency of warm peanut butter, creates volcanoes with steeply sloping sides. The slow-moving lava may sometimes cool to solid rock while it is still inside the crater of the volcano. If this solidified lava blocks the **vent** (opening), it leads to a build-up of gases in the magma trapped below. As the pressure from the volcanic gases increases, it may cause the volcano to bulge. Eventually, the volcano may suddenly burst apart, exploding gases and chunks of hot lava high into the air.

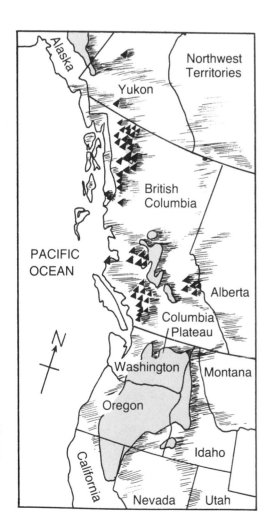

The shaded parts of the map represent hardened volcanic lava, such as the Columbia Plateau that covers most of the state of Oregon. The triangles represent volcanoes that have been active during the last 3 million years.

These volcanic eruptions are among the most dramatic events on Earth. They hint at the massive forces that can transform the shape of the Earth's crust, destroying land as well as forming it. When Mount St. Helens blew its top in May 1980, it sent a column of dust and ash more than 19 km into the sky and totally flattened nearly 400 km² of surrounding forest. The blast instantly turned millions of tonnes of solid rock into dust.

The eruption of Mount St. Helens melted ice and snow on the volcano's peak, producing boiling mud that rushed down the mountain's slopes.

Where Are Volcanoes Located?

What powerful forces cause the Earth's crust to fold and crack, thrusting up mountains and building volcanoes? This question puzzled geologists for many years. One early attempt to explain the process proposed that mountains are thrust up by the shrinking of the Earth. The idea was that the Earth's interior gets smaller as it cools, making the outer crust wrinkle up like the skin of a dried prune. If this were the explanation, we would expect to find mountains distributed at random all over the Earth's surface. If you study a map of the world, however, you will see that mountains and volcanoes are found only in certain locations, and not in others. In the next Activity, you can discover if there is any pattern in this distribution.

Mapping Mountains and Volcanoes

Problem

Is there any pattern in the worldwide distribution of mountains and volcanoes?

Procedure

1. Copy the distribution of volcanoes shown in the map onto an outline map of the world.

2. On your map, shade or colour in the following mountain ranges: Rockies, Andes, Himalayas, Alps, Urals, and Appalachians. Use an atlas or globe to help you.
3. Keep your map for Activity 4-11.

Finding Out

1. (a) Which continents have the fewest volcanoes?
   (b) In which parts of North and South America are most of the volcanoes located?

2. Does there appear to be any connection between volcanoes and oceans? Give a reason for your answer.
3. List the mountain ranges that are associated with volcanoes.
4. In which areas are there mountain ranges without volcanoes?
5. Is the worldwide distribution of mountains and volcanoes random? Explain your answer.

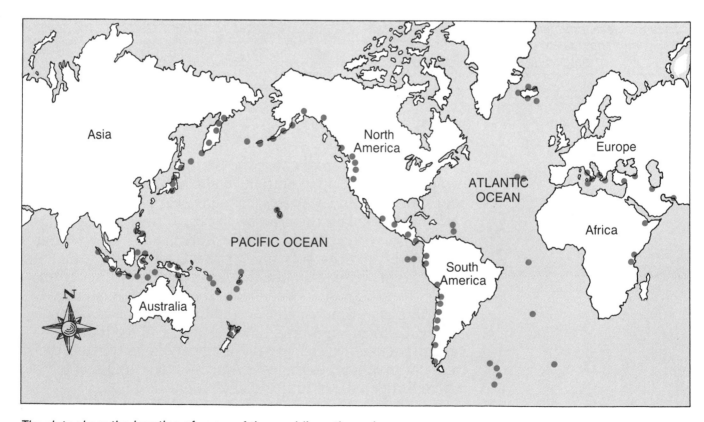

The dots show the location of some of the world's active volcanoes.

Checkpoint

1. (a) Write a sentence that describes the age of a friend, using the term "absolute age."
   (b) Maria is 15 years old. John is 11, and Louise is 23. Describe the relative age of each person, compared with your age.

2. The samples of rock in the diagram were taken from a single core of the sedimentary rock shown below the samples. The core was obtained by drilling to a depth of 30 m with a special hollow drill. Which sample—A, B, or C—is probably the oldest? Which is the youngest?

3. (a) Why are fossils found in sedimentary rock but not in igneous rock?
   (b) Why might you be less likely to find a fossil of a worm than of a snail?

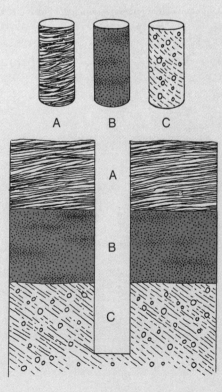

4. In several different locations in North America, dinosaur footprints have been found in slabs of rock.
   (a) What is this kind of fossil called?
   (b) How are such fossils formed?

5. Huge, shelled creatures called ammonites were once common in the seas covering much of the Earth. In places as different today as southern England and western Mexico, rocks shaped precisely like ammonite shells have been found in rock quarries and eroded hillsides.
   (a) What is this kind of fossil called?
   (b) How are such fossils formed?

6. (a) Draw the outline of:
   • an old mountain range; and
   • a young mountain range.
   (b) What causes the difference in appearance between old and young mountain ranges?

7. Look at the drawing of Mount Kerkeslin on page 185. Which process do you think happened first—the folding or the uplifting of rock? Explain your reasoning.

8. How could you tell the difference between a mountain that was formed by a volcano and one that was built by folding and uplifting?

(c) Is it possible that somebody in a million years' time might find fossilized remains of a lion living today? If so, how might this happen?

The Trembling Earth

One day in the spring of 1964, terrified residents of Anchorage, Alaska, saw the pavement begin to roll and heave as giant cracks opened up in the ground. Underground gas and water lines snapped apart. Buildings twisted and collapsed onto people fleeing into the streets. One end of a school building dropped 6 m, and several luxury homes built on a bluff slipped into the churning ocean. For nearly 4 min, the region was shaken by one of the biggest earthquakes ever recorded. Nearly 200 km away, at Valdez, giant waves set off by the vibrations slammed into the harbour. A crowd of people on the pier was washed away and a 10 000 tonne freighter was swept inland. The effects of the earthquake were felt as far away as Texas, where people saw the water in swimming pools slosh back and forth.

When the Earth moves, the damage can be terrible. If the earthquake occurs in a populated area, it can kill hundreds or thousands of people and cause millions of dollars of damage. An earthquake in China in 1976 killed about 600 000 people, while 20 000 died in an earthquake in Mexico City in 1985.

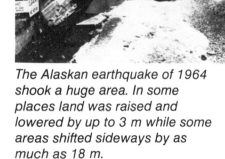

The Alaskan earthquake of 1964 shook a huge area. In some places land was raised and lowered by up to 3 m while some areas shifted sideways by as much as 18 m.

The earthquake that hit the area around San Francisco in October 1989 destroyed buildings, bridges, and roads. Sixty-eight lives were lost.

Measuring Earthquakes

The study of earthquakes has given geologists valuable information about what goes on deep below the Earth's surface. Most of this information comes from measuring the vibrations set off by earthquakes. To think about the nature of these vibrations, consider this: Have you ever tapped on a wall to find out if the wall is hollow or solid? The sound made by the tap gives you the answer. Try pressing your ear to your desk and tapping the desk. Then press your ear against a book and tap the book. The tapping produces vibrations that you hear as sounds. Vibrations moving through different materials produce different sounds. Using this principle, geologists can infer the structure of the Earth's crust. They don't listen to the sound of earthquakes—they measure the vibrations caused by earthquakes, using an instrument called a **seismograph**. The vibrations measured are caused by **seismic waves**, produced when energy is transferred away from the focus of the earthquake in all directions. The **focus** of the earthquake is the point inside the Earth where the energy is first released that causes the earthquake to occur.

A seismograph records vibrations as a series of zigzag lines, producing a visual record called a **seismogram**.

The frame and recording cylinder of a seismograph are set on solid rock. They vibrate with movements of the Earth. The recording device, which may be a pen, a beam of light, or an electric pulse, is held steady by a heavy pendulum or spring.

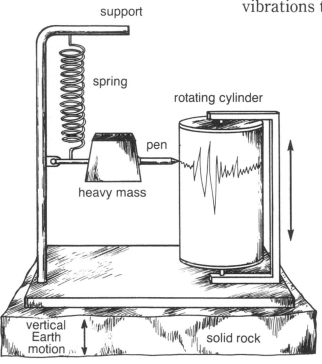

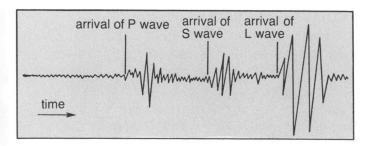

A typical seismogram of an earthquake.

Waves that Jolt

Earthquakes and the vibrations they cause occur when the Earth is suddenly jolted as if hit by a huge hammer. The jolting and rolling movements of the Earth that people experience during an earthquake are produced by the waves that travel through the Earth from its focus. Fast-moving **compression waves**, also known as **P waves**, are the first to reach the surface of the Earth and are thus the first waves recorded on a seismograph. They move along rapidly like a spring whose ends are first pushed together, then pulled apart. Matter is

The strength of an earthquake is usually measured on the Richter scale. Each number on this scale represents an amount of energy released by the earthquake. A tremor measuring 2 on the scale is the lowest that can be felt by most people. Earthquakes with a value of 7 or more are very dangerous.

Compression waves (also called P waves) travel rapidly through solids, liquids, and gases.

Shear waves (also called S waves) move from side to side in the shape of an S. They cannot travel through liquids.

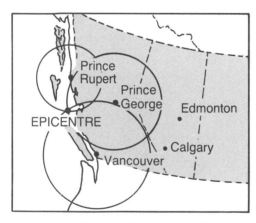

Seismic recording stations in Prince Rupert, Prince George, and Vancouver, British Columbia, calculate their distances from an earthquake. The earthquake's epicentre is where these distances intersect.

squeezed together at the head of the wave and spreads apart behind it. P waves can travel through all forms of matter—solids, liquids, and gases. Next, slower-moving **shear waves**, also called **S waves**, reach the surface of the Earth and are recorded. These waves vibrate from side to side in an S-shaped motion. S waves *cannot* pass through liquids. A toy Slinky can be used to show the action of P waves and S waves. From their different types of action, can you see why P waves are faster than S waves?

Surface waves, also known as **L waves**, are the last to arrive at a seismograph. They are the result of the whole Earth in the area vibrating like a bowl of jelly. They travel not through, but more slowly along, the surface of the Earth; thus, they are the last waves to be detected by the seismograph. The illustration on page 195 shows how the three different types of waves may appear on a seismogram. As you can see, the P waves arrive at the seismic recording station first because of their rapid speed.

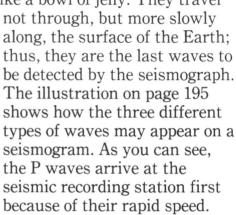

How Strong and How Far?

The size of the zigzags on the seismogram tells how strong the quake was. How can the **epicentre**, or point on the surface directly above the earthquake's focus, be determined? To locate the exact position of the earthquake's epicentre, records from three or more seismograph stations must be used. The further a seismograph is from an epicentre, the greater the time difference between the arrival of P waves and S waves at the station. Each station determines how far an epicentre lies from it, based on this information. On a map of the area, the seismologist draws a circle around each of three seismograph stations, using the distance of each station from the epicentre. Where the three circles intersect is the earthquake's epicentre. As you can see, only with information from three or more stations can the epicentre's location be determined.

Building a Seismograph

Problem

How does a seismograph work?

Materials

support stand
ring clamp
felt pen (fine tip)
string
small mass
sheet of cardboard (about
    28 cm × 21 cm)
roll of adding machine tape
masking tape

Procedure

1. Assemble the apparatus as shown in the diagram. The pen should just touch the paper.
2. Have one person pull the adding machine tape slowly and steadily under the pen while a second person creates "quakes" by striking, with an open hand, the top of the desk or bench on which the seismograph sits. Do not directly touch or move the apparatus itself. Try to create vibrations of varying intensity.

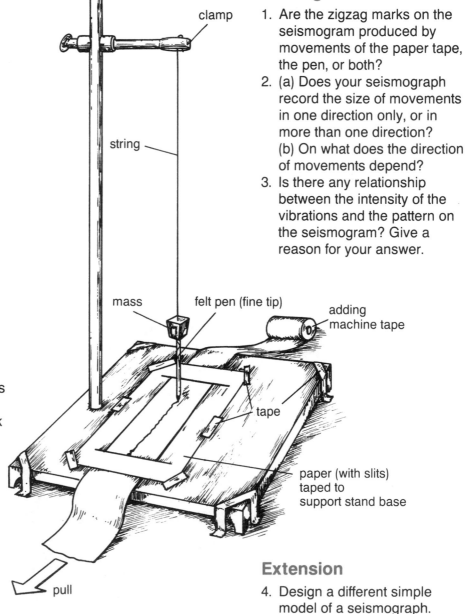

clamp

string

mass

felt pen (fine tip)

adding machine tape

tape

paper (with slits) taped to support stand base

pull

Finding Out

1. Are the zigzag marks on the seismogram produced by movements of the paper tape, the pen, or both?
2. (a) Does your seismograph record the size of movements in one direction only, or in more than one direction?
   (b) On what does the direction of movements depend?
3. Is there any relationship between the intensity of the vibrations and the pattern on the seismogram? Give a reason for your answer.

Extension

4. Design a different simple model of a seismograph. Sketch your design and, if time permits, build it and then test it.

Although scientists cannot accurately predict when an earthquake will happen, there is evidence that some animals can sense forthcoming quakes. For many years, the Chinese have recorded unusual behaviour among various animals during the hours before an earthquake strikes. Rats and mice run from buildings. Cattle, sheep, and horses will not enter their pens. Fish jump out of the water, and dogs seem disturbed. What do you think these animals might be sensing?

Where Are Earthquakes Located?

Seismographs used by scientists around the world show that there are hundreds of small Earth tremors (shaking movements) every day. Many earthquakes occur in the floor of the ocean, and most are too small to be felt. Although an earthquake could occur almost anywhere, the majority of strong earthquakes are recorded in a zone that runs around the Pacific Ocean. Places such as California, on one side of the Pacific Ocean, and Japan, on the other side, have suffered particularly destructive earthquakes during this century.

The location of earthquakes is closely connected with the location of faults. One of the best-known faults in the world is the San Andreas Fault, which runs for 700 km along the west coast of North America. The area along this fault experiences earthquakes frequently, although scientists cannot predict exactly when an earthquake is likely to happen. A quake occurs when sections of crust on each side of the fault suddenly shift position relative to one another. Massive amounts of energy are released as a huge area of land is shifted up and down or from side to side. Careful measurements have shown that the land to the west of the San Andreas Fault is gradually moving north at a rate of about 2 cm a year relative to the land east of the fault.

Aerial photograph of the San Andreas Fault, near the west coast of North America. Large earthquakes along this famous fault struck the city of San Francisco in 1906 and 1989.

Mapping Earthquakes

Problem

Where do most earthquakes occur?

Procedure

1. Copy the location of earthquakes shown in the illustration onto the map of volcanoes and mountains you prepared in Activity 4-9.

Finding Out

1. Which areas on Earth have a concentration of major earthquakes?
2. Does there seem to be a relationship between the location of mountain ranges, volcanoes, and earthquakes? Explain your answer.
3. Which mountain ranges have little or no earthquake activity near them?

The location of earthquakes around the world.

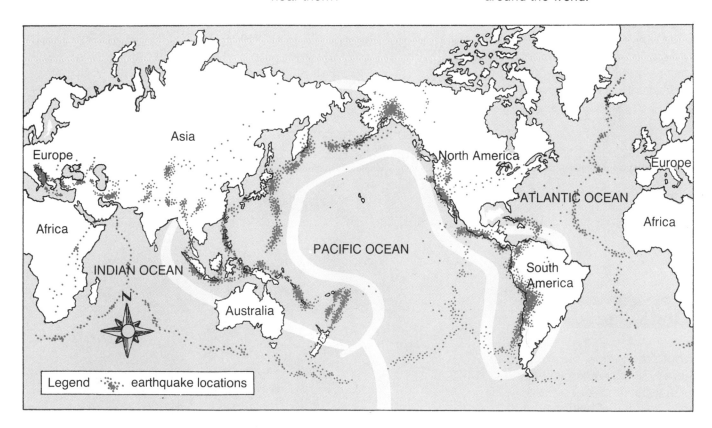

1. What is the risk of earthquakes in the area where you live? Do some research in newspapers or reference books to find out.
2. Some cities in earthquake zones, such as San Francisco, Vancouver, and Tokyo, have buildings that are designed and constructed to withstand minor shocks and tremors. Find out what techniques are used to "earthquake-proof" buildings.
3. What can people do to protect themselves before an earthquake starts, or after one has begun?
4. Apart from the movement of the Earth itself, what other dangers might follow after an earthquake hits a populated area, and why?

A Model of the Earth

Seismograph records are like windows to the Earth's interior. By measuring the speed and direction of seismic waves that travel through the ground, geologists can reconstruct the characteristics of the Earth beneath our feet. For example, you learned that S waves do not travel through liquid. Because S waves have been detected travelling through most of the Earth's crust, we can infer that most of the crust is solid. This means that the liquid magma that produces volcanoes is not found everywhere beneath the outer crust, but is found only in isolated pockets.

Measurements of seismic waves have produced a model of the Earth's internal structure. The model resembles a hard-boiled egg. As the diagram shows, the Earth's crust is a very thin outer shell, no more than 60 km thick. Below that is a layer called the **mantle**, represented by the white of the egg. The mantle is the thickest layer, extending down about 2900 km from the base of the crust. It is made of denser material than the crust. The centre of the Earth, represented by the egg yolk, is called the **core**. Unlike a real yolk, the Earth's core has two layers. The outer part of the core is thought to be liquid because S waves do not pass through it. The inner core, about 1200 km across, is solid.

What's the temperature like down there? Oil drillers know that the oil pumped from deep wells is hot. This kind of evidence and measurements recorded by geologists have shown that the Earth's temperature increases deeper and deeper towards its core. The inner core is thought to reach temperatures as high as 5500°C.

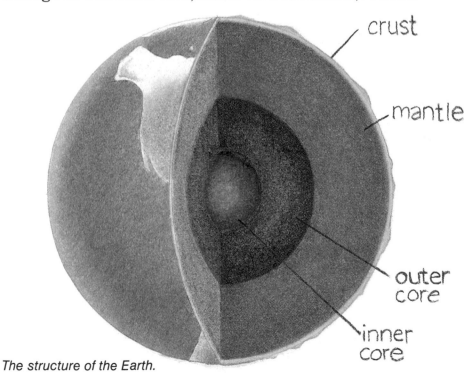

The structure of the Earth.

You have discovered that most of the mountain building, volcanic eruptions, and earthquakes that we can see occur along the edges of continents where mountain chains meet the ocean. (Geologists think that the mantle in these areas may be hotter than elsewhere. They hypothesize that currents of heat rise from the mantle and circulate through the overlying rock crust. The Earth's fierce inner heat provides the force that makes the thin crust buckle, fold, and split.) As you will discover in the next Topic, there is evidence that the entire crust is actually broken into several huge pieces that move and interact in response to currents of heat produced deep inside the Earth's mantle.

Did You Know?

Many earthquakes occur in the floor of the ocean. Although we do not feel these earthquakes directly, they may create waves that can have devastating effects on shorelines thousands of kilometres away. The huge waves caused by undersea or coastal earthquakes are called *tsunamis*. These waves travel outward from the site of the earthquake, much like the ripples that spread from a stone dropped in a pond. A tsunami races through the water at about 800 km/h. When it reaches a shoreline, it is forced to slow down, and its tremendous energy is converted into towering waves up to 30 m high.

Tsunamis are caused by underwater or coastal earthquakes.

Science and Technology in Society

Reducing the Damage of Quakes

A west-coast Canadian city has a problem—a strong possibility of an earthquake in the near future. Imagine that you have just been asked to design a structure that wouldn't collapse during an earthquake. How would you even begin such a challenging task?

If you were to think about what happens during an earthquake—the ground shifts, cracks, and buckles—your first concern might be to think of ways to minimize the building's contact with the ground! Is that possible? Don't all buildings need to be firmly "planted" on the ground?

Dr. Bogue Babicki, a Vancouver engineer, noticed that trees are rarely harmed during earthquakes. The trunk of a tree is a strong, flexible central column. Although it may sway violently during an earthquake, the lighter branches that radiate out from the column can move about freely without being damaged.

Dr. Babicki decided to apply these observations to the design of an earthquake-resistant building—the Westcoast Building owned by the Westcoast Transmission Company Limited in Vancouver.

How is this building similar to a tree? The "trunk" of the Westcoast Building is a hollow concrete core that contains the elevators, heating ducts, and electrical wiring for the building. The 15 floors are suspended from steel cables attached to the "crown" (top) of the trunk (core). So, like the branches of a tree, the floors move more freely during an earthquake. As one local citizen put it, "I don't know what holds the floors up; they must be hanging from something." Like a tree, only the core of this remarkable building needs to be in touch with the ground.

Earthquake vibrations caused the pavement shown in this photograph to shift and buckle.

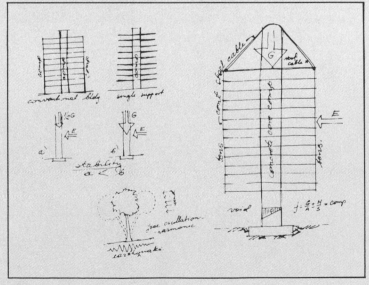

An architectural drawing of the Westcoast Transmission Building.

Teams of engineers are constantly studying buildings in earthquake-prone areas to learn more about why certain buildings fall down while others do not. The information can be used to design better earthquake-resistant buildings. Information is collected from special seismic monitoring equipment installed in and around the buildings. The data are fed into computers that then simulate the behaviour of buildings during an earthquake.

Another way engineers determine how a particular building will react in an earthquake is by placing models of the building on a special "shake" table. The buildings are shaken to see how they react. The researchers have learned that the simpler and more symmetrical a building, the safer it is. If possible, the building should be somewhat flexible; for example, materials such as steel, wood, and reinforced concrete can all bend a little without breaking. Brick buildings, however, break apart very easily. Like a tree, it's important that all parts of the building be securely interconnected. Often people are injured by balconies and stairways breaking away from buildings.

Buildings located on solid rock are more likely to withstand an earthquake than buildings standing on thick soil and sediment. Solid rock will vibrate only a little, but softer ground tends to vibrate much more violently. The October 1989 earthquake in San Francisco was a tragic reminder of this fact. The buildings that suffered the most damage were those built on the soft earth of a former landfill site.

Scientists at earthquake research centres are analysing the data collected from the San Francisco earthquake. Such analysis should help architects, engineers, and city planners design safer structures. While earthquakes can't be prevented, citizens in earthquake zones around the world are learning the importance of being prepared.

Think About It

There are many innovative methods of constructing earthquake-resistant buildings. Based on your understanding of earthquakes, and your previous studies of structures and design, draw and/or build your own model of an earthquake-resistant building.

The Westcoast Transmission Building in Vancouver.

Earthquake damage in San Francisco, California, in October 1989.

Continents that Move

Observe the shape of the Atlantic Ocean on a map of the world. The coastlines on either side of the ocean look as though they could fit together. People noticed this pattern when world maps were first drawn more than 300 years ago. It made them wonder whether North and South America had once been joined with Europe and Africa to form one huge continent!

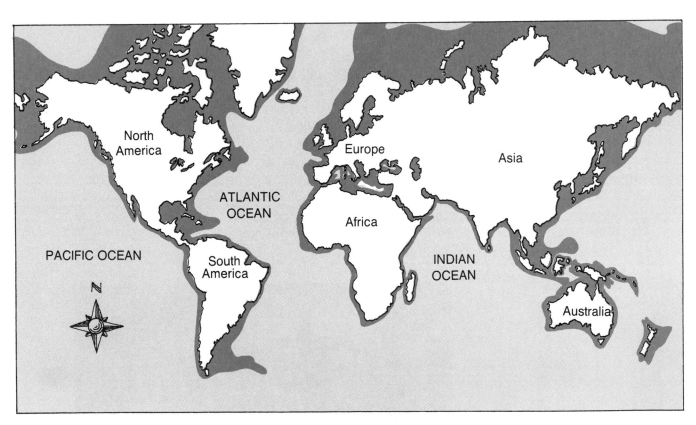

A map of the world. The shaded areas show the continental shelves. These are the shallow underwater edges of the continental land masses where the land drops steeply away to the ocean floor.

In 1915, a German scientist and explorer named Alfred Wegener expressed the idea that is now known as the **theory of continental drift**. He suggested that there had once been a single land mass, or "supercontinent," which later broke up. The different parts of this supercontinent had slowly drifted apart to form the continents we know today. Wegener backed up his idea by pointing out that the types of rock found in the mountains of northern Europe are similar to those found in the Appalachian Mountains on the opposite side of the Atlantic. Similarly, rocks on the west coast of Africa match those on the east coast of South America. The same kinds of animal and plant fossils are also found in rocks on both sides of the ocean.

Although this evidence was interesting, it was not enough. Wegener's idea did not satisfactorily explain how continents could possibly "drift" through solid rock. Because of this, most scientists dismissed the idea as being too far-fetched. When Wegener died in 1930, the idea of continental drift was almost forgotten. It was not until the 1960s that new evidence from the seabed made scientists think about Wegener's ideas once again.

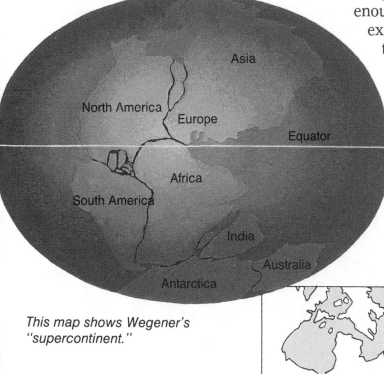

This map shows Wegener's "supercontinent."

Evidence for Wegener's idea came from matching up similar rock types and formations on opposite sides of the ocean.

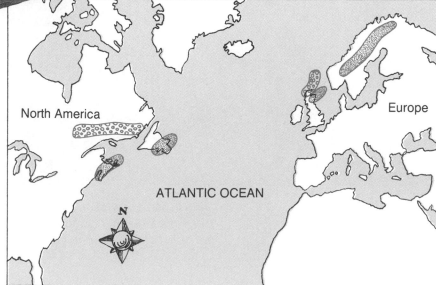

Probing

Try piecing the continents together. Trace the outlines of the continents from a map of the world onto a piece of paper. Cut along the eastern shorelines of North and South America, and along the western coasts of Greenland, Europe, and Africa. Try to fit the pieces together like a jigsaw puzzle. How well do the coastlines match up? How might you account for any gaps between the pieces?

Sea-Floor Spreading

Several important discoveries provided clues to the puzzle of moving continents. The first discovery was that a huge volcanic mountain range runs underwater along the middle of the Atlantic Ocean. This feature, called the **Mid-Atlantic Ridge**, is much longer and higher than any mountain range found on land. Temperature measurements along the ridge show that it produces more heat than other areas of the sea floor. The ridge is also covered with recently formed volcanic rock, much younger than that found on land or at further distances from the ridge.

Another significant discovery was that deep **ocean trenches**, many hundreds of kilometres long, run along the edges of some oceans. The deepest of these trenches drops 11 000 m below sea level. No valleys of this depth are found on the continents. For example, compare this with the Grand Canyon, which is 1700 m deep.

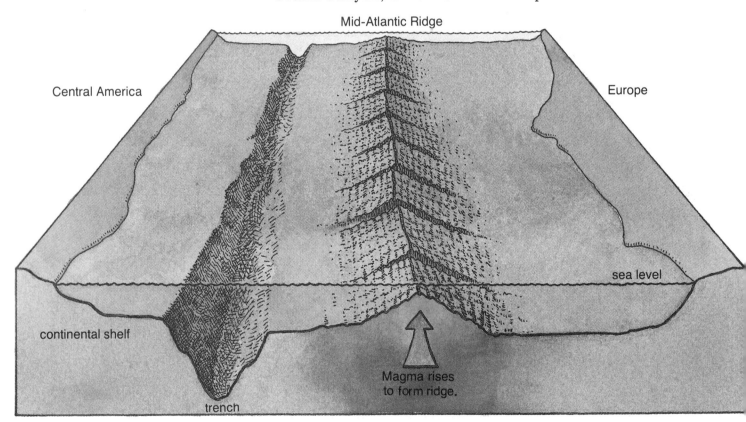

Here is a cross section of the Atlantic Ocean. The Mid-Atlantic Ridge runs down the centre of the ocean. A deep sea trench lies off the coast of Central America.

Before the 1900s, little was known about the ocean floor. Then, in the early 1900s, sonar was invented. In sonar systems, an electronic instrument attached to the underside of a ship sends out high-frequency sound waves. Echoes of these sounds bounce off the ocean floor. By measuring the time it takes for echoes to return to the ship, the sonar system can quickly compute the distance from the ship to the ocean floor. Thus, the depth of the ocean at that point can be easily determined.

Putting together the evidence, scientists have developed the **theory of plate tectonics** to account for these and other features. The theory proposes that the Earth's crust is broken into several large sections called **tectonic plates**. The mid-ocean ridge marks a boundary between two such plates. Magma rising from the mid-ocean ridge produces new crust, which pushes the plates apart. The sea floor spreads, and the ocean gets wider.

The Earth is not getting bigger, however. If new crust is produced in one place, it must disappear somewhere else. This happens where plates come together at the deep ocean trenches. Here, one plate slips down beneath the other and is dragged back into the Earth's mantle to be melted into magma. The system can be thought of as a continually moving conveyor belt. Crust material is thrust up at the mid-ocean ridge, moves across the sea floor, and is "swallowed" again at the trenches. This action is shown in the diagram below. To help you visualize this idea further, make a model of it in the next Activity.

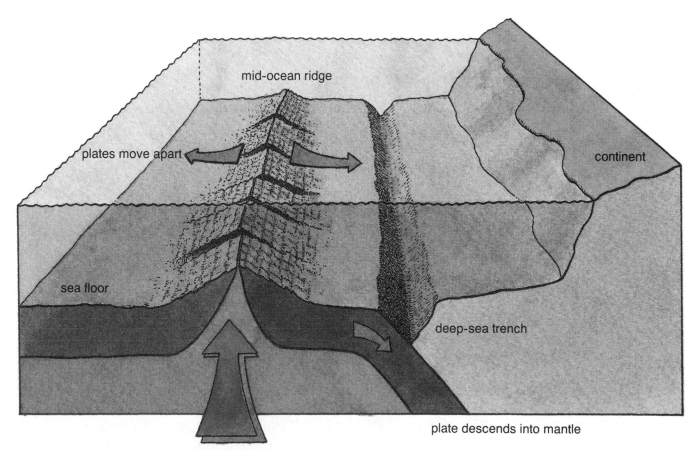

Currents of heat in the mantle cause the motion of the Earth's plates.

Activity 4-12

Sea-Floor Spreading

Problem

How can you make a model to show sea-floor spreading?

Materials

sheet of paper (21 cm × 28 cm)
coloured markers
scissors
tape

Procedure

1. Fold a sheet of paper in half lengthwise. Cut along the fold to produce two strips approximately 10 cm × 28 cm each.

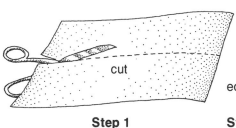

Step 1

2. Tape the two strips together as shown.

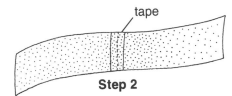

Step 2

3. Push two desks together. Hold the paper strips vertically under the crack between the desks and push the two separate ends up until about 4 cm from each end shows above the top of the desk.

4. Fold the ends of the paper down on the desk top as shown. Colour the visible ends with a solid colour or a pattern.

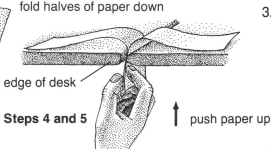

fold halves of paper down

edge of desk

Steps 4 and 5   ↑ push paper up

5. Push up on the paper below the desk until another 4 cm or so appears above the desk top. Fold the paper down and fill in the new section of the strip with a different colour or pattern.

6. Repeat the procedure two or three times.

Finding Out

1. In your model of sea-floor spreading, what is represented by:
   (a) the crack between the desks; and
   (b) the paper?
2. Which rock on the sea floor is:
   (a) oldest; and
   (b) youngest?
3. In your model, which section of rock would be closest to an ocean trench?

A Unifying Theory

The theory of plate tectonics does more than provide an explanation of how continents might move. It also answers questions such as: What causes volcanoes? Why are volcanoes found in long belts at the edges of continents? Why are earthquakes often found in the same areas as volcanoes? What causes movements along faults? What causes rock to fold and produce mountains? These questions, once thought to be unrelated, are all connected by this one unifying theory.

Look back at your map of mountain ranges, earthquakes, and volcanoes. Most of these features occur along the edges of plates. Volcanoes are produced in two places: where plates move apart and where they come together. The movements of plates are also responsible for earthquakes. Younger folded mountains occur in the same areas. The enormous forces that pushed them up are caused by a collision between one plate and another. Older mountains, such as the Appalachians, may have grown up along ancient plate boundaries that have since moved or closed up.

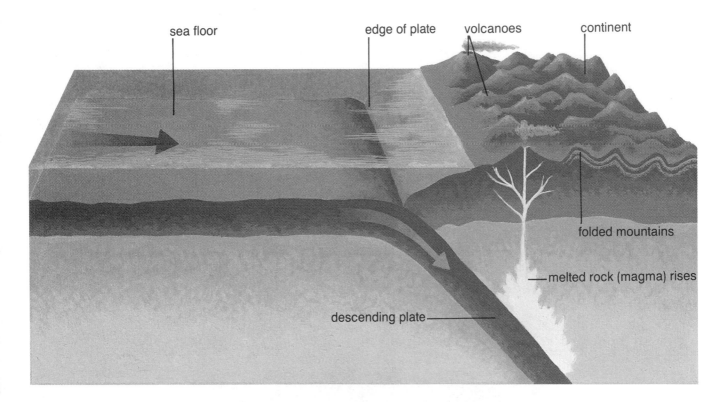

The movement of the plates helps to explain folded mountains, volcanoes, and earthquakes, as well as the shifting of continents.

Finding answers to scientific questions often takes many years—even generations—of painstaking work. The observations, measurements, calculations, and ideas of many different scientists were involved in developing the theory of plate tectonics. Evidence for the theory was built up bit by bit, from studies of rocks and minerals, maps, and deep-sea exploration. The ideas of one person, Alfred Wegener, started other people thinking along the right track. It is fascinating to wonder how many clues to other unsolved problems are waiting for someone with an inquiring mind to notice them and point them out!

Working at Solving Earth's Mysteries

"When I was 15, I went prospecting for gold. The mapping and prospecting we did took us into the wild country north of Lake Superior. I didn't know much about geology then, but I knew I loved the rugged outdoor life."

These early experiences aroused Dr. Tuzo Wilson's curiosity about the natural world. His curiosity led him to geophysics—a field of study combining both geology and physics. The knowledge he gained from both subjects would one day help him make important discoveries about the movement of the Earth's crust.

"But back then, the study of geology was confined mainly to examining rocky outcrops and recording your observations on maps. Blundering through the bush with your hammer, it was easier to identify a rock than it was to recognize a fault that stretched for kilometres. It wasn't until the development of aerial photography in the 1930s that we could get a bird's-eye view of the country—a view that would let us see big geological features like faults."

Dr. Wilson is best known for his explanation of "transform faults," the geological feature that permits the movement of the Earth's plates. These large fractures cut across many plate boundaries, permitting plate movement. Dr. Wilson has won many honours for his contributions to the theory of plate tectonics, including having a submerged volcano off Canada's west coast named after him, as well as a range of mountains in Antarctica.

After an outstanding career in teaching and research, Dr. Wilson was asked to become the director of a museum of modern science—the Ontario Science Centre. Here, for 11 years, he shared his experience, knowledge, and enthusiasm for science with students of all ages.

"The problem with geology now is that we know what is going on, but we don't know why. To understand the Earth's changes, you need to look beneath the surface formations to the deeper mysteries inside the Earth." Dr. Wilson is still trying to unravel some of the Earth's geological mysteries. "I didn't expect all of this when I started out. In fact, I was quite a shy little boy. You never know what you might achieve."

Checkpoint

1. Sketch a model of a seismograph and explain how it works.

2. Which of the following statements is correct? Write each correct statement in your notebook.
   (a) Earthquakes cause volcanoes.
   (b) Volcanoes cause earthquakes.
   (c) Earthquakes cause tsunamis.
   (d) The movement of plates causes both earthquakes and volcanoes.

3. (a) Give an example of the geological evidence that Wegener used in his idea of continental drift.
   (b) Why did many geologists in the early part of this century find it easy to dismiss Wegener's idea?

4. How does the theory of plate tectonics help explain:
   (a) folded mountains;
   (b) volcanoes; and
   (c) earthquakes?

5. Use the comic strip below to answer the following questions.
   (a) What was Tuzo Wilson's important observation about the Hawaiian Islands?
   (b) What inference did he make, based on his observation?
   (c) What theory is supported by Dr. Wilson's inference?

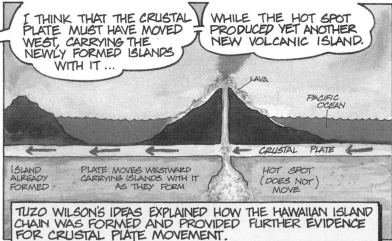

Focus

- Rocks are made up of minerals, which can be identified by their properties.
- Igneous rock is formed by the cooling of lava or magma.
- Sedimentary rock is formed by the compression of eroded sediments.
- Metamorphic rock is formed when rock is changed by heat and pressure.
- The three families of rock are constantly changed and recycled.
- The relative age of rocks can be determined by their relative positions in the Earth's crust.
- The absolute age of rocks can be determined by measurements of radioactive decay.
- Fossils are evidence of ancient life on Earth.
- Mountains may be formed by the folding and uplifting of rock, or by the accumulation of erupted igneous rock.
- Earthquakes and volcanoes occur mostly along the edges of continents where there are faults in the Earth's crust.
- The Earth's crust consists of several large, interlocking slabs called tectonic plates.
- Tectonic plates constantly move, carrying continents with them.
- Where plates come together, volcanoes, earthquakes, folded mountains, and deep ocean trenches form.

Backtrack

1. Use the clues below to find the correct terms to complete the word puzzle. The highlighted letters in the puzzle spell another word. Define the meaning of this word.

   (a) Molten rock beneath the Earth's crust.
   (b) Type of rock formed by layers of sediment.
   (c) Solid mineral with a regular geometric shape and smooth flat faces.
   (d) Crack in the Earth's crust along which the Earth moves.
   (e) Naturally occurring pure substance found in rock.
   (f) Process of mountain building in which rock layers are bent.
   (g) Instrument used to record earthquakes.
   (h) A principle used to determine the relative age of rock layers.
   (i) Violent vibrations on the surface of the Earth.
   (j) Type of rock formed by the cooling of molten rock.
   (k) Mountain formed by erupting lava.

   (a) □ ■ ■ ■ ■
   (b) ■ □ ■ ■ ■ ■ ■ ■ ■
   (c) ■ ■ ■ ■ □ ■ ■
   (d) ■ □ ■ ■ ■
   (e) □ ■ ■ ■ ■ ■ ■
   (f) ■ □ ■ ■ ■ ■ ■
   (g) ■ ■ ■ ■ ■ ■ ■ □ ■ ■
   (h) ■ ■ ■ ■ ■ □ ■ ■ ■ ■ ■ ■
   (i) ■ ■ ■ ■ □ ■ ■ ■ ■
   (j) □ ■ ■ ■ ■ ■ ■
   (k) ■ ■ ■ □ ■ ■ ■

2. (a) What is the Earth's crust?
   (b) What is a rock?
   (c) What are the three major types of rocks, and how is each formed?

3. Write down three questions that you could ask to help identify the minerals in a sample rock.

4. Suppose you find a sample of igneous rock that contains many large crystals. Where might the rock have been formed? Give a reason for your answer.

5. Why does a mineral's cleavage help you to identify it?

6. How is the crystal size of minerals affected by whether magma cools rapidly or slowly?

7. How do sedimentary rocks such as shale, sandstone, and conglomerate differ?

8. Describe how the principle of superposition can be useful to a geologist or a fossil collector.

9. Last year, a rock hunter found a piece of rock that contained the shape and outline of a fish. The details of the fish's scales and fins could be clearly seen. Describe how the fish's shape might have been preserved in the rock.

10. What is the geological time scale?

11. How are radioactive elements used to help tell when a rock was formed?

12. Describe at least two processes that help form mountains.

13. How are different types of volcanoes formed?
14. What happens at the focus of an earthquake to cause an earthquake on the Earth's surface?
15. (a) What is a fault, and what causes it?
(b) How does the occurrence of volcanoes and earthquakes relate to the presence of faults?

Synthesizer

16. (a) Describe the interior of the Earth.
(b) How does our knowledge of S waves help explain whether the various parts of the Earth's interior are solid or liquid?
17. Ivan and Maria visited the Grand Canyon during their holiday. "It's amazing," said Maria. "This whole area was once underwater." What evidence might lead her to this inference?

18. The arrowhead in the photograph was made by some of the native peoples of North America from an igneous rock called obsidian. What two properties of this rock might have made it particularly suitable for this purpose?
19. A geologist was showing a friend two pieces of rock. "This one I found on the surface of the Earth, but it was formed deep underground," said the geologist. "And this one I found deep underground, but it was formed on the surface."
(a) What family might each rock belong to?
(b) Explain the changes that each rock might have gone through from the time it was formed until the geologist found it.
20. Each of the following words is the correct answer to a question. Write a suitable question to match each answer.
(a) a volcano
(b) a folded mountain
(c) a fault-block mountain
21. You have just moved to a new town at the foot of a mountain. You would like to know how the mountain was formed, and how old it is. Describe what evidence you would need in order to answer these questions.

22. "An earthquake could happen any time, any place," said Toni. Give your opinion of this statement, including reasons for your answer.
23. In sedimentary rock beds, fossils of dinosaurs are found far below the first fossils of early humans. Suppose your younger brother has just been reading about dinosaurs. He says to you: "I'll bet the Stone Age people found dinosaurs really scary." What would be your explanation to him?
24. Describe two geological processes that occur deep underground. Explain how scientists infer that these processes have happened without observing them first-hand.
25. "To understand geology, you must have a different sense of time."
(a) What do you think is meant by this statement?
(b) Explain why you agree or disagree with it.
26. Write a short explanation of the theory of plate tectonics, using all the following terms: plates, mid-ocean ridge, deep sea trench, sea-floor spreading.

Managing Plant Growth

Most of the living things on Earth get the energy they need from plants. Millions of different species of plants exist—from towering trees to ground-hugging ferns, mosses, wildflowers, weeds, and herbs.

Ever since human beings ceased to be simply hunters of animals and gatherers of plant foods, we have managed the growth of plants to meet certain needs. We use plants such as cotton to supply fibres for making thread and cloth. Some chemicals in plants are a source of medicinal drugs. The strong fibres in wood from trees make it an ideal construction material. Wood fibres are also used in making paper and cardboard. Most importantly, we use the chemical potential energy of many plant products as food.

About 10 000 years ago, people began to plant seeds of food crops near their homes, managing plant growth with primitive tools: sticks and stones. Simple, laborious methods of planting and harvesting crops have been replaced over the centuries by new methods and machines. As well, scientific knowledge of how plants "work" has led to new technologies—methods of starting new plants as well as ways of improving their growth. In this Unit, you will use some of this technology to manage plant growth. For example, you will explore several ways of starting new plants and encouraging their growth. Throughout the Unit you will learn about what plants need in order to grow, stay healthy, and reproduce.

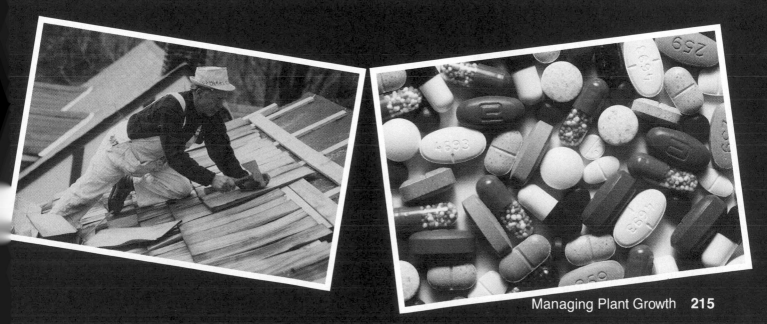

Starting New Plants

For every apple, strawberry, or tomato that you eat, a plant had to grow. In this Topic, you'll look at some ways in which new plants are produced. These methods are used to start plants in gardens, forests, fields, greenhouses, and homes.

Have you ever wondered what goes on underground after seeds have been planted? In Activity 5-1, you will observe the germination of a seed. **Germination** is the process in which a seed sprouts and develops into a tiny new plant.

Observing Germination

PART A
Problem

What changes can you observe when a seed germinates?

Materials

seeds (beans, peas, or other suitable variety)
250 mL beaker (or clear plastic drinking glass)
small pot (made of plastic, clay, or peat) or paper cup with a drainage hole punched in the bottom
tray to hold beaker and pot
potting soil or sand
paper towel
masking tape

Procedure

1. Label the beaker and the pot with the names of the students in your group, the kind of seeds, and the date.
2. Crumple a piece of paper towel and place it loosely in the beaker. Put two or three seeds between the paper and the glass, at about the same depth but in different positions, as shown in the illustration.

3. Place potting soil or sand into the pot to a depth of about 1 cm from the top. Place the same kind and number of seeds in the soil as you had used in the beaker.
4. Add about 50 mL of water to both the beaker and the pot. Then place the beaker and the pot on the tray.
5. Over the next week, keep the paper towel and the soil moist but not so wet that the seeds are under water.
6. Observe the development of the seedlings (tiny new plants). Each day, write your observations in your notebook, and draw sketches of the seedlings.
NOTE: Save your seedlings for use again in Activity 5-3.

Finding Out

1. What emerges from a seed first?
2. In this Activity, you have two manipulated variables. What are they?
3. Did the position of the seed affect its germination in any way? If so, how?
4. Compare germination in soil with germination in a moist paper towel. What difference(s), if any, did you observe?

Finding Out More

5. What can you infer about the development of the seeds in moist soil compared with those with moisture but no soil?
6. What do you think happens within a seed as it germinates?

PART B

Design a similar Activity to compare the effects of different conditions on the germination of seeds. Decide which variables you want to investigate: for example, different depths of planting, different temperatures, different degrees of moisture, different light conditions, or different ages of seeds. Determine how you will measure and record these differences. Then carry out your experiment.

Finding Out

1. How does the condition you investigated affect the germination of seeds?
2. How can you be sure that you have controlled all the other variables so that only the condition you varied in the experiment affected the result?

Finding Out More

3. How could you discover the best combination of conditions for the germination of a particular type of seed?

Starting Plants from Cuttings

In Activity 5-1, did you notice, a few millimetres above the growing root tip, an area in which hairlike structures grow? This area, which ends where the root is lengthening, is called the **root hair zone**. New root hairs are produced every day, as the root grows. The root hair zone always remains about the same length, as the root grows longer and older root hairs shrivel. At its very tip (called the **root cap**), the root is growing new cells. These new cells are not mature enough to produce root hairs.

Sometimes new plants are not started from seeds, for various reasons. For example, you might want to grow a new plant quickly, rather than waiting for a seedling to mature. In a case such as this, a new plant can be started by **vegetative reproduction**—the use of parts of plants to produce a plant almost identical to an existing plant. This is done by taking a small part, known as a **cutting**, from a stem, leaf, or root. In Activity 5-2, you will start some new plants from stem cuttings.

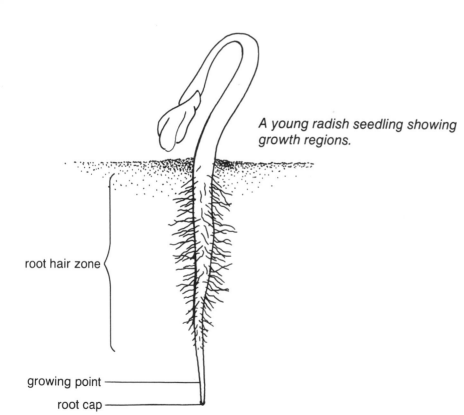

A young radish seedling showing growth regions.

root hair zone
growing point
root cap

Taking a Stem Cutting

Problem

How do stem cuttings produce a new plant?

Materials

plastic bag
2 popsicle sticks
7.5 cm plastic pot or a suitable container with drainage holes
appropriate plants, such as geranium, coleus, impatiens, or begonia
single-edged razor blade
mixture of soil, peat moss, and vermiculite
large elastic band
beaker or jar

Procedure

1. Use the razor blade to cut a section of stem 8 cm to 12 cm long on a slant just below a node. (A **node** is a small bump on the stem where a leaf was, or is still growing. This region will develop roots more readily than other areas of the stem.) Cutting at an angle will increase the surface area for the absorption of water.

> **CAUTION:** When you use the razor blade, be sure to cut away from yourself (and anyone else).

2. Remove the leaves from the bottom 4 cm of your stem cutting. (Otherwise, these leaves will come in contact with the soil and will rot.) Do not remove the top leaves.

3. Set your cutting aside while you prepare soil for it. Gently pat the soil mixture into the pot until it is about 3 cm from the top. This will allow room for water when you water your plant.

4. Carefully insert the cutting into the soil and gently pack the soil around the stem with your fingers. Also place one or two cuttings in a beaker of water so that the development of the roots can be easily observed.

5. Water the soil until excess water drains through the holes at the bottom of the pot.

6. Place two popsicle sticks in the soil to support the plastic bag over the cutting. Use an elastic band to hold the plastic bag around the pot. This plastic "tent" will keep moist air from escaping, which will slow the loss of water from the cutting. (You'll learn more about this water loss in Topic Five.)

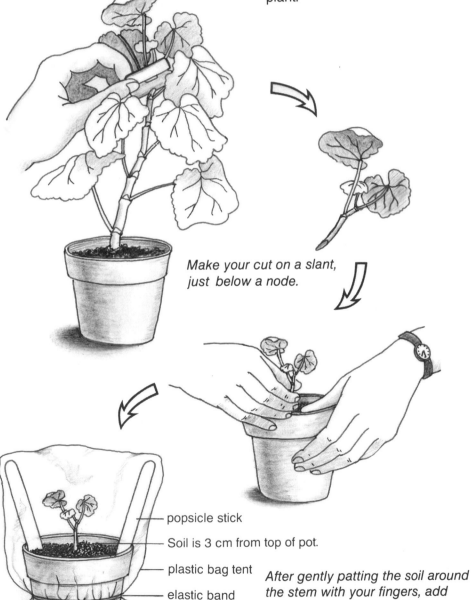

Make your cut on a slant, just below a node.

— popsicle stick

— Soil is 3 cm from top of pot.

— plastic bag tent

— elastic band

After gently patting the soil around the stem with your fingers, add water to the soil and then cover the cutting with a plastic bag.

Finding Out

1. Observe the formation of new roots in the beakers of water. How long did it take for roots to develop?
2. (a) Did all the plants develop roots at the same rate?
(b) What factors do you think affected the development of the roots?
3. (a) Which kinds of plants in your class developed roots the fastest?
(b) Which plants in your class developed roots the slowest?
4. Did any of the plants die? If so, suggest possible reasons why they died.
5. Compare the growth of stem cuttings that were in soil with those that were in water.

Underground Activity

It is amazing that leaves at the very tops of tall trees can get the water they need for photosynthesis from the soil. **Photosynthesis** is the production of food by organisms having the green pigment, **chlorophyll**. The process of photosynthesis can be stated in a word equation:

$$\text{carbon dioxide + water} \xrightarrow[\text{chlorophyll}]{\text{light}} \text{starch + oxygen}$$

The term photosynthesis is derived from three Greek words:

photos = light
syn = together
thesis = putting

Photosynthesis is the "putting together" of complex substances, using carbon dioxide and water, in the presence of light and chlorophyll.

How do the roots manage to collect the water needed by the leaves in order for photosynthesis to occur? How are other materials in the soil absorbed by the roots? In this Topic, you will investigate the structure of plant roots in order to understand how they function to absorb and transport that most important substance—water, along with other materials dissolved in it.

This tree's roots function to get water from the soil, all the way up to the leaves at the top of the tree.

Examining Root Growth

Problem

How do roots grow?

Materials

seedlings from Activity 5-1, and
  older seedlings
string
ruler
pen

Procedure

1. Each group of students will use the three seedlings from the beaker in Activity 5-1. (If you need to use the plants in sand or potting soil, you will have to remove the sand or soil very carefully with a gentle stream of water. Do this over a container so that the soil will not wash down the drain.) Measure the total height of growth above the stem.

2. Draw and label sketches of each of the seedlings. Include your measurements of height.

3. Use a piece of string to measure the total length of the roots and all the main root branches of each seedling. (Hint: To measure the total root length, place the string at the bottom of a long root. Use a pen to mark the string at the top of the root. Use the pen mark as the starting place to measure the next root. When you have measured all the roots and root branches in this way, measure the entire length of the string you used.)

4. Add up the total root length of all three seedlings, and divide by 3 to find the average root length of seedlings at this age.

5. Now measure the height and total root length of a seedling that has been growing for two weeks more than your seedlings. Record these measurements, along with a labelled diagram, in your notebook.

Finding Out

1. What is the purpose of finding the average root length of the seedlings?
2. How does the root system change as the seedling grows in height?
3. How does the growth in height compare with the root growth?

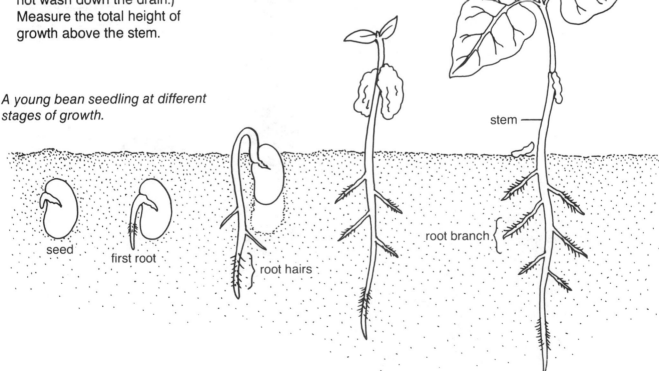

A young bean seedling at different stages of growth.

seed first root root hairs root branch stem

How Materials Move In and Out of Plant Cells

Both water and dissolved substances in soil move into the root hairs of plants. Exactly how does this happen?

A thin living layer called the **cell membrane** lines the surface of each plant cell. (The cell membrane is, itself, surrounded by a non-living cell wall.) The cell membrane controls the passage of substances, such as gases and dissolved chemicals, both into and out of the cell. The cell membrane is said to be **differentially permeable**. This means that it allows only certain substances to enter and leave the cell. (To learn more about the structure of plant cells, refer to Skillbuilder Five, *Working with a Microscope*, on page 342.)

Recall that the process of diffusion is responsible for the gradual mixing of substances. In the following Activity, you will observe diffusion through a differentially permeable membrane. Here, a piece of dialysis tubing and a piece of glass tubing are used as a model for the action of a cell membrane.

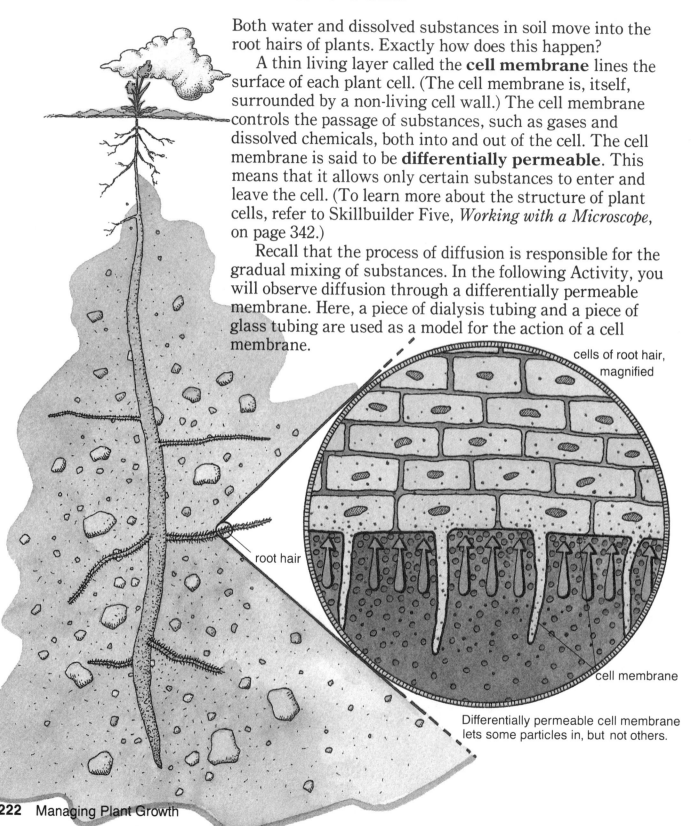

cells of root hair, magnified

root hair

cell membrane

Differentially permeable cell membrane lets some particles in, but not others.

Diffusion through a Membrane: Demonstration

Problem

How do substances diffuse through a differentially permeable membrane?

Materials

10 cm of dialysis tubing
strong sugar solution (corn syrup or molasses)
50 cm of glass tubing or a thistle tube, fitted with a one-holed rubber stopper
twist tie
beaker of distilled water
support stand and clamp
small piece of masking tape

Procedure

1. Soak the dialysis tubing in water for a few minutes. Rub it between your thumb and forefinger to open it.
2. Tie a knot in one end of the tubing, about 1 cm from the end.
3. Fill the tubing with the strong sugar solution.
4. Use a twist tie to attach the dialysis tubing to the rubber stopper containing the glass tubing (see the diagram).

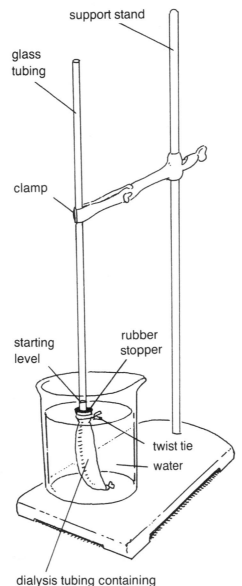

support stand

glass tubing

clamp

starting level

rubber stopper

twist tie

water

dialysis tubing containing sugar solution

5. Rinse the outside of the dialysis tubing with water.
6. Lower the dialysis tubing into the beaker of water and clamp the glass tubing or thistle funnel vertically.
7. Place masking tape on the glass tubing to mark the starting level of the sugar solution.
8. Mark the level again after 20 min.

Finding Out

1. Describe what happens to the sugar solution in the dialysis tubing during the 20 min.
2. Was there any evidence that water diffused through the tubing? Explain your answer.
3. Was there any evidence that sugar diffused through the tubing? Explain your answer.

Finding Out More

4. Use the particle theory to explain what you observed in this Activity.
5. How does the particle theory help explain the function of the cell membrane?

Osmosis—A Special Kind of Diffusion

How can a plant that looks like the one on the left be made to look like the one below it? Add a little water to the soil around the wilted plant and let osmosis do the job. **Osmosis** is the diffusion of water particles through a differentially permeable membrane. You saw evidence of osmosis in Activity 5-4.

Look at the diagram below that shows a model for osmosis. There is a higher concentration (greater number) of water particles on the left side of the membrane compared with the right side. The water particles on the left side tend to move (diffuse) to an area where there are fewer water particles—the right side. Thus, the water particles cross the membrane into the sugar solution. The sugar particles cannot pass through the membrane because they are too large. Water passes from an area of high concentration to an area of low concentration through the differentially permeable membrane until water particles are evenly distributed on both sides of the membrane.

A model to explain osmosis. The arrows show the main direction of movement of water particles.

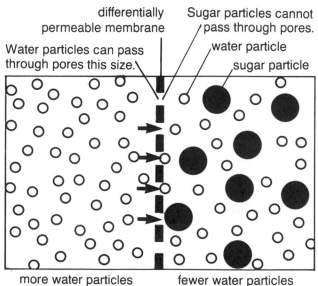

differentially permeable membrane

Sugar particles cannot pass through pores.

Water particles can pass through pores this size.

water particle

sugar particle

more water particles on this side of membrane

fewer water particles on this side of membrane

Checkpoint

1. Use the definitions given below to complete the word puzzle. The highlighted letters will spell a word that describes the diffusion of water particles through a differentially permeable membrane.

(a) ■■■■■■■■□■
(b) ■■■■ ■■■■□
(c) ■■■■■■■■■■■■■■
  ■■■□■■■■■
(d) ■■■■■■■■■■
  ■■■■□■■■■■■■
(e) ■■■■□■■■■■■■■■
(f) ■■■■□■■■
(g) ■■■■■□■■■

(a) The process in which a seed sprouts and develops into a tiny new plant.
(b) Hairlike structures that develop above the growing root tip.
(c) A characteristic of the cell membrane that allows only certain substances to enter and leave the cells.
(d) The use of parts of plants to produce a plant almost identical to an existing plant.
(e) The production of food by organisms having the green pigment, chlorophyll.
(f) A small part of a stem, leaf, or root used to produce a new plant.
(g) The gradual mixing of the particles of substances.

2. Name one condition that seeds need in order to germinate.

3. (a) What is the function of the cell membrane in a root hair cell?
(b) Which characteristic of the cell membrane enables it to perform its function?

4. How could a knowledge of osmosis help to promote plant growth if fertilizer solutions are applied to soils?

5. The illustration directly below represents the normal condition of a root hair cell (Side A), surrounded by soil water (Side B).
(a) In which direction will the large particles tend to move?
(b) In which direction will the water particles tend to move?
(c) Make a sketch to show how the number of the particles on the inside and outside of the cell will compare after some time.

6. The illustration directly below represents fertilizer particles in soil water surrounding a root hair.
(a) In which direction will the particles of fertilizer tend to move?
(b) In which direction will the water particles tend to move?
(c) Make a sketch to show the approximate numbers of particles on each side of the cell membrane after some time.

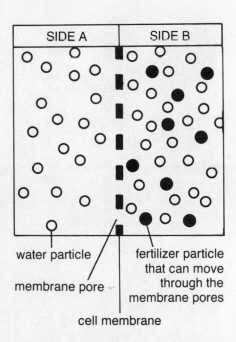

SIDE A	SIDE B

water particle
membrane pore
cell membrane
fertilizer particle that can move through the membrane pores

SIDE A	SIDE B
ROOT HAIR CELL	SOIL WATER

large particle
water particle
soil particle
membrane pore
cell membrane

Growing Plants in Soil and Without It

When you look at a solid chunk of rock like granite or limestone, it is difficult to imagine that the soil on the Earth's surface was formed largely from rocks such as these. The weathering of rocks begins the process of soil formation. The weathered rock fragments mix with water and decaying organisms. Over time, soil as we commonly think of it is formed.

What exactly is in a handful of soil? How can you improve soil for growing plants? How can plants be grown *without* soil? In this Topic, you will find answers to these questions.

Soils supply many of the substances that plants and other organisms need in order to grow and thrive: water, minerals, and air. What are the most important characteristics of soil for the survival of different kinds of plants? Do the following Activities to discover some differences in soil characteristics and their effects on plant growth.

Soil forms slowly. In most places, only about 250 kg to 500 kg of soil per hectare are formed in a year. However, where the soil has been cleared of plants in order to build highways, it is common for thousands of kilograms of soil per hectare to be eroded in a year's time.

Activity 5-5

Investigating Soil

Problem

Do plants grow better in some soils than in others?

Materials

healthy seedlings or cuttings of equal size
a variety of soils, such as clay, sand, silt, and loam
an assortment of soil additives, such as peat moss and vermiculite
flats or pots

Procedure

1. Make a hypothesis about the soil characteristics that you think will best promote plant growth. Write your hypothesis in your notebook.
2. Design an experiment to test your hypothesis. Plant several seedlings in the soil mixture you selected. As a control, plant some seedlings in either sand or clay. Compare the growth of plants in this mixture with your experimental group of plants. Write your experimental design in your notebook. Include the period of time for the experiment.
3. With your teacher's approval, set up your experiment.

Finding Out

1. In every science class period, examine your plants. In your notebook, write your observations of their development. Be sure to keep all the variables the same for both groups of plants: equal water, equal exposure to light, the same temperature, etc.
2. What difference(s) do you observe between your experimental plants and the control?

Finding Out More

3. What do you infer has caused any observable differences between the experimental plants and the control?

Comparing Soil Characteristics

Problem

How does soil from your schoolyard compare with potting soil from a store?

Materials

a pail of schoolyard soil
a bag of potting soil
2 pieces of cloth (each about 15 cm²)
string
2 paper cups
microscope
2 cover slips
2 glass microscope slides
balance
2 beakers (each 50 mL)

Procedure

PART A: Using Your Senses

1. Hold a sample of each type of soil in your hands. Use your senses of sight, smell, and touch to describe three differences between the two types of soil. Record your observations in your notebook.

PART B: Will the Same Volume of Different Soils Have the Same Mass?

NOTE: You may wish to refer to Skillbuilder Three, *Measuring Matter*, on page 333 before beginning Part B.

2. Label one paper cup "potting soil" and the other "schoolyard soil."

3. Measure and record in your notebook the mass of each paper cup.
4. Measure exactly 50 mL of each of the soils into the appropriate paper cup.
5. Record the mass of each soil-filled cup.
6. Subtract the mass of each cup to determine the mass of each soil sample.
7. Record the mass of each soil sample in your notebook.

PART C: Do the Two Soils Hold the Same Amount of Water?

8. Wrap each of the soil samples in a piece of cloth and tie the cloth closed with string. In your notebook, record the mass of the dry soil in its cloth bag.
9. Half fill each paper cup with water. Soak each bag of soil in the water.
10. Add water until each soil sample is completely soaked.
11. Hold the bag over the cup until water stops dripping from the bag, as shown in the illustration. Then record the mass of the wet soil.
12. Subtract the mass of the dry soil from the mass of the wet soil. This mass represents the maximum amount of water that the soil can hold. Record this amount for each soil sample.

PART D: Looking Closer

NOTE: If you need to review proper use of a compound microscope, do Skillbuilder Five, *Working with a Microscope*, on page 342 before beginning Part D.

13. Wet your finger and dip it into the potting soil. Touch the microscope slide with your wet finger.
14. Cover the wet soil on the slide with a cover slip. Observe the soil under the microscope.
15. Sketch what you observe. On your sketch, label which type of soil is represented.
16. Repeat Steps 13 to 15 using the other soil sample.

Components of Soil

Soil is more than just dirt! Spaces between soil particles (the dirt) contain both air and water. The solid soil particles are:

(1) minerals, formed from rocks; and
(2) organic matter, resulting from the decay of organisms.

The size of soil particles varies: from very large, as in sand; to medium, as in silt; to very small, as in clay.

The air in soil contains oxygen, which is needed by the cells of the root to carry out their functions. Too much water decreases the amount of space available for oxygen, causing the roots to die. That is why overwatering is the most common cause of death in house plants. The importance of air to root growth is shown in the illustration.

The water in soil is necessary for photosynthesis to take place in the leaves. Soil water also contains the dissolved materials that plants need to grow and to carry out their functions.

Finding Out

PART A

1. (a) What are some characteristics of soil?
   (b) Which characteristics differ between the two soil samples?

PART B

2. For equal volumes of each type of soil, which soil had a smaller mass than the other?
3. (a) Why did one soil have less mass than the other?
   (b) What does this difference in mass tell you about the way the soil particles are "packed" together?
   (c) How does this affect the ability of the soil to hold water and air?

PART C

4. Which of the two soils held more water?
5. Why do you think the two soils held different amounts of water?

PART D

6. (a) Look at your sketches of the magnified soil samples. Identify and label soil particles, air, and water, as represented in each sketch.
   (b) What differences between the two soils can you see?

These two groups of tomato plants were grown under identical conditions, except that the group on the right had air bubbled through the water surrounding the roots. How did the air affect the growth of the plants?

Improving Soil for Plant Growth

Whether a soil is "good" depends, for one thing, on the type of plant. For most garden plants, a good soil is about 50% solid material, 25% water, and 25% air.

One way to improve soil for growing plants is to add materials such as peat moss, vermiculite, or perlite. Peat moss consists of the dead, crumbled sphagnum mosses that once grew in bogs. Because peat moss is spongy, it increases the amount of water that the soil can hold. Vermiculite and perlite are porous materials that separate soil particles and increase the amount of air in the soil. You can add these materials to soil to improve its characteristics for growing plants. Soil should also be drained of excess water so that air can get to the roots.

Plant Nutrients

Soil must provide the nutrients that a plant needs. **Nutrients** are substances that supply plants with what they need for growth and reproduction; these substances are dissolved in water absorbed through the roots. Nutrients in soil are set free by the erosion of the rocks from which the soil was produced. Some soils may contain better combinations of nutrients than others, depending upon the minerals forming the rocks in an area. The illustration shows that plants cannot survive with water alone. They need six nutrients in large amounts and at least six other nutrients in small amounts. Each nutrient has a different effect on plant growth.

TO HAVE REACHED MY MAGNIFICENT STATE OF HEALTH, I HAVE ABSORBED LARGE AMOUNTS OF THESE NUTRIENTS...

SMALL AMOUNTS OF THESE NUTRIENTS HAVE ALSO CONTRIBUTED TO MY OVERALL HEALTH...

nitrogen (N)
phosphorus (P)
potassium (K)
calcium (Ca)
magnesium (Mg)
sulphur (S)

boron (B)
chlorine (Cl)
copper (Cu)
iron (Fe)
manganese (Mn)
zinc (Zn)

By using a soil test kit, the presence or absence of nutrients in a sample of soil can be determined. Special laboratories conduct tests on soil samples and will provide a detailed report on the quality of a soil sample. This information could be very important to a greenhouse operator or a farmer if soil is found to be deficient in a particular nutrient.

Over time, a soil's nutrients can be used up. One way to return nutrients to the soil is to add fertilizer. There are two types of fertilizers: organic and inorganic. **Organic fertilizers**, such as animal waste (manure) or a plant crop that is ploughed under the soil, are natural sources of nutrients. **Inorganic fertilizers** are manufactured products made from a number of chemicals.

SAMPLE SOIL TEST RESULTS

1. Available Nutrients

NUTRIENT	VERY LOW	MEDIUM	HIGH
Nitrogen	less than 3.2 kg/hectare	22 kg/hectare	over 22 kg/hectare
Phosphorus	less than 2.2 kg/hectare	16 kg/hectare	over 43 kg/hectare
Potassium	less than 22 kg/hectare	70 kg/hectare	over 174 kg/hectare

2. Fertilizer Recommendations

Add 2.5 kg of 21-0-0 per 100 m².

A soil test kit is used to determine the presence or absence of nutrients in a sample of soil.

A soil testing lab can tell you which nutrients to add to your soil to improve plant growth.

The three numbers on this bag of fertilizer (10-6-4) tell you that it contains 10% nitrogen, 6% phosphorus, and 4% potassium. The percentages of nutrients are always listed in alphabetical order. The other 80% of the fertilizer is filler—a material that neither contributes to nor harms plant growth.

The three main nutrients provided in fertilizers are **nitrogen**, **phosphorus**, and **potassium**. A fertilizer high in nitrogen is used on lawns in the spring to encourage the growth of healthy green leaves. A fertilizer high in phosphorus is used to start seedlings. A fertilizer high in potassium stimulates flowering and the development of fruit. As shown in the photograph, the three numbers on a bag of fertilizer indicate the percentages of nitrogen, phosphorus, and potassium that the fertilizer contains.

If any nutrient is missing, the plant may show visible symptoms of the deficiency. For example, without enough magnesium or iron, a plant's leaves may become pale or they may have yellowish blotches. Such problems can be corrected by spraying the nutrients on the leaves or by adding the nutrients to the soil. In the following Activity, you will analyse the results of some experiments that show the importance of the various nutrients that plants get from soils.

Probing

Another factor that affects plant growth is soil acidity. Many plants can grow well only in a soil that is moderately acidic. Some examples of acid-loving plants are birch, pine, and some oaks. Plants such as azalea, dogwood, gardenia, and rhododendron require acidic soils. Other kinds of plants do better in moderately basic soils. Geraniums, lawn grass, and many garden vegetables are examples of such plants. Find out about pH and its effects on soils. Do most of the crops in your area grow better in acidic or basic soils?

Wild geraniums grow best in moderately basic soils.

Rhododendrons grow best in moderately acidic soils.

Activity 5-7

Comparing the Effects of Nutrients

Problem

In a research laboratory, experiments were set up in which pure chemicals were used to supply the nutrients to plants. This ensured that no unknown nutrients were present as impurities in the chemicals. Each group of plants was treated in exactly the same way, except that one nutrient was missing from the solutions used to bathe each group of experimental plants. The control group received a complete solution containing all the nutrients. The illustration shows the results of the experiment. How do different nutrients affect plant growth?

Finding Out

1. What differences exist between the growth of the control plants and that of plants lacking one of the nutrients?
2. What differences exist among the plants lacking nitrogen, phosphorus, and potassium?
3. What do these results indicate about the relationship between nutrients and plant growth?

Finding Out More

4. Why is the term "essential nutrient" sometimes used to describe nitrogen, phosphorus, and potassium?
5. Would the results have differed if a different kind of plant had been used for the experiment? Give a reason for your answer.

The effects of a lack of particular nutrients on the growth of lettuce. The plants on the right are the control: They received all the nutrients.

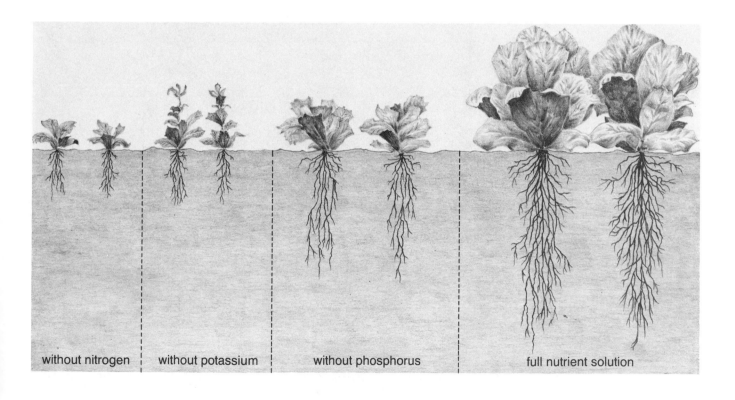

without nitrogen | without potassium | without phosphorus | full nutrient solution

Soil, Water, and Technology

Soil is used to help produce almost all of the food that we eat. However, some of this important soil is being constantly eroded. For example, in some parts of the Canadian Prairies, about 30 000 kg of soil are lost per hectare each year—by water erosion alone. Wind erosion has also removed much of the topsoil from many dry areas. In this Topic, you will see examples of how some technologies may help to save soil and how other technologies help grow more food crops. Lastly, you will look at some ways in which technologies have been harmful.

Soil lost by erosion can be lost forever.

Benefits of Technology

To reduce the loss of soil by erosion, a number of technologies have proved helpful. These include contour farming, strip farming, shelter belts, and terracing. In **contour farming**, ploughing and cultivating are done at right angles to the slopes of the land so that water is caught between furrows instead of running down them. In **strip farming**, only alternating strips of land are cultivated with a crop to be harvested, leaving grass or hay growing between these strips of the crop plant. **Shelter belts**— rows of trees planted around or on certain sides of fields— have been found to be effective in reducing erosion by wind. On land that slopes a great deal, **terracing**, the planting of crops on a series of "steps," helps prevent water from carrying soil along with it down the slopes.

In contour farming, water is caught between furrows instead of running down the slope and therefore eroding soil.

In strip farming, grass or hay is left growing between strips of the crop plant.

Terracing reduces erosion of soil by water.

Shelter belts reduce erosion of soil by wind.

Some farmers in Canada also now use a technology called zero tillage. Traditional cultivation of land by means of a plough turns the soil over, loosening it so that air and water can enter. However, this exposes the soil to erosion by both wind and water. In the **zero tillage** method, a seed drill simply plants the seeds under the remains of the old crop—no ploughing is done. Since old plants are not removed from the land, their roots continue to bind the soil so that less soil is lost to wind and water erosion. Also, since the soil is covered, less soil water evaporates.

A modern seed drill.

This simplified diagram shows how a seed drill works:
1. The first disc opens a narrow groove in the soil.
2. The next disc adds fertilizer to the groove.
3. The next disc opens a groove, about 5 cm from the first groove, for the seeds.
4. The planting disc adds the seeds to the groove.
5. The press wheel then presses the soil around the seeds.

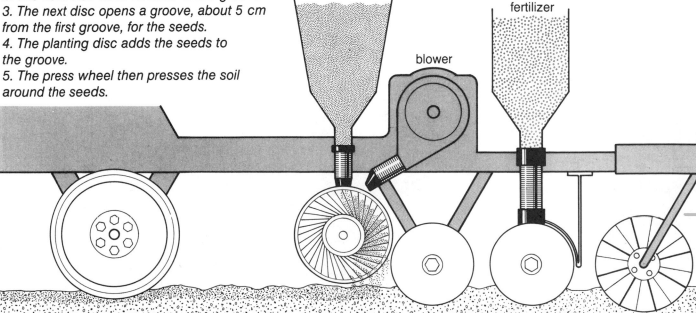

press wheel   planting disc   seed groove opener   fertilizer disc   first disc

seeds   blower   fertilizer

Irrigation systems are used to grow more food crops.

In some areas that have insufficient rainfall, farmland is **irrigated** (supplied with water by artificial means). Some irrigation systems are stationary, like interconnected lawn sprinklers; other systems travel across fields, spraying water in all directions.

As they grow, plants remove nutrients from the soil. For example, a bushel of harvested corn contains about 0.5 kg of nitrogen. The soil from which it was harvested has lost that amount of nitrogen. To improve crop yield, fertilizers, especially inorganic ones, are added to the soil. Fertilizers have been used extensively throughout the world since about 1945.

In some places where soil is in short supply, another technology is being explored. **Hydroponics** is a technology in which plants are grown without soil. Instead, they are grown in water alone, or in a material such as sand, gravel, sawdust, or peat moss. Nutrients are carefully measured, added to water, and then, in dissolved form, are made available to the plant's roots.

This hydroponic garden is growing underground in a mine in Sudbury, Ontario.

These petunias have been grown hydroponically.

Growing Plants Without Soil (A Class Project)

Problem
How can plants be grown hydroponically (without soil)?

Materials
seeds of fast-growing plants, such as lettuce
clean sand, vermiculite, or perlite
nutrients prepared for hydroponic solutions
aquarium air pump
aquarium heater
large container, such as a plastic bucket
plastic window screen
peat moss
small pots
string

Procedure
Set up your hydroponic garden as shown in the illustration.

Finding Out
1. Keep accurate records of the garden's growth. Your class's growth records should include notes on:
(a) the steps followed in making the garden;
(b) what the nutrient solution contains;
(c) the types of plants to be grown;
(d) the measurements of plant growth;
(e) which kinds of plants grew best; and
(f) any problems encountered.
2. Did some gardens produce more growth than others? If so, suggest a reason or reasons why.

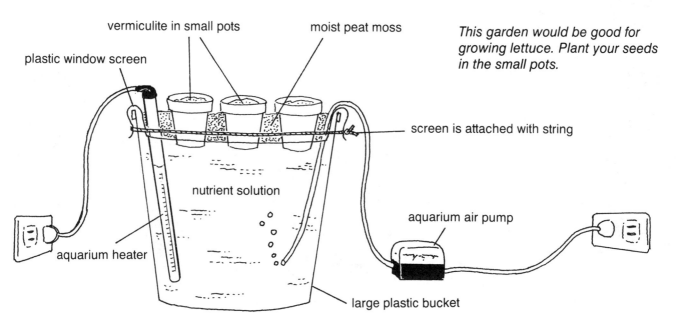

This garden would be good for growing lettuce. Plant your seeds in the small pots.

plastic window screen
vermiculite in small pots
moist peat moss
screen is attached with string
nutrient solution
aquarium heater
aquarium air pump
large plastic bucket

Using Technology Appropriately

While technologies have solved some problems in plant growth, they have also created new ones. For example, use of fertilizer to increase crop yield has had an unexpected side effect. Just as fertilizer increases growth of crops, it also increases algal growth in waterways. Fertilizer dissolved in rain and irrigation water can run from fields to rivers and lakes, often causing so much algal growth in these waters that many forms of life cannot survive in them.

Also, irrigating soils increases the amount of salts in the soil, sometimes so much as to be harmful to plant growth. This occurs because irrigation water usually contains small amounts of salts dissolved from minerals in the Earth. When the irrigation water evaporates from the soil or from the surfaces of plant parts, what is left? The solutes — in this case, the salts dissolved in the water. Eventually, in some places, you can even see salt crystals on the surface of the soil. As the salt accumulates, the soil becomes too salty to support the growth of many types of plants.

Technologies such as contour farming and strip farming have been found to be impractical in some areas, and technologies such as hydroponic gardening are not practical in others. Hydroponics is often a very expensive technology since it requires the addition of nutrients and, in many places, artificial lighting.

A disadvantage of zero tillage is that the soil sometimes retains too much water, and this method controls weeds less effectively compared with traditional ploughing.

As you can see, each technology must be used where it is appropriate. If overused or if used in the wrong places, a particular technology can cause problems. Scientists continue to look for ways to try to ensure that the Earth's ever-growing population receives the nourishment it needs by improving technologies, and by trying to ensure that they are used appropriately.

Saline (salty) soil cannot support the growth of many types of plants.

Checkpoint

1. In your notebook, match each definition in List A with the correct term in List B.

LIST A	LIST B
(a) The loss of soil by wind and water.	phosphorus
(b) An agricultural technology that uses a seed drill to plant seeds—no ploughing is done.	shelter belts
(c) Something plant roots need in soil, besides water and nutrients.	zero tillage
(d) A 10-20-5 fertilizer contains 20% of this nutrient.	air
(e) A technology in which rows of trees are planted around or on certain sides of fields to reduce erosion of soil by wind.	terracing
(f) The planting of crops on a series of "steps" to help prevent erosion of soil by water running down slopes.	erosion

2. (a) What are the three main components of soil?
(b) What is the role of each component?

3. (a) What are the three main nutrients in a bag of commercial fertilizer?
(b) What do the three numbers on a bag of fertilizer tell you?

4. (a) What type of fertilizer would you use to make a lawn a rich green colour?
(b) What type of fertilizer would you use if you wanted to help a young plant develop a healthy root system?

5. What could happen to a plant if you give it too much fertilizer? Explain your answer.

6. Raja had taken great care in growing several tomato plants, yet the results were very disappointing, as shown in the illustration. The plants had plenty of leaves, but some of the leaves were spotted with yellow. As well, the plants had very few flowers and even fewer tomatoes.
(a) What can you infer about the nutrients in the soil in which Raja planted the tomatoes?
(b) What nutrients would you advise Raja to add to the soil?

7. List some technologies used to increase the growth of crops, and describe one technology.

8. (a) What is zero tillage?
(b) What are some advantages of this technology?

9. (a) What is hydroponics?
(b) Why might hydroponics be useful in some parts of Canada?

Transporting the Essentials

A plant's roots, as you have seen, are efficient absorbers of water and nutrients from the soil. Transporting these materials up to the leaves for photosynthesis, as well as transporting food back down from the leaves after it has been produced, are other tasks to be performed. Just how does a plant transport materials from roots to leaves, and from leaves to all other plant parts? These "waterworks" of the plant are investigated in this Topic.

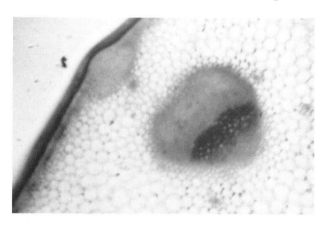

This micrograph is a highly magnified view of the cells making up stem tissues in a plant.

Think about the last time you ate a piece of celery. What were your immediate sensations as you bit into the celery?

- When you chew celery, thousands of cells called **parenchyma tissue** are crushed, producing the sound you hear. These are thin-walled, bubbly, living cells that store food in green plants.
- **Xylem tissue (vessels)** made up of thick-walled, dead cells transport water and nutrients from the roots to the leaves of the celery.
- **Phloem tissue** made up of small living cells transports food produced in the leaves up and down the stem, supplying cells with needed food.
- **Collenchyma tissue** made up of thick-walled, living cells strengthens the stems (stalks) of the celery.

These cells and tissues carry out the same functions in all plants.

Now use a microscope to observe more closely what it was you sensed when you last ate some celery.

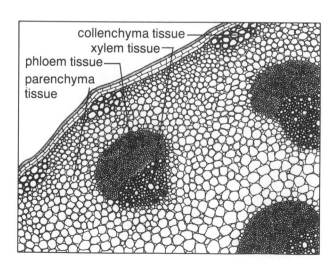

collenchyma tissue
xylem tissue
phloem tissue
parenchyma tissue

Activity 5-9

Examining Cells

Problem
What gives celery its crunch?

Materials
fresh celery placed in red food
   colouring overnight
single-edged razor blade
glass microscope slide
cover slip
microscope

Procedure
1. Take a piece of celery that has been placed in food colouring overnight. Use a razor blade to cut as thin a section of celery as possible across the celery stalk.

CAUTION: A razor blade is extremely sharp. Be very careful when you cut the thin section of celery! As an extra precaution, cover the non-cutting edge of the razor blade with masking tape.

2. Place your section in a drop of water on a microscope slide. Then add a cover slip to the slide, as shown in the diagram below.
3. Look at the section under a microscope at low power. What do you think the red "dots" indicate?

Finding Out
1. In your notebook, draw a diagram of what you see under the microscope. Label your diagram of the magnified celery stalk (refer to the illustration).
2. Write down the functions of each of the structures you have labelled.

celery

taped edge

razor blade

drop of water

cover slip
thin section

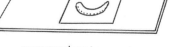

prepared wet mount

The Plant's Transport System

The transport system within a plant extends from the roots, up through the stems to the leaves, flowers, and fruit. This system forms a network of pipelike structures made up of xylem and phloem tissue. These structures bring to every cell the water and nutrients each of them needs to live and to grow.

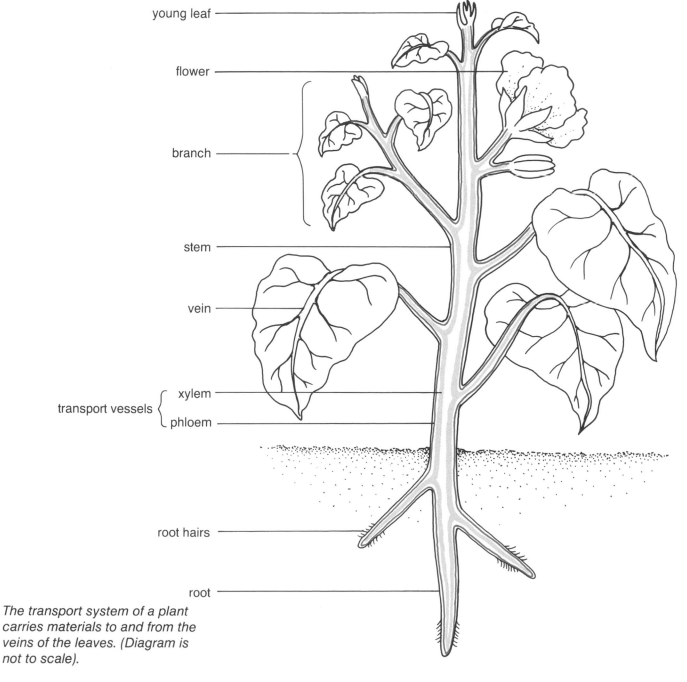

young leaf

flower

branch

stem

vein

transport vessels { xylem
phloem

root hairs

root

The transport system of a plant carries materials to and from the veins of the leaves. (Diagram is not to scale).

Transpiration

One important process that helps move water and its dissolved nutrients up through the xylem is transpiration. **Transpiration** is the evaporation of water from cells at the surface of plant parts (for example, leaves). You can observe that water is lost through transpiration by placing a plastic bag over a plant, as shown in the photograph.

Try the next Activity at home or in your classroom to determine the effect of leaves, if any, on the transport of water up the plant.

What evidence suggests that a plant gives off water by transpiration?

Activity 5-10

Transpiration: Pulling Water through the Plant

Problem

What role do leaves play in pulling water up through a plant?

Materials

2 leafy stalks of celery
red food colouring
2 beakers (each 400 mL)
   or glass jars
single-edged razor blade

Procedure

1. Place one leafy stalk of celery in a beaker or jar with a little water containing red food colouring.
2. Remove the leaves from a second stalk of celery; place this stalk in a beaker containing water and food colouring as well.
3. Place both stalks in a sunny place or under a bright light.
4. After approximately 3 h, cut a number of cross sections to see how far the food colouring rose in each stalk.

Finding Out

1. How far did the food colouring rise in each stalk?
2. What can you infer from this experiment about the effect of leaves on the movement of liquid through the transport system of a plant?

celery stalk with leaves

celery stalk without leaves

food colouring in water

During the growing season, a forest of maple trees gives off enough water by transpiration to cover the ground to a depth of 70 cm (if the water were to lie on the ground without soaking in or evaporating).

GIMME JUST A LITTLE TRANSPIRATION, BABY, SO I DON'T DRY OUT!

Forces that Move Water through a Plant

Leaves lose water vapour to the surrounding air by the opening of tiny holes, called **stomata** (singular: **stoma**), in the leaves. As this water vapour escapes during transpiration, the air spaces within the leaf become drier, permitting more water to evaporate from the cells in the interior of the leaf. These cells now have less water than their neighbouring cells. By osmosis, water will move from cell to cell, all the way to the nearest xylem vessel. The pulling force produced by transpiration pulls water up the xylem vessel from the roots, all the way to the leaves where it is lost through transpiration.

Osmosis in the root hairs also helps to keep water moving upward. When a tree is cut down in the spring, water flows out of the cut surface of the trunk because of this force produced in the roots. These and other forces keep the water moving upward.

More About Stomata

A land-living plant needs to lose water by transpiration to move water up the xylem from the soil to the leaf. However, if too much water is lost, the plant will die. How do plants control water loss? Some species have leaves that are covered with a waxy material, reducing the loss of water.

Plants also control the amount of water lost by means of the stomata, in the leaves, stems, flowers, and fruit. Stomata can open during transpiration and close at other times to reduce water loss. In Activity 5–11, you will investigate this important plant feature—the stomata.

The cactus plant has thin, spiny leaves covered with a waxy material that helps reduce transpiration, thus enabling the plant to live in hot, dry desert regions.

Looking at Stomata

Problem

What do stomata look like?
NOTE: If you have not studied Skillbuilder Five, *Working with a Microscope*, on page 342, you should do so now, before beginning this Activity.

Materials

leaf of a house plant or crisp
    lettuce
methylene blue stain
microscope
glass microscope slide
forceps
cover slip
dropper

Procedure

1. Fold a leaf or a piece of crisp lettuce. Look for a thin, clear layer ("skin") on the inside curved surface where the leaf was folded.

2. *Pull* (don't scrape!) the thin transparent layer gently away with your fingernails. (A small piece will do.)
3. Place a drop of water on a microscope slide. With forceps, place the transparent layer of the leaf in the water.
4. Use a dropper to add a drop of methylene blue stain to the water, and cover the slide with the cover slip.
5. Focus the leaf under the lowest power of the microscope. Then carefully switch the magnification to 100X, observing the objective lens from the side to be sure it clears the cover slip.
6. Compare the stomata with the illustrations shown here. Within the cells surrounding the stomata, called **guard cells**, you will see small green

dots called **chloroplasts**. Notice that the other cells at the leaf's surface lack chloroplasts. Photosynthesis occurs in the chloroplasts.

Finding Out

1. In your notebook, make a drawing of a stoma. Label each of the following: the two bean-shaped structures, or "guard cells;" the green dots in the guard cells, or "chloroplasts;" and the opening between the two guard cells, or "stoma."
2. Make a drawing of a cell around the stoma. Label the thick wall around the cell, "cell wall," and label the spherical structure in the cell, "nucleus." The nucleus controls the chemical processes of the cell.

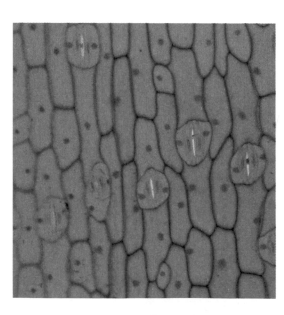

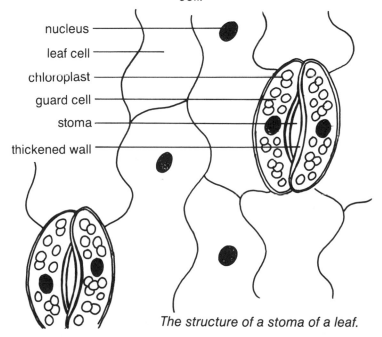

nucleus
leaf cell
chloroplast
guard cell
stoma
thickened wall

The structure of a stoma of a leaf.

Leaves—Using the Sun's Energy

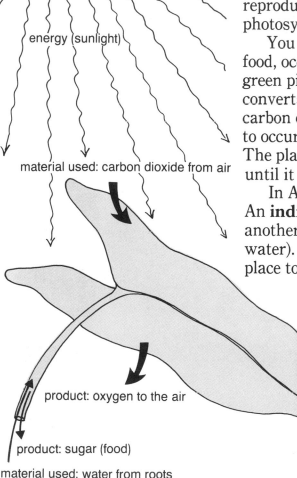

energy (sunlight)

material used: carbon dioxide from air

product: oxygen to the air

product: sugar (food)

material used: water from roots

- Water and nutrients move up the xylem to the leaf.

- Carbon dioxide enters the leaf through the stomata.

- Chloroplasts in the leaf use the water, the carbon dioxide, and the energy of the Sun to produce food and oxygen.

- The food produced is used by the plant to grow and reproduce. The oxygen produced is used by organisms in respiration.

You have investigated how food, nutrients, and water are transported up and down through plant parts, ensuring that the entire plant is well supplied. In this Topic, you will look closely at leaves, the main plant structure in which the food is produced. Energy for all plant processes—growth, reproduction, etc.—is stored in the food produced by photosynthesis.

You have learned that photosynthesis, the production of food, occurs in green plants, in the presence of light. The green pigment, chlorophyll, captures the Sun's energy and converts it into chemical energy stored in food. Water and carbon dioxide are the substances needed for photosynthesis to occur. The food first produced by the plant is a sugar. The plant then converts the sugar into starch for storage until it is needed for growth.

In Activity 5-12 on the next page, an indicator is used. An **indicator** is a substance that can detect the presence of another substance (for example, oxygen, carbon dioxide, or water). When an indicator is used, a visible change takes place to indicate the presence of a specific substance.

Is light needed for starch to be produced in a leaf? To test for the presence of starch, the indicator, iodine, is used. As you observed in Unit Three, starch and iodine combine to produce an inky, blue-black colour. No other substance causes iodine to change colour in this way. If the iodine becomes blue-black, then starch must be present.

Light and Photosynthesis: Demonstration

Problem

Is light necessary for starch production in photosynthesis?

Materials

healthy plant such as a geranium (taken from a dark cupboard where it has been kept for about 48 h)
mask (cardboard or aluminum foil)
paper clips
3 beakers
test tube
test tube holder or clamp
iodine solution
ethanol
hot plate
forceps
dropper
watch glass or petri dish

Procedure

1. Attach a mask to part of a leaf of the plant, as shown.
2. Place the plant in sunlight or under artificial light until your next class period.

> **CAUTION:** Iodine is a corrosive substance. Do not touch it or spill it. Ethanol is flammable, poisonous, and volatile. There must be no open flames in the classroom!

3. (a) In your notebook, describe the appearance of the leaf with the mask attached.
   (b) Remove the mask. Describe the appearance of the leaf beneath the mask.
4. Your teacher will use the procedure shown to test the leaf for starch (see the diagrams below).
5. Describe the leaf:
   (a) before the iodine was applied; and
   (b) after the iodine soaked in.

(a) Remove the chlorophyll from a leaf, using a water bath.

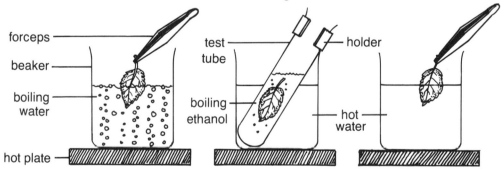

1. Dip leaf in boiling water.   2. Extract chlorophyll in boiling ethanol.   3. Dip leaf in hot water.

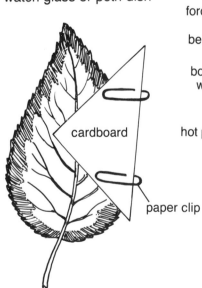

cardboard

paper clip

A part of a leaf is masked to keep out light.

(b) Use a gentle stream of water to spread the leaf flat for the iodine test.

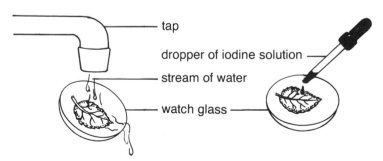

tap

dropper of iodine solution

stream of water

watch glass

Steps in testing a leaf for starch.

Cellular Respiration

You have learned that photosynthesis produces food in the green cells of plants and algae, *storing* chemical energy. A basic life process that occurs in *all* living things, both plants and animals, is called **cellular respiration**. This process *releases* the stored energy of food for growth, repair, and reproduction. The overall word equation for cellular respiration is:

food + oxygen $\longrightarrow$ carbon dioxide + water

As you can see, the products of this process are the raw materials for photosynthesis. The products of photosynthesis, likewise, are the raw materials for respiration. The most important fact to remember is that each process produces the materials that are needed for the other.

Gas Exchange in Plants

During the day, both photosynthesis and cellular respiration occur in plants. On a bright, sunny day, photosynthesis occurs much faster than cellular respiration, producing an excess of both food and oxygen. At night, only cellular respiration occurs, and some of the food produced during the day is used by the plant while it is in darkness. The diagram summarizes the two processes of photosynthesis and cellular respiration.

Finding Out

1. Draw sketches of the leaf:
   (a) with the mask attached;
   (b) after the mask was removed; and
   (c) after the starch test.
   Label the areas of the leaf that became blue-black as well as those areas that did not change colour.
2. Which areas of the leaf contain starch?
3. Why was it important to remove the chlorophyll from the leaf by placing it in hot ethanol?
4. In which areas did photosynthesis take place?
5. In which areas did photosynthesis not take place?
6. From this experiment, what can you infer is necessary for photosynthesis?
7. Why do you think the plant you used had been kept in a dark place for a period of time?

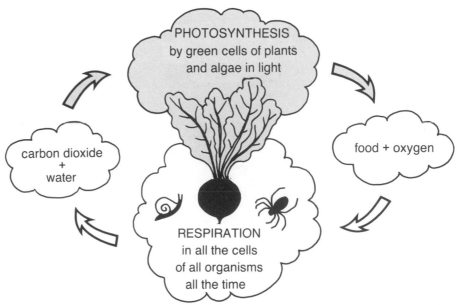

The cyclic interrelationship between photosynthesis and cellular respiration.

Plant Needs—A Summary

Plants must have adequate water in order for the stomata to stay open. This condition is necessary so that the plant can take in carbon dioxide for photosynthesis. When you see that plants are wilting, you know that they need water. Without water, they will not be photosynthesizing, even if the sun is shining. To encourage their growth, plants must have adequate water, sunlight, carbon dioxide, and nutrients.

Fluorescent lights in a greenhouse burn at night to increase the "day length" for growing plants.

This carbon dioxide generator burns natural gas to increase the amount of carbon dioxide in a greenhouse.

Checkpoint

1. In your notebook, write the term corresponding to each definition below. The highlighted letters will spell out something that is essential to the survival of green plants— the spaces between guard cells that open and close to control the amount of water lost or retained by plant structures, especially leaves.

(a) ■■■■■■□
(b) ■■■□■■■■■■■■
(c) ■■■□■■
(d) ■■■■□
(e) ■■■■■■□■■■■
(f) ■■■■■■■■■■□■
(g) ■■■■■■■□■■■■

(a) Pipelike structures made up of xylem cells.
(b) The use of the Sun's energy by green plants to produce food.
(c) Small, living cells that transport food produced in leaves up and down the stem of a plant, supplying all cells of the plant with food.
(d) Dead cells making up vessels in a plant, which transport water and minerals from roots to leaves.

(e) Carbon dioxide is produced by this process that occurs in plant cells, as well as in cells of other organisms.
(f) The plant cell structures containing chlorophyll, in which photosynthesis occurs.
(g) The process by which water is lost from plant structures, primarily the leaves.

2. What energy conversion takes place in photosynthesis? (Hint: Recall from Unit Two the kinds of energy conversions that can occur.)
3. What are the products of cellular respiration?
4. What energy conversion occurs in cellular respiration?
5. Describe the test for starch.
6. How could you find out if a plant is producing food?
7. (a) Why does a plant need carbon dioxide in order to grow?
(b) How does a plant produce oxygen?
(c) How would you find out if a potato is made up of starch?
(d) Why will a plant growing in the shade lose less water than one growing in sunlight?

8. Pruning involves cutting away overgrown branches from a tree or plant. How would pruning affect the rise of water in a tree trunk or plant stem?
9. (a) Label the events that occur at 1, 2, and 3 in order for transpiration to occur.
(b) Make your own drawing with labels and arrows to show where materials are taken in and released in order for photosynthesis to occur.

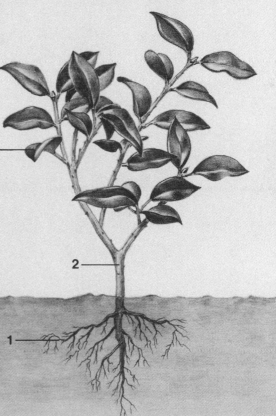

Science and Technology in Society
The Healing Powers of Plants

During the long, cold winter of 1534, the French explorer Jacques Cartier and his crew struggled to survive in what Europeans at that time called New France—now part of Canada. Unprepared for the harshness of winter in the New World, the poorly nourished explorers became victims of scurvy, an exhausting disease that causes skin eruptions, pain in the arms and legs, and extreme tenderness in the gums. Twenty-five of the 110 men camped on the frozen banks of the St. Lawrence River perished before a band of Iroquois Indians showed them a cure. The remedy consisted of a tea rich in ascorbic acid (vitamin C) made from the bark and needles of the white cedar tree.

Most people probably think of food or landscaping as the most obvious uses for plants, but plants also supply us with many important medicinal drugs. Some of these drugs have been used for centuries. In many societies, healers are respected for their practical knowledge of the hundreds of plants used to treat illnesses. If you go into a traditional Chinese drugstore, for example, you will find rows of jars filled with dried leaves and roots used to prepare medications. One such root comes from an herb called ginseng, used as a tonic in the Far East.

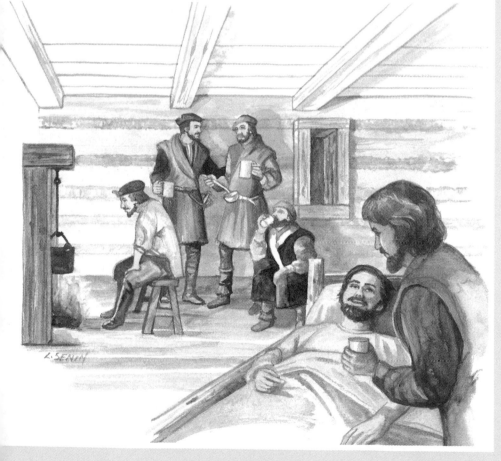

Jacques Cartier and his crew suffered from scurvy, a disease caused by a lack of vitamin C.

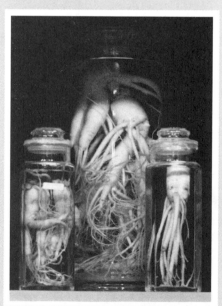

Ginseng is a common item in traditional Chinese drugstores.

Although native to North America as well as to China, the ginseng root is not used very much as a medicine by North Americans. However, several extremely important modern drugs were discovered when scientists began to study some of the plants used in traditional medicines.

For example, in Europe, the dried leaves of the foxglove plant have been used since 1775 to treat angina, a serious heart disease once known as "dropsy." Today, doctors use an extract of the foxglove—digitalis—to stimulate heart muscle contraction in patients with cardiac disorders.

When 17th-century European explorers reached South America, they encountered inhabitants who used the bark of an evergreen tree to prevent malaria, a mosquito-borne tropical disease that causes high fevers. The bark of the cinchona tree yields a bitter granular substance, known as quinine, that is still used in antimalarial pills.

If you suffered from a headache or a fever recently, the bark of another tree may have helped you feel better. Although now synthesized—that is, manufactured from other chemicals—aspirin was originally prepared from an acid in the bark of the willow tree. Its present synthesis is possible because of our knowledge of the chemical structure of the natural substance. The bark's medicinal powers were known to many North American Indian societies, who chewed the willow bark to relieve pain.

The plants mentioned here are not isolated examples. The World Health Organization has listed more than 20 000 species of plants that have some medicinal value.

Plants are such an important source of medicines that more than one-quarter of the prescription drugs in your local pharmacy probably contain chemicals that are either extracted from plants or that imitate plant substances by synthesis.

Think About It

1. Research some plants that were used as medicines by native people in your area.
2. Look up "curare" in a reference book such as an encyclopedia. Where does it come from and what is it used for?
3. List some plant products containing vitamin C that you would find in a grocery store.

A substance extracted from the foxglove plant is used to treat heart disease.

The bark of the black willow tree contains a substance that relieves pain.

Plant Reproduction

Up until now, you've been studying the structures and processes within a single plant. Now let's look at how a plant produces more plants, in two different ways: by means of seeds produced in flowers (sexual reproduction); and by various vegetative methods (asexual reproduction). These are the two types of reproduction among living things.

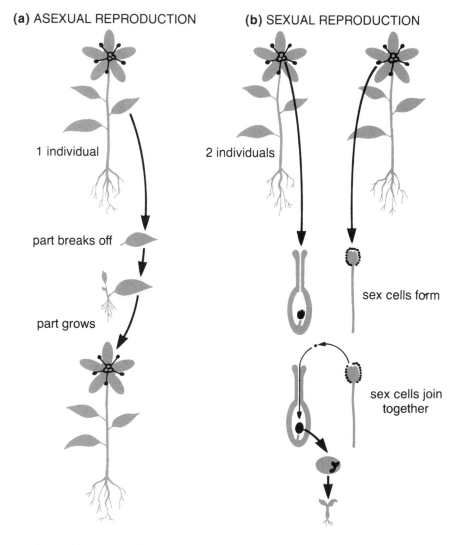

(a) ASEXUAL REPRODUCTION

1 individual

part breaks off

part grows

almost identical individual

(b) SEXUAL REPRODUCTION

2 individuals

sex cells form

sex cells join together

new individual

Sexual Reproduction

As shown on page 254, in **sexual reproduction**, a new individual is produced by the combining of material from two parents. In plants, as in animals, a **sperm** moves towards an **egg**. **Fertilization** occurs when the egg and sperm nuclei (the central part of each cell) unite to start the development of the offspring. By repeated cell division, the fertilized egg grows from a single cell into a many-celled **embryo** (a tiny new plant before it develops into a seedling).

The variation resulting from the union of the nuclei from two different parents is important. New combinations of characteristics occur in the offspring. From this rich variation, scientists, farmers, and gardeners can select the offspring with the most suitable characteristics to survive and reproduce.

The flower is the structure that makes sexual reproduction in flowering plants possible. (Other plants also reproduce sexually, but do not have flowers. For example, a pine tree produces seeds within cones.) Although grasses and trees such as oaks and birches may not appear to produce flowers, they do. A wide variety exists in flower appearance, but the function of the flower is the same. Notice the typical parts of the flower and their functions, listed below.

- The **stamen** contains the male part of the flower. It produces pollen, a yellow, powdery substance. Pollen is produced in the top of the stamen, in a structure called the **anther**.
- The **pistil** contains the female part of the flower. The top of the pistil is called the **stigma**. It produces a sugar that is used by the pollen to grow a tube. The **pollen tube** delivers the sperm down to the **ovary**. This is the enlarged part of the pistil where the female sex cells (eggs) are produced. The eggs are fertilized by the sperm from the pollen tube. The transfer of the pollen from the anther to the stigma is called **pollination**.
- The **petals** of the flower attract insects that carry the pollen from one plant to another. Some plants, like grass, have no petals and the pollen is carried by the wind.

In Activity 5–13, you will look closely at a flower to study its parts.

The parts of the flower.

Flower Structure and Function

Problem

- What are the reproductive parts of a flower?
- How does fertilization occur in flowering plants?

Materials

simple flower
forceps
eye dropper
microscope slide
microscope
sugar solution
stirring rod
cover slip
hand lens
single-edged razor blade

Procedure

1. The diagram shown here is a typical flower. The flower that you use may not be exactly like this.
2. Use a hand lens to examine your flower. Using forceps, as needed, carefully take the flower apart and set the parts on a page of your notebook.
3. Use the diagram to help you identify the parts of your flower. In your notebook, draw a diagram of each part of your flower. Label each part and its function.

4. Examine the anther with a hand lens. Add a drop of sugar solution to a microscope slide. The sugar solution will imitate the sugary surface of the stigma. (The pollen tube uses the sugar to produce energy for growth.) Place a yellow anther in the drop of solution and stir it around with a stirring rod.
5. Remove the anther and add a cover slip over the drop of solution. Examine the pollen under a microscope. Draw a diagram of what you see at first. Every 5 min during your class period, examine the slide to note any changes. Draw a diagram of any changes that occur.
6. Use the razor blade to cut open the ovary of the flower.

7. Draw a diagram of what you see. If the ovary is mature, you may observe a number of chambers inside it. These chambers contain the seeds that are forming. Label your diagram to show the chambers and the seeds.

Finding Out

1. (a) Is the ovary divided into parts? If so, how many?
   (b) When the ovary matures, forming a fruit, how do you think it will look? Draw a diagram of a fruit that could be formed from this ovary.
2. Each pollen grain develops a pollen tube containing the sperm. The pollen tube grows downward to the ovary. State the purpose of this growth.

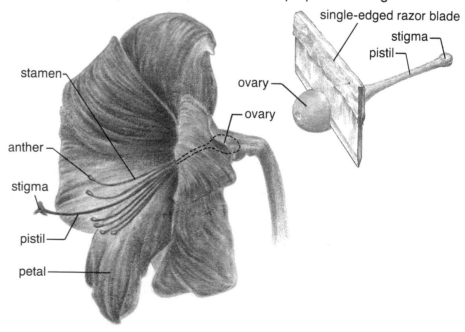

A typical flower.

Germination

Seeds are the product of fertilization in flowers. Each small seed "package" consists of three parts:

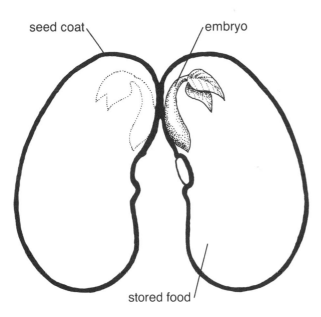

seed coat

embryo

stored food

The halves of a bean seed, showing the parts (not to scale).

1. The **embryo**, a tiny new plant, features a new combination of characteristics, different from any that have existed before. The embryo exists in a resting stage, called **dormancy**, in which its life processes have slowed down. Cellular respiration proceeds so slowly that the embryo may survive for many years in this state.
2. The **food reserve** consists of concentrated, dried materials such as proteins, starch, and oils. When water reactivates this food supply, the embryo germinates and the seedling has a source of energy that will supply its needs as it grows into a self-sustaining plant. This concentrated food reserve makes seeds attractive as a food source for other organisms, including humans.
3. The **seed coats** are two tough layers that protect the seed until suitable conditions for germination occur.

Different kinds of seeds require different conditions in order to germinate. These conditions include temperature, water, and light. For example, some seeds will not germinate unless they have undergone cold conditions, such as freezing—a condition that might kill other kinds of seeds. The seeds of some pines will not germinate unless the heat of a forest fire releases them from their cones.

How do we know before we plant it that a particular seed is **viable** (capable of growth)? Since seeds have different characteristics, some seeds may be more vigorous than others. Some seeds might carry fungus that will kill them. Farmers, foresters, and greenhouse operators have to know in advance how many of the seeds that they plant will germinate. To determine the percentage of seeds that will germinate, nurseries conduct a germination study.

Suppose a nursery has a choice of three different brands of radish seeds to be sold. Is each brand of seeds equally viable? In the next Activity, you will carry out an experiment to determine the viability of radish seeds.

Probing

Find out how the seeds of a corn plant differ from the bean seed shown above. As well, find out how the seeds of cone-producing plants differ from those of flowering plants.

Determining Seed Viability

Problem

What percentage of three brands of radish seeds will germinate?

Materials

3 beakers containing 3 different
   brands of radish seeds in water
3 shoe boxes
paper towels
plastic wrap
elastic bands or string
masking tape

Procedure

1. Make three germination boxes for the entire class to use by lining three shoe boxes with plastic wrap. (If your class is large, you might need six boxes—two boxes for each brand of radish seeds.) Label each box with the name of a different brand of seeds.
2. Count out 20 seeds of one brand that have been soaked in a beaker of water overnight.

Table 5-1

BRAND OF RADISH SEEDS	NUMBER OF SEEDS THAT GERMINATED	NUMBER OF SEEDS USED	PERCENTAGE OF SEEDS THAT GERMINATED
1			
2			
3			

3. Place your seeds on four moist (but not soaking wet) paper towels and roll the towels up into a tube. Secure the tube with an elastic band or string. Write the initials of your group members on a piece of masking tape. Hold it in place with the elastic band or string.
4. Carefully place the paper-towel tube on its side in the appropriate germination box.
5. Repeat Steps 2 to 4 for the other two seed brands.
6. In three or four days, count and record the number of seeds that have germinated in your paper-towel tube.

Finding Out

1. Copy Table 5-1 into your notebook. Fill in the middle two columns.
2. Calculate the percentage of seeds that germinated. For example:

$$\frac{15 \text{ seeds germinated}}{20 \text{ seeds used}} \times 100 = 75\%$$

3. Compare the germination percentage of each brand of seeds with that of the other two brands.
4. Which brand of seeds seems to be most viable?

Finding Out More

5. (a) Which brand of seeds would you recommend that people buy?
(b) What other information do you need in order to make your decision, if any?

Extension

6. What are the ideal conditions for the germination of a particular type of seed? Design an experiment to test your predictions.

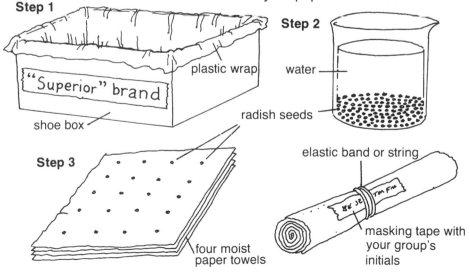

Step 1
"Superior" brand
plastic wrap
shoe box

Step 2
water
radish seeds

Step 3
four moist paper towels
elastic band or string
masking tape with your group's initials

Asexual Reproduction

Recall your use of cuttings to form new plants. This is an example of vegetative reproduction (a type of **asexual reproduction**). In this type of reproduction, the new plant is almost identical to the original plant. Greenhouses use stem cuttings and leaf cuttings to produce many plants with the same characteristics considered to be desirable.

Grafting is another use of vegetative reproduction. A shoot or bud from one tree is inserted (grafted) into another in such a way that it will grow there. Cuttings from a desired crop, such as Golden Delicious apples, are grafted onto the trunk of a tree that has a hardier root and also several years' head start in growth. You can buy an apple tree to which five or six varieties of apple fruit have been grafted so that you can pick fruit both early and late in the season. As another example, garden varieties of roses are also grafted onto hardier, wild rose roots.

Plants produced using bulbs and tubers are other examples of vegetative reproduction. **Bulbs** are short underground stems surrounded by many scales (modified leaves). Tulips and daffodils are garden plants usually started from bulbs. **Tubers** are swollen underground stems. Potatoes are an example of tubers.

Cloning is a way of producing organisms by asexual reproduction in the laboratory. In **cloning**, a single cell is removed from an organism, placed in a solution, and allowed to multiply. From a single cell, a whole new organism can be produced. For example, a new carrot plant can be produced from one root cell. Some important questions you may have about cloning are: exactly how is it done, what is the value in doing it, and on what species should it be permitted? You may be interested in investigating more about cloning as a science project.

Spy apple stem inserted into cut area on Spartan apple branch

Spartan apple branch cut back

grafting process complete

seal to prevent infection

Grafting a stem from a Spy apple onto a stem of a Spartan tree.

Probing

1. An onion bulb readily forms roots. Support one with toothpicks on a glass filled with water. What do you observe?
2. A potato is an example of a tuber, a type of underground stem. Plant the "eye" of a potato, along with a little of the starchy tissue, in a pot of soil and watch it grow.

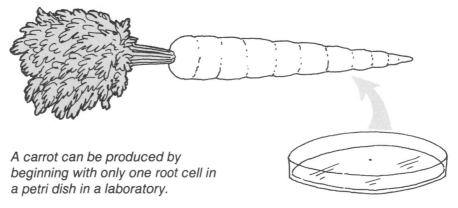

A carrot can be produced by beginning with only one root cell in a petri dish in a laboratory.

Troubleshooting Plant Problems

Finding out what is wrong with a plant would be easy if it could just tell you!

Plants *do* tell you what they need by developing visible signs called **symptoms**, such as yellow spots on leaves, when they are getting too much or too little of something they need, or if something is damaging them. Symptoms are clues that tell you what is wrong with the plant.

Some plant problems are due to too much or too little light or water, an excess of nutrients, or too fcw nutrients. Other problems are due to pests. Generally, any organism that humans consider to be undesirable is called a **pest**.

As you will see in Activity 5–15, there is often more than one way to get rid of a pest. **Pesticides**, chemicals developed to kill pests, may be used, as well as alternative methods. Pesticides are sometimes specific to a kind of organism. For example, **insecticides** are pesticides used to decrease the number of insect pests; **herbicides** are used to eliminate bothersome plants; and **fungicides** may be used against fungi such as rusts. Today, people are trying to use methods other than pesticides whenever possible because of problems with pesticide use. (You will study some of these problems in Unit Six and in future courses.)

A healthy head of cabbage, and one suffering from the feeding of cabbage butterfly larvae.

You're the Plant Doctor! (Diagnosing and Treating Sick Plants)

Problem

What are some symptoms of unhealthy plants, and how can you help them recover?

Procedure

1. Obtain several unhealthy-looking plants for examination.
2. In your notebook, prepare a table to record information about each of the plants you examine. Make columns headed by: "Name of Plant," "Symptom," "Diagnosis," and "Recommended Treatment."
3. Make a list of characteristics that you consider to give a plant a healthy appearance. Compare several healthy and unhealthy plants.
4. Read the descriptions of plant symptoms printed in the following diagnosis chart for the plants as you examine them.
5. In your table, record each unhealthy plant's symptoms, and your decision about needed treatment. Then answer the Finding Out questions on page 266.

CAUTION: Your task is to diagnose and *recommend* treatment. Do not carry out any treatment unless instructed to do so by your teacher.

In this Topic, you will learn how to interpret some symptoms of unhealthy plants. You will use these symptoms to diagnose some plant problems and determine how to give plants the care that they need. In this Activity, you will need to know how to use the diagnosis chart on pages 262 to 265. This chart includes symptoms of plant problems, ways to diagnose the problems, and some possible ways to treat the problems.

As you observe unhealthy plants, use this chart to try to decide what their problems are; try also to decide how to help them become healthy. First, read each symptom. If it applies to the plant you are observing, go to "If yes" under the symptom description. Make the appropriate diagnosis, based on careful observation, and note the treatment or treatments you would select. Then go on to the next symptom. If the "yes" description does not match your plant's problem, proceed immediately to the next symptom.

In some cases, you will find that a symptom may have more than one possible cause. Then you'll decide which cause has more likely produced the symptom in the plant you are observing. As well, you may find that some diagnoses have several different "no" possibilities. Like so many problems, the best way to solve your plant problems is to start looking, and think about what you observe. Using the diagnosis chart, begin your task.

Diagnosis Chart: *Diseases and Pests of Indoor Plants*

SYMPTOM 1

Does the plant droop, with its leaves hanging over the edge of the pot like those shown here?

IF NO →

SYMPTOM 2

Are the leaves turning yellow?

IF   YES

IF   YES

This could be caused by unsuitable light.

OR

OR

DIAGNOSIS

The roots are dying of suffocation and root rot due to too much water. Touch the soil. If wet:

DIAGNOSIS

The plant wilted because the soil is too dry. Touch the soil. If dry:

DIAGNOSIS

Too much bright light damages the chlorophyll, so leaves turn yellow. If the plant has been in bright light:

DIAGNOSIS

Too little light does not allow the plant to make chlorophyll, so leaves turn yellow. If the plant has been in low light:

TREATMENT

Let the plant dry out; ensure that the roots have proper drainage and air; change the soil; and/or remove dead roots.

TREATMENT

Water on a regular schedule.

TREATMENT

Move the plant out of direct sunlight.

TREATMENT

Move the plant into a brighter location.

IF NO →

SYMPTOM 3

Are there coloured spots on the leaves?

IF YES

DIAGNOSIS

Coloured spots might indicate a viral disease.

↓

TREATMENT

Remove and burn infected leaves or the whole plant.

IF NO →

SYMPTOM 4

Are there furry patches on the leaves?

IF NO →

IF YES

This could be caused by an unsuitable amount of fertilizer.

OR

DIAGNOSIS

Too much fertilizer draws the water out of the roots by osmosis in the reverse direction.

↓

TREATMENT

Rinse the soil with plenty of fresh water, and allow it to drain well.

DIAGNOSIS

If plants have too little magnesium, manganese, and iron, required to make chlorophyll, their leaves will turn yellow.

↓

TREATMENT

Apply appropriate plant fertilizer as directed on the package.

DIAGNOSIS

Furry spots could be a fungus such as a white mildew.

↓

TREATMENT

Remove infected leaves; if the problem persists, dust the plant with a fungicide.

IF NO

SYMPTOM 5

Are there holes, like windows, that do not go all the way through the leaves?

IF NO

SYMPTOM 6

Are there bites out of the leaf, or big holes?

IF NO

IF ↓ **YES**

DIAGNOSIS

Caterpillars (larvae of moths or butterflies) eat big holes in leaves. Weevils (snout beetles) eat notches around the edges of leaves.

Weevil ×4

TREATMENT

Remove the insects.

Tent caterpillar (approx. actual size)

IF ↓ **YES**

DIAGNOSIS

These holes are caused by leaf miners—tiny larvae of moths, flies, or beetles—that live and eat in the middle of the leaf.

TREATMENT

Apply a systemic insecticide (one that will be carried to the insects through the plant's transport system) to the soil.

(a) Spider mites look like tiny red dots. They suck plant juices, damaging leaves and buds and sometimes killing the plant. They are not insects, but spiderlike creatures having eight legs. Look for a web of tiny lines on the leaf or bud.

DIAGNOSIS

Spider mites or their webs were found on the plant.

Spider mite ×40

TREATMENT

There is no simple treatment; a special chemical specific to mites is required.

(b) Bugs are insects that have piercing and sucking mouthparts. Many of them suck plant juices from leaves, buds, flowers, and fruits, both indoors and outside. Bugs, in the adult stage, have membranous wings that overlap at the tips and are thickened at the base.

DIAGNOSIS

Insects of this kind (called true bugs) were found on the plant.

True bug ×1.5

TREATMENT

Spray or dust with an insecticide, such as rotenone, or "fossil flower" (not really flowers but fossil diatoms, known also as diatomaceous earth).

SYMPTOM 7

Does the plant show none of the previous symptoms but just looks generally "sick," with drooping leaves, leaves falling off, etc.? Many kinds of tiny organisms attack house plants. Examine the plants closely to see if any of the organisms shown here are present.

IF YES

IF YES

(f) Scale insects cover themselves with a brown, gold, yellow, or white scale made of wax or shellac. They move very slowly, or not at all.

DIAGNOSIS

Scale insects were found on the plant.

Scale insect ×5

TREATMENT

The same as for mealybugs.

(c) Aphids ("plant lice") are tiny, soft-bodied insects (2 mm long) —green, white, or black—that cluster on tender young shoots or the undersides of leaves.

DIAGNOSIS

Aphids were found on the plant.

Aphid ×5

TREATMENT

Wash the plant gently with soapy water, or simply spray it with water to dislodge the aphids. Alternatively, treat it with an insecticide such as pyrethrum.

(d) Whiteflies are tiny insects (2 mm to 3 mm long) that fly up in a swarm when the plant is disturbed.

DIAGNOSIS

Whiteflies were found on the plant.

Whitefly ×7

TREATMENT

Without disturbing the whiteflies, gently place the plant into a plastic bag. Spray pyrethrum powder (or put a piece of "no pest" strip) into the bag, and tie it tightly. Leave it overnight. Repeat every 5 d until no whiteflies remain.

(e) Mealybugs are tiny insects (2 mm long) that cover themselves with a white, cottony, waxy coating. Inside this tent, they suck plant juices.

DIAGNOSIS

A cottony coating with mealybugs inside was found on the plant.

Mealybug ×9

TREATMENT

Since sprays and dusts do not get through their tent, mealybugs must be treated individually. Dip a cotton swab or paintbrush into ethanol and touch each insect with the alcohol to kill it. Repeat this action every few days, until there are no more mealybugs.

1. (a) Did other members of your class reach the same diagnosis and recommended treatment for each unhealthy plant?
   (b) If there were differences, explain how you came to different diagnoses or treatments in at least one case, after discussing the case with a classmate who had suggested a different diagnosis or treatment.
2. Why is only one symptom sometimes not enough to diagnose what is wrong with a plant?

Controlling Plant Pests

From Activity 5-15, you learned that some of the symptoms that a plant develops may be caused by too much or too little of something in the environment: light, water, or fertilizer. But often, a plant's illness is caused by another living thing: for example, an insect, a fungus, or a viral disease.

You have seen some examples of common pests you might encounter as you grow plants. Once you have learned how to identify each pest, you can consult reference books to learn about its life cycle. Knowing the life cycle of a pest helps you to determine its weakest stage of development, when it is easiest to get rid of the pest.

Alternatives to Pesticides

You may have noted in the treatment sections of the diagnosis chart that there are several ways to control pests. In some cases, pesticides are needed, but in many cases, other methods of control are just as effective.

As well as control methods in the chart, note that many common pests survive the winter in weeds. To control these pests, weeds can be dug up instead of using herbicides. We can also simply accept a certain amount of damage to plants caused by insects: it isn't necessary or possible to try to eliminate all insects. And remember that some insects are the "good guys"! They actually help us get rid of some of the pests. Look for and encourage ladybird beetles, which eat aphids and other small insects. They spend the winter in dead leaves. Watch for the big black ground beetles; they are called "caterpillar hunters" for good reason—they eat many destructive caterpillars. Encourage the praying mantis; it can eat a grasshopper every day. The assassin bug sucks the juices out of other bugs.

Besides these helpful insects, spiders and centipedes are predators that feed on pests. Gardeners and greenhouse operators in many parts of the world encourage toads to stay around: they consume large quantities of insects. And birds are relentless seekers of insects. Encourage all these predators as **biological controls** (using other living organisms to control the numbers of the pest species).

These organisms act as biological controls for pests: (a) assassin bug;
(b) mountain bluebird; (c) ladybird beetle; (d) toad; and (e) praying mantis.

Did You Know?

Here are two other examples of biological controls. A Saskatchewan farm family that grows strawberries has found that geese work as well as herbicides in controlling the weeds in their strawberry fields. The geese eat the weeds but do not seem to like the taste of strawberry plants. The result? No weeds and lots of strawberries!

In gardening, you can grow plants that repel insects near other plants that you want to protect. For example, garlic keeps insects away. Marigolds kill soil nematodes (roundworms) that might attack the roots of other plants. Marigolds also keep some beetles away from beans, and help tomatoes grow better. In parts of the world where hornworms are a problem, dill is often planted next to tomato plants to attract hornworms away from the tomato plants.

Working with Plant Life

Gail Rhynard is a garden designer. In an interview, she had this to say about her work.

As a child I loved being in the garden. Both my father and grandfather were keen gardeners. My favourite childhood photo is of me in a prairie garden, surrounded by flowers. I think wherever you grow up, you are influenced by the landscape around you. In my work as a garden designer, I use a lot of plants that were a part of my childhood in Manitoba.

Many of the plants you see in Canadian gardens have actually come from other countries. Most Canadian gardens consist of straight-lined beds of imported flowers surrounding a rectangular piece of lawn. These gardens can be beautiful, but I tend to do less formal landscaping. I try to design a garden that looks as though it grew there naturally. To achieve this, I use native plants, arranged in an informal way. Native plants are those that grew here originally before the country was settled, like trilliums, downy service berries, and black-eyed Susans.

There are many large trees where I live and work. In trying to find plants that grow well under all that shade, I often select native plants that might grow naturally in the understory of a Canadian deciduous forest. I look at the type of soil, drainage patterns, amount of sunlight, and moisture available at the garden site, and I work with these conditions in mind. The resulting woodland garden flourishes without much intervention. That means that fertilizers and pesticides can be used sparingly, if at all.

I've learned a lot about natural garden design by walking in the woods, looking to see where certain plants grow, and noting the specific conditions they need in order to thrive.

Since my education was in fine arts, I needed some extra training for my current profession. I took courses in horticulture, garden construction, and design from the landscape architecture department of a technical college.

Universities, colleges, and vocational centres across Canada offer a wide range of courses and programs that lead to many careers in this area. Some colleges offer apprenticeship programs where, for example, you might work three to four days a week as a landscape architect's assistant, and then go to school for one or two days.

If you are interested in this kind of work, try to get a summer job with a landscape architecture firm or with your community's parks department. You might discover, as I did, that this creative, vigorous outdoor work is exactly the career for you!

Checkpoint

1. In your notebook, match each item in List A with the appropriate description in List B.

LIST A	LIST B
(a) pistil	Chemicals used to decrease the number of insect pests.
(b) stamen	The part of a flower that produces pollen.
(c) germination	The use of other living organisms to control the numbers of a pest species.
(d) symptom	The beginning of a seed's growth.
(e) aphid	A common plant pest.
(f) biological controls	Chemicals developed to kill pests.
(g) pesticides	The part of a flower that produces seeds.
(h) herbicides	Chemicals used to eliminate bothersome plants.
(i) insecticides	Indicates an illness.

2. What is the purpose of a germination study?
3. Define:
   (a) asexual reproduction
   (b) sexual reproduction
   (c) fertilization
   (d) dormancy
4. Why is the variation that results from sexual reproduction important?
5. What would be some symptoms in a plant that was given too much water and one that was given too little water?
6. Diagnose what might be wrong with plants that have the following symptoms:
   (a) The plant droops, yet the soil feels wet.
   (b) There are furry white spots on the leaves.
   (c) The leaves are yellowish and are dropping off the plant.
   (d) A cluster of tiny green insects swarms on the young plant.
7. What are some alternatives to using pesticides?
8. (a) Examine these photographs and try to identify the pest that is attacking each plant.
   (b) Consult the diagnosis chart on pages 262 to 265 and, in your notebook, write a recommended treatment for each problem you identified in (a) above.

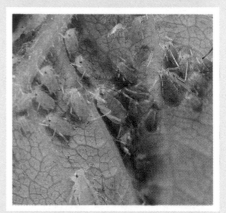

Focus

- Vegetative reproduction (a type of asexual reproduction) produces plants from stems or leaves, without seeds.
- Cuttings can be used to start new plants.
- Green plants have certain basic structures in common: leaves, stem, roots, and flowers.
- Managing plant growth requires a knowledge of the functions of each structure.
- In photosynthesis, a plant uses light energy from the Sun, carbon dioxide, and water to produce oxygen and food.
- Photosynthesis takes place in green bodies called chloroplasts in the cells of each leaf.
- In cellular respiration (in both plants and animals), oxygen and food are used to produce carbon dioxide, water, and energy for life and growth.
- Water moves by osmosis into the root hairs of a plant, climbs up the xylem tissue of the stem, and is evaporated from the leaves by transpiration.
- Knowing how transpiration occurs permits people to place plants in conditions that either reduce or increase transpiration, depending on the type of plant.

- Soil supplies a plant with water and nutrients necessary for growth. The most important nutrients are nitrogen, phosphorus, and potassium.
- Dissolved nutrients can be added to materials other than soil to produce plants hydroponically.
- People use their knowledge of the effect of each nutrient on plant growth to determine which nutrients a plant needs; for example, one to increase root growth, one to help produce more leaves, etc.
- Sexual reproduction by means of flowers produces seeds.
- Asexual reproduction results in very similar offspring from one organism. In sexual reproduction, different characteristics of two individuals combine to produce varied offspring.
- Symptoms of ill health in plants are evidence of unsuitable growth conditions or attack by pests.
- With a knowledge of all the major factors that are important in the proper functioning and growth of a plant, people can treat unhealthy plants to make them healthy, once again.

Backtrack

1. Describe two ways in which people use techology to help in managing plant growth.
2. List the materials that:
   (a) a plant needs to carry out photosynthesis;
   (b) are products of photosynthesis;
   (c) a plant needs to carry out cellular respiration; and
   (d) are products of cellular respiration.
3. Plants have a transport system that brings water and nutrients from the roots to the leaves and flowers. Explain how water:
   (a) moves into a root hair;
   (b) moves up a stem; and
   (c) is lost from leaves.
4. Describe the importance of transpiration to the "waterworks" of a plant.
5. Soil is important for plant growth.
   (a) What are the three main components of soil?
   (b) What is the function of each component?
6. What are some ways that technology can improve soil for plant growth?
7. Describe two ways of producing new plants without seeds.
8. A farmer, gardener, or greenhouse operator who manages plant growth must be on the alert for plant pests.
   (a) List three types of pests that damage plants.
   (b) Describe three different ways of getting rid of plant pests.

9. List the functions of the numbered flower structures shown in the illustration.

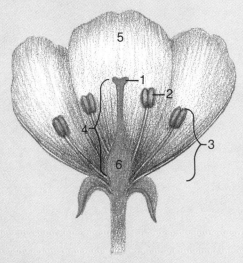

Synthesizer

10. Three plants of the same kind were given different numbers of hours of light per day for six weeks. Look at the results of this experiment shown in the illustration and answer the following questions.
(a) What can you infer about the amount of light needed to produce flowers in this species?
(b) Give a report to a florist, telling the florist the amount of light you would recommend for this species if customers want the fullest-looking plants with the most foliage, or leaves.
(c) A florist decides to place all the species of plants in her greenhouse in light for 12 h per day. State why you would or would not advise this action, giving your reasons.

11. Select three of the following and design an Activity that would allow you to show that each of the statements is true.
(a) To make a tall plant shorter, roots can be developed on the middle of the stem of a growing plant.
(b) Removing the top 1 cm of a plant will result in a short, bushy plant.

8 h of light per day

(c) Apple seeds will be more likely to germinate if they experience a cold period lasting a few months.
(d) Seeds collected in the spring will more likely germinate than those collected in the fall.
(e) Some kinds of seeds will germinate only if the seed travels through the digestive system of an animal. (A dilute acid can be used to imitate an animal's digestive system.)
(f) A dandelion flower does not need to be pollinated to produce seeds.
(g) To keep a plant flowering, you can cut off all the old flowers that are producing seeds.

12 h of light per day

18 h of light per day

Environmental Interactions

Have you ever kept living things in a small aquarium? All you need is some gravel, dechlorinated water, water plants, and a few fish and snails. If you place your aquarium by a window or under a lamp, you now have a miniature world. Although it looks peaceful, there is a lot going on in the aquarium. In this Unit, you will learn how the living things in an aquarium—and, in fact, living things on the entire planet—survive by interacting with different parts of their surroundings.

Living things do not just exist against a background landscape. They continually take in materials and energy from their environment and release waste materials. As organisms grow, build homes, eat, or are eaten, they channel energy and materials from one place to another. Like the different parts of a huge machine, organisms, materials, and energy interact together as a single system. No part of this system can be altered without affecting other parts. Think what might happen to the water or plants in your aquarium if you add or remove some fish.

Many human activities affect the environment and the interactions that occur within it. For example, destruction of forests and grasslands affects the organisms that live there. In this Unit, you will investigate many types of interactions that occur in the environment, and you will think about environmental problems and how to confront them. If we understand the interactions in the environment, we can take steps to keep the Earth a fit place for all organisms to live.

What Organisms Need to Survive

Imagine that your classroom is a large box and that everything outside it has disappeared. Nothing can get into or out of the room. How long could you survive? What would you need inside the room to help you to stay alive? You would probably put food, water, and air high on your list. These are basic things that most organisms need to survive. These basic things come from the **environment**, an organism's surroundings. In an enclosed classroom, you might quickly use up your supply of one or more of these things. In nature, however, the conditions needed for life are constantly maintained by the interactions occurring among different parts of the environment. The network of interactions that links the living things and the non-living things in an environment is called an **ecosystem**.

In what ways do people depend on the environment for their survival?

One way to study an ecosystem is to divide the environment into living and non-living parts. The living, or **biotic**, parts of the environment consist of plants, animals, and micro-organisms. We depend on living things for food and for some of the materials we use in making clothes and

The science of ecology is the study of the relationships among living things and their environment. The word "ecology" comes from two Greek words: "*oikos*" (home) and "*logos*" (to study). Why is "ecology" a good name for this science?

building shelters. Our survival also depends on the non-living, or **abiotic**, parts of the environment. The abiotic components of the environment include air, water, soil, sunlight, temperature, wind speed, and whether an area is hilly or flat.

You already know many of the ways in which different parts of the environment depend on, interact with, and influence one another. For example, the erosion of soil by rain is an interaction between two abiotic parts of the environment. A grasshopper eating a plant is an interaction between two biotic parts of the environment. The process of photosynthesis is an interaction between a biotic part of the environment (green plants) and abiotic components (sunlight, water, and carbon dioxide). The network of interactions of all the biotic and abiotic components of an area forms the area's ecosystem.

The buttercup shown in the illustration interacts with many different things: the type of soil, the slope of the land, the amount of rainfall and sunshine, the temperature and wind, the micro-organisms in the soil, and the animals and other plants in the field. A change in any part of its environment may determine whether the buttercup can continue to survive there. For example, if a tall plant (a biotic component) grows nearby, it may shade the buttercup from the Sun (an abiotic component).

In the following Activity, list some of the biotic and abiotic parts of the environment around your school, and consider some of the relationships that may exist among them.

The environment can be divided into biotic and abiotic parts.

ABIOTIC ENVIRONMENT

sunlight

air

water

soil

BIOTIC ENVIRONMENT

animals

plants

micro-organisms

What Is in Your Schoolyard?

Problem

What are the biotic and abiotic parts of your schoolyard environment?

Materials

notebook
pen or pencil
hand lens

Procedure

1. Before going outside, make a list of all the different types of living things you predict might be observed around your school building (for example, ants, dandelions, sparrows, pine trees, etc.).
2. Draw two columns in your notebook, with the headings "Biotic" and "Abiotic."

3. (a) Walk slowly around your schoolyard and list or draw all the kinds of organisms you can find there in 20 to 30 min. Record your observations in the first column.
(b) In the second column, record the abiotic factors that you observe. For example, are there any supplies of water? Is the soil clay-like or sandy? Is the ground level or hilly? Is it shady or sunny?
NOTE: Do not pick or break any plants or walk through flower beds. If you turn over a rock or log to see what is underneath, be sure to replace the rock or log carefully before you leave.

Finding Out

1. Look at your original list of organisms. Compare it with the list you made in the schoolyard. What living things did you find that you did not predict would be present?
2. What is the total number of different types of
(a) plants
(b) animals
(c) other living things found by you? found by your class?
3. Briefly describe how one of the abiotic factors might affect:
(a) a plant; and
(b) an animal.
4. How might one of the animals you found affect one of the plants?
5. How might one of the plants affect one of the animals?

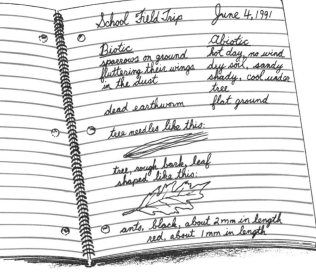

Even if your schoolyard is mostly paved over, you can still find many living things if you look carefully.

The Influence of the Abiotic Environment

It is a hot summer day with a slight breeze. You decide to give your household fern a treat and put it outside. Later that day, you observe that the leaves of the fern are brown and curled at the edges, and the plant is drooping. What do you infer? By moving the fern, you have put it into a different environment. In the summer, it is cooler, darker, and perhaps more humid indoors than it is outside. The abiotic conditions inside your house or apartment may thus be more like those in a forest, where most kinds of ferns grow in nature. In the hot Sun, or in a breeze, ferns quickly lose moisture through their thin leaves. The leaves burn and the plant wilts. If the fern is left standing in the hot Sun for too long, it may eventually die.

All living things survive only within certain limits for each environmental factor. For example, a plant may die if the temperature drops below 0°C or goes above 40°C. The range within which an organism can survive is called the organism's **range of tolerance**. An organism may have a wide range of tolerance for one factor, such as temperature, and a narrow range of tolerance for another, such as type of soil. Different species have different ranges of tolerance for each environmental factor. These things together determine

Finding Out More

6. Explain why you might get different results in your survey if you conducted it:
   (a) at night;
   (b) during the winter; and
   (c) during the summer holidays.
7. (a) Name a kind of animal or plant that is found in your province, but does not live near your schoolyard.
   (b) Why do you think it does not live there?
   (c) What changes would you need to make in the environment to make it possible for this kind of organism to live near your schoolyard?
8. Name one way in which a plant or an animal in your schoolyard might be affected if:
   (a) a pond were added to your schoolyard; and
   (b) a tall wooden fence were built all around your schoolyard. Explain your answers.

Did You Know?

You might think there are very few living things in your schoolyard, but remember that many organisms are very small or microscopic. For example, one hectare (10 000 m²) of rich soil may contain as many as 300 million small organisms such as mites, worms, and insects.

To the north of the coniferous forest in Canada is an area called the tundra. As shown in this photograph, no trees grow in this area. Use a reference book to find out what abiotic factors might prevent the growth of trees in the tundra.

where an organism can live. A cactus, for example, can survive in hot and dry conditions that would kill a fern. Organisms usually thrive best in conditions near the middle of their range of tolerance and grow less well when living near the extremes.

A single abiotic factor may have a major influence on where a particular organism can survive. Even if all other conditions in the environment are suitable, an organism may not be able to live where it is too hot, too cold, too dark, too salty, too wet, or too windy.

Suppose you observe a particular type of plant living in place A, but not in place B. You wonder why it doesn't live in place B. The reason might simply be because the organism has never reached that area and therefore has never had a chance to live there. It might be kept out of the area by disease, competition, or the constant risk of being eaten. Or it might be absent because the abiotic conditions in place B are unsuitable in some way. To find out, you could measure and compare the abiotic conditions in the two places.

In the next Activity, you will compare some of the abiotic factors in the north and south parts of the Prairie Provinces, and then relate these factors to differences in the types of vegetation growing in these two areas. You will also be given samples of soils from two different areas. Try to determine in which area each sample could be found.

How do the abiotic conditions in these two environments differ?

Activity 6-2

Comparing Different Environments

Problem

How do abiotic parts of the environment differ between the north and south of the Prairie Provinces?

Materials

maps on this page
2 samples of soil, labelled A and B
2 jars or beakers (each 500 mL)
timing device with a second hand
large can with holes punched in the bottom
200 mL graduated cylinder
water

Procedure

1. Examine the three maps showing hours of sunshine, precipitation, and general soil type (whether dry-climate or wet-climate) in the Prairie Provinces. In your notebook, make a table to compare each of these three factors in area A and area B as shown on the maps.

2. Examine the two samples of soil. In your notebook, record the characteristics of each sample that you can observe with your senses.

3. Using the equipment provided or devising your own experimental design, determine a method of measuring the ability of each type of soil to hold water. Before you begin, predict which sample will hold more water. Carry out your experiment and record your results.

Finding Out

1. The map directly below shows the main type of vegetation found in each part of the Prairie Provinces. Which type of vegetation grows where there is:
   (a) most sunlight?
   (b) least sunlight?
   (c) most precipitation?
   (d) least precipitation?
   (e) dry-climate soil?
   (f) wet-climate soil?

2. (a) Which of your soil samples holds more water?
   (b) Infer which sample of soil might come from area A and which from area B. Give a reason for your answer.

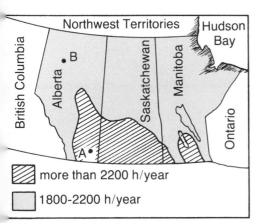

more than 2200 h/year
1800-2200 h/year

Bright sunshine hours in the Prairie Provinces.

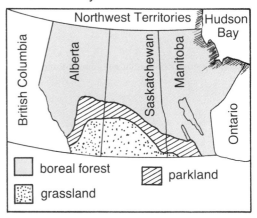

Distribution of vegetation in the Prairie Provinces.

boreal forest
grassland
parkland

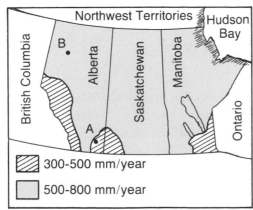

Annual precipitation in the Prairie Provinces.

300-500 mm/year
500-800 mm/year

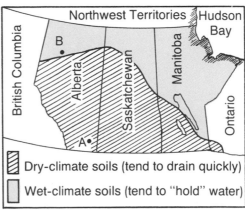

Distribution of soil type in the Prairie Provinces.

Dry-climate soils (tend to drain quickly)
Wet-climate soils (tend to "hold" water)

Where Organisms Live

How would you describe the place where you live? There are many ways to answer this question. You could describe your house or apartment, your town, your province, or the whole country of Canada. You live in all these places, as the address in the illustration shows. Each line of the address describes just a part of the line that follows it.

In the same way, you can draw many boundaries in the environment around you. You can choose to study any part of this, from the environment in a small puddle of water to the environment of the entire planet. Each smaller environment influences larger environments in different ways, just as you influence and are influenced by your town, your country, and your planet.

a. Student
101 College Street
Mytown
Alberta
Canada
North America
Planet Earth
Solar System
Milky Way Galaxy
Universe

The Biosphere

The largest ecosystem that ecologists study is called the **biosphere**. It includes all the places on the planet where living organisms can survive—from the ocean depths to high in the atmosphere, and from the poles to the equator. The biosphere can be pictured as a layer of life covering the entire planet. All parts of this huge global ecosystem are connected by circulating air and water currents and the movements of organisms.

Some Interactions in the Biosphere

In these and many other ways, each part of the biosphere affects other parts:

- Most of the oxygen in the Earth's atmosphere is produced by the trees of the tropical rain forests and the photosynthesizing microscopic life of the oceans.
- A large volcanic explosion in one part of the world can send enough dust and gases into the atmosphere to affect the weather in other parts of the world, thousands of kilometres away.
- Migrating birds can carry the seeds of plants from one continent to another, attached to the mud on their feet, or in their feathers or digestive systems.

Take just one small area in the entire biosphere, such as a tropical rain forest, and look at smaller and smaller parts within it. How might the smaller ecosystems affect the larger ones? How might other parts of the biosphere affect the smaller ecosystems?

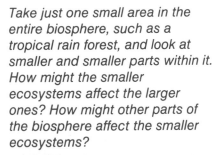

Biomes

If you wanted to see a wild polar bear, where would you start looking? Most probably, you would head north. You are unlikely to begin your search in the Prairies or the coniferous forest, because you know that these environments are unsuitable for polar bears. Obviously, the environment differs from area to area around the world. Different areas tend to have their own characteristic climate, soils, plants, and animals. Biologists call these large areas **biomes**. Polar bears live in the tundra biome. The Prairies are part of the grassland biome. Examples of most of the world's other biomes are also found in North America.

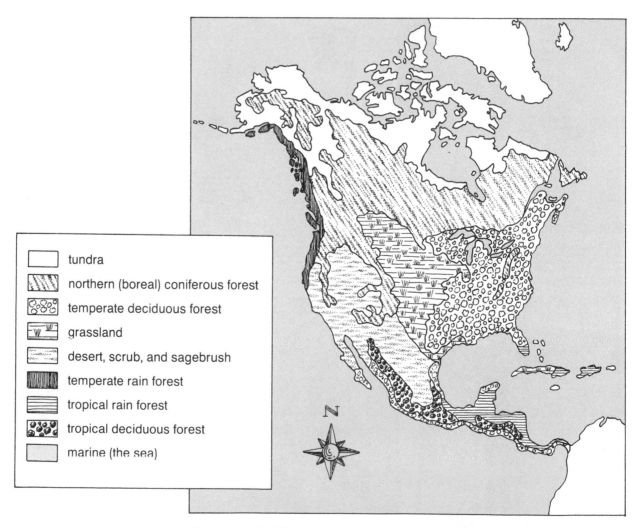

tundra

northern (boreal) coniferous forest

temperate deciduous forest

grassland

desert, scrub, and sagebrush

temperate rain forest

tropical rain forest

tropical deciduous forest

marine (the sea)

There are 12 different major biomes around the world. Examples of most of them are found in North America. What environmental factors do you think determine where one biome ends and another begins? Which biome do you live in?

Probing

If you put a message in a bottle and throw it into the Milk River in southern Alberta, it may end up in the Gulf of Mexico. Look in your atlas. Alberta's Milk River flows into the Missouri-Mississippi River system, which empties into the warm sea waters near New Orleans. If the water became polluted in the Milk River, where might that pollution have an effect on the environment?

As you can see from the map, most biomes are described by the type of vegetation that is most common in that area. The type of vegetation that grows in a biome depends mainly on the climate and the soil. The types of animals that live in a biome depend mainly on the type of vegetation.

The boundaries of each biome occur where there is a change in the conditions of the climate or soil. One of the biggest influences on climate is distance from the equator. In general, as you move from the equator to the Earth's poles, the climate gets colder and drier, and, as a result, there are fewer different species of plants and animals. You can see the same type of changes in the environment if you climb a mountain. With increasing altitude (height), it gets colder and drier. Because of this, you can pass through as many different biomes going up the side of the Rockies as you can driving from southern Canada to the Arctic.

(c)

(d)

(a)

(b)

A typical view of several major biomes: (a) northern coniferous forest; (b) desert, scrub, and sagebrush; (c) temperate deciduous forest; and (d) grassland.

Habitats and Micro-environments

Within each biome, there are many different habitats in which organisms may live. In the organism's "address," a **habitat** is like the home town—the place where an organism spends its time and carries out its activities. The habitat may be a pond, a field, or a forest. The size of a habitat varies according to the size and habits of the organism. For example, a wolf's habitat may include hundreds of square kilometres of forest. A spider's habitat may be a single bush or tree. A micro-organism may pass its entire life in a few square centimetres of soil.

Within a particular environment, there may be smaller areas or **micro-environments** that have their own distinct abiotic conditions. Some organisms having a small range of tolerance for a particular condition may live in such micro-environments. For example, in a forest environment, the area beneath a fallen tree will be cool, dark, and damp. Various insects and other small organisms that need these conditions to survive are found only in such restricted areas in the forest.

A pond environment can be divided into smaller micro-environments. Some organisms are found only at the bottom of the pond, while others live at the water's edge or on the pond's surface.

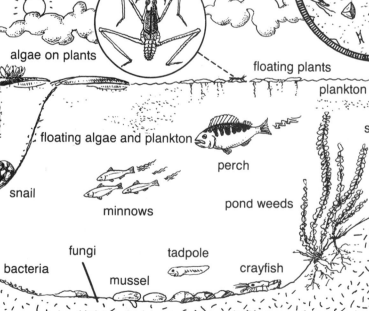

kingfisher

cat-tail

water lily

algae on plants

water strider (magnified)

plankton (magnified)

floating plants

plankton

scum of algae

insects

floating algae and plankton

snail

minnows

perch

pond weeds

bacteria

fungi

mussel

tadpole

crayfish

in the soft mud, roundworms, bloodworms, bacteria, fungi

Analysing Micro-environments

Problem

How do conditions vary among micro-environments around your school?

Materials

thermometer
tape measure
wooden stake (about 1 m long)
hammer
notebook
pen or pencil
elastic band or masking tape
string
light meter (commercial or homemade)
wind meter (commercial or homemade)
gardening spade

Procedure

1. You will be studying the same area that you looked at in Activity 6–1, but this time in more detail. Your goal is to measure the highest and lowest levels of temperature, wind, moisture, and light within the study area. Begin by looking around the area for spots that you think are especially warm, cool, windy, calm, wet, dry, bright, or shady.

Measuring wind velocity with a homemade wind meter.

2. Measure and record the air temperature at ground level in a warm spot and in a cool spot. Leave the thermometer in each place for a few minutes before taking your reading. In your notebook, describe the location of each reading (for example, the distance in metres from the school entrance).

3. At a suitable spot, use the hammer to drive a stake into the ground to a depth of at least 30 cm. Using an elastic band or masking tape, fasten a thermometer to the stake, with the bulb at a height of 30 cm above ground level. Record the temperature found here.

4. Record the temperature at ground level (where the stake enters the ground).

5. Wriggle the stake around in the ground to make a hole, then withdraw the stake. Tie a piece of string to a thermometer. On the string, mark a length of 30 cm from the bulb of the thermometer. Lower the thermometer until the bulb is 30 cm below the ground. After a few minutes, record the temperature. Refill the hole.

6. Locate the area that you think is most moist, and the area that appears to be driest. At each area, estimate the soil moisture by digging a handful of soil from the surface of the ground and squeezing it. If the soil holds together, it is very moist. If it holds together somewhat, it is moderately moist. If it falls apart, it is dry. Record whether there is a difference in soil moisture at the two locations you selected.

7. Measure and record the highest and lowest wind speeds you can find between ground level and up to 2 m above the ground. Describe the abiotic conditions of the test area.

8. Measure and record the highest and the lowest light levels you can find within this same distance above the ground. Describe the abiotic conditions of the test area.

Finding Out

1. For each high and low measurement, briefly explain what might be making this spot the warmest, coldest, windiest, etc.

2. On a graph, plot your measurements of temperature above, below, and on the ground. What can you infer about the kinds of organisms that would live in each micro-environment?

3. (a) Was there a difference between the amount of moisture in the soil samples? (b) If so, what effect do you think this difference has on the kinds of organisms that live in each area?

4. Did you record more than one of your high and low measurements in the same micro-environment? (For example, was the brightest spot also the warmest or the driest?) If so, explain why these factors may be related to each other.

Finding Out More

5. (a) How might your high and low measurements change during a day? (b) Describe how these changes might affect specific species of organisms.

Extension

6. Many animals can create micro-environments for themselves by activities such as digging burrows beneath the soil. Investigate one example of an animal that modifies its environment in some way and write a brief report on it. How does the modification of its environment help the animal to survive?

Checkpoint

1. (a) List three examples of the biotic components and two examples of the abiotic components of the pond environment shown in the photograph below.
   (b) Describe one micro-environment of a pond and name two organisms that might be found there.

2. What abiotic factors could affect the survival of a group of pine trees growing at the edge of a cliff?

3. List (a) the abiotic factors and (b) the biotic factors that you have interacted with today in your environment.

4. Using the term "range of tolerance," explain why hummingbirds do not live in northern Canada in winter.

5. (a) In which biome was the photograph directly below taken?
   (b) Name two animals you would expect to see in this biome.
   (c) Name one animal and one plant you would not expect to see in this biome. Give a reason for your answers.

6. List the biomes that can be found in:
   (a) British Columbia;
   (b) Alberta; and
   (c) Quebec.

7. (a) What is the habitat of a grasshopper?
   (b) What is the habitat of an earthworm?

8. (a) In what micro-environment of a pond would you expect to find a leech?
   (b) What micro-environment of a dog's body serves as a flea's habitat?

Obtaining Energy and Nutrients

It takes more than warmth, air, water, and a suitable habitat to keep an organism alive. Living things also need a source of energy to fuel their growth and activities, as well as materials for growth and repair. They get their energy and materials from food. But living things obtain food from their environment in two very different ways.

Green plants, algae, and some micro-organisms can make their own food using resources from the abiotic environment alone. By means of photosynthesis, they produce simple sugars from carbon dioxide and water. Because they can produce their own food in this way, these organisms are called **producers**. They form an important link between the abiotic and the biotic environment.

Animals and most micro-organisms must get their food from the biotic environment. They do this by consuming (eating) other organisms. Because of this, they are called **consumers**.

How does each of these organisms obtain its food?

In any ecosystem, all consumers depend directly or indirectly on producers. Consumers that feed directly on producers, such as deer and rabbits, are called **primary consumers**. Other consumers, such as wolves, frogs, and spiders, are meat eaters. They get their energy by eating primary consumers. Meat eaters are called **secondary consumers**. They still depend on producers, but indirectly. Some kinds of animals feed mostly on secondary consumers (for example, hawks that eat birds that eat insects). These animals are called **tertiary consumers** (meaning "third-level" consumers).

Although these categories are useful for analysing ecosystems, not all organisms fit rigidly into one category or another. For example, there are many organisms that eat plants *and* animals. They are both primary and secondary consumers. Think of some examples of organisms that eat both plants and animals.

Food Chains and the Flow of Energy

What happens when you eat an orange, or when a frog eats a worm, or when a grasshopper eats a leaf? When any animal eats, materials pass from one organism to another. It is sometimes useful for scientists studying feeding relationships to think of food as energy. By doing this, they can discuss all feeding in terms of energy units, no matter what animal is eating, or what food it eats, or how much it consumes.

In your previous studies, you measured the energy stored in food. By eating or by being eaten, organisms channel energy from one part of the environment to another. Using this idea, scientists can estimate the flow of energy through an ecosystem by observing and measuring feeding relationships. This information can be used to answer such questions as:

- How much energy does a particular organism or group of organisms need to survive?
- How does the amount of food energy in one environment compare with that in another?
- Where does the energy in an ecosystem come from?

In a later Topic, you will see how the amount of energy available in food can be related to the numbers of different kinds of animals that can live in an area.

The movement of food energy in an ecosystem from producers through the different levels of consumers is called a **food chain**. Every organism is part of one or more food chains. The illustration shows one food chain on land and one in water. Notice that both food chains begin with the energy of the Sun. The arrows indicate the direction of energy flow. With a few exceptions, found in the ocean depths, every living thing on Earth can be said to "feed" on the energy of the Sun.

The flow of energy through two different food chains, one on land and one in water.

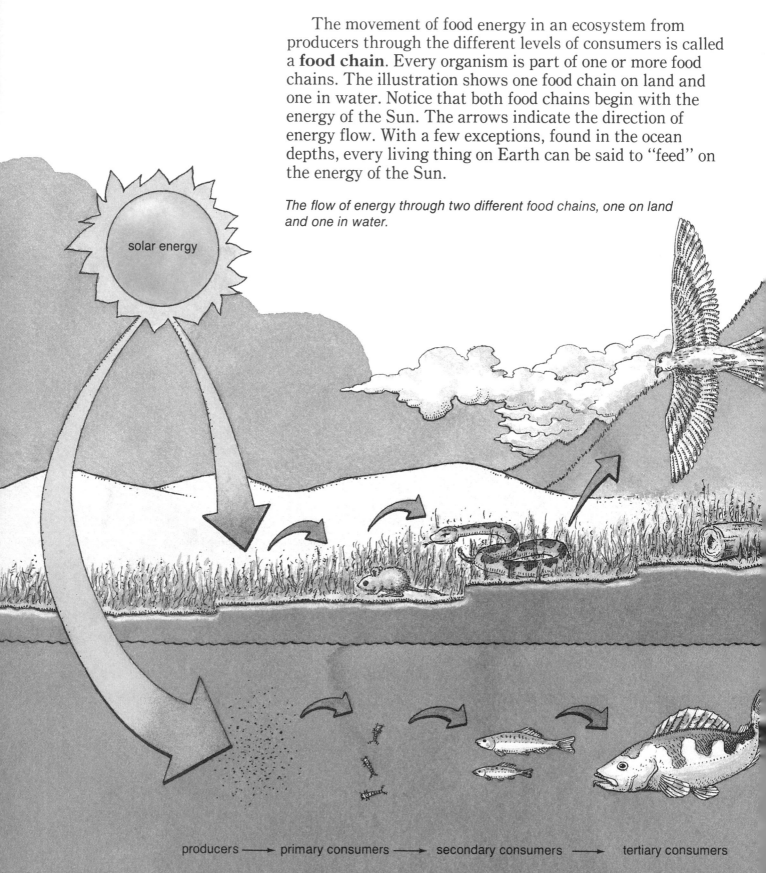

producers ⟶ primary consumers ⟶ secondary consumers ⟶ tertiary consumers

Feeding relationships in ecosystems are rarely as simple as a single food chain. Most producers are eaten by more than one kind of consumer. Most consumers eat, or are eaten by, more than one kind of organism. The small rodent (field mouse) in the illustration, for example, might eat several different types of grasses and other plants and insects, too. The rodent may be eaten by an owl, a coyote, a badger, a weasel or a mink, as well as by a rattlesnake! Thus, a food chain is usually intertwined with other food chains to form a network called a **food web**. In the next Activity, you will use a scientific model to help you track the flow of energy from organism to organism in a food web.

A food web.

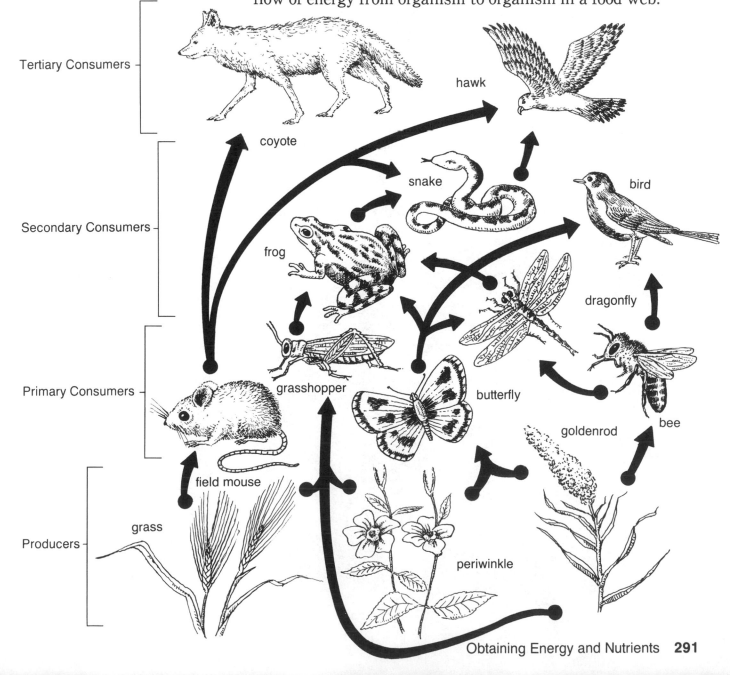

Tertiary Consumers

Secondary Consumers

Primary Consumers

Producers

coyote

hawk

snake

bird

frog

dragonfly

grasshopper

butterfly

bee

field mouse

goldenrod

grass

periwinkle

Activity 6-4

Eat and Be Eaten

Problem

How are organisms linked together in a food web?

Materials

sheet of thick cardboard (about 30 cm²)
9 push pins or thumbtacks
3 strands of cotton thread, each a different colour (about 150 cm of each colour)
9 adhesive labels
ruler
coloured pens or pencils
scissors

Procedure

1. Divide your board into three horizontal rows. Label the bottom row "Producers," the second row "Primary consumers," and the top row "Secondary consumers."

Table 6-1   *Plants and Animals of the Prairies*

Producers	grasses, snowberry, prickly pear cactus, aspen, prickly rose, sage, willow, dandelion
Primary consumers	grouse, grasshopper, rabbit, ground squirrel, pronghorn antelope, prairie dog, vole, mouse
Secondary consumers	horned lark, meadowlark, badger, weasel, coyote, rattlesnake, western toad, fox, hawk

2. Push three push pins into the "Producer" row. Write on each of three labels the name of a producer selected from Table 6-1. Stick one label beneath each push pin.
3. Repeat Step 2 for the "Primary consumer" and "Secondary consumer" rows on your board.

4. Cut three strands of thread of one colour about 50 cm in length. This colour represents the energy flow from one of your producers.
5. Wrap a few turns of one thread around the push pin representing a producer.
6. Run the thread to a primary consumer that feeds on the producer and wrap it around the push pin a few times.
7. Run the thread from the primary consumer to a secondary consumer that feeds on it. Wrap the thread around the push pin a few times.
8. If you think your producer can be eaten by one or both of the other primary consumers on your board, repeat Steps 5 to 7.
9. Repeat Steps 4 to 8 for each of the other two producers on your board, using different coloured thread for each one.
10. Copy the completed food web into your notebook, using coloured pens or pencils. Draw arrows beside each link (thread) in your food web to show the direction of energy flow.

The Nutrient Cycle

So far, you have considered food only as an energy source. Food also contains nutrient materials, such as carbon, nitrogen, calcium, and phosphorus. Organisms need these materials for growth and repair. Unlike energy, which comes from the continuous supply of sunlight, there is no source of nutrients outside the biosphere itself. Why doesn't this limited supply of nutrients run out?

The answer to this puzzle is a group of organisms that feed on dead and waste matter. These organisms are called **decomposers**. Most of them are microscopic bacteria and fungi that live in huge numbers in the soil. You learned about some of their activities during your previous study of micro-organisms and food. Decomposers feed by producing weak acids that break down dead tissue into smaller chemical particles. This process releases nutrient materials and gases into the soil, water, and air, where they can be used by producers. In this way, every organism that dies is recycled. The nutrient materials are never used up—they simply shuttle back and forth between the biotic and abiotic environment in an endless cycle.

Finding Out

1. The food web you have made shows energy flow from the producer level to higher consumer levels. Where do the producers get their energy from?
2. What might happen to other species in your food web if:
   (a) one of the producers is removed?
   (b) one of the primary consumers is removed?
   (c) one of the secondary consumers is removed?
3. How could one of the animals that is a secondary consumer also be a tertiary consumer?

Finding Out More

4. Suppose that a poison is sprayed onto some plants. How might some of this poison end up inside the body of a tertiary consumer such as a hawk?

Extension

5. Think of two species to add at the tertiary consumer level. How might they be affected by removing a secondary or primary consumer?

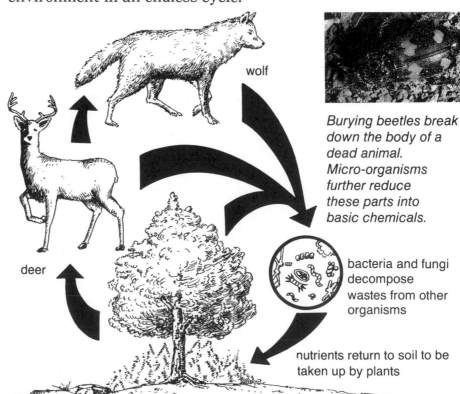

wolf

deer

Burying beetles break down the body of a dead animal. Micro-organisms further reduce these parts into basic chemicals.

bacteria and fungi decompose wastes from other organisms

nutrients return to soil to be taken up by plants

Nutrients are cycled between the biotic and abiotic parts of the environment.

Tracing Chemicals in Food Chains

One way to discover where nutrients go in nature is to introduce into the food chain a chemical that can be traced. For example, a group of plants could be watered with a solution containing a particular chemical. The plants take up the chemical through their roots. Later, different organisms in the area can be collected and tested for the presence of the chemical. Animals that eat the plants, and the animals that eat the plant-eaters, will all have traces of the chemical in their bodies.

Studying Feeding Behaviour

How do scientists find out what different organisms eat? There are several ways of doing this. In some cases, animals can be observed directly as they feed. Many animals, however, are difficult to observe over long periods. They may feed infrequently or only at night. In these cases, scientists may infer an animal's eating habits from indirect evidence. For example, the plant-feeding cotton boll weevil is found only on cotton plants and on no other type of plant. It is therefore reasonable to infer that this insect feeds only on cotton plants.

Another approach is to collect representative animals from an area and examine the contents of their digestive systems. The remains of plants or animals in their stomachs are evidence of what they have been feeding on. Alternatively, the animal's digestive waste, or feces, can be collected and analysed. Both these techniques can be misleading, however, if some items in the animal's diet are digested more rapidly or more completely than others.

Owls have a habit that allows scientists to determine the kinds of foods they eat. Some time after a meal, they cast up undigested parts of their food through their mouth in the form of pellets. Pellets can often be found at the base of a tree or other place where the owl sits to digest its food. The pellets consist of bits of feathers, bones, fur, and the hard parts of insects. By pulling pellets apart and identifying the contents, scientists can tell what an owl has been eating. In the next Activity, you will investigate what one such owl has eaten.

Did You Know?

The next time you drink a glass of milk, consider this—the calcium in the milk might have originally been part of the toe bone of a dinosaur living 70 million years ago!

Looking at Owl Pellets

Problem

What does an owl eat?

Materials

owl pellet
paper towel
forceps
hand lens
identification keys

Procedure

1. Place an owl pellet on a paper towel. Then carefully tease apart and examine the pellet or study the illustration of the contents of a pellet shown here.
2. Answer the following questions.

Finding Out

1. Describe and, if possible, identify each item in the pellet.
2. How many different individual organisms do these remains represent? Give reasons for your answer.
3. Explain how this analysis might mislead you about the owl's diet.

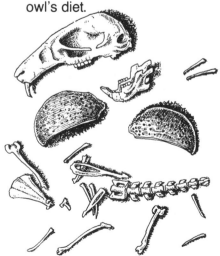

The remains of an owl pellet.

Other Interactions Among Living Things

Organisms sometimes affect other living things in their environment in unexpected ways. For example, certain birds that eat insects are often found following large animals such as cattle. Why do they do this? As cattle plod along, they stir up small insects and other animals from the ground with their hooves. When the insects jump or fly away, the birds dart in and capture them. The birds take advantage of the cattle to obtain food for themselves.

Many organisms live closely together with others in relationships such as this, which may benefit one or perhaps both partners. This type of relationship is called **symbiosis**. One of the organisms usually depends on the other for food, shelter, or protection. Three main types of symbiotic relationships have been observed in nature. .

Why do birds such as these cattle egrets follow groups of large animals such as cattle and rhinos?

This clown fish has a commensal relationship with a sea anemone.

1. **Commensalism** is a relationship in which one species benefits and the other neither benefits nor is harmed. For example, some species of tropical fish can live safely among the tentacles of sea anemones, although these tentacles quickly paralyse and kill any other fish that touches them. The clown fish benefit by being protected from their enemies. They can also feed on scraps of food left over from the anemone's meal. The anemone gets no obvious benefit from the relationship.

2. **Mutualism** is a relationship in which both species benefit. For example, a fungus and an alga live closely together to form a lichen—the colourful, crusty growths often seen on bare rocks. Together, the fungus and alga are able to survive in harsh environments where neither organism would be able to live on its own. If you look at a lichen under a microscope, you will see that the top and bottom layers are made of closely packed fungal threads. These threads hold the organisms together and protect the lichen from drying out. Just under the upper surface of a lichen are the green cells of the alga. The alga makes food for both organisms by the process of photosynthesis.

A lichen.

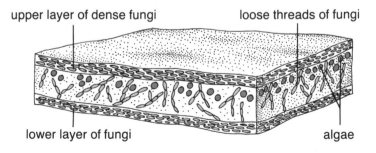

upper layer of dense fungi   loose threads of fungi

lower layer of fungi   algae

Lichens consist of two organisms living together in a relationship that benefits both.

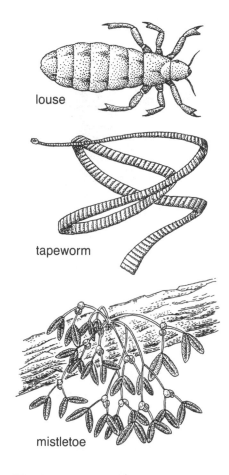

louse

tapeworm

mistletoe

The louse, the tapeworm, and the mistletoe are parasites.

3. **Parasitism** is a relationship in which one species benefits and the other is harmed, although not usually killed. The partner that benefits is called the **parasite**, and the other partner is called the **host**. Some parasites, such as lice, live and feed on the body of their host. Others, such as tapeworms, live inside their host, absorbing nutrients from the host's food. Some plants are also parasites. For example, mistletoe is a parasite that grows on trees, sending roots into its host, instead of into soil, to draw out water and nutrients.

Niches

Imagine what might happen in your community if all the bus drivers disappeared. Or all the police officers. Or all the ice-cream manufacturers. You would notice an effect right away, even if you personally never took a bus, or needed a police officer, or ate ice cream. Within a community, each group of people has a part to play. The activities of each group affect all the other groups in the community. Similarly, in nature, each species plays a particular part in the ecosystem it shares with other organisms. Some are producers, some are consumers, some are decomposers, some are parasites, and so on. The jobs, or roles, of an organism make up what is called its ecological **niche**. Every type of organism has its own niche, and no two niches in the same ecosystem are exactly the same. A complete description of an organism's ecological niche includes where it lives, how it feeds, what it feeds on, and how it affects its environment.

What would happen if all the police officers in your community suddenly disappeared?

The ground squirrel is a rodent that has an important niche in its prairie ecosystem.

Consider some of the activities that are part of the ground squirrel's niche on the Prairies. The ground squirrel is a primary consumer, feeding on grasses. It digs tunnels that help stir up the soil, letting air and water penetrate more easily. Unused ground squirrel tunnels provide shelter for other animals, such as rattlesnakes. The ground squirrel is a host for fleas, ticks, and other parasites. It may also be a meal for a hawk or other secondary consumer that lives on the Prairies.

One way to understand the meaning of the term "niche" is to imagine what would happen if the ground squirrel were suddenly removed from its habitat. The ground squirrel's "jobs" would then be left undone: Grasses would not be eaten, tunnels would not be dug, and fleas and hawks would not be fed. Although other organisms also do some of these things, no organism does them all in the same way the ground squirrel does.

Endangered Species

What are the most important organisms in a forest ecosystem? Which organisms could the forest do without? The trees are the most obvious living things in the forest. They are producers, and provide essential food and shelter for many types of animals. Without the trees, these other organisms could not survive. But the trees could not survive without microscopic fungi living in the soil of the forest floor. These fungi are decomposers. They break down dead and rotting material and release the nutrients that the trees need for their growth. Because each species of organism has its own niche, every species helps ensure the survival of others.

It is estimated that today, on a worldwide basis, one species per day is becoming extinct. Most of these extinctions are the result of the destruction of habitats.

The American scientist Paul Ehrlich once compared an ecosystem to an airplane. The species in an ecosystem are like the rivets (bolts) that keep an airplane held together. What happens to an airplane if the rivets start to pop out as the plane is flying? A few rivets may not be missed, because the plane is made with extra rivets for strength and safety. After a certain point, however, the loss of one more rivet could lead to a serious accident. Similarly, in an ecosystem, the loss of species could eventually lead to a damaged environment in which most organisms can no longer survive.

Many human activities have caused other species of organisms to become rare, in danger of disappearance, or **extinct** (completely died out). A species is extinct when no living members can be found anywhere in the world. Often, species disappear from large areas but may still be found in small numbers in some parts of their previous range. They are then said to be "locally extinct" or **extirpated**. When a species survives only in game parks or zoos, it is said to be "extinct in the wild."

Species may disappear from an area because they are overhunted by people. This happened to the plains bison during the last century. About 2.5 million bison were killed every year between 1870 and 1875. By the end of the century, only 500 plains bison remained. Other species have disappeared because their habitat has been altered by people. For example, the passenger pigeon, a beautiful, once-common bird, was hunted extensively in the 1800s, but its extinction was due to the burning and cutting of beech-oak-maple forests for farming.

The bison was once found in vast numbers across the Prairies, from the Rockies to eastern Manitoba. It now lives in only a small part of northern Alberta and the Northwest Territories.

A passenger pigeon.

Activities such as draining swamps, cutting down forests, damming rivers, and building cities and highways alter environments. Usually, organisms that lived in the area before it was altered cannot live there afterwards. The disappearance of large numbers of species could eventually alter the world's environment to such an extent that it may no longer be able to support human life. You will learn more about the effect of human activities on the environment in Topic Six.

Activity 6-6

Going, Going, Gone!

Problem

- What causes the extinction of a species?
- How does its extinction affect humans?

The giant panda, the African elephant, and the whooping crane are species that have been endangered by human actions.

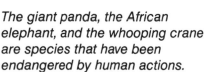

Procedure

Select a species of plant or animal that either has disappeared from an area where it was once common, or that seems to be disappearing from an area due to human actions. Use newspaper articles, magazine articles, and reference books to investigate the reasons for the disappearance of the organism. Prepare your own article based on the information you find. Your article should include answers to the following questions.

1. Is the organism becoming locally extinct or is it becoming extinct worldwide?
2. What is the organism's habitat, and what niche in its ecosystem does the organism occupy?
3. How might the disappearance of this species affect:
   (a) other organisms? and
   (b) humans?
   (Hint: If you decide to report on an organism that has already disappeared, you might wish to research either the passenger pigeon or the dodo bird—two species now extinct due to human actions.)

Checkpoint

1. Name a producer, a primary consumer, and a secondary consumer.
2. Draw an example of a food web, including all the organisms in the illustrations below.
3. What is the function of decomposers?
4. "All flesh is grass." In your own words, explain the meaning of this quotation.
5. Where does your energy come from? Be specific in your answer.
6. In each of the statements below, say whether the relationship described is parasitic, commensal, or mutualistic. Define each of these terms.
   (a) Young spruce and fir trees grow well in the shade provided by aspens.
   (b) Athlete's foot is an irritating skin growth caused by a type of fungus.
   (c) The ants that live in spiny acacia trees feed on a special part of the leaves, but protect the tree from all other insect pests.
7. What is the difference between a habitat and a niche?
8. Explain how the extinction of one species might affect several other species.

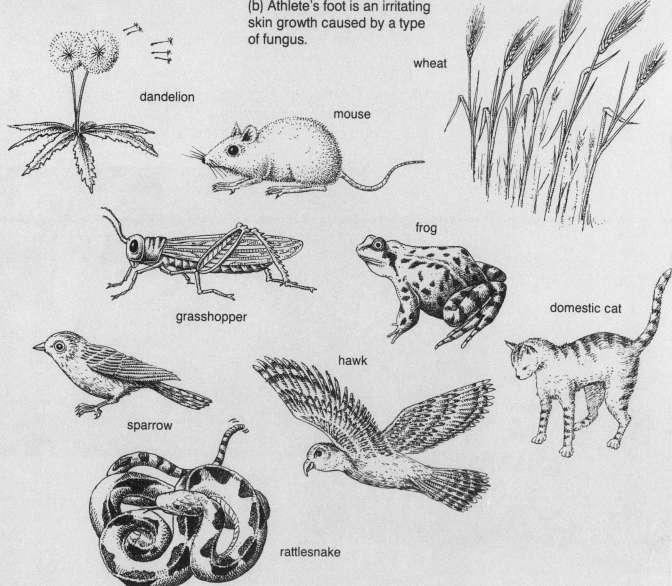

dandelion

wheat

mouse

grasshopper

frog

sparrow

hawk

domestic cat

rattlesnake

The Numbers of Living Things

What kinds of organisms are found in the greatest numbers where you live? On a walk through your neighbourhood, you are likely to see many plants such as grasses, dandelions, and various bushes and trees. These are common almost everywhere, even in cities. You may see several species of birds such as sparrows and pigeons that feed on plant seeds. Insects such as bees and flies are also common in most places. You are less likely to see animals such as eagles or foxes.

In this Topic, you will learn how scientists estimate the numbers of different kinds of organisms that live in an area. You will also discover reasons why some organisms are always found in much greater numbers than others.

Why are some organisms found in greater numbers than others?

Measuring Populations

All the individual organisms of a species that live together in a habitat make up a **population** of the species. In the same habitat, there will be populations of many other different species. Together, these populations of different species form a **community**. For example, a woodland community might include populations of deer, squirrels, mosquitoes, cedars, maples, owls, and wolves.

Scientists are interested in population sizes as a way of understanding how organisms interact with one another and their abiotic environment. For example, a large population of ground squirrels will dig more holes, eat more grain, and provide more food for secondary consumers than a small population of ground squirrels. But there are many other reasons why people might want to know the numbers of certain types of animals or plants in an area. A forester needs to know how many trees are in an area scheduled for cutting. A hunter may want to know the population of ducks in a marshland. A farmer may want to know if the population of grasshoppers in the fields is increasing. How could you determine these numbers?

It is usually difficult or impossible to actually count all of the individual organisms in a large area, especially if the organisms move about a lot. Ecologists have therefore developed several techniques to help them estimate population size. Most of these methods involve counting the organisms in small **samples** that represent a larger area. These accurate counts are then multiplied to give an estimate of the numbers for the entire area.

Suppose you are managing the public parks in your community. You want to know if the number of dandelions on the lawns is increasing from year to year so that you can decide if you need to control them. In the next Activity, you will learn a method that is often used for estimating populations of plants.

The levels of biological organization from individual organisms to the ecosystem.

individual   population   community   ecosystem

Activity 6-7

Quadrat Sampling

Problem

What is the population of dandelions on a lawn?
NOTE: This Activity can be carried out on a lawn or meadow near your school. If there are no dandelions growing there, you can study another suitable plant, such as clover or plantain, both of which commonly grow as weeds in grassy areas.

> **CAUTION:** Do not pick plants, leave litter, or otherwise damage the area during your study.

The dandelion is a common plant in many areas.

Materials

4 metal pegs (made from wire coat hangers bent to form a loop at one end)
string (a little more than 4 m long)
tape measure or metre stick

Procedure

1. Calculate the area of the lawn or field you are studying by measuring two adjacent sides (in metres) and multiplying the figures together. This gives the area in square metres.
2. Toss one of your pegs into the area in any direction or use a brightly coloured object if the grass is long. Where the peg lands determines where you will count your sample.
3. Construct a **quadrat**, or square sampling area, starting from the peg you tossed. This peg should become the lower left corner of your quadrat. Drive four pegs into the ground, starting with the peg that was tossed, to form the corners of a square measuring 1 m². Tie a length of string firmly to the pegs to outline a square. Make sure the corners are all at right angles.

4. Count all the individual dandelion plants that are growing within your quadrat. If your line runs across a plant, count it only if more than half the plant lies inside the square. Record your tally.
5. Depending on the size of the lawn and the number of students in your class, repeat Steps 2 to 4 two or three times.
6. Total all the dandelion counts obtained by the class. Obtain an average number of dandelions per quadrat by dividing this total by the number of samples taken.
7. Multiply the average population of dandelions in a quadrat by the number of square metres in the lawn. The answer will be the estimated total population of dandelions in the lawn.

Other Methods of Estimating Populations

The quadrat sampling method is useful for estimating populations of low-growing plants, but it is not very practical in an area with trees or scrubby bushes. In these areas, scientists may instead use the **line transect** method. This involves running a straight line of string through the area being studied. At regular intervals along the line, every plant that touches the string, or grows directly above or below it, is identified and counted. This information gives an estimate of which species are most common in the area.

Finding Out

1. Why do you think it was important to choose your sample areas at random?
2. Suggest one way in which the accuracy of your population estimate might be improved.

Finding Out More

3. (a) What biotic and abiotic factors might affect the population of dandelions on the lawn?
   (b) Explain how each factor might act to increase or decrease the population.

Plants growing along a line transect are recorded at regular intervals.

Running a Line Transect

Suppose you are a forest ranger, studying the vegetation on the slope of a river valley to find out how the plants help prevent soil erosion. There are four main species of bushy plants growing on the slope. You want to know which of these plants is the most common. You run a line transect and record the plants at ten equal intervals along the transect. The results of this survey are shown in Table 6-2. The four types of plants are labelled A, B, C, and D. Each "x" indicates that the plant was growing along the transect. Use the data in the table to answer the questions that follow.

Finding Out

1. Which type of plant—A, B, C, or D—was:
   (a) most common?
   (b) least common?
2. Did the two least common plants grow on the same part of the slope?
3. Did the two most common plants grow on the same part of the slope?

Finding Out More

4. A forest ranger noted that the slope investigated in this Activity had very little erosion. In a similar line transect she did on another slope nearby with a great deal of erosion, the main species of plant was Plant B.
   (a) What inferences might she make about this plant's ability to prevent erosion?
   (b) What recommendations might she make about methods to reduce erosion on the nearby slope?
   (c) What further studies might she want to carry out before making any recommendations?

Table 6-2 *Results of Line Transect on Valley Slope*

POINT ON LINE	PLANTS GROWING AT EACH POINT			
	A	B	C	D
1	x	x		x
2	x	x		
3	x		x	
4	x		x	x
5			x	
6	x			
7	x		x	
8			x	
9	x			
10	x		x	x

Estimating Animal Populations

Unlike plants, animals do not usually stay in one place. This makes it more difficult to estimate the size of animal populations. One technique, used for some animals that gather in groups, is to estimate numbers from a photograph of the group. For large animals such as caribou, the herd is photographed from an aircraft. A flock of birds may be photographed as it flies overhead. If the group is spread over a large area, a series of several photographs may be needed. To simplify the counting task, a grid of squares drawn on a transparent sheet is laid over the photograph. The number of animals in each square is counted and recorded separately, then totalled. What is the number of birds in the flock shown in the illustration?

Suppose an ecologist needs to know the number of grasshoppers in a field. A technique often used to estimate the population of small animals such as this is called the **mark-recapture method**. First, a sample of grasshoppers from a small area of the field is captured using a sweep net. The captured insects are marked with a dot of coloured paint or with some other harmless substance, then released where they were caught. The next day, at the same time, the same area is swept with a net. Some of the grasshoppers captured the second day will have been caught before and will have a mark on them. Others will be caught for the first time and will be unmarked. From the ratio of marked to unmarked insects, an estimate of the total population of grasshoppers in the field can be calculated. Here is an example.

1. Day One: 50 grasshoppers were captured, marked, and released.
2. Day Two: 64 grasshoppers were captured; 8 had been marked, 56 were unmarked.

To discover how many birds are in this flock, count the number in each square and then total these numbers.

Since 8 out of 64 or 1/8 of our sample captured on Day Two had been marked, then we can assume the ecologist marked 1/8 of all the grasshoppers on Day One. Therefore, the 50 grasshoppers the ecologist caught on Day One must be 1/8 the total grasshoppers in the field. So 50 grasshoppers × 8 = 400 grasshoppers, the total population in the field.

3. To express this grasshopper population estimate mathematically, you can do the following calculation. (Use "gh" to represent the total grasshopper population you're determining.)

$$\frac{50}{gh} = \frac{8}{64}$$

$$8gh = 50 \times 64$$

$$gh = \frac{50 \times 64}{8}$$

$$gh = 400$$

In the following Activity, you will devise your own method of estimating the "population" of kidney beans in a jar.

Using a sweep net to sample insects in a field.

Activity 6-9

How Many Beans?

Problem
How can you estimate the population of beans in a jar?

Materials
large, wide-mouthed jar half filled with kidney beans
waterproof marker, liquid paper, or quick-drying paint

Procedure
1. Estimate how many beans are in the jar by observation alone. Record your estimate.
2. Devise a method of estimating the bean population by using the mark-recapture method.

3. Confirm the accuracy of your estimate by actually counting all the beans in the jar. (This task can be divided among the class.)

Finding Out
1. How accurate was the population estimate obtained: (a) by observation alone? and (b) by the mark-recapture method?
2. How could you increase the accuracy of your method?
3. Name two factors in a real population of animals that might make this method unreliable. Explain your answer.

Populations and Food Chains

What factors determine how many of each kind of organism may share the same habitat? For example, why might there be a population of 500 deer in a particular woodland community and not 100 or 1000? The numbers of deer might be affected by abiotic factors in the area, such as forest fires or the amount of snowfall. The size of the deer population might also be affected by their interactions with other organisms that live in the woodland. For example, there may be a small population of deer if there are:

- few of the organisms that deer feed on; or
- many of the animals that eat deer.

Would you expect a forest community to have more wolves than deer, or more deer than wolves? What might happen if there were a population of 100 wolves and a population of 100 deer? A community such as this could not exist for long. An adult wolf requires about 1.8 kg of meat per day. One hundred wolves therefore require 180 kg of meat per day. That is roughly the quantity of meat provided by four deer. If the wolf population consumes four deer per day, it would consume all the deer in the forest in only 25 days—not enough time for the deer to reproduce and increase their numbers. The wolves would soon have to find other food, or move out of the area, or die of starvation.

In general, the population size of any kind of organism is limited by the amount of food available to it. For this reason, a community usually has higher numbers of the organisms that are eaten than of the organisms that eat them. If you put these numbers into a food chain, this means there must always be more producers than primary consumers, more primary consumers than secondary consumers, and more secondary consumers than tertiary consumers. These relationships form a **pyramid of numbers**, with a broad base and a small tip. The pyramid of numbers can serve as a model of the feeding relationships in a food chain.

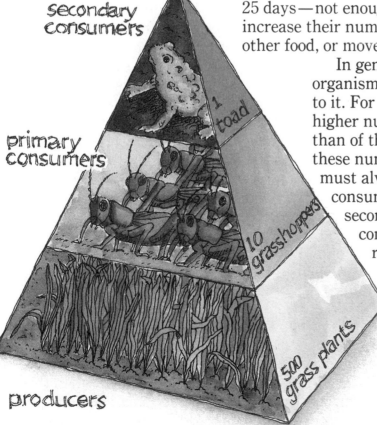

A pyramid of numbers. Which organisms are the most numerous? Which are the least numerous?

secondary consumers

1 toad

primary consumers

10 grasshoppers

500 grass plants

producers

0.1 g/m²

secondary consumers

0.6 g/m²

primary consumers

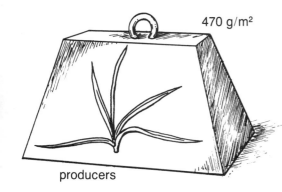

470 g/m²

producers

A pyramid of biomass shows the total amounts of material available in different populations of organisms.

Biomass

Imagine that the students in your classroom form a population that lives on fish. How many fish would you need to provide enough food for all the students for one week? If the fish were small, like sardines, you might need about 12 fish per student per day. A single larger fish, such as a salmon, might feed three or four students per day. Or you might squeeze a single whale shark into your classroom. At 18 m in length and 40 000 kg in mass, this one fish could keep an entire class of 30 students alive for a year or more!

This example demonstrates that representing a food chain by using a pyramid of numbers does not tell the whole story. In the food chain of fish ⟶ students, you could have a population of hundreds or thousands of small fish supporting the same population of students as one large fish would support.

To know the amount of food needed by organisms at each level of a food chain, ecologists go a step beyond using a pyramid of numbers. They actually measure the amount of material—the total mass—of the population at each level of a food chain. First, they take a sample of a population and from this sample, they estimate the total number of individuals in a population. Then they multiply the population by the average mass of the individuals in the population. The result is called the population's biomass. **Biomass** is a measure of the total mass of a population at a given time. For example, a population of 100 fish with an average mass of 10 kg each has a total biomass of 1000 kg. Note that a very few large fish could provide the same biomass to a consumer at the next higher level of a food chain. For example, a population of 10 fish with an average mass of 100 kg also has a biomass of 1000 kg.

A **pyramid of biomass** can serve as a model of the amount of material (the biomass) at each level of a food chain. As you can see from the illustration of such a pyramid, the amount of material gets less at each higher level of a food chain. Where has the missing biomass gone? If you have ever weighed yourself before and then several hours after a meal, you know that you do not increase in mass by the mass of the food you eat. The material in the food is broken down to provide energy for life functions such as cellular respiration, excretion, and muscular activity. Much of the energy from food is lost to the environment as heat, just as the energy in gasoline produces heat when the gas is burned in a car engine. Only a very small percentage of the food you eat is actually changed into new biomass.

Ecosystems and People

In this Unit, you have studied many of the interactions that exist within ecosystems. This Topic gives you an opportunity to explore one ecosystem in depth, looking closely at the relationships within it. You will then complete your analysis of ecosystems by investigating some of the ways human actions affect the environment.

An Ecosystem in Action

You are now going on an imaginary field trip to a habitat that is common across the Prairies: the slough (pronounced "slew"). As you read about the organisms, soils, and climate of this area, review the ideas that you have learned so far in this Unit. What are the biotic and abiotic parts of this ecosystem? How do the populations of organisms in the slough community interact with one another, and with the abiotic environment? What influences the numbers of each species in the community? Before answering the questions at the end of the Activity, you may want to do some extra reading about this ecosystem, look at field guides to prairie animals and plants, or watch a movie about the Prairies. For each organism or abiotic feature that you read about, think of at least one other living or non-living part of the environment that interacts with it. In this way, you will soon be able to determine many important interactions that maintain this ecosystem.

A prairie slough.

Case Study: The Prairie Slough

Problem

What examples of interactions can you discover in a prairie slough ecosystem?

Abiotic Environment

Sloughs are shallow lakes and ponds that are widely found across the Prairies. These bodies of water have a distinct community of plants and animals, many of which are not found on the surrounding plains. Sloughs form wherever there is a low-lying bit of land. In the spring, they fill up with water from the melting snow or rain. Sloughs can be as small as a classroom, or as large as 2 km across. Most are shallow and the smaller ones may dry out by mid-summer. There are no streams running in or out of the sloughs. There are fewer sloughs in the western Prairies because this area receives less precipitation. The soil around the sloughs is a thick, dark-brown clay. Because sloughs are in low-lying land, fertile soil from nearby farmland or grassland is washed or blown into them. This nutrient-rich soil supports a varied community of plant life.

Plant and Algal Life

Sloughs contain many water-loving plants and algae—from tiny green algae and duckweed floating on the surface, to tall, waving bulrushes growing around the edges. Near the shore grow water buttercups, common slough grass, wild barley, and sedge. The quantity of plant and algal growth depends partly on rainfall. Sloughs in the wetter eastern Prairies are often bounded by a thick band of sedge and other water reeds. Sloughs in the western Prairies are generally more open, with less dense vegetation.

Animal Life

The water of the sloughs is full of microscopic organisms. They provide food for slightly larger organisms, such as water fleas and water mites. In their turn, the water fleas and mites are hunted by insects called water striders that skim across the surface. Some insects, such as mosquitoes and dragonflies, lay their eggs in the sloughs. The larvae of these insects live and feed in the water. When fully grown, they climb out and turn into adult insects. The decaying plant and algal life of the pond

forms a feast for water snails, which nibble their way along the slimy underwater stems.

Among the larger animals around a slough, the most common are the ducks and wading birds. Mallards and coots prefer the wetter sloughs, where they can hide among the thick vegetation at the edges. The bulrushes also make ideal perches for blackbirds. Around the more open sloughs of the west, shorebirds such as curlews and killdeer are common. They nest among hummocks of grass, and feed on small animals, such as insects and snails. There are usually no fish in the sloughs. Muskrats burrow into the soft banks to make their dens. They collect water plants to eat and to use as bedding. Mink and snakes come to drink and hunt frogs, and coyotes look for nesting ducks.

Now that you know some of the abiotic and biotic parts of a typical slough environment, review what you've learned by answering the questions on the following page.

Finding Out

1. In your own words, briefly describe how the abiotic factors of (a) precipitation and (b) the slope of the land, affect the plant community of a slough.
2. Draw a simple food web for a slough ecosystem. Include at least two different producers, two primary consumers, two secondary consumers, and one tertiary consumer.
3. Name two ways in which animals at the slough use plants and algae for a purpose other than food.
4. Describe the niche of a water snail.
5. (a) Why do you think there are usually no fish in a slough?
   (b) Do you think farmers could use the sloughs on their land to raise fish? Why or why not?
6. Do you think water fleas or water striders are likely to be more numerous in a slough community? Explain your answer.

Finding Out More

7. Leopard frogs and mosquitoes are two common species in the sloughs. Bullfrogs and black-flies are not found in prairie sloughs, although they are common in the ponds and rivers of eastern Canada. Read the descriptions of these two species in (a) and (b), and explain what biotic or abiotic factor(s) might prevent each from being able to survive in sloughs.

(a) The bullfrog is the largest North American frog. It usually lives near bodies of still water. The frogs lay their eggs in water in spring, and the tadpole stage lasts from one to three years. The adult frogs feed mostly on insects.

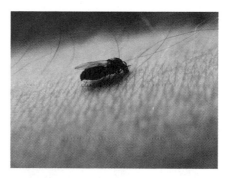

(b) Black-flies lay their eggs in running water in the summer. The eggs hatch the following spring, and the tiny larvae develop quickly. They cling to rocks to avoid being swept away by the current. After they have turned into adult flies, they go off in search of a meal of blood from deer, caribou, cattle, or humans.

8. In the 1950s, there were about 8 million sloughs across the Prairies. In the 1980s, there were about 2 million.
   (a) What factors might have caused this decline?
   (b) What effect do you think this change might have had on:
   • the total duck population of the Prairies? and
   • the duck population of individual sloughs?

Extension

9. Choose *one* of the following tasks:
   (a) Conduct some research on one of the organisms that lives in a slough. Find out details about its locomotion, digestion, reproduction, senses, behaviour, and growth. Present a report showing how the various characteristics of the organism allow it to survive in the slough environment.
   (b) Invent a new animal or plant that is able to live somewhere in the slough. Consider what part of the slough it lives in, how it obtains its food, and whether it is eaten by other organisms. Prepare a sketch or a written report that describes your organism, and explain how it interacts with at least one abiotic and one biotic factor in its environment.

People and the Environment

Humans, like all other living things, depend on the environment for food, shelter, air, and water. As we obtain these needs, we alter the environment in various ways. The development of technologies such as engines, computers, airplanes, and automobiles has allowed people to change the environment and use energy on a far greater scale than ever before. These developments have brought great benefits to many people, but have also led to many unexpected consequences. For example, the removal of resources and the manufacture, use, and disposal of products often produce waste materials that pass into the soil, water, and air. Anything added to the environment that is harmful to living things is considered a **pollutant**.

Farming, fishing, forestry, and mining have provided us with many products to meet our needs. On the other hand, they have led to some unintended consequences.

For example, pesticides were considered a great discovery of the 20th century because of their effectiveness in killing insects and other pests. They have been used extensively both to increase crop yield and to prevent diseases (by killing insects that carry disease-causing micro-organisms such as malaria). However, it is now known that pesticides can be pollutants, causing serious problems when they get into food chains, just as can mercury and other poisonous chemicals released by industrial processes.

Poisons in the Food Chain

You have learned that materials in the environment are cycled through food chains. Because of this, chemical pollutants added to the environment in one place may turn up in the bodies of organisms in another place some distance away. Many of these human-made chemicals cannot be easily broken down by living things. They therefore remain in the bodies of the organisms.

Before the 1960s, few people thought that a pesticide used to kill insects might end up killing birds, and might potentially harm people as well. At that time, studies began to show that pesticide levels in animals increased as they passed along food chains. You will discover the ecological reasons for these findings in the next Activity.

Pollution in rivers and streams may kill fish and other organisms.

Activity 6-11

Tracking Poisons

Problem

How does a pesticide build up in the bodies of different kinds of organisms in the food chain?

Procedure

Carefully study the following paragraphs and the illustration that accompanies this Activity. Then answer the questions on page 317.

In 1939, the chemical DDT was discovered to be a powerful insecticide. From that time until the 1960s, it was extensively used both to prevent disease and to increase crop yield, by killing insects.

In the 1950s, scientists began to notice that some bird species were decreasing in number. Scientists made several discoveries as they probed this problem. They found high levels of DDT in the fat of many hawks, falcons, and eagles. (DDT is very soluble in fat, so it can easily accumulate in an animal's fat cells.) In the nests of these birds they observed eggs with shells so thin that they had broken before the eggs could hatch. Through experiments, scientists found out that DDT interferes with the ability of the mother bird's body to provide calcium to harden the shells of the eggs.

The illustrations show one example of how the use of DDT to control an insect pest also caused negative effects on populations of other animals, such as hawks.

Finding Out

1. Draw a food chain that includes earthworms, robins, and hawks.
2. The amount of DDT in the body of an earthworm is one unit. Suppose that a robin eats five worms a day. If all the DDT stays in the robin's body, how many units of DDT will it have in its body after six weeks? Write this number on your food chain.
3. A hawk catches and consumes 12 robins over the summer. How many units of DDT will it have in its body? Write this number on your food chain.
4. By how many times has the amount of DDT increased from the body of a worm to the body of a hawk?
5. What will happen to the DDT when the hawk dies?

Finding Out More

6. Imagine the following situation. An insect pest is sprayed with poison but does not immediately die. A type of bird that feeds on these insects builds up large quantities of the poison in its body. Many of the birds die. The population of insect-eating birds becomes very small.
(a) Predict what will happen to the population of insects.
(b) In your own words, explain how the use of an insecticide could increase the population of insect pests.

1. *An insect called the coddling moth is a pest of apple orchards.*

2. *In the 1940s, 1950s, and early 1960s, DDT was sprayed on the apple trees to eliminate the coddling moth.*

3. *The leaves of the apple trees, still DDT-covered, fell to the ground in the autumn. The leaves were dragged into the ground by earthworms and were later eaten. The DDT became stored in the fat cells of the earthworms.*

4. *Small birds, such as robins, ate the earthworms and the DDT became stored in the birds' fat cells.*

5. *Hawks, falcons, and eagles ate many of these smaller birds. DDT accumulated in their fat cells. When the females laid eggs, the DDT prevented proper eggshell thickening, and no young hawks, falcons, and eagles were hatched.*

Did You Know?

The use of DDT in Canada was severely restricted in 1967, but it is still used extensively in some parts of the world. Small quantities of DDT are now found in organisms throughout the world—even in penguins living in the Antarctic. It is also found in humans. This finding further demonstrates the way in which all parts of the biosphere are interconnected.

Biological Indicators

The levels of chemical pollutants in the air, soil, or water at a certain location are often difficult to measure because the pollutants quickly spread over large areas. Because of this, scientists regularly measure the amount of pollutants in the bodies of certain animals and plants. These organisms serve as **biological indicators**. They tell scientists how various pollutants move through the environment, and whether they have built up to levels that might be dangerous to people and other organisms.

Air Pollution

How clean is the air you breathe? If you live in a city, the air probably contains waste gases that come from the burning of fuel used in automobiles and in industries. If you live in the country, the air may contain dust or chemical sprays from farmers' fields. All the tiny solid and liquid bits that cause air pollution are called **particulates**. People are not usually aware of air pollution unless the air actually appears hazy. In the next Activity, you will collect some particulates from the air to find out how abundant they are, and you will try to identify them.

Fit to Breathe?

Problem

How abundant are particulates in the air you breathe?

Materials

3 microscope slides
petroleum jelly
popsicle stick
felt-tip marker
masking tape or duct tape
magnifying glass or microscope
cover slip
wind meter

Procedure

1. Three or four students will work together to compare results. Each student should smear a thin layer of petroleum jelly on one side of a microscope slide.
2. Decide on a location for each of your group's slides.

> **CAUTION:** The location for each slide must be safe and approved by your teacher.

3. Carefully tape the slide for which you are responsible to a location outside your school building, with the jelly side facing up. You could tape it to a window ledge, a tree, a fence, or some other location where it is unlikely to be disturbed.

4. After one day, collect the slide. Use a magnifying glass or a microscope to examine the materials that have stuck to your slide, and to the slides of other members of your group. Sketch the appearance of the particulates on each slide and try to identify them. Crystal-like particulates are most likely fragments of soil. Tiny flat specks may be ash from chimneys. Small oval shapes may be pollen. There may also be small particulates from plants and insects.

5. Record which of the locations used by your group showed the greatest number of particulates, which had the least, and which had an amount in between. (You will need to devise a scale for comparing numbers. For example, up to a certain number of particulates = low particulate pollution, etc.)

6. Compare your results with those of other groups.

Finding Out

1. What type of particulates are most common in the air near your school?
2. Where were the most particulates collected?
3. Was there any pattern in the distribution of particulates near your school? If so, try to describe the pattern.
4. What is the possible source of the various particulates that you collected?

Finding Out More

5. Predict how the pattern of airborne particulates and air pollution might change according to the weather or some other factor. Set out your air-pollution "traps" at different times to test your ideas.

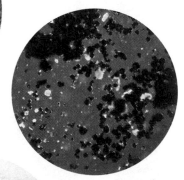

These photographs show highly magnified views of some of the particulates you might find on your slide. From left to right: pollen; dirty raindrop; mould; and fly-ash oil.

Finding Answers to Environmental Problems

Pollution, endangered species, erosion, loss of forests. . . , the list of environmental problems is a long one. You may have heard or read about some of those in the list above, or they may be new to you. But what is the cause of so many problems?

In your study of ecology in this Unit, you have learned these two important things.
1. People depend on the environment for their needs.
2. Every human activity has an effect on the environment.

It is from these two facts that environmental problems arise. And it is by using these facts that some solutions have been and will continue to be found. If you understand the connections among parts of an ecosystem, you can take steps to minimize the harmful effects of human activities. You can also take action to promote activities that are beneficial to the environment.

For example, suppose you buy a large amount of paper, then throw the paper in the garbage after you have finished with it. Your actions have several effects on the environment. Paper is made from living things—trees. The demand for more paper results in increased logging activities in the forest. This affects other organisms in the forest ecosystem, together with the forest soil and water.

Individual actions can often make a difference.

The disposal of waste paper results in more pollution, whether your local garbage is buried or burned. As an alternative, you can buy recycled paper whenever possible, and save your used paper for recycling. You could also cut down on your demand for paper by not buying things that are overpackaged, and by not using paper wastefully. These actions will reduce your harmful impact on the environment.

Activity 6-13

Taking Action

Problem

What action(s) can be taken to reduce a harmful impact on the environment?

Procedure

The photographs at the beginning of this Topic show examples of farming, fishing, forestry, and mining—four major ways that people make use of the Earth's resources. These activities, while providing benefits, also have major effects on the environment. Investigate an environmental problem associated with one of these activities. You may choose a problem that has already been solved, or one that still exists. Write a report explaining what action has been taken or can be taken—either by individuals, governments, or companies—to try to solve the problem.

You can present your report in the form of a poster or brochure intended to make the public more aware of environmental problems and how to find solutions to them. In your report, be sure to include:
(a) What causes (or caused) the environmental problem?
(b) What are (or were) some obstacles to improving the situation?
(c) How can the harmful effect of the activity be reduced (or how was it reduced)?
(d) What actions can be taken (or were taken) by individuals?
(e) What are (or were) the expected results of their actions?

Science and Technology in Society
Operation Burrowing Owl

It's hard to believe that this tiny bird with long spindly legs and huge yellow eyes actually makes its home under the ground, but the burrowing owl does just that. It nests in abandoned badger and ground squirrel holes on the Prairies.

This "short fat owl on stilts," as it has been called, doesn't dig its own burrow. Instead it takes over old burrows and refashions them. The male uses his feet, beak, and wings to scrape dirt out of the burrow. He then lines the burrow with feathers, dried plants, and cow dung. From the mound of dirt by the burrow, or atop a fence post, the 22 cm owl can search for food in the prairie grasses.

But the burrowing owl is in trouble. It is considered a threatened species. The number of burrowing owls left on the Prairies is so low that the survival of the species is in jeopardy. The species is threatened because its habitat, the prairie grasslands, is becoming smaller and smaller.

As the grasslands are converted to farmland or developed for human habitation, badgers and ground squirrels move away or in some cases are poisoned. For the owls, this means fewer burrows. In addition, because the owls eat small rodents as well as their own mass in grasshoppers every day, they are affected by the pesticides used to control grasshoppers and rodents. These pesticides have killed some owls and have reduced their reproductive success.

What can be done? Many farmers and landowners are joining a project called "Operation Burrowing Owl." When they join, they agree to protect the owl's nesting sites for at least five years and to use only pesticides considered harmless to the owl.

Students on the Prairies are getting involved by building urgently needed homes for the owls. Special wooden nesting boxes are constructed and buried in pastures at least 15 cm below the ground with a tunnel that gradually slopes up to the surface. To make the new occupants feel at home, a small dirt mound is provided next to the opening for the owls and owlets to sit on.

Students are also helping to band the owls. Each bird is banded with a numbered aluminum leg band to assist in later identification.

One family of owls in Saskatchewan was quickly removed from the path of road construction, and relocated a short distance away in the equipment compound of the Department of Highways! Local residents worked through the night building a nesting box for the birds. In the morning, road workers dug a hole for the box. The female, one chick, and seven eggs were carefully installed in their new home and road construction went ahead on schedule. A few weeks later, seven chicks emerged from their box.

The owls can adapt to a variety of unusual locations. "We have 15 pairs of owls on our front lawn and we take the best care of them that we can," says Walter Bedford, a cattle and grain farmer. "They are interesting little birds and don't hesitate to run at the family dog." The Bedfords were one of the many families honoured by Prince Philip of the United Kingdom (president of the World Wide Fund for Nature) for their participation in Operation Burrowing Owl — a program that may not only secure a future for this species but demonstrates what can be accomplished when individual citizens take the time to get involved.

Think About It

1. Consider the diet of the burrowing owl. Give some reasons why farmers might want to encourage this owl to nest on their properties.
2. Other prairie animals such as the long-tailed weasel, grey fox, wolverine, and western woodland caribou are in need of protection. Find out what efforts are being made to protect one of these species of animals.

Concerned students, farmers, and landowners on the Prairies are trying to save the burrowing owl.

Prince Philip honouring participants in Operation Burrowing Owl.

Working with Nature Photography

Do you like going for walks in the woods or exploring wilderness areas? John and Janet Foster do. They are wildlife photographers who travel to remote wilderness regions of Canada to capture on film the beauty and wonder to be found there. They have filmed and hosted many television documentaries and have written two books about Canada's wilderness regions. Janet Foster is the author of three books for children: *A Cabin Full of Mice, The Wilds of Whip-poor-will Farm*, and *Journey to the Top of the World*.

In a recent interview, John and Janet spoke about their careers. "Our photography has grown out of our interest in nature and a desire to record and share what we see. We hope that our work will create a sense of wonder and excitement, which will in turn create the desire to preserve and protect wilderness areas."

The Fosters carry a variety of camera equipment with them so that they can record animals at a distance or close up. Sometimes they have to disguise themselves with blinds and other devices so that they don't alarm the animals. Once, on the Yukon tundra, they draped themselves in mosquito netting, crouched low, and hoped that the caribou coming their way would think they were rocks. As the herd drew near, it parted and flowed like a river around them.

Another time, on Ellesmere Island in the high Arctic, they had a close encounter with a musk-ox. What they didn't know at the time was that the musk-ox was using its body language to tell them to move back. Suddenly, the musk-ox exploded into action. John tried to escape the charge by leaping across a wide, water-filled depression. Unfortunately, he landed face down in the middle of the icy water! But at least the musk-ox did not pursue him.

If you are fascinated by the natural world, a good way to pursue your interest is to join a field naturalist club. Later on in school, you could combine your studies in science with many other disciplines, such as film, photography, writing, or fine arts. Such a diversified program of study should open up many exciting career possibilities for you.

Checkpoint

1. In your notebook, write out the sentence below, inserting the words "population," "community," and "ecosystem" as appropriate in place of the black squares.
   A ■ of wolves living in the tundra ■ of the far north is part of a ■ that includes caribou, birch trees, and reindeer moss.

2. On a field trip, you see a flock of sparrows feeding on some grass seeds in a meadow.
   (a) What technique would you use to estimate the population of sparrows?
   (b) What technique would you use to estimate the population of grass plants?

3. (a) What is meant by sampling a population?
   (b) Why is sampling used by ecologists?
   (c) How might you sample an insect population?

4. Name three things that could affect the numbers of mice living in a barn. Include at least one biotic factor and one abiotic factor.

5. (a) What is biomass?
   (b) Explain why biomass is a more useful measure for ecologists than numbers of individuals in a population.
   (c) Which population of fish in the illustration has the greater biomass?

6. Why doesn't your mass increase by 100 g after you eat a 100 g sandwich?

7. Name two ways in which humans have an impact on the biotic and abiotic parts of the environment.

8. (a) Name two pollutants found in the area where you live.
   (b) Name one way in which the effect of one of these pollutants on the environment could be reduced.

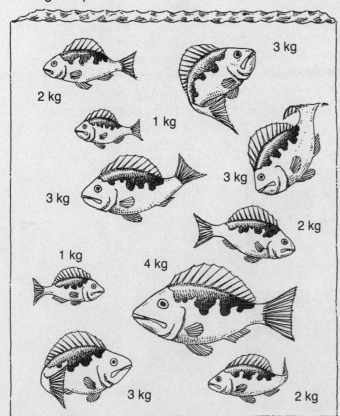

2 kg
3 kg
1 kg
3 kg
3 kg
2 kg
1 kg
4 kg
3 kg
2 kg

POPULATION A

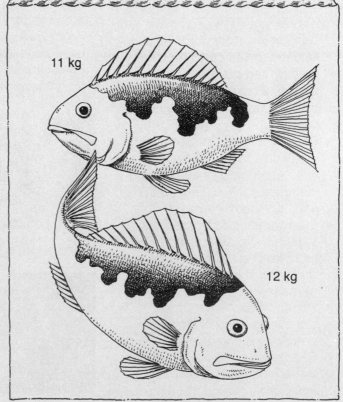

11 kg
12 kg

POPULATION B

Focus

- Living things interact with their environment in order to survive.
- The environment includes biotic (living) and abiotic (non-living) parts.
- Green plants and algae obtain the materials and energy they need from the abiotic environment, and are called producers.
- Biomes are large areas that share the same biotic and abiotic characteristics.
- Habitats are the places where organisms live, and niches describe the role of each species in the ecosystem it shares with other organisms.
- Animals obtain the materials and energy they need by consuming other organisms and are called consumers.
- Energy and materials pass from one organism to another through food chains and food webs.
- Organisms called decomposers break down the tissues of dead organisms and release materials back into the abiotic parts of the environment.
- Many organisms live closely together with others in symbiotic relationships that may benefit one or both partners.
- Populations of different organisms living in the same area form a community.
- Population sizes are estimated by various methods of sampling.
- In general, the populations of organisms at the top of a food chain are smaller than those at the bottom, forming a pyramid of numbers.
- Biomass is a useful measure of the amount of energy and materials at each level of a food chain.
- Energy is lost at each step up a food chain.
- Pollution resulting from human activities has a major impact on the environment.
- Pesticides accumulate as they pass up a food chain, and the levels of pesticides in organisms are biological indicators of the quality of an environment.
- People can minimize the harmful impact of their activities on the environment if they take appropriate steps based on awareness of the interactions among parts of the ecosystem.

(a) *Lamprey feeding on a trout.*

(b) *Tent caterpillar eating a leaf.*

Backtrack

1. List three components of the biotic environment and three components of the abiotic environment that allow you to survive.
2. In your notebook, match each of the words in List A with two terms from List B.

LIST A	LIST B
biome	surface of pond
ecosystem	woodland
micro-environment	tundra
	prairie
	rotting log
	pond

3. What are the main differences between a producer, a consumer, and a decomposer?
4. Draw a sketch to illustrate how nutrients are cycled through an ecosystem. (Include both biotic and abiotic parts of the environment.)
5. Name and define the symbiotic relationship shown in each of these photographs.

(c) *Bee collecting pollen from a flower.*

6. Suppose you set up a mini-ecosystem in a jar. It contains gravel, water, plants, fish, snails, and micro-organisms. What might happen to the populations of the remaining organisms if:
(a) the fish are removed?
(b) the plants are removed?

7. Explain why pesticides may accumulate in the bodies of animals as they pass through a food chain.

Synthesizer

8. Design an experiment to find the range of tolerance of small insects to one environmental factor. Your method must not harm the insects. Sketch the apparatus you would use and briefly describe the procedure, including how you would record your data.

9. Complete the following short story, telling how an increase in the population of a species of your choice affected both the biotic and the abiotic environment.
"During the night of March 3, 2033, the number of [organism of your choice] in the world suddenly increased. When people woke up in the morning, they discovered ten times as many [organisms] as there had been before."

10. (a) Design a survival kit that would allow you to live in a warm, dry, bare cave for one month, having no contact with the outside world. List the items you would put in your kit, along with a reason for each item.
(b) Which item in your kit could you live without? Remove it from your list. What other item is not essential to your survival? Continue asking yourself this question and removing items until you have a list that contains only the minimum necessary for you to survive for one month.
(c) List any environmental factors already in the cave that are essential to your survival.

11. In the library one day, you find an atlas that was printed a hundred years ago. One of the maps shows the biomes of the world. You compare this map with a similar map in a modern atlas. You notice that the biomes of North America are similar on both maps. In the modern map of Africa, however, the tropical rain-forest biomes are smaller and the desert biomes are larger.
(a) Explain what factors may have caused the changes you observed in Africa.

(b) Why has there been no apparent change in North America?
(c) "Modern biome maps should have an extra biome to indicate where human activities have replaced all the original plants and animals." Explain the reasoning of the person making this statement.
(d) Draw a map of North America showing the boundaries of the biomes as they may appear a hundred years from now. Explain your reasoning for this biome distribution.

12. Shortly after a logging company started removing trees from the slopes of a river valley, people noticed that there were fewer fish in the river. They inferred that removing the trees had caused changes in the environment that eventually affected the fish. List as many ways as you can think of in which removing trees might affect fish. Suggest how it might be possible to allow loggers to remove trees without harming the fish.

13. When rivers become polluted, they often have low amounts of oxygen dissolved in the water. Therefore, most organisms can no longer live in them. However, leeches and certain insects can live in such water. Explain how an ecologist could make use of this knowledge.

Skillbuilder One

The SI Units

The system of measurement that is used throughout most of the world today is the *Système international d'unités* (SI). This system was developed in France in 1791 and was revised and modernized in 1960. We often refer to it as the metric system: The name comes from the base unit of length, the metre. Table A shows the units of measurement that are used in this book.

A good swimmer can swim about 50 m in 60 s.

A small car has a mass of about 1000 kg.

We have 60 ha of land, divided into 10 fields.

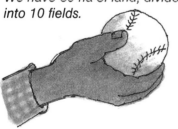

It takes about 1 N of force to lift this baseball.

Table A *Some SI Quantities, Units, and Symbols*

QUANTITY	UNIT	SYMBOL
length	kilometre	km
	metre*	m
	centimetre	cm
	millimetre	mm
mass	kilogram*	kg
	gram	g
	tonne	t
area	square metre	m²
	square centimetre	cm²
	hectare	ha
volume	cubic metre	m³
	cubic centimetre	cm³
	litre	L
	millilitre	mL
time	second*	s
temperature	degree Celsius	°C
force	newton	N
energy	kilojoule	kJ
	joule	J

*NOTE: These are base units. Other SI units are derived from base units such as these.

The SI is easy to use and understand because all the units of measurement are derived from base units. Any unit can be divided or multiplied by 10 to give smaller or larger units. A prefix is used to show the relationship between units. Table B shows common metric prefixes and gives some examples.

This satellite orbits the Earth at an altitude of 36 000 km.

69 cm

This German shepherd has a mass of 33 kg and has a shoulder height of 69 cm.

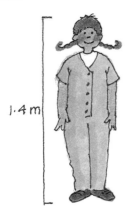

1.4 m

This girl is 1.4 m tall.

Table B

PREFIX	SYMBOL	FACTOR BY WHICH THE UNIT IS MULTIPLIED	EXAMPLE
mega	M	1 000 000	
kilo	k	1 000	1000 m = 1 km
hecto	h	100	
deca	da	10	
—	—	1	
deci	d	0.l	
centi	c	0.01	0.01 m = 1 cm
milli	m	0.001	0.001 m = 1 mm

NOTE: one tonne (t) = one megagram (Mg); one hectare (ha) = one square hectometre (hm²)

Converting Units

To convert from one unit to another, you need to move the decimal point. The examples in Table B show this. The decimal moves to the right when the new unit is smaller. The decimal moves to the left when the new unit is larger. Study the three sample problems below to think about how to convert from one unit to another; then practise your own skills in Skillbuilding Practice 1-1.

1. 3 m = ? cm

Solution Because 1 m = 100 cm, you should move the decimal two places to the right. Therefore, 3 m = 300 cm.

2. 2463 g = ? kg

Solution Because 1000 g = 1 kg, you should move the decimal three places to the left. Therefore, 2463 g = 2.463 kg.

3. 0.4 km = ? cm

Solution Because 1 km = 100 000 cm, you should move the decimal five places to the right. Therefore, 0.4 km = 40 000 cm.

Skillbuilding Practice 1-1

Test Your Metric Skills

1. (a) 1 mL = ? L
   (b) 10 mL = ? L
   (c) 100 mL = ? L
   (d) 1000 mL = ? L
2. A shoe box is 20 cm long.
   (a) What is the length of the shoe box in millimetres?
   (b) What is the length of the shoe box in metres?
3. Solve the following problems.
   (a) 25 mm = ? cm
   (b) 350 cm = ? m
   (c) 10 mg = ? g
   (d) 786 355 cm = ? km
   (e) 3.2 kg = ? g
   (f) 55 km = ? m
4. An Olympic-sized swimming pool is 50 m long. Give its length in centimetres.
5. A bunch of carrots has a mass of 0.6 kg. What is the mass of the bunch of carrots in grams?
6. Young children receive about 5.5 kJ of energy from their food each day. How many joules of energy is this?

Models in Science

Do you understand a problem more easily if it is presented in the form of a diagram? Many people do. For some problems, you need to have either an actual picture or a mental image before you can solve them. Pictures, diagrams, or other means of representing something are types of **models**; images like these help you understand things you cannot observe directly.

Models don't have to look like the thing they represent. For example, a city street map is a type of model; in this model the streets are simply coloured lines. The map doesn't show any buildings, and you don't learn from it what the streets look like. Although it gives no details of the city's appearance, a street map can be a very useful model when you're trying to find your way in an unfamiliar place!

Engineers make three-dimensional models of structures they intend to build and they use the models to test their plans. A model of the Toronto City Hall, for example, was tested in a wind tunnel at the Institute for Aerospace Studies at the University of Toronto before the building was actually constructed. As a result of the test, the original plans were changed. The end walls were made stronger to ensure that the building could withstand strong winds.

Toronto City Hall.

Mental models can be as useful as physical models. Do you accept the idea that there are radio waves in the air around you? You can't see or feel or taste these waves, but if you turn on a radio, you get sound. Scientists have devised a model to explain radio waves. The model accounts for how radio waves work. Because of their understanding of the model, scientists and technologists can use radio waves for many useful purposes.

Models are also helpful in representing things that are either extremely large or extremely small. For example, the model on this page shows the five inner planets of our solar system. It helps us to visualize the relative sizes and positions of the planets as they orbit the Sun. The model is not exactly like the real thing. The scale used to show the size of the planets is 2000 times the scale used to show the size of the orbits. (If the same scale were used for both planets and orbits, either the planets would be too small to see, or the model would be too large to fit into a football stadium!) The Sun is also not shown to scale. (The diameter of the Sun is about ten times the diameter of Jupiter.) In spite of its limitations, the model helps us to visualize the relative sizes and positions of the planets as they orbit the Sun.

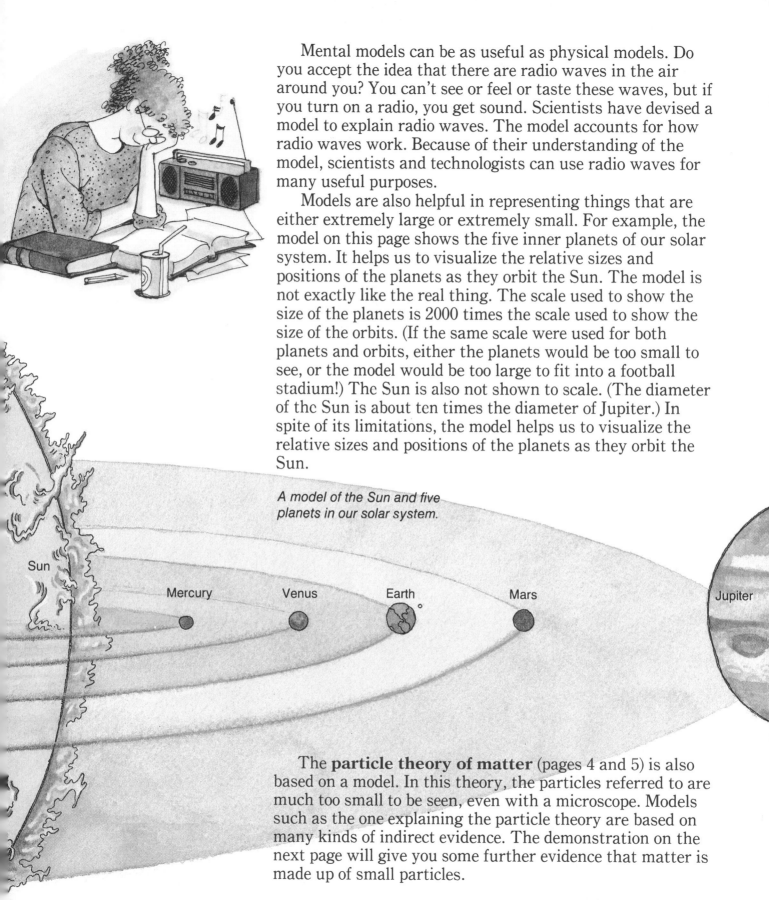

A model of the Sun and five planets in our solar system.

Sun   Mercury   Venus   Earth   Mars   Jupiter

The **particle theory of matter** (pages 4 and 5) is also based on a model. In this theory, the particles referred to are much too small to be seen, even with a microscope. Models such as the one explaining the particle theory are based on many kinds of indirect evidence. The demonstration on the next page will give you some further evidence that matter is made up of small particles.

Brownian Motion: Demonstration

Materials

smoke chamber
source of smoke
microscope
bright light source

Procedure

1. Set up the apparatus as shown here.
2. When some of the smoke has been drawn into the chamber, observe carefully and describe the motion of the specks of smoke.
3. Concentrate on one speck and describe its motion.

Finding Out

1. Make a diagram to show what must be happening to an individual speck of smoke to cause it to move as you observed.
2. This type of motion of small specks is called **Brownian motion**. Explain how Brownian motion helps you infer whether air is made up of particles.

The motion of specks of smoke can be observed by using a smoke chamber.

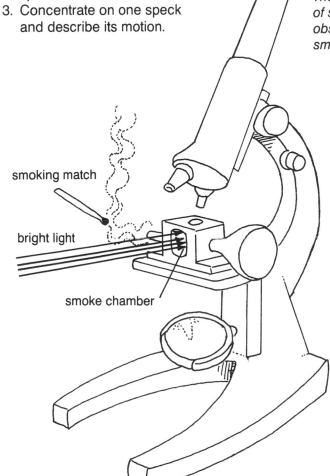

smoking match

bright light

smoke chamber

Extension

3. To help you visualize the size of the particles making up matter, suppose you have accidentally burned a cherry pie. The charred cherry pie is mostly carbon. To get a single particle of carbon, you need to cut the pie in half, cut one of the halves in half, cut one of these pieces in half, and so on. After about 90 cuts, you would have a single particle of carbon. Take a piece of paper (round or square) about the size of a pie. Cut it in half as many times as you can. How many more cuts would you have to make in order to get a piece of paper the size of a carbon particle?

Measuring Matter

Mass

The amount of matter in an object is its **mass**. You can measure mass by using a balance. In your science classroom, you may have balances similar to the ones shown here. Once you are familiar with the equipment, try the following exercise.

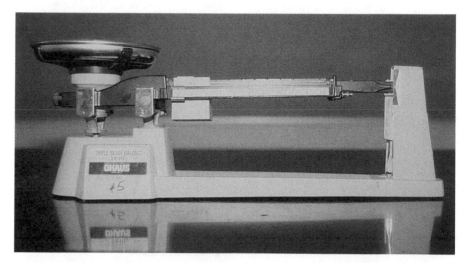

Triple-beam balance.

Equal-arm balance.

1. Obtain four solid objects from your teacher. Determine the mass of the first object and record it in your notebook. Then estimate the mass of each of the other objects. Use the balance to check how close your estimates were to the actual masses.

2. A raisin has a mass of about 1 g. Approximately how many raisins are there in a package containing 1 kg of raisins?

3. (a) A car has a mass of 1.6 Mg. What is its mass in kilograms?
   (b) If an average human has a mass of 70 kg, how many humans would be needed to balance a car on an equal-arm balance (a very large one)?

4. Estimate approximately how many kilograms of solid food you eat in one week.

5. Describe how you would measure the mass of a given amount of liquid. Assume that you can use a balance and that you have a container for the liquid. List the steps you would take to determine the mass of the liquid.

6. (a) Pour some water into a beaker, and estimate the mass of the water, using only your senses.
   (b) Using a second, dry container, follow the steps you outlined in Step 5 above, to determine the mass of the water. How close was your estimate?

Volume

Units of Volume

Volume is an amount of space. The volume of an object is the amount of space it occupies. Because the base unit of length in the SI is the metre, the unit of volume is the cubic metre (m^3). A cubic metre is the space occupied by a cube 1 m × 1 m × 1 m. This unit of volume is used to measure large quantities, such as the volume of concrete in a building. In your experiments, you are more likely to use the cubic centimetre (cm^3) or the cubic decimetre (dm^3) to record the volume of a solid object.

You can easily calculate the volume of a rectangular prism if you know its length, width, and height.

$$volume = length \times width \times height$$

If all the sides are measured in centimetres (cm), the volume will be in cubic centimetres (cm^3). If all the sides are measured in metres, the volume will be in cubic metres (m^3).

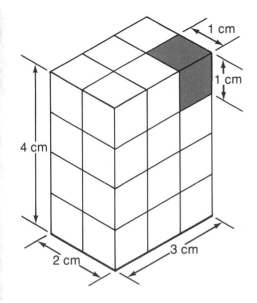

For the small cubes shown in the diagram, it is most convenient to measure the sides in centimetres. You can calculate the volume in cubic centimetres.

volume = 1 cm × 1 cm × 1 cm = 1 cm³

You could calculate the volume of the large block in cubic centimetres or in cubic metres, whichever is more convenient.

volume = 2 cm × 3 cm × 4 cm = 24 cm³
volume = 0.02 m × 0.03 m × 0.04 m = 0.000 024 m³

All these units are **cubic units** of volume. When measuring the volume of liquids, **capacity units** are often used instead of cubic units. The basic unit of volume for liquids is the litre (L). A common related unit is the millilitre (mL). You've probably seen capacities in litres and millilitres printed on the containers of products such as milk, juice, and soft drinks. In your science classroom as well, you use millilitres and litres.

> Cubic units and capacity units are related.
> $1 \text{ cm}^3 = 1 \text{ mL}$
> $1 \text{ dm}^3 = 1 \text{ L}$
> $1 \text{ m}^3 \ = 1 \text{ kL}$

You can measure the volume of a liquid directly in a graduated cylinder, by reading the markings on its side. The upper surface of the liquid is curved where it touches the side of the container; this curved surface is called the **meniscus**. You should read the level of the liquid at the *lowest point* of the meniscus. For an accurate measurement, you should have your eye at this level.

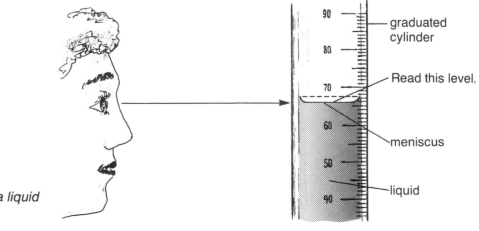

Reading the volume of a liquid accurately.

1. State an appropriate SI unit to measure the volume of:
   (a) the air in your lungs;
   (b) a soft drink in a bottle;
   (c) sand in a dump truck;
   (d) shampoo in a squeezable tube; and
   (e) a brick.

2. Examine the diagram of the aquarium.
   (a) Calculate its volume in cubic centimetres.
   (b) What is the aquarium's maximum capacity in litres?

Materials

overflow can
graduated cylinder
irregularly shaped objects (small and large)
water
dissecting needle (optional)

PART A

Procedure

1. With your finger over the spout, fill the overflow can above the level of the spout. Place the can on a level surface and allow the excess water to drain out into a sink.

2. Hold a graduated cylinder under the spout, and carefully lower the object into the water. If necessary, push the object gently under the surface of the water by using a dissecting needle or a pencil. Catch the water from the overflow can in the cylinder.

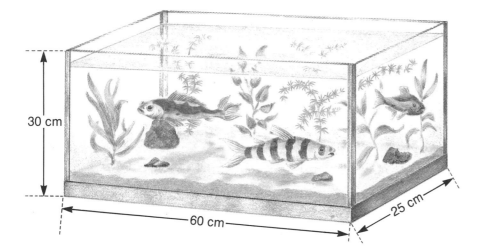

Volume of Irregular Solids

How accurately can you estimate volume? Try estimating the volume of several irregularly shaped objects such as a rock, a piece of chalk, a spoon, and an eraser. You can measure the volume of solid objects such as these by determining how much liquid they displace. There are two similar methods: **overflow** (useful for large objects), and **displacement of water** (useful for smaller objects). Try these methods in the following exercise.

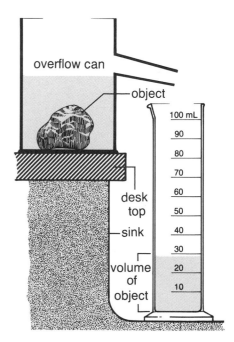

Determining volume by overflow.

3. Measure the volume of water in the cylinder. This volume is equal to the volume of the irregularly shaped solid.

PART B

1. Pour some water into a graduated cylinder and measure its volume. Record the volume in your notebook.
2. Tilt the graduated cylinder slightly, and gently slide a small object into it. If necessary, push the object beneath the surface of the water by using a dissecting needle or a pencil.
3. Read the volume at the surface of the water. Calculate the difference from the original volume. The increase in volume is equal to the volume of the irregularly shaped object.

Finding Out

1. Now that you know the volumes in millilitres of these irregularly shaped solid objects, write their volumes in cubic centimetres.
2. What method would you use to find the volume of the following?
   (a) an orange
   (b) a grape
   (c) a portable tape recorder

3. (a) What problem might arise if you tried to use displacement to find the volume of a piece of soap? What could you do to minimize the problem?
   (b) List at least two other objects for which overflow or displacement are not suitable methods to use in determining the volume. Explain your reasoning.

Extension

4. Use two different methods to determine the volume of the same regularly shaped objects. By comparing the following methods, determine which is more accurate.
   (a) Determine the volume of each object by overflow or displacement.
   (b) Measure the dimensions of the objects and calculate their volumes. (The abbreviations you should use are: l for length, w for width, h for height, and r for radius.)

   volume of rectangular prism = $l \cdot w \cdot h$

   volume of cylinder = $\pi \cdot r^2 \cdot h$

   volume of sphere = $\frac{4}{3} \cdot \pi \cdot r^3$

   (c) Which method seems more accurate? Give a reason for your answer.

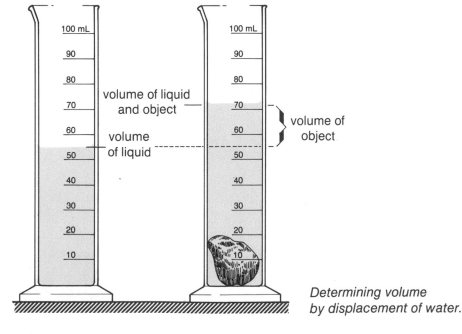

Determining volume by displacement of water.

Graphing

Interpreting Graphs

Being able to understand and make sense of data is an important skill in science. In an experiment or in your research, you may collect large amounts of numerical data. If you plot the data on an appropriate graph, the shape of the line will allow you to recognize patterns and see trends. If you plot two sets of data on the same graph, you will find it easy to make comparisons. Try the following exercises for practice in interpreting graphs.

Skillbuilding Practice 4-1

A Fast Start

In preparation for a race, the owners of a speedboat wanted to find out how quickly their boat would accelerate. They clocked its speed every 2 s as it started from rest. Their measurements are shown on the graph.

1. (a) What was the speed of the boat after 2 s?
   (b) What was the speed of the boat after 8 s?
   (c) What is the maximum speed of the boat?
2. (a) At what time was the speed of the boat increasing most rapidly?
   (b) Describe how the boat's speed changes over time.
3. How long does it take before the speedboat reaches a steady speed?

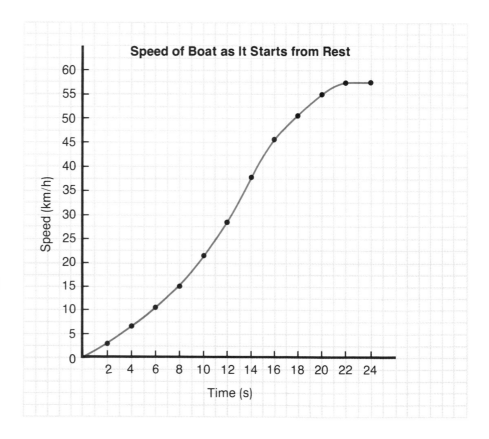

Speed of Boat as It Starts from Rest

Daily Temperatures

The southernmost tip of Canada is Point Pelee, a peninsula that extends into Lake Erie in southern Ontario. Here, the climate is different from anywhere else in Canada, and as a result, the vegetation and wildlife are unique. To prepare the data for this graph, daily high and low temperatures were measured at Point Pelee over several years. Each month, the average daily high and the average daily low temperatures were calculated. After several years, all the data for each month were averaged. The result of these calculations is shown on the graph, with one line representing the average daily high temperatures and the other showing the average daily low temperatures.

Birdwatching at the southern tip of Point Pelee, Ontario.

1. During how many months is the average daily high temperature below freezing (0°C)?
2. During how many months is the average daily low temperature below freezing (0°C)?
3. In what month(s) is there the greatest difference between average daily high temperature and average daily low temperature?
4. In what month(s) is there the smallest difference between average daily high temperature and average daily low temperature?

Average Daily High and Low Temperatures at Point Pelee, Ontario

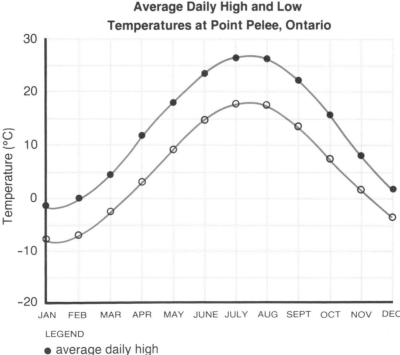

LEGEND
- • average daily high
- ○ average daily low

Steps in Making a Graph

1. Collect the data to be graphed. The data consist of pairs of numbers, called **variables**. Arrange the pairs of numbers in two columns in a table.
2. Prepare the axes. Draw a vertical line and a horizontal line that meet at the **origin**. Decide which is the **manipulated variable** (the condition that is set and systematically regulated by the experimenter), and label the horizontal axis with this quantity and its units. Label the vertical axis with the **responding variable**, the condition to be measured, along with its units.
3. Mark the scales on both axes. You should keep in mind that all data should fit on one piece of graph paper and that the graph should be large enough to fill most of the page. It is not necessary for the scales to start at zero if this is not suitable for the data.
4. Plot the points on the graph. For each point, make a dot surrounded by a small circle. (If you are plotting more than one set of results on one graph, use a different shape to surround the second set of points, or use a different colour for the points belonging to each set of data.)
5. Draw a smooth line through the points.
6. Complete the graph. Add a title. If there is more than one line on the graph, include a legend to identify the sets of points.

Preparing Graphs

1. A researcher, working for a tennis-ball manufacturer, wants to know how high a tennis ball will bounce when it is dropped from different heights. The ball is dropped from heights of 0.5 m, 1.0 m, 1.5 m, and 2.0 m, and the rebound height is measured. Show how each axis of the graph should be labelled.

2. An engineer designing a new spigot (tap) for oil barrels needs to know the time it takes to drain a barrel through different-sized holes. The time it takes to drain a barrel through holes with diameters of 1.0 cm, 2.0 cm, 3.0 cm, 4.0 cm, and 5.0 cm is measured. Show how each axis of the graph should be labelled.

3. A ball was dropped from various heights. The height to which it bounced was measured each time. The results are shown in Table C. Prepare a graph of these data.

Table C

DROP HEIGHT (cm)	REBOUND HEIGHT (cm)
10	8
20	16
30	24
40	32
50	40

4. Before deciding which of two bows to buy, an archer measured the force in newtons (N) needed to pull back the strings of the two bows different distances. The results are shown in Table D. Present this information in the form of a graph.

Table D

DISTANCE BETWEEN STRING AND BOW (cm)	FORCE REQUIRED (N)	
	BOW A	BOW B
20	0	0
30	18	26
40	35	51
50	53	75
60	71	102
70	87	123
80	100	150

5. (a) Table E gives temperature data for Fort McMurray, Alberta. Plot the data on a graph.
   (b) The graph and the four questions in Skillbuilding Practice 4-2 on page 339 refer to similar data for Point Pelee, the southernmost tip of Canada. Answer the same four questions, using your graph of the Fort McMurray temperatures.
   (c) In what ways are these two graphs similar and how are they different?

Table E *Average Daily High and Low Temperatures at Fort McMurray, Alberta*

MONTH	MAXIMUM (°C)	MINIMUM (°C)
January	-17	-27
February	-9	-22
March	-2	-16
April	9	-5
May	17	2
June	21	7
July	23	10
August	21	8
September	15	3
October	9	-2
November	-4	-13
December	-12	-22

Working with a Microscope

A water-filled flask can act as a magnifying lens.

Light microscopes make objects appear larger than they are because they contain lenses. A **lens** changes the path of light as the light travels through it. A drop of water can act as a lens and so can a flask filled with water. Both of these are simple magnifying devices, or microscopes.

In a compound microscope, light passes through at least two systems of lenses. For example, in the microscope shown in the diagram, light passes through one of the three objective lenses, then through two lenses in the eyepiece. Examine the diagram, then try to identify the various parts of the microscopes shown in the photograph on page 343.

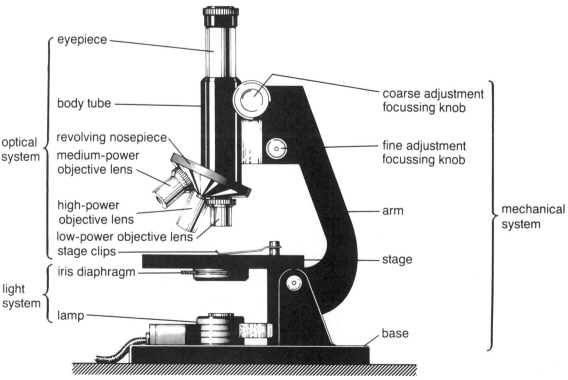

The parts of the compound microscope.

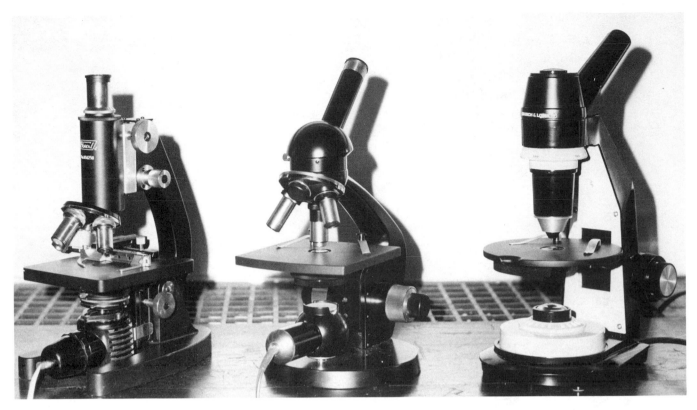

These are all compound microscopes.

Hints for Handling a Microscope

A microscope is a valuable and delicate instrument. Review the parts of the microscope shown in the diagram and read the following hints so that you can use a microscope properly.

1. Use both hands to carry a microscope. Use one hand to hold it vertically by the metal arm, and use the other hand for extra support under the base.
2. Place the microscope on the surface of a cleared lab bench or a clean desk.
3. Keep the microscope in an upright position at all times. Tell your teacher if your microscope is dirty or if the parts do not move freely. Do not try to force any parts of the microscope to move. If you are examining a liquid, use only a small drop. Keep the stage clean and dry.
4. Start focusing by using the low-power objective lens. (To focus means to make something sharp or clear.) *Observe the microscope from the side as you use the coarse adjustment knobs.* Lower the lens as close as possible to the stage without touching it, as shown in the photograph on the next page.

5. When you focus, look through the eyepiece and slowly turn the coarse adjustment knobs so that the lens moves *upwards* from the stage. The fine adjustment knobs may then be used to sharpen your view of the object.
6. When you have finished using the microscope, remove the glass slide, place both stage clips so that they point forwards, and ensure the low-power lens clicks into place below the eyepiece.
7. Cover your microscope when it is not in use.

This student is demonstrating why the high-power lens should never be used with the coarse adjustment knobs. Both the high- and medium-power lenses are long enough to touch the slide if they are lowered too much, perhaps breaking the slide and/or the lens. Only the low-power lens should be lowered using the coarse adjustment knobs!

Using the Microscope

Skillbuilding Practice 5-1 will give you experience in preparing a slide for viewing and in using a microscope. You will observe a **wet mount**, a glass slide that has been prepared using water and a cover slip. A wet mount spreads the water to produce a very thin layer for viewing under a microscope.

PART A
Preparing a Wet Mount

Materials
letter such as "a," "e," or "r", cut from a newspaper
water
dropper
plastic cover slip
microscope slide

Procedure

1. Using the dropper, place a small drop of water on a clean glass slide.
2. Lay the newspaper letter carefully on top of the water.

prepared letter on drop of water

microscope slide

3. Hold the plastic cover slip between your thumb and forefinger. Touch one edge of the cover slip to the slide at the edge of the water, as shown.

cover slip

4. After the water has spread to the corners of the cover slip, slowly lower it onto the slide so that the letter is covered.

PART B
Using the Microscope

Materials
compound microscope
wet mount of a newspaper letter
glass slides and cover slips
facial tissue
a piece of Velcro
other materials you'd like to view

Procedure
1. Turn on or adjust the light source of your microscope.
2. Make sure the low-power lens is "clicked" into position.
3. Lay the slide with your wet mount under the stage clips, so the cover slip faces up and the letter faces you. Make sure the letter is over the opening on the stage.
4. Focus with the low-power lens, using the coarse adjustment knobs.
   NOTE: If you have air bubbles in your **field of view**—the area that you can see—prepare a new wet mount. Be sure you *slowly* lower the cover slip onto the slide to avoid air bubbles.

> **CAUTION:** Never focus downwards.

5. In your notebook, draw what you see. Draw a circle around your diagram, and label it to show its magnification under the low-power lens. (Hint: The magnification of your eyepiece lens multiplied by the magnification of your low-power lens gives the *total* magnification.)
6. As you look through your microscope, slowly move the glass slide slightly to the right, then to the left. Describe in your notebook what happens, in each case, to the letter you are observing.
7. Now observe the letter through your microscope's medium-power lens by bringing it into position. Make sure that you feel the "click" that tells you the lens is in place.

> **CAUTION:** When using the medium- and high-power lenses, focus only with the fine adjustment knobs. Always move the lens *away* from the slide.

8. In your notebook, draw what you see, placing a circle around it and labelling it.
9. Using the high-power lens, repeat the procedure.
10. Prepare and observe wet mounts of several other materials. Draw and label a diagram for each material.

Finding Out
1. When you move a slide in a certain direction, what happens to the position of the object you are observing under a microscope?
2. Under which lens was your field of view largest? In other words, under which lens could you view the whole newspaper letter or the greatest amount of it?
3. How many times is an object enlarged or magnified under your microscope by using:
   (a) the low-power lens? and
   (b) the high-power lens?

Cell Structure and Function

Before microscopes were invented, only about 400 years ago, people didn't know that living things are made of cells. During the 17th and 18th centuries, scientists used early microscopes to discover many kinds of cells, especially single-celled micro-organisms. Gradually, scientists came to realize that all living things are made up of cells. By the mid-19th century, the **cell theory** was developed. It states that:

1. Cells are the basis of structure for all living things.
2. Cells are the basis of function for all living things.
3. All cells are formed from pre-existing cells.

Cells vary greatly in size. One of the smallest cells is the pneumonia bacterium (0.0001 mm). The ostrich egg is probably the largest single cell (75 mm). The longest cells in the human body are nerve cells, which can be up to 1000 mm long. A human egg cell measures about 0.2 mm across. Because they have so many different functions, cells also have many different shapes.

All cells, no matter what their size or shape, have three main parts that are responsible for much of the basic structure and function of the cell.

- The **cell membrane** regulates the passage of certain substances into or out of the cell. It also separates one cell from other cells. Under a microscope, the cell membrane looks like a very thin line.
- The **cytoplasm** contains all the other cell structures, or **organelles**, that are essential for a cell to function. It is a jelly-like material where many processes are occurring all at once, rather like a factory. The cytoplasm receives materials from the cell membrane and expels waste materials back out through the cell membrane. Within the cytoplasm are many smaller structures in which important processes occur. Some of these smaller structures can be seen under a classroom microscope, but a more powerful microscope is required to see the details of these structures.
- The **nucleus** is the "control centre" of the cell. It organizes and directs the functions of the cell and is essential for the production of new cells. Within the nucleus are the chromosomes containing the genes that are responsible for all inherited characteristics. Under a microscope, the nucleus looks like a dark blob.

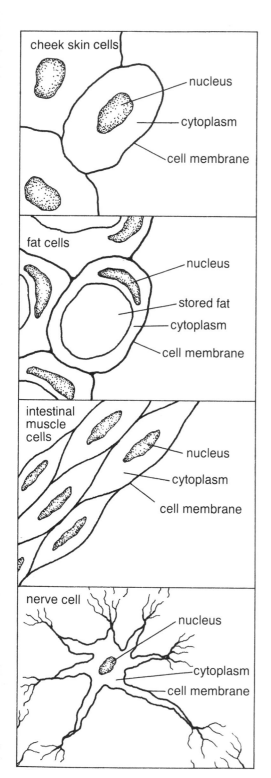

Different kinds of human cells (not drawn to scale).

Plant cells have an additional structure outside the cell membrane, called the **cell wall**, which animal cells do not have. When you look at plant cells, you can see this structure easily. Usually the cell membrane and the cell wall are so close together you can't see the difference between them using a light microscope. Whereas the cell membrane is a living part of the cell, the cell wall is non-living (made up of material produced by the cell).

When you look at cells under a microscope you may be able to identify several other organelles.

- Within the nucleus, you may see a darker area called the **nucleolus**. This organelle is involved with the transfer of information from the nucleus to the cytoplasm.
- **Vacuoles** are organelles surrounded by a membrane and filled with different substances. In plant cells these may be large and easy to see. In most animal cells they are small. (However, in certain animal cells, large vacuoles are used to store fat, as shown on page 346.)
- In plant cells only, you may be able to see **chloroplasts**. These organelles contain the green pigment called chlorophyll, which is used in photosynthesis.

The diagrams show a typical animal and plant cell, as you might see them under a microscope. When viewed under a light microscope, organelles in cells, other than those described above, look like granules.

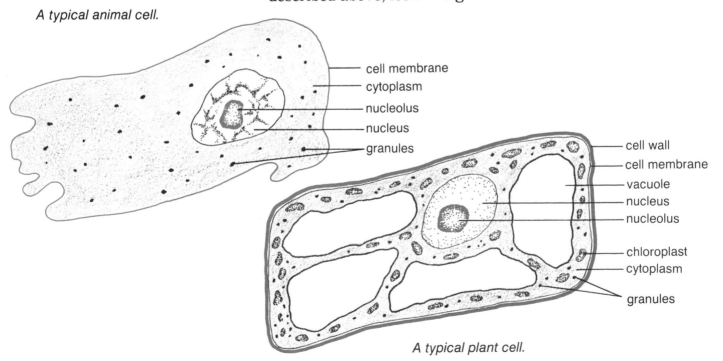

A typical animal cell.

cell membrane
cytoplasm
nucleolus
nucleus
granules

cell wall
cell membrane
vacuole
nucleus
nucleolus
chloroplast
cytoplasm
granules

A typical plant cell.

Looking at Animal and Plant Cells

PART A
Problem

What can you see in a living plant cell?

Materials

forceps
microscope slide
cover slip
compound microscope
paper towel or tissue
iodine solution
dropper
water
small section of white onion (with outer dry skin removed)

Procedure

1. Put a small drop of water on a slide.
2. Using the forceps, strip a small, thin section of skin (membrane) from your onion. It will come off easily if the inner curved surface of the onion is folded, as shown.
3. Continue using the forceps to place the membrane on the drop of water. Be careful to have a single layer. Don't let the membrane fold over.
4. Place another small drop of water on top of the onion membrane.
5. Place the cover slip on the slide.
6. View your prepared slide with the compound microscope using the low-power objective lens.
7. Make a diagram of at least three cells and label any parts you can see.

> **CAUTION:** Iodine is a corrosive liquid that will stain skin, clothing, desk tops, and floors. Take care to avoid spilling. Quickly wipe up any accidental spills, and rinse the area with water.

8. Remove the slide from the microscope and carefully draw off the water by placing a piece of paper towel or tissue at one edge of the cover slip.
9. Using the dropper, place a small drop of iodine solution at one edge of the cover slip. Allow it to spread underneath the cover slip.

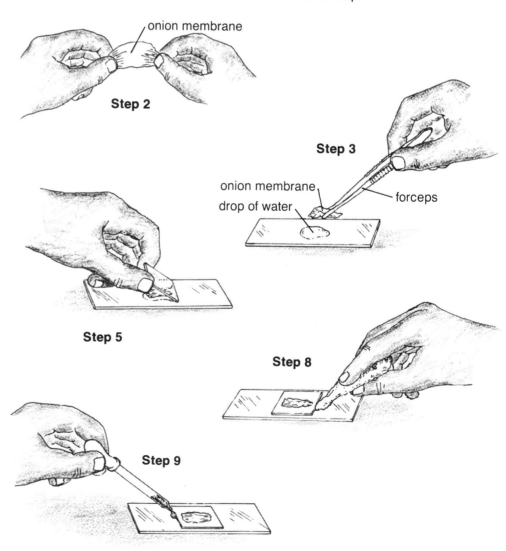

Step 2 — onion membrane

Step 3 — onion membrane, drop of water, forceps

Step 5

Step 8

Step 9

10. View the slide again using first the low-power, then the medium-power, and finally the high-power objective lens.
11. Make a diagram of one cell as it appears under the high-power lens. Label the nucleus, cell wall, and cytoplasm.

Finding Out

1. What cell structures could you see without the iodine?
2. What cell structures could you see more easily after adding iodine?

Extension

3. Using forceps, peel a piece of thin skin from a section of either a tomato or a green pepper. Then carefully use a scalpel or a single-edged razor blade to scrape the inner surface of the skin to remove the flesh. The skin should be clear. Place the skin carefully on a slide so that the outer surface is uppermost. Add two drops of iodine solution, then position the cover slip. Observe your slide under all magnifications, starting with low power. Make a diagram of two cells that are beside each other, and label all visible parts.

CAUTION: A scalpel (or single-edged razor blade) is extremely sharp.

Scrape the inner surface of the tomato skin to remove the flesh. The skin you examine under the microscope should be clear (transparent).

4. Examine a prepared slide of a water plant such as *Elodea* or *Spirogyra* under low power. Find an area in which the cells appear quite distinct, then move the slide until that area is in the centre of the field of view. Examine the area under medium power. Make a large, labelled diagram of one cell.

PART B
Problem

What can you see in an animal cell?

Materials

prepared microscope slide(s) of one or several of the following: human skin cells, human smooth muscle cells, frog blood cells
compound microscope

Procedure

1. Place the prepared slide on your microscope stage. Observe the slide first with low-, medium-, and then high-power lenses.

Finding Out

1. Make a diagram of two or three cells as they appear under high power.
2. Label any structures you recognize.

Finding Out More

3. What is the general shape of the cells?
4. Can you see all structures clearly within the cell? If not, explain why you think some may be difficult to observe.
5. Describe the ways in which these cells look different from the cells you observed in Part A.

Cells Working Together

The cells that make up most organisms are specialized to carry out different functions. Cells that are specialized to perform a certain function often form **tissues**. For example, a microscopic muscle cell in your arm acting alone would not be able to pull your arm up or extend it, but together with thousands of other similarly specialized cells, it forms a part of muscle tissue that can fulfill these functions quite efficiently. Tissues that are specialized for the same function together make up **organs**. The various organs that are specialized to perform certain tasks then act together, ensuring a **system** carries out its function. Most kinds of living organisms are dependent upon several different systems for their survival. For example, most organisms have a system to circulate nutrients and oxygen; a system to respond to stimuli; and a system to digest food.

the circulatory system

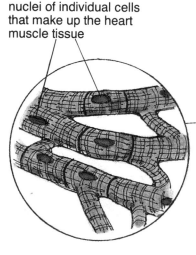

nuclei of individual cells that make up the heart muscle tissue

the heart—an organ

heart muscle—a tissue

Cells specialized to perform a certain function together form a tissue. Tissues function together to make up organs. Various organs work together to ensure that a system, such as the circulatory system, carries out its function.

Glossary

How to Use the Glossary

The numbers in parentheses after each definition tell you where to find the glossary word in the text. The first number is the Unit or Skillbuilder number; the number after the dash is the page number in the text. For example, at the end of the definition of **abiotic**, the number (6-275) tells you that this term occurs in the text in Unit Six on page 275. The following Pronunciation Key is used for several difficult words to help you pronounce them.

Pronunciation Key

a = **a**cid, m**a**sk	i = s**i**mple, th**i**s
ae = r**ai**n, s**a**me	oh = h**o**me, l**oa**n
ah = c**a**r, f**a**ther	oo = sh**oo**t, t**u**be
aw = h**o**t, l**aw**n	u = s**u**n, w**o**nder
e = m**e**t, sh**e**lter	uh = l**e**mon, foc**u**s
ee = cl**ea**n, sh**ee**t	uhr = t**ur**n, st**ir**,
ih = b**i**te, m**y**	w**or**ry, ins**er**t

abiotic describes non-living parts of the environment, such as soil and water. (6-275)

absolute age an exact age, which can be given in years or fractions of a year. (4-172)

accelerated aging a type of testing in which products are used repeatedly in order to determine how well they may withstand years of normal use. (3-124)

alloy a mixture consisting of two or more metals. For example, brass is an alloy of copper and zinc. (1-14)

anther the top part of the stamen of a flower, where pollen is produced. (5-255)

anticline an upfold of a rock layer. (4-186)

antifreeze a solution used in many automobile radiators to prevent freezing; usually consists of water and ethylene glycol. (1-48)

artificial materials human-made materials (also known as synthetics) such as plastics; distinguished from natural materials, such as cotton. (3-117)

asexual reproduction a method of reproduction in which a part of an individual breaks off, developing into a new individual; for example, the leaf of a plant, or budding in some other organisms (yeast, hydra, etc.). (5-259)

atom the smallest particle of an element that has all the properties of that element. (1-4)

balance an instrument used to measure the mass of an object by comparing its mass with that of a known mass. (SB3-333)

biohazardous infectious material WHMIS usage: organisms such as certain viruses, bacteria, fungi, and protozoa, which cause disease, and the toxins produced by such organisms. (Introduction-xiv) (3-134)

biological control the use of other organisms to reduce the numbers of a pest species; for example, encouraging the presence of ladybird beetles that eat aphids, and spiders that eat many pest species. (5-266)

biological indicators organisms whose presence or absence can be used to indicate how polluted an environment is. As well, in some cases, the amount of a pollutant in the organism can be measured to determine if the pollutant has reached a level considered to be dangerous. (6-318)

biomass the total mass of living material in a population. (6-310)

biome a large area of the Earth that has characteristic climate, soils, plants, and animals. (6-282)

biosphere the total area of the Earth in which living things are found. (6-280)

biotic the living parts of an organism's environment; in other words, all other organisms in the environment. (6-274)

boiling the rapid bubbling and change of state (liquid to gas) that occurs at a specific temperature when a liquid is heated. (1-44)

boiling point the temperature at which a liquid changes to a gas. (1-44)

boycott to refuse to buy certain products. (3-149)

bulb a short, underground stem, surrounded by scales (thick, fleshy leaves); used to start a new plant. (5-259)

Canadian Standards Association (CSA) an organization that tests a wide range of products against standards, to ensure the products' safety and reliability. (3-130)

capacity units units such as the litre and millilitre; commonly used to measure the volume of liquids. (SB3-335)

carding the brushing of fibres with a toothed instrument that separates them before they are spun into yarn. (3-118)

cast a type of fossil made when sediment slowly fills a mould, showing the original form of the organism. (4-185)

cell the basic unit of which all living things (and those that have been living) are made. (SB5-346)

cell membrane the thin structure surrounding a cell that regulates the passage of substances into or out of the cell. (5-222) (SB5-346)

cell theory   a theory stating that cells are the basic structural and functional units of all living things and that they develop from existing cells.   (SB5-346)

cell wall   a rigid structure of non-living material surrounding the cell membrane of plant cells, but not animal cells.   (SB5-347)

cellular respiration   the cell process in which oxygen and food release energy for use by the organism.   (5-249)

characteristic   a feature or property of a substance or living thing.   (1-2)

chemical   a commonly used term referring to any substance. For example, oxygen, carbon dioxide, and hydrochloric acid are chemicals.   (4-157)

chemical energy   the form of energy stored in foods and fuels.   (2-87)

chlorophyll [KLOHR-oh-fil]   the green pigment, produced in green cells of plants and algae, that converts the energy of sunlight into the chemical energy of food.   (5-220)

chloroplasts   the organelles in the cells of green plants and some protists. It contains chlorophyll. (5-246) (SB5-347)

cinder cone   a type of volcano built up by bits of ash and cinder that pile up around the volcanic crater.   (4-189)

Class 1 lever   a lever in which the fulcrum is between the load and the effort force.   (2-62)

Class 2 lever   a lever in which the fulcrum is at one end, the load is in the middle, and the effort force is at the opposite end from the fulcrum.   (2-62)

Class 3 lever   a lever in which the effort force is between the fulcrum and the load.   (2-63)

cleavage   the tendency of a crystal to split most easily along a plane (flat surface) parallel to its flat sides or faces.   (4-160)

cloning   the asexual reproduction and subsequent growth of a new individual from one cell of a single organism.   (5-259)

collenchyma tissue [kuh-LENG-ki-muh TI-shoo]   a plant tissue in which the cells have thickened walls for added strength and support.   (5-241)

colloid   a mechanical mixture in which the tiny solid pieces or droplets are too small to settle but are larger than dissolved particles. The solid pieces or droplets remain suspended in the mixture. Milk is an example of a colloid.   (1-16)

combustible   WHMIS usage: easily set on fire (Introduction-xiv) (3-134)

commensalism   a relationship between two species in which one benefits and the other neither benefits nor is harmed.   (6-296)

community   a group of interacting populations of two or more different species that live together in the same area.   (6-303)

compacted   describes being squeezed together; rock fragments are compacted by the mass of sediment and water on top of them to form a larger mass of solid rock.   (4-166)

composite cone   a type of volcano made from alternating layers of cinder and hardened lava, forming a steep mound.   (4-190)

compound microscope   a microscope that uses a series of glass lenses to increase magnification; the type of microscope used in most schools.   (SB5-342)

compression waves   also known as P waves; fast-moving earthquake vibrations (seismic waves) that travel through the Earth's interior.   (4-195)

concentrated   describes a solution containing relatively more dissolved solute compared with another solution.   (1-35)

concentration   the amount of solute dissolved in a solvent.   (1-35)

condensation   the change of state from a gas to a liquid.   (1-6)

conglomerate   a type of sedimentary rock formed from pebbles and small stones.   (4-166)

conservation of energy   energy is neither created nor destroyed; it can be easily changed from one form to another.   (2-91)

consumer   a buyer of products and services (3-104). Also, in food chains, an organism that obtains its food by eating another organism.   (6-289)

consumer survey   a technique of questioning consumers to help determine the quality of a consumer product.   (3-125)

continental drift   the theory stating that continents have moved and are continuing to move slowly over the surface of the Earth.   (4-205)

contour farming   a technology of ploughing and cultivating the land at right angles to the slope so that water does not run off but is caught in furrows.   (5-234)

control   the variable that does not change in a scientific test; it is compared with the variables that do change.   (3-111)

core   the centre of the Earth, made up of a liquid and a solid layer.   (4-200)

corrosive material   WHMIS usage: a material (e.g., sodium hydroxide, hydrochloric acid) that wears away another material   (Introduction-xiv) (3-134)

crude oil   another name for petroleum, the liquid formed underground from matter that was once living.   (1-32)

crust   the outer layer of the Earth, from 5 to 60 km thick.   (4-156)

crystal   a naturally occurring piece of a solid, with straight edges, flat sides, and regular angles.   (1-27)

crystallize   to form into a crystal. This occurs as a solution evaporates, leaving a crystalline solute.   (1-27)

cubic units   units such as cm^3 and m^3 that are commonly used to measure volume, especially of solids.   (SB3-335)

cutting   a leaf or a piece of a stem that is cut from a plant in order to start a new plant.   (5-218)

cytoplasm [SIHT-oh-plaz-uhm]   the jelly-like material within a cell that contains other cell organelles. It receives materials from the cell membrane, and carries waste materials back out through the membrane. (SB5-346)

dangerously reactive material WHMIS usage: a material that undergoes a vigorous chemical reaction (Introduction-xiv) (3-134)

decay in radioactivity, the transformation of a radioactive element into a different element by giving off particles and energy. (4-3). Also, in soil, the decomposition of dead organisms. (5-229)

decomposer an organism that feeds on material that had once been living, either dead matter or waste matter. (6-293)

differentially permeable permits the movement of some particles through it but not others. For example, the cell membrane is differentially permeable. (5-222)

diffusion the gradual mixing of substances caused by the random movement of particles (1-4); therefore, the tendency of particles to move from a region of higher concentration to one of lower concentration (that is, from where there are more to where there are fewer particles) until mixing is complete. (5-224)

dilute describes a solution containing relatively little dissolved solute compared with another solution. (1-35)

dissolving the complete intermingling of the particles of two or more substances so that the substances appear as one. (1-12)

distillate the liquid formed and collected by the cooling of a gas. (1-28)

distillation the evaporation of a liquid followed by condensation of its gaseous form; used as a means of separating a substance from a mixture. (1-28)

dormancy a state in which an organism is alive but not active or growing. Seeds and the eggs of many insects may be dormant for a period before they begin to grow. (5-257)

driven gear the gear wheel to which the driving force is applied in a gear train. (2-81)

driving gear the gear wheel that supplies the driving force in a gear train. (2-81)

earthquake violent vibrations on the surface of the Earth, usually caused by movements along faults. (4-194)

ecology the study of interactions in the environment. (6-275)

ecosystem a network of interactions linking living (biotic) and non-living (abiotic) things. (6-274)

efficiency a measure (usually expressed as a percentage) of the amount of useful output energy from a machine, compared with the input energy needed to run the machine. (2-96)

effort force the amount of force that must be exerted in order to overcome the force of resistance on a load; the force required to do work. (2-57)

egg a cell that, when fertilized by a sperm, develops into an embryo. (5-255)

elastic potential energy the energy stored in a spring or other elastic device. (2-89)

electrical energy the energy of moving electrical particles. (2-87)

element a pure substance that cannot be further subdivided; composed of only one kind of particle. (4-157)

embryo the early stage in the development of a new individual. (5-255)

emulsifier a substance in an emulsion that keeps one liquid mixed with another so that they do not separate. (1-24)

emulsion the name given to a colloid in which tiny droplets of one liquid are suspended in another liquid. Hand lotion is an example of an emulsion. (1-16)

endangered species a kind of organism in immediate danger of extinction. An example is the blue whale. (6-298)

Energuide Number a guide, for consumers buying new appliances, that rates in kilowatt hours the amount of energy an appliance will use in a typical month; usually appears as a label on the appliance. (2-99)

energy the ability to do work. Energy exists in many forms, including thermal, light, sound, mechanical, electrical, elastic, chemical, magnetic, and nuclear. (2-56)

environment an organism's surroundings. (6-274)

epicentre the point on the Earth's surface above the point (focus) from which an earthquake originates. (4-196)

era unit of time in the geological time scale. Different eras last for different lengths of time. (4-180)

erosion the process by which soil and particles of rock are broken up and carried away by water, ice, or wind. (4-230)

essential nutrient a substance needed for the healthy life or growth of an organism. (5-230)

ethical based on moral principles. (3-149)

evaporation the change of state from a liquid to a gas. (1-6)

extinction the disappearance of a species from the Earth. (6-299)

extirpation the local extinction or the disappearance of a species from a part of its former range. (6-299)

extrusive rock rock formed from lava that hardened on the Earth's surface; also known as volcanic rock. (4-163)

faces the flat, smooth sides of a crystal. (4-106)

fair test a test in which all variables remain exactly the same except for the one variable being measured. (3-110)

families three major groups into which rocks may be classified: igneous, sedimentary, and metamorphic. (4-162)

fault a break in the Earth's crust along which movement of the crust may occur. (4-186)

fault-block mountain   a mountain produced when rock is lifted vertically along a fault.   (4-187)

fertilization   the union of an egg and sperm in sexual reproduction.   (5-255)

field test   a test carried out under normal conditions of use, rather than in a laboratory.   (3-124)

filter   a device used to separate parts of a mechanical mixture by holding back the larger pieces of one or more of the substances comprising the mixture.   (1-20)

filtrate   the material that passes through a filter.   (1-20)

filtration   the separation of the parts of a mixture by holding back the larger pieces.   (1-20)

flammable   WHMIS usage: very easily set on fire. (Introduction-xiv) (3-134)

flocculator   a substance that can make small pieces of a material stick together in clumps so that the material can be separated from a mixture. Alum is an example of a flocculator used in water-treatment plants.   (1-20)

flower   the sexual reproductive structure of a flowering plant.   (5-254)

focus   the point underground where energy is first released to cause an earthquake.   (4-196)

fold   the bending and tilting of sedimentary rock layers.   (4-184)

food chain   a series of organisms, beginning with a producer, each of which uses for food and thus obtains energy from the organism before it in the chain.   (6-290)

food web   a series of interconnected food chains, showing many feeding relationships among organisms.   (6-291)

force   any push or pull, measured in newtons (N).   (2-56)

force advantage   the advantage that is provided by a machine when the effort force is smaller than the force of gravity on the load being moved.   (2-66)

fossil   the rock-like remains or traces of an organism. (4-174)

fossil fuel   any fuel obtained from material that was once living, such as oil, coal, and natural gas.   (2-93)

fractional distillation   a technique used to separate liquids that boil at different temperatures.   (1-32)

fractionating column   a tower in which a mixture of liquids (for example, crude oil) is separated by the process of fractional distillation.   (1-32)

fracture   in geology, a rough, uneven break in a mineral.   (4-160)

freezing   the change of state from a liquid to a solid; solidification.   (1-6)

fulcrum   the point that supports a lever and upon which a lever pivots.   (2-61)

fungicide [FUN-ji-sihd]   a substance used to kill fungi. (5-260)

fungus [FUN-gus] (plural: fungi [FUNG-ih])   a type of micro-organism that includes yeast and mushrooms.   (5-257)

gas   a state of matter. A gas has no definite shape or volume. A gas takes the shape and volume of its container. Oxygen is a gas.   (1-2)

gas exchange   the exchange of carbon dioxide and oxygen from the surfaces of leaves. Also, the exchange of oxygen and carbon dioxide from the surfaces of lungs, gills, and some skin surfaces in animals.   (5-249)

gear train   two or more gear wheels that mesh so that rotary motion and force from one gear can be transferred to another gear.   (2-80)

gear wheel   a wheel with precisely manufactured, identical teeth arranged around its edge. It is used to transfer rotary motion or force to another gear wheel.   (2-80)

geological time scale   a scale, covering thousands of millions of years, which represents Earth's history, based largely on fossils found in different rock formations.   (4-180)

geology   the study of the Earth.   (4-210)

germinate   to sprout, as when a seed starts growing. (5-216)

graduated cylinder   a container used to measure volume. Its outside is marked off to indicate the capacity units of a substance in millilitres (mL).   (SB3-335)

grafting   inserting a shoot or bud from one variety of tree or shrub into the stem or root of another tree or shrub so that the shoot or bud will grow there.   (5-259)

graph   a diagram of numerical data that shows changes or comparisons. A graph is used to organize numerical information to make it easier to understand.   (SB4-338)

gravitational energy   the energy of falling objects. (2-88)

guard cells   paired bean-shaped cells that surround the openings (stomata) on the surfaces of leaves, and some other plant parts. These cells control the rate of transpiration by opening and closing the stomata. (5-246)

habitat   the natural home of an organism.   (6-284)

hardness   a characteristic of minerals. A scale is used to determine hardness; if one mineral will scratch another mineral, that shows the first mineral has greater hardness than the mineral that was scratched.   (4-158)

heat   the energy transferred from a hotter substance to a colder one.   (1-6)

herbicide   a substance used to kill unwanted plants such as weeds.   (5-260)

horizontal axis   the number line of a graph that runs from left to right. The horizontal axis shows the manipulated variable. It is often called the x-axis. (SB4-340)

host   an organism that is used for food or shelter by a parasite.   (6-297)

hydroelectricity   electricity that is generated from falling or rapidly flowing water.   (2-92)

hydrometer [hih-DRAW-met-uhr]   a device used to estimate the concentration of a solution.   (1-36)

hydroponics   a technology for growing plants in nutrient solutions, rather than in soil.   (5-237)

hypothesis   a model or idea that explains why something always happens in the natural world.   (1-4)

igneous rock a type of rock formed by the cooling of magma (molten rock). (4-162)

incandescent [in-kan-DES-ent] gives off light due to an object's high temperature. (2-96)

inclined plane a type of simple machine; in its simplest form, a sloped ramp that reduces the effort force needed to lift a load from one level to another. (2-57)

indicator a substance used to detect the presence of another substance. For example, iodine is an indicator of the presence of starch. (5-247)

inference a possible explanation for the cause of an event, based on a set of observations. (1-2)

inorganic fertilizer a manufactured product for promoting plant growth, containing essential nutrients. (5-231)

insecticide a substance used to kill insects. (5-260)

insoluble unable to dissolve (in a particular solvent). (1-12)

intrusive rock a type of rock formed from magma that hardened beneath the Earth's surface. (4-163)

irrigation the technology of bringing water to the land in order to promote plant growth. (5-237)

joule the standard SI unit of measurement of energy; abbreviated J. (2-96)

kidney stone a hard mineral deposit formed in the kidneys. (1-28)

kilowatt hour a unit of measurement for the energy used by an appliance; abbreviated kW·h.

kinetic energy the energy present in a moving object. For example, a rock rolling down a hill has kinetic energy. (2-88)

L waves *see* surface waves. (4-196)

lava hot melted rock that flows onto the Earth's surface, usually from volcanoes. (4-163)

lens the part of a microscope that changes the path of light in order to magnify an image. (SB5-342)

lever a type of simple machine; in its simplest form, a straight, rigid bar that pivots on a fulcrum. (2-57)

lichen [LIKE-uhn] a fungus and an alga growing together, and depending on each other. (6-296)

life cycle the stages of development that an organism goes through during its life. The life cycle of a human being includes birth, infancy, childhood, and so on. (5-266)

light energy the form of energy that is visible to the eye; most light energy comes from the Sun. (2-87)

line graph a graph that has a line drawn through the points plotted on it. A line graph shows changes in variables in relation to each other. (SB4-338)

line transect a method of estimating plant populations by counting and identifying the plants that grow along a straight line. (6-305)

liquid a state of matter. A liquid has a definite volume, but no definite shape. A liquid takes the shape of its container. Water is a liquid. (1-2)

load the object to be moved or lifted by a simple machine. Its mass is usually measured in grams or kilograms and the force of gravity on it is measured in newtons. (2-57)

lustre a description of how a mineral shines under light. (4-158)

machine a device that uses energy to perform useful work. (2-54)

magma hot melted rock found at great depths below the Earth's surface. (4-163)

magnetism a force that acts on objects in the invisible field around a magnet. (1-19)

manipulated variable the condition that is controlled by the experimenter in an investigation. (SB4-340)

mantle the thickest layer of the Earth, lying just below the crust. (4-200)

mark-recapture a method of estimating the size of a population of small animals by marking a sample, releasing it, and later recapturing a second sample. (6-307)

mass the measure of the amount of matter in an object, usually measured in grams (g) or kilograms (kg). (SB3-333)

matter anything that has mass and occupies space (has volume). (1-2)

mechanical energy the energy associated with mechanical systems; it may be either kinetic or potential. (2-89)

mechanical mixture a mixture in which two or more parts can be seen with the unaided eye. (1-10)

melting the change of state from a solid to a liquid. (1-6)

melting point the temperature at which a liquid changes to a solid. (1-44)

meniscus [mi-NIS-kuhs] the curved surface of a liquid where it touches the sides of a container. (SB3-335)

metamorphic rock a type of rock formed below the Earth's surface when rock is altered by heat, pressure, or chemical reactions. (4-162)

micro-environment a small area of an environment that has different conditions (such as temperature and/or humidity) compared with the larger environment of which it is a part. (6-284)

Mid-Atlantic Ridge a large, volcanic mountain range that runs underwater along the middle of the Atlantic Ocean. (4-206)

mineral a pure, naturally occurring solid substance found in rocks (4-157); minerals can dissolve in water, often becoming nutrients for organisms. (5-239)

mixture a material made up of two or more substances. A mixture can be either a mechanical mixture or a solution. (1-7)

model a picture, diagram, or other means of representing something. For example, the particle theory is a mental picture of the nature of matter. (SB2-330)

Mohs' hardness scale a standard set of minerals of varying hardness, used to measure the hardness of all other minerals. (4-158)

molecule two or more atoms joined together to make the smallest particle of a pure substance that can exist by itself. (1-5)

mould a type of fossil; a cavity made by the imprint of an organism or its tracks. (4-185)

mudstone sedimentary rock made from fine clay or mud. (4-166)

multiplying gear a gear train that increases the rotational speed of a device. For example, a hand-operated food mixer uses a multiplying gear. (2-82)

mutualism a relationship between two species in which both species benefit from the relationship. (6-296)

newton the standard SI unit of measurement of force; abbreviated N. (2-56)

niche the role of an organism in its environment. (6-297)

nitrogen a nutrient essential in plants and animals for the making of proteins for growth. (5-232)

non-renewable resource a material, such as a metal or petroleum, which exists in limited quantities and may eventually be completely used up. (3-146)

nucleolus [NOO-KLEE-uh-lus] an organelle within the nucleus of a cell; it is involved with the transfer of substances containing "information" from the nucleus to the cytoplasm, where proteins are produced that make up the entire cell. (SB5-347)

nucleus [NOO-klee-uhs] an organelle within a cell that contains the chromosomes carrying genes that are responsible for all inherited characteristics; sometimes called the "control centre" of the cell. (SB5-346)

nutrient a substance that organisms require for life, growth, and reproduction. (5-230)

ocean trenches deep parts of the ocean floor found along the edges of some continents. (4-206)

ore rock containing minerals in a high enough concentration to make it worthwhile for mining. (4-160)

organ a structure made up of tissues performing the same function. For example, the liver is an organ. (SB5-350)

organelle within a cell, a structure that performs a specific function; for example, nucleus, chloroplast, cell membrane, etc. (SB5-347)

organic fertilizer a natural substance that supplies essential nutrients to soil, for example, manure. (5-231)

organism a living thing. (6-272)

origin the point on a graph where the x-axis and the y-axis meet. (SB4-340)

osmosis the diffusion of water through a differentially permeable membrane. (5-224)

ovary in a flower, the lower part of a pistil, in which the seeds develop. (5-255)

oxidizing substance WHMIS usage: a substance that causes combustion or contributes to the combustion of another material. (Introduction-xiv) (3-134)

P waves *see* compression waves. (4-195)

parallel gear a gear train in which the gears are of equal size; used to reverse the direction of a rotation. (2-82)

parasite an organism that obtains food or shelter from another organism. It sometimes harms, but usually doesn't kill, the other organism. (6-297)

parasitism a relationship between two species in which one benefits and the other may be harmed. (6-297)

parenchyma tissue [puh-RENG-ki-muh TI-shoo] in plants, a tissue made of thin-walled cells that store water and starch. (5-241)

parent rock a rock that becomes altered to form metamorphic rock. (4-168)

particle theory a theory stating that all matter is made up of extremely small particles in constant motion. (1-4) (SB2-331)

particulates tiny solids or liquid drops that produce air pollution. (6-318)

pest any organism that human beings consider to be a nuisance or harmful. (5-260)

pesticide a substance used to kill one or more types of pests. (5-260)

petal one of the large, showy parts of a flower, often coloured, that attracts insects for pollination. (5-255)

petrified fossil a fossil formed when minerals completely replace the original porous remains of an organism. (4-176)

petroleum an oily liquid mixture found underground, produced from the remains of organisms that once lived. (1-32)

petroproducts substances produced using petroleum as the raw material; for example, plastics, gasoline. (1-32)

phloem tissue [FLOH-em TI-shoo] a plant tissue made up of living cells; it transports food produced in the leaves to cells throughout the plant. (5-241)

phosphorus a nutrient that stimulates the growth of seedlings. (5-232)

photosynthesis the process, occurring in the green parts of plants and other organisms, that uses the Sun's energy to convert water and carbon dioxide into food and oxygen; requires the presence of chlorophyll. (5-220)

pinion the smaller of two gear wheels in a gear train. (2-80)

pistil the female reproductive structure of a flowering plant. (5-255)

plate a large section of the Earth's crust. (4-207)

poisonous WHMIS usage: causing immediate and serious harmful effects to humans and other organisms. (Introduction-xiv) (3-134)

pollen tube the tube that develops downward through the pistil in order for fertilization in flowering plants to occur. (5-255)

pollination the transfer of pollen from the male part of a seed-producing plant to the female part of a plant in order for fertilization to occur. (5-255)

pollutant anything added to the environment that is harmful to living things. (6-316)

population the number of individuals of a species that live together in one area. (6-303)

potash a mineral found in underground deposits; used as a fertilizer because of its potassium content. (1-26)

potassium a nutrient required by green plants; needed by flowering plants to stimulate flowering and the development of fruits. (5-232)

potential energy stored energy, such as chemical energy, available to be converted to other forms. (2-89)

primary consumer a consumer that eats producers. (6-289)

principle of superposition the principle by which any sedimentary rock in a horizontal section of layered rock is considered younger than the rock just beneath it. (4-174)

producer an organism that can produce its own food from materials in the abiotic parts of the environment. Green plants and other organisms with chlorophyll are producers. (6-288)

property a characteristic of a material. For example, oxygen gas is colourless. (4-157)

pulley a type of simple machine; in its simplest form, a wheel with a groove along its edge to receive a rope; used either to reduce the effort force needed to lift a load or to allow the lifting of a load by pulling down rather than lifting up. (2-57)

pure substance matter in which all particles are identical. (1-11)

pyramid of biomass a model that shows the total mass of the producers and consumers making up each level of a food chain. (6-310)

pyramid of numbers a model that shows the structure of a food chain. There are large numbers of producers at the base of the pyramid, fewer primary consumers above them, and still fewer secondary and tertiary consumers at the top. (6-309)

quadrat a small sampling area (usually a square metre), used for estimating populations of small organisms. (6-304)

radioactive dating the process of using a radioactive element to find the age of an object. For example, scientists can calculate when rock was formed by measuring the proportions of a radioactive element compared with the element into which it is transformed. (4-181)

radioactivity the release of particles and energy from the nucleus of an atom, such as an atom of the element uranium, changing it to another element. (4-181)

random sampling the technique of taking samples at random or non-selectively. (3-124)

range of tolerance the upper and lower limits of an abiotic factor, such as temperature, within which an organism can survive. (6-277)

recycling using discarded materials such as paper, glass, and metal to make more materials. (3-147)

reducing gear a gear train that decreases the rotational speed of a device. (2-82)

relative age the age of something or someone compared with the age of something or someone else; for example, a student 15 years of age is old relative to a student 12 years of age. (4-173)

reliable describes a test that can be depended on for accurate results. (3-124)

renewable resource a natural material such as wood or cotton that comes from living things and thus can, with proper management, be harvested for an unlimited time into the future. (3-146)

repeatable describes a test that has been done over and over again, achieving similar results. (3-124)

reproduction the production of offspring by living things. (5-254)

residue the material that remains following filtration and distillation. (1-20)

responding variable the condition that changes in an investigation because of changes to the manipulated variable. (SB4-340)

reusing using a product such as a bottle more than once. (3-147)

Richter [RIK-tuhr] **scale** a scale for measuring the amount of energy released when an earthquake occurs. (4-196)

rock cycle over long periods of time, any piece of the Earth's crust may be transformed into any of the three families of rock—igneous, sedimentary, or metamorphic—depending on conditions. Thus, each family is linked to the others in a cycle. (4-170)

root hair zone in a plant, the region just above the tip of a growing root, where root hairs increase the amount of exposed surface a root has, for absorption of water and minerals. (5-218)

S waves *see* shear waves. (4-196)

sample in science, a randomly selected group, representing an entire population of organisms. (6-303)

sandstone sedimentary rock formed from particles of sand. (4-166)

saturated describes a solution that contains the maximum amount of solute that will dissolve at that temperature. (1-5)

science a search for explanations; knowledge of the structure and patterns that explain the nature of the world around us, based on curiosity, objectivity, and experimentation. (Introduction-xv)

screw a type of simple machine; essentially an inclined plane wrapped around a cylinder. (2-57)

secondary consumer an organism in a food chain that eats primary consumers (those that eat producers).

A hawk that eats seed-eating mice is a secondary consumer. (6-289)

sedimentary rock a type of rock formed by the accumulation of sediments. (4-162)

sedimentation a separation process involving the settling of the heavier pieces in a mixture. (1-20)

seed a structure consisting of an embryo, nutrient material, and a protective seed coat; the part of a flowering plant that will develop into a new plant under suitable conditions. (5-257)

seed coat a tough, protective layer that surrounds a seed. (5-257)

seismic waves vibrations spreading out from an earthquake's focus, due to the energy released at the focus. (4-195)

seismogram [SIHZ-moh-gram] a visual record of earthquake vibrations, usually recorded as a series of zigzag lines. (4-197)

seismograph an instrument for measuring earthquake vibrations. (4-195)

sexual reproduction the process in which a new individual is formed by the union of material (egg and sperm) from two other individuals. (5-255)

shale a fine-grained sedimentary rock, also known as mudstone. (4-166)

shear waves also known as S waves; earthquake vibrations that travel through the Earth's interior in an S-shaped motion. (4-196)

shelter belt a row of trees planted in a field to reduce wind erosion. (5-235)

shield cone a low, dome-shaped volcano made from hardened lava flows. (4-189)

SI the abbreviation for the *Système international d'unités*; that is, the metric system. (SB1-328)

simple machine a device that transfers or transforms energy to perform a useful function. The six types of simple machines include lever, inclined plane, wedge, pulley, wheel-and-axle, and screw. (2-57)

slate a metamorphic rock formed from shale. (4-168)

slough [sloo] a shallow lake or pond found mainly in the Prairies; sloughs are not fed by streams and often dry up in the summer. (6-311)

soil naturally occurring material consisting mainly of minerals, from rocks and from the decay of organisms. (5-226)

solar energy energy from the Sun. Light is one form of solar or radiant energy. (2-92)

solid a state of matter. A solid has a definite shape and volume. Ice is a solid. (1-2)

solidification the change of state from a liquid to a solid; also called freezing. (1-6)

solubility the amount of a solute that will dissolve in a given amount of a solvent at a certain temperature. (1-42)

soluble able to dissolve (in a particular solvent). (1-12)

solute the substance in a solution that is present in the lesser quantity. For example, in a solution of a solid in a liquid, the solid is the solute. (1-12)

solution a mixture of two or more substances that looks as though it were all one substance, due to the solubility of one or more solutes in a solvent. (1-10)

solvent the substance in a solution that is present in the greater quantity. For example, in a solution of salt in water, water is the solvent. (1-12)

sound energy the form of energy that permits us to hear. Sound energy travels as vibrations through a medium such as air. (2-88)

species a kind of organism. Members of the same species are very similar and, in general, can reproduce only with members of their own species. (4-178)

speed advantage a speed increase provided by a machine. For example, a wheel-and-axle is used to produce a speed advantage; occurs if a load moves a greater distance than the distance of the effort force exerted on it. (2-66)

sperm the male sex cell specialized to fertilize an egg in sexual reproduction. (5-255)

spot testing the random selection of products for testing. (3-124)

sprocket a gear wheel turned by a looped chain, as on a bicycle. (2-83)

stamen the male reproductive part of a flower consisting of a thread-like stalk and the anther in which the pollen is produced. (5-255)

states of matter the forms in which matter can be found: solids, liquids, and gases. (1-2)

stigma the sticky tip of the pistil of a flower, on which pollen grains land. (5-255)

stoma [STOH-muh] (plural: stomata) a tiny opening between a pair of guard cells found on the surfaces of leaves, and often other plant parts. These openings allow water to pass out of the plant, and carbon dioxide and oxygen to pass into and out of the plant. (5-245)

streak the powdery mark left by some minerals when they are scraped against a hard surface. (4-158)

strip farming the technology of preventing soil erosion by the cultivation of alternate strips of land on a slope, thus leaving strips of grass or hay in order to absorb runoff water. (5-234)

sublimation the change of state from a gas directly to a solid or from a solid to a gas, without passing through a liquid state. (1-6)

subsystem one of the working parts that make up a complex machine. For example, the crank on a pencil sharpener is a subsystem of the sharpener. (2-57)

surface waves also known as L waves; a type of earthquake vibration that travels along the Earth's surface. They are the last waves to be detected on a seismograph. (4-196)

suspension a cloudy mechanical mixture in which small solid pieces or droplets are scattered throughout another substance (the parts may settle out when the suspension is left standing). Tomato juice is an example of a suspension of a solid in a liquid. Smoke is a suspension of a solid in a gas. (1-16)

symbiosis [sim-bih-OH-sis]   a relationship between two species that may benefit one or both partners.   (6-295)

symptom   a visible sign of a disease or of the action of a pest.   (5-260)

syncline   a downfold of a rock layer.   (4-186)

system   a complex machine made up of simpler working parts, each of which may be made up of one or more simple machines.   (2-57) Also, in a living thing, a system is made up of specialized organs. Together they perform a body function, such as digestion (by the digestive system).   (SB5-350)

technological   describes techniques or inventions that solve practical problems; usually these are based on applying scientific knowledge.   (Introduction-xv)

terracing   the technology of preventing soil erosion on a slope by planting crops on a series of level steps.   (5-235)

tertiary consumer [TUHR-shuhr-ee kawn-SOO-muhr]   an organism that eats secondary consumers. For example, an eagle, which eats foxes and other animals that themselves eat other animals, is a tertiary consumer.   (6-289)

test   a comparison of the characteristics of one product against those of another product, or against standards.   (3-110)

theory   when a hypothesis is supported again and again by experimental results, over time, it becomes accepted as a theory.   (1-4)

theory of plate tectonics   the theory that the Earth's crust is broken into large sections called plates, which move relative to one another.   (4-207)

thermal energy   the total energy of all the particles of a material.   (2-88)

threatened species   a kind of organism that may still be abundant in its habitat, but is declining in numbers. The grizzly bear and green turtle are examples.   (6-322)

tissue   a group of cells specialized to perform a certain function. For example, nerve tissue and muscle tissue are comprised of cells specialized in different ways.   (SB5-350)

toxic   WHMIS usage: poisonous; causing skin or eye irritation to humans or other organisms, or causing long-term harmful effects (e.g., cancer).   (Introduction-xiv) (3-134)

transpiration   the loss of water by evaporation from the surface of plant cells.   (5-244)

trilobite   a type of extinct sea-living organism, related to crabs and crayfish, commonly found as a fossil.   (4-178)

trouble spot   the feature of a consumer product that is most likely to fail or wear out first.   (3-113)

tsunami [soo-NAH-mee]   a huge wave caused by an undersea earthquake.   (4-201)

tuber   a swollen underground stem that starts new plants by vegetative reproduction.   (5-259)

unifying theory   a theory that connects many observations once thought to be unrelated.   (4-208)

urine   the waste fluid excreted by humans and other animals.   (1-28)

vacuole   within a cell, an organelle surrounded by a membrane and filled with various substances.   (SB5-347)

variable   any changeable factor that may influence the outcome of a scientific test.   (3-110) (SB4-340)

vegetative reproduction   a type of asexual reproduction in which a new plant is produced using part of a leaf, stem, or root.   (5-218)

vent   the opening in a volcano through which lava flows.   (4-190)

vertical axis   the number line on a graph that runs from the bottom to the top. The vertical axis shows the responding variable. It is often called the y-axis.   (SB4-340)

vessels   long, hollow tubes of dead xylem cells that, with other tissues, form the pipe-like transport system of a plant.   (5-243)

viable [VIH-uh-bl]   capable of growth. Seed viability is the measure of the percentage of seeds able to germinate.   (5-257)

volcano   a type of mountain having a vent or opening through which lava, solid rock, cinders, ash, and gases may erupt.   (4-188)

volume   the amount of space occupied by a substance.   (SB3-334)

wedge   a type of simple machine; a form of inclined plane, consisting of a V-shaped piece of material.   (2-57)

wet mount   a glass slide prepared for viewing through a microscope, using water, the object to be viewed, and a plastic cover slip.   (SB5-344)

wheel-and-axle   a type of simple machine; in its simplest form, a large wheel and a smaller wheel mounted on a common axis so that the wheels rotate together.   (2-57)

work   the result of a force being exerted on an object and the object moving in the general direction of the force.   (2-56)

xylem tissue [ZIH-luhm TI-shoo]   a plant tissue made up of thick-walled, hollow dead cells that transport water and dissolved minerals from the roots up through the stem to the leaves, flowers, fruits, and seeds.   (5-241)

zero tillage   the technology of preventing wind or water erosion of soil by leaving an old crop undisturbed when new seeds are inserted into the ground using a seed drill.   (5-236)

Index

Credits

Key to abbreviations: t = top; b = bottom; c = centre; l = left; r = right.

Illustration

Suzanne Bohay: xii, 163, 164, 168, 180, 181, 190, 195, 196, 197, 279, 310. **Pat Cupples:** 12, 13, 21(c), 35, 49, 216, 217, 230, 245, 260, 328, 329, 330, 331(t), 332(r), 334, 340, 350. **Heather Ednie:** 114, 132, 135, 151. **Norman Eyolfson:** 74, 84, 111, 113, 117, 206, 207, 222, 284, 290, 291, 293, 294, 301, 312–313, 317, 325, 331(b). **Carlos Freire:** 4, 5, 30, 42, 43, 44, 45(t), 56, 62(bl), 64, 80(br, based on MacCauley, *The Way Things Work*, 1988, p. 43), 308(b). **Full Spectrum:** 11, 17, 26, 37, 38, 39, 40, 41, 45(b), 51(tr), 52, 53, 161, 264(tl), 276, 280, 335, 338, 339, 344, 346, 347, 348. **Celia Godkin:** 218, 219, 221, 224, 225, 242, 243, 246, 247, 248, 249, 271. **Dan Hobbs/Angry Cow:** 89, 110, 143, 148, 156, 177, 186, 187, 200, 309. **William Kimber:** 106, 107, 138, 223, 226, 227, 228, 229, 238, 244, 258, 259, 332(l). **Paul McCusker:** 72, 77, 91, 170, 171, 172, 173, 182, 211, 274, 285, 292, 303, 304, 305, 308(t), 319. **Russell Moody:** 58, 59, 60, 61, 62, 63. **Julian Mulock:** 3, 6, 19, 31, 32, 34, 66, 67, 69, 76, 80(tl, cl, bl), 82, 83, 144, 145, 174, 175, 178, 179, 185, 192, 193, 199, 204, 205, 208, 209, 275, 282, 296, 297. **Loreta Senin:** 112, 119, 120, 121, 126, 130, 131, 139, 141, 147(b), 149, 252. **Peter van Gulik:** 8, 20, 21(l & r), 28, 29, 51(l), 70, 71, 78(r), 79, 88, 92, 233, 236, 240, 241, 250, 251, 254, 255, 256, 257, 264, 265, 336, 337, 342.

Photography

Alberta Public Affairs: 2(l), 273(c), 298, 311. **Animals, Animals:** 281(bl-Michael Fogden), 300(l-Ray Richardson), 326(tl-Donald Specker, bl-John Paling, © Oxford Scientific Films). **Arco Solar, Inc.:** 92. **George W. Argus:** 253(r). **B.C. Hydro:** 93(br). **Black Star:** 189(t-Victor Englebert). **Boeing Canada, de Havilland:** 15(br-Tony Honeywood). **Canadian Cycling Association:** 153(Pam Bishop). **Canadian Standards Association:** 104, 105(t & bl), 130, 131, 136, 137(l). **Canadian Tire:** 96. **Canapress Photo Service:** xvi(Maclean's), 1(tr), 2(c & r), 6, 14(b), 18(cr & cl), 55(tl), 105(tc), 129, 146, 175, 194, 203(r-Maclean's), 297. **Canon:** 122. **Roger J. Cheng:** 319(cl, cr, r). **Daniel Crichton:** 50(b). **City of Edmonton/ Environmental Services:** 20(c). **City of Toronto Archives:** 330. **Consumers Distributing:** 15(cl). **Crane:** 125. **Dennison Mines:** 315(bl). **Dickinsfield Neighbourhood School, Ft. McMurray, Alberta:** 128. **Dominion Textiles:** 117. **Earth Scenes:** 235(tr-Michael & Barbara Reed). **Environment Canada:** 147(t). **First Light:** xv(Larry Lee/West Light), xvi(Jim Russell), xvii(Thomas Kitchin), 18(bl-Patrick Morrow), 300(c-Patrick Morrow), 318(t-Tom Tracy), 339(Wayne Wegner). **Focus Stock Photo:** 235(bl-D.W. Boult), 237(t-Agripress), 239(Agripress), 269(Agripress). **Fundamental Photographs:** 27(cr-Paul Silverman). **J.E. Gardner:** 278(bl). **Gordon Gore:** 63, 65, 66, 69, 70, 73, 75, 77, 81, 84, 85, 86, 87, 90, 102, 103(tl, tc, tr, cl), 342. **Bill Hause:** 276. **Labour Canada:** 134, 152. **Murray Lang:** 232(tl), 236, 241, 244, 250, 252, 261, 262, 263(r), 264, 269(t & b). **Levi Strauss:** 118(br). **MAH Neuchatal-Suisse:** 78(l & c). **Robert B. Mansour:** 59, 105(br), 108(l), 109(bl), 137(r). **Masterfile:** xvi(Oliver Massart/ Daily Telegraph), 22(l-J.A. Kraulis), 27(t-Dr. Jeremy Burgess/ Science Photo Library), 155(tl-Dick Rowen/Science Source, tc-Bill Brooks), 188(Mike Dobel), 191(Kraft/Explorer/Science Source), 201(Tony Stone/Worldwide), 237(br-Anne Mackay). **Miller Comstock:** 1(tl), 1(br-Croydon), 14(cl-D.J. Heaton), 48(l), 97(Armstrong Roberts), 116(r-Armstrong Roberts), 118(tl-

Armstrong Roberts), 215(bl, br, tr-Robert Hall, tl-Eric Hayes, cr-W. Griebeling), 232(bl-R. Krubner/Roberts, br-J.D. Taylor), 235(br-E. Otto), 253(l), 267(tr-Mario A. Madau). **NASA:** 103(br), 281(tl). **Birgitte Nielsen:** xv, 1(bl), 7, 9(l & t), 13, 15(cr & tr), 17, 18(br), 26(tr), 36, 51, 55(bl & br), 79(r), 98, 101, 127, 140, 142, 150, 263(l), 268(r), 273(br), 344, 349. **Nikon Canada:** 123. **Ontario Ministry of Transport:** 46. **Ontario Science Centre:** xvii, 55(tr), 57, 79(l), 88, 210. **Peabody Museum:** 299(r). **Alex Penner:** 155(br), 157(t), 158, 160(tl), 165(r), 176(l), 179(tl & cl), 333. **Arlene Penner:** 27(b), 48(r), 157(c), 161, 162, 163, 165(l), 166(tr & bl), 167, 169, 171, 186, 267(tc). **Petro Canada:** 25. **Pioneer Electronics:** 116(l). **Alan Pitcairn:** 215(c). **Quinn:** 322(r), 323. **Raleigh Industries:** 68. **Reuters/ Bettmann Newsphotos:** 202. **Gail Rhynard:** 268(l). **James D. Rising:** 283. **Royal Ontario Museum:** 50(t-Egyptian Dept.), 213(Dept. of New World Archeology). **Saskatchewan Property Management Corp.:** 26(b). **Sault Star Photo:** 324. **SCC Photocentre:** 316. **Amy Seiden:** 71(b). **Travel Alberta:** 33. **Valan Photos:** xvii(Kennon Cooke; Chuck Gordon), 20(tl-Dennis W. Schmidt), 55(tc-Arthur Strange), 93(t-Richard Nowitz), 108(tr-Ed Hawco, br-Alan Wilkinson), 109(t, c, br-Ed Hawco), 115(Kennon Cooke), 155(bl-John Cancalosi, tr-Don McPhee), 160(tr, br, c, bl-John Cancalosi), 166(tl & cl), 176(t), 179(r-Mildred McPhee), 183(B. Templeman), 184(Thomas Kitchin), 189(b-Joyce Photographics), 198(Stephen J. Krasemann), 215(cl-Stephen J. Krasemann), 220(Francis Lepine), 224(V. Wilkinson), 234(A.B. Joyce), 235(tl-Jeannie R. Kemp), 237(bl-V. Wilkinson), 246(Harold V. Green), 267(bl-Harold V. Green, br-V. Wilkinson, tl-J.A. Wilkinson), 273(tl & tr-Harold V. Green, bl-J.R. Page), 278(t-Stephen J. Krasemann, br-John Fowler), 281(tr & bc-Arthur Strange, br-V.R. Tymstra), 287(l-Dennis W. Schmidt, r-Jeff Foote), 288(l-Wayne Lankinen, c-John Johnson, r-Jeff Foote), 293(J.A. Wilkinson), 295(Stephen J. Krasemann), 296(t-Fred Bavendam, b-V. & J.A. Wilkinson), 299(l-J.A. Wilkinson), 300(r-J.A. Wilkinson), 302(l-Dennis W. Schmidt, r-Wayne Lankinen), 307(J.R. Page), 314(t-J.A. Wilkinson, b-Martin Kuhnigk), 315(tl-Wayne Shiels, br-J. Eastcott/V. Momatiuk, tr-Thomas Kitchin), 318(b-Kennon Cooke), 319(l-Harold V. Green), 320(l-Phillip Norton, r-V. Wilkinson), 322(l-Aubry Lang), 326(r-Harold V. Green). **Vancouver Province:** 203(l). **L.T. Webster/Libra Photographics:** 71(t & c). **John Wiley & Sons Canada:** 9(r & b), 14(tl), 22(r), 23, 24, 27(cl), 231, 343. **Tracy Wong:** 100.

Special thanks to **Philip Baer**, science teacher at Annette Public School, and all students who participated in photo sessions.